TEST SCORING

TEST SCORING

Edited by

David Thissen
The University of North Carolina at Chapel Hill

Howard Wainer
Educational Testing Service

LEA LAWRENCE ERLBAUM ASSOCIATES, PUBLISHERS
2001 Mahwah, New Jersey   London

Lawrence Erlbaum Associates, Inc., Publishers
10 Industrial Avenue
Mahwah, NJ 07430

Cover design by Kathryn Houghtaling Lacey

Library of Congress Cataloging-in-Publication Data

Test scoring / edited by David Thissen, Howard Wainer.
    p.   cm.
Includes bibliographical references and index.
ISBN 0-8058-3766-3 (hardcover : alk. paper)
    1. Examinations—Scoring. I. Thissen, David. II. Wainer, Howard.
LB3060.77.T47   2001
371.26—dc21   00-053525
                                                                    CIP

Books published by Lawrence Erlbaum Associates are printed on acid-free paper,
and their bindings are chosen for strength and durability.

Printed in the United States of America
10 9 8 7 6 5 4 3 2 1

Contents

Preface

At the threshold of the 21st century, educational and psychological tests and their scores hold a more prominent place in society than ever before. Tests are taking an increasingly important place in education and educational policy. Students take more tests, and the consequences associated with the scores are associated with higher stakes: A majority of U.S. states have, or are considering, statewide tests that are part of promotion or graduation decisions. Results obtained from the National Assessment of Educational Progress (NAEP) guide educational policy at the national level, and results from statewide assessments similarly support policy decisions at the state and local levels. Increasing emphasis on tests and their scores may also be observed in many other countries.

Although these educational uses of testing may be most visible in the media, other uses of psychological testing are on the increase as well. For example, in recent years results obtained with psychological tests and questionnaires have become the primary outcome measures in many medical trials, as drugs are designed whose purpose is an improvement in the quality of life. As another example, certification tests are required for entry to an increasing number of occupations and careers. As a single illustration, the assessments that certify computer professionals have grown in just a few years from nonexistence to become some of the largest volume testing programs in the world.

With the increasing use of tests comes greater complexity in their scoring: Large-scale tests often require multiple test forms for which scores must be reported in a comparable way. Some computerized adaptive tests (CATs) may be the ultimate in tests with multiple forms; CATs may be designed in such a way that each examinee is administered an essentially unique collection of items. The increasing importance of tests has attracted widespread interest in their content and structure, and contemporary assessments often include a wide variety of questions and activities that may be evaluated in an even wider variety of ways. Performance exercises and open-ended test questions augment or supersede more objectively scored items, such as multiple-choice questions, in many contexts.

This volume is about test scoring: combining the coded outcomes on individual test items into a numerical summary of the evidence the test provides about the examinee's performance. Our emphasis, expressed in the book's vocabulary and our choice of examples, is on large-scale educational measurement, but the topics and procedures we describe may be applied in any of a number of measurement contexts. We draw from the classic literature of the traditional test theory, where we find useful concepts that are nearly a century old, as well as from psychometric developments of the past decade, which has produced both refinements of old techniques and entirely novel technologies.

Chapter 1 provides a more detailed overview of the contents of this volume. Chapter 2 discusses test scores, and their reliability, from the perspective of traditional test theory, and chapters 3 and 4 describe the statistical estimates that are used as test scores and indexes of their precision in the context of item response theory (IRT). Taken together, chapters 2–4 are intended to provide an integrated description of the properties of test scores developed using either the traditional theory or IRT—for which purpose those chapters stand on their own. In *Test Scoring*, these chapters include the topical coverage that is prerequisite for the novel developments in chapters 7–9. In chapters 7 and 8 we extend IRT methods to provide alternative scoring systems for tests that comprise different kinds of items. In chapter 9 we describe the computation of "augmented scores": scores for small subsets of items (subscores), using the multivariate generalization of Kelley's regressed true score estimates, optionally in combination with IRT. Because details of the application of the procedures based on IRT depend on the dimensionality, or factor structure, of the test being scored, we include in chapters 5 and 6 an overview of contemporary methods for item factor analysis.

The concepts introduced in this volume are applied in a handful of examples using assessments and data drawn from the statewide educational testing programs of North Carolina and Wisconsin. These examples were selected to illustrate the results that may be obtained using the procedures we describe; most of the examples appear in two or more chapters, forming the threads of a spider web that holds *Test Scoring* together, and show how the parts are integrated into a whole.

This book was inspired by questions raised by the testing directors of many state assessment programs as well as others actively engaged in the design, construction, administration, or use of large-scale educational assessments. As a result, we address a diverse audience: those who are concerned with the integration of assessment and educational policy, those who design and develop tests, those who provide the technical procedures for administration and scoring, and (at least some) end users of assessment results, who wish to be familiar with the technical aspects of reported scores and summaries.

In addition, we hope that this volume will find an audience among researchers and graduate students in education and the social sciences. The quality of measurement in education and the social sciences appears ever in need of improvement; this volume makes some contributions toward that goal, and, more importantly, it may inspire others to provide even better procedures.

Test Scoring was created at the instigation, and with the support, of the State Collaborative on Assessment and Student Standards (SCASS) Technical Guidelines for Performance Assessment (TGPA) consortium of the Council of Chief State School Officers (CCSSO). Under the able management first of Ed Roeber, and subsequently of Phoebe Winter, the SCASS group provided the real-life context for the creation of this book. Frank B. Evans was chair of the study group that instigated this work, and has been a wonderfully patient and supportive guide throughout its creation, along with the other original members of the committee: Jim Hertzog, Edgar Morgan, Ellie Sanford, and Gloria Turner. Other SCASS participants too numerous to name exhaustively, but including James Friedebach, Linda Hansche, Sue Rigney, and Liru Zhang, provided us with a good deal of food for thought. Financial support was provided by the National Center for Education Statistics (NCES) and the National Science Foundation (NSF) through the National Institute of Statistical Sciences (NISS); thanks are due to Jerry Sacks and Alan Karr of NISS. We are further grateful to Bob Brown, Suzanne Triplett, Lou Fabrizio, Chris Averett, and Ellie Sanford for their support of, and confidence in, us as we developed many of the methods described in this book and first applied them in the statewide testing programs of the North Carolina Department of Public Instruction.

In addition, we thank Peter Behuniak, R. Darrell Bock, Eric T. Bradlow, Jan de Leeuw, Jonathan Dings, Richard Hill, Eiji Muraki, James O. Ramsay, Louis Roussos, and Yiu-Fai Yung for helpful comments on earlier drafts of the book and for informative suggestions that may have helped clarify our thinking or presentation. Any errors that remain are, of course, our own.

We close with the dedication of this book to all of those who seek to use the technology of educational and psychological testing to improve life, and the hope and trust that some of those hardworking people will improve on the techniques and explication we offer here.

—David Thissen
—Howard Wainer

Chapter 1

An Overview of *Test Scoring*

David Thissen
University of North Carolina at Chapel Hill

Howard Wainer
Educational Testing Service

A test score is a summary of the evidence contained in an examinee's responses to the items of a test that are related to the construct or constructs being measured. The sort of summary desired, and the extent to which that summary is intended to generalize beyond the specific responses at hand, depend strongly on the theoretical orientation of the test scorer. There are, broadly speaking, two schools of thought on this matter. One point of view is the purely empirical: It sees the test score as a summary of responses to the items on the test and generalizes no further. An alternative approach views the item responses as indicators of the examinee's level on some underlying trait or traits; in this context, it is appropriate to draw inferences from the observed responses to make an estimate of the examinee's level on the underlying dimension(s).

This latter point of view is consonant with a long tradition of psychological scaling, and has developed into modern item response theory (IRT). Although cogent arguments can be made for a purely empirical outlook, for reasons of utility, theoretical generalizability, and grace, the authors of this book fall, unapologetically, into this latter class. Thus, in this book about "test scoring," we consider many algorithms to compute test scores, in addition to the time-honored number-correct score; although these procedures may differ one from another, they have a common goal: optimal use of the evidence provided by item responses to infer the level of performance of the examinee.

> *Following a decision that all students in North Carolina should demonstrate competence in the use of computers by the end of the eighth grade, the North Carolina Test of Computer Skills is designed to assess whether this goal has been met. Planned for statewide administration, with as many as 100,000 examinees per year, several forms of the test are constructed. Each form includes a 70-item multiple-choice section that measures factual knowledge about computer use, as well as performance assessment sections requiring the examinee to enter text using the keyboard, perform specified editing operations on a second block of text, and answer questions that require the use of a database system and a spreadsheet application. The multiple-choice section is conventionally machine scored; the responses associated with the performance exercises are assigned grades by trained raters, using specially designed rubrics.*
>
> *At about the same time, in Wisconsin, an experimental reading test is constructed for third-grade students. In addition to the traditional multiple-choice questions following a reading passage, this item tryout form includes open-ended questions that require brief written responses, as well as a novel item type that asks the students to make a drawing that reflects part of their comprehension of the story; there is also an open-ended item that is a follow-up to the drawing, asking for an explanation.*

How should tests like these be scored? Tradition suggests that the multiple-choice sections can be scored by counting the number of correct responses, but that solution does not extend readily to tests of the complexity just described. In classroom examinations, combinations of selected-response and constructed-response items have often been scored by the arbitrary assignment of a certain number of points for each, but that procedure may not be acceptable for a large-scale testing program, in which scoring may be subject to extensive public scrutiny, and professional standards of precision are expected to be met. When we ask "How should tests like these be scored?" in the context of large-scale assessment, we usually mean, "How should tests like these be scored, in such a way that we can state the precision of measurement, assure ourselves that scores on alternate forms are interchangeable, and, if required, provide diagnostic subscores that may be useful to suggest the direction of further instruction?" One goal of the methods described in subsequent chapters is to offer alternative psychometric approaches for scoring complex assessments.

Many large-scale assessment programs serve part of the need for accountability in the educational system; often these tests serve other needs as well. Assessment programs tend to be complex when they serve a variety of needs, for a variety of constituencies. A recent development is that assessment programs often combine multiple-choice tests with various open-ended formats, or with performance exercises, or even with portfolio materials, or some of the latter formats are administered and scored without any multiple-choice component at all. The motivation for these varying test formats arises in part from the desire to measure aspects of proficiency that may not be captured by traditional multiple-choice tests; attainment of that goal may still be evaluated by conventional psychometric criteria. However, varying formats are also motivated, in part, by the belief that the use of particular assessment formats in accountability programs may have consequences for instruction; the use of some kinds of assessment, because they encourage teachers to utilize a broader range of classroom activities, may be associated with higher quality educational experiences.

We anticipate that in the near future increasing numbers of testing programs will attempt to construct instruments combining multiple-choice, open-ended, and other kinds of assessments. There is widespread agreement that tests comprising multiple-choice items alone may not have the salutary effects on educational attainment that are anticipated as consequences of many educational accountability systems. There is also a developing consensus that the use of various kinds of open-ended or performance assessments, or portfolios, does not exhibit the degree of precision or generalizability that is required for many purposes, especially those that involve scoring individual test takers (see, e.g., Koretz, McCaffrey, Klein, Bell, & Stecher, 1992). Assessments that combine item types can borrow strength from each: Multiple-choice or other machine-scored formats, such as grid-ins, can be used to provide the breadth of domain coverage that is only practical using a large number of small items, while rater-scored open-ended items or performance tasks may be used to encourage educational attention to complex tasks. Combined scores may be used to show that both breadth and depth are important.

Complex assessments raise difficult psychometric questions that are focused on issues involved in combining and reporting scores for multifaceted tests, because many traditional approaches to score summarization and score reporting prove to be inadequate. One reason that assessment programs face challenges when they combine item types is that the psychometric theory underlying such combinations is both incomplete and incompletely disseminated. The theory will probably remain forever incomplete; however, a goal of this monograph is to extend dissemination of the theory and techniques that exist, as well as to describe some procedures that are new here.

WHO DO WE EXPECT WILL USE THIS BOOK?

This volume was created at the urging (and with the support) of the State Collaborative on Assessment and Student Standards (SCASS) Technical Guidelines for Performance Assessment (TGPA) consortium of the Council of Chief State School Officers (CCSSO). This group, including the testing directors of many state assessment programs as well as others actively engaged in the design, construction, administration, or use of large-scale educational assessments, raised many of the questions for which we attempt to provide answers in subsequent chapters. As a result, we address a diverse audience: those who are concerned with the integration of assessment and educational policy, those who design and develop tests, those who provide the technical procedures for administration and scoring, and (at least some) end users of assessment results, who wish to be familiar with the technical aspects of reported scores and summaries.

In addition, we hope that this volume will find an audience among researchers and graduate students in education and the social sciences. The quality of measurement in education and the social sciences appears ever in need of improvement; this volume makes some contributions toward that goal, and, more importantly, it may inspire others to provide even better procedures.

What Background Do We Expect of the Readers?   We expect, first of all, that the reader is already interested in, and familiar with, educational and psychological measurement. There are many excellent "first books" about testing; volumes such as those by Anastasi and Urbina (1997) and Cronbach (1990) are the latest editions of time-honored texts for the first course in educational and psychological measurement, and we assume that the reader is familiar with the basic concepts covered in those books. Beyond that, we expect most readers will have been exposed to some graduate study of test theory; books such as those by Suen (1990) or Nunnally and Bernstein (1994) cover many topics in test theory that we do not consider here, and are complementary to this volume.

We consider test scoring to be a statistical enterprise, and assume that the reader is familiar with standard statistical language and techniques, at least at the level that is conventionally presented in the first-year graduate statistics sequence in education or the social sciences. Understanding of the concepts of basic probability, expectation, variance, covariance, correlation, and linear regression are essential to the comprehension of any of the chapters of this book with the exception of this one. Thorough understanding of these topics as presented in standard statistical textbooks, such as those by Hays (1994), Moore and McCabe (1993), or Shavelson (1996), provides an adequate basis to understand many of the statistical procedures in this book.

Some sections of this book involve mathematics that is beyond that expected for elementary noncalculus presentations of statistics. Specifically, the chapters on item response theory make use of differential and integral calculus (at least at the level of notation), and the chapters that involve factor analysis and multiple subscores use matrix algebra. We expect that the more technically inclined readers will be comfortable with the relatively elementary calculus and matrix algebra that we use, and those less technically inclined can probably skip those sections and gain some understanding of the consequences of the techniques we describe through the many examples throughout the book. Readers seeking a brief summary of the matrix algebra used in a few sections of this volume may wish to consult Bock's (1975) chapter 2, Lunneborg and Abbott's (1983) chapters 2–4, Maxwell's (1977) chapter 3, or the appendices on matrix algebra in the books by Lawley and Maxwell (1971), Tabachnick and Fidell (1996), Pedhazur (1982), or McDonald (1985), to list just a few examples.

In a subsequent section of this chapter, we provide "executive summaries" of each of the other chapters. Those summaries indicate the topics that are included in each chapter, the ways those topics are related to each other, and the technical depth of each. We suggest that readers make use of this chapter-level overview to select a path through this book that is compatible with their purposes.

However, before we review our own book, we digress to include a brief essay on our view of the nature of educational assessment.

WHAT IS A TEST ABOUT?

A fundamental tenet of educational measurement is that the inference to be drawn from the student's test performance refers, not to the particular exercises that make up the test, but to the *domain* of exercises that the test represents. If the domain is well defined, either by an algorithm for generating an indefinite number of exercises, or by a sufficiently large corpus of exercises written or selected according to some specification, the extent of the student's mastery of the domain is indexed unambiguously by the proportion of its exercises that the student is expected to perform satisfactorily. (Bock, Thissen, & Zimowski, 1996, p. 1)

The Test as a Sample Representing Performance

The central idea of a test is that a relatively small sample of an individual's performance, measured under carefully controlled conditions, may yield an accurate description of that individual's ability to perform under much broader conditions, over a longer period of time. This idea is most straightforwardly represented in the domain-reference description of a test offered by Bock et al. (1997). The particular example that Bock et al. use is among the clearest available for domain reference: the traditional spelling test. The example involves a spelling test constructed by drawing a simple random sample of 100 words from an early secretary's word book (Leslie & Funk, 1935), and administered as is traditionally done: Each word is read, used in a sentence, and read a second time, after which the examinees write the word on an answer form. With the test constructed in this way, the proportion of words spelled correctly by each examinee is an estimate of the proportion of the entire domain (in this case, the 25,000 words in the original book) that he or she would spell correctly.

For this simple test, everything is clear: The motivation for the short test is that it is not reasonable for examinees to be required to spell thousands of words, and any knowledge of statistics at all tells us that asking each examinee to spell some sample of the words will serve the purpose of measuring the person's spelling proficiency. The domain is clear: It is the list of words in the original volume. The sampling procedure is clear: It is a simple random sample.

The best test score to use, surprisingly enough, is not so obvious. The observed proportion of words spelled correctly by each examinee could be used as the test score, and is an unbiased estimate of the proportion of the words in the domain that examinee would spell correctly. However, Bock et al. (1997) found that use of the models and methods of item response theory (IRT) provided scale scores that could be used to compute more accurate estimates of domain performance than the usual proportion-correct score.

The question of the accuracy of test scores is a crucial one: The *Standards for Educational and Psychological Testing* (American Psychological Association, 1985, p. 20) state that

> For each total score, subscore, or combination of scores that is reported, estimates of relevant reliabilities and standard errors of measurement should be provided in sufficient detail to enable the test user to judge whether scores are sufficiently accurate for the intended use of the test.

What of more complex assessments? The relevant domain is not nearly as well defined for many tests of educational achievement as it may be for spelling. What does "accuracy" mean when part of the assessment is a short essay written by the student in response to a particular prompt, and rated by one or two judges? What is the domain of "writings" that the student could (even hypothetically) perform successfully or unsuccessfully? It remains clear that in asking a student to do a single 20-minute writing task, we are trying to make an inference about how well that student would write on other occasions (comprising a sort of domain), so "accuracy" is a measure of how well that inference can be made. But it is a challenge to decide how to score a particular essay, and report an index of uncertainty for that score, in such a way that both the score and its measure of uncertainty are meaningful, and possibly comparable with those obtained by other students who wrote other essays at other times.

When the assessment includes multiple-choice items, other difficulties arise. Because no important domain of achievement is defined in terms of a set of multiple-choice questions, some mechanism is necessary to translate performance on the multiple-choice items to any meaningful domain. In addition, it is clear that examinees may "guess" some correct answers; it might be best if the test score somehow accommodated that fact, and if the measure of uncertainty reported with the test score did so as well.

What further complexities arise when the assessment is truly complex? For example, what does "accuracy" mean for the computer skills test that we mentioned in the introduction to this chapter, or for a reading comprehension test that includes drawings as responses?

The fact is that the test theory that has been developed over the past eight decades deals with many of the issues we have raised thus far surprisingly well. However, contemporary assessments that combine several types of items, such as multiple-choice items, short and extended constructed-response items, and/or portfolio materials, challenge even the most well-developed psychometric tools. We attempt to draw together relevant material already developed in psychometrics with new ideas specifically developed for the latest large-scale assessments, to provide options for scoring tests.

WHAT IS THIS BOOK (AND EACH OF ITS CHAPTERS) ABOUT?

Psychometric Bases for Test Scoring

A great deal of psychometrics has been developed over the past eight decades that is relevant for scoring complex assessments and for evaluating the accuracy of the resulting scores. However, much of that work is not conveniently accessible. Chapters 2, 3, and 4 provide a summary of relevant traditional and modern psychometrics, as it pertains to scoring tests. These chapters are also intended to provide the background for the new developments in subsequent chapters.

Chapter 2, True Score Theory: The Traditional Method. Traditional test theory, based on the concept of the *true score*, has been the subject of many book-length treatments; the best for many purposes are those by Gulliksen (1950/1987) and Lord and Novick (1968). In chapter 2, after a statement of the basic ideas of true score theory, we pursue only a subset of the theory in some detail: the principles underlying the estimation of *reliability* in the contexts of different kinds of tests. We emphasize reliability for two reasons: The first is that, within the confines of the traditional test theory, the reliability estimate forms the basis of statistical statements about the precision of the test scores. The second is that (properly estimated) reliability describes an upper limit on the validity of those scores; for scores on tests that comprise a mixture of components, careful consideration of the structure of the test, and the combination rule for the scores, is necessary to choose a reliability estimate that is, in fact, related to validity.

As a prelude to the content of subsequent chapters, in chapter 2 we consider two specific uses of reliability estimates in detail. The first of these involves the use of reliability in the choice of *weights* for the parts of tests involving multiple components. In sections on that topic, we introduce a novel criterion for weighting—the *Hippocratic criterion*—as well as the classic solution for optimal weighting. (The section of chapter 2 on optimal weighting makes use of matrix algebra, which is the only convenient way to state the solution both explicitly and generally. Aside from this section, the technical level of chapter 2 is essentially that of standard introductory statistics.)

The second emphasis of chapter 2 is on Kelley's (1927, 1947) *regressed estimates of the true score*. As originally proposed, Kelley's true score estimates rarely see practical use. However, Kelley's equation is discussed in detail because the concepts involved are also used in the computation of *scale scores* using IRT, as discussed in chapters 3 and 4, as well as in the IRT approach to score combination that is the subject of chapters 7 and 8; chapter 9, on *augmented subscores*, is entirely about the multivariate generalization of Kelley's true score estimates.

Chapter 2 concludes with a description of the relation of the reliability estimate to various ways to characterize the precision of reported test scores. In chapter 2, and throughout the book, the concepts described are illustrated with numerical examples.

Chapter 3, Item Response Theory for Items Scored in Two Categories. Item response theory (IRT) is the basis for test construction and score reporting for many contemporary tests. Early in chapter 3, we provide a brief historical description of the development of IRT, because it is important to understand the principles on which its computations are based. Most applications of IRT involve *strong models* for the responses to test questions—that is, assumptions are made that the probabilities of the item responses can be accurately described using specific parametric functions. These parametric functions are not arbitrarily selected; there are sound theoretical reasons, supported by extensive empirical data, for each choice. We describe the theory in chapter 3, in a lengthy aside in what is otherwise a relatively applied volume, because understanding of the theory should form the basis for any decision about whether IRT provides an appropriate mechanism for scoring any particular test.

In subsequent sections of chapter 3, we describe the computation of *scale scores* based on item response patterns, or on summed scores. We explain alternative methods for the computation of scale scores in detail, because those methods remain the same, and are crucial, in our treatment of scale scores for polytomous IRT models in chapter 4, the techniques for score combination that we introduce in chapters 7 and 8, and the IRT versions of augmented subscores presented in chapter 9. It is easiest to describe the basics of IRT scale score computation using models for dichotomous data, so all of that material is concentrated in chapter 3 and not subsequently repeated.

Chapter 3 requires the use of differential and integral calculus, at least at the level of notation—that is, the reader must understand the meaning of the symbols representing derivatives and integrals. However, we illustrate the computation of scale scores in fairly extensive numerical detail, in an effort to demystify calculations that are merely extensive and tedious, rather than complex. In practice, all of the computations for IRT scale scores are done with computer software; the goal of chapter 3 is to explain what the computer programs are doing. Chapter 3 includes several illustrations based on real test data, to provide concrete examples of the results of the use of IRT's scale scores.

Chapter 4, Item Response Theory for Items Scored in More Than Two Categories.   Many performance assessments involve a relatively small number of performance exercises as "items"; the responses to each such exercise are usually scored in more than two categories. In chapter 4, we describe the most commonly used IRT models for such large items: Samejima's (1969) *graded model*, and a class of models based on Bock's (1972) *nominal model*. The description of these models is relatively brief, because both rest on the underlying theoretical development of IRT that is presented in chapter 3.

The computation of scale scores for items scored in more than two categories is also described in chapter 4, but this description is very brief, because all of the computations are the same as those described in detail in chapter 3. In chapter 4, most of the new material associated with items scored in more than two categories is presented in the context of the examples.

The final large section of chapter 4 introduces the concept of the *testlet*—a "large item" that is created by the test developer (either in advance, or during data analysis) to score several questions on a test as a unit.

Testlets provide a mechanism for the appropriate application of many of the useful features of IRT for assessments that may not comprise similar, independent, homogeneous items. Testlets are usually scored in more than two categories; however, because they use exactly the same IRT models that were developed for other kinds of items scored in more than two categories, no new models are needed.

Some of the examples in chapter 4 illustrate the computation of scale scores for combinations of performance exercises with multiple-choice sections. In chapter 4, those computations are based on response-pattern scoring; in chapters 7 and 8, we use the models described in chapters 3 and 4 as the basis for other, novel ways to score tests that mix multiple-choice and constructed-response item types. In chapter 9 we use scale scores based on items with more than two categories in subscore estimation.

What Is Being Measured?

To what extent do different item types measure different aspects of proficiency?

> There are many modes of possible assessment, each with its strengths and weaknesses. Multiple choice items are economically practical and allow reliable, objective scoring but may emphasize recall rather than generation of answers. Constructed response items are more difficult to score objectively and reliably, but provide a task that may have more systemic validity. Portfolio assessment requires smaller leaps of faith to specialize to a specific situation, but loses ground in the areas of objectivity, equity, generality and standardization. It is likely that many future assessments will be made up of combinations of such items. Combinations may allow the concatenation of the strengths of each while compensating for weaknesses. (Wainer & Thissen, 1993, pp. 103–104)

Before the responses to any set of items are combined into a single score that is taken to be, in some sense, representative of the responses to all of the items, we must ascertain the extent to which the items "measure the same thing." This question is more salient in tests that mix item types, because a number of claims have been made about what different kinds of items measure.

Contemporary techniques of factor analysis permit evaluation of the extent to which open-ended assessments may measure different aspects of proficiency than do traditional multiple-choice items. Factor analytic studies (Bennett, Rock, & Wang, 1991; Thissen, Wainer, & Wang, 1994) have shown that although there is some evidence of a "free-response factor," that factor is often so highly correlated with the "multiple-choice factor" that it can be better estimated with the more reliable multiple-choice questions than it can with free-response questions. This is because the contribution to total error associated with the statistical bias caused by measuring the "wrong thing" is smaller than the contribution to error from the unreliability of the free-response items. (In casual terms, we can define *validity* as measuring the right thing, and *reliability* as measuring the thing right. The results obtained with some combinations of multiple-choice and free-response items are examples in which measuring the thing wrong yields larger errors of measurement than measuring the wrong thing.)

However, the meaning of scores obtained with different item types may well differ for some assessments and/or in some contexts. What information can inform the test constructor about the likely usefulness and meaning of scores that combine item types, for a particular test? Modern factor analytic techniques for test items (some of which are reviewed by Mislevy, 1986), combined with Cattell's (1956, 1974) time-honored *item-parceling* procedure, are very useful here. Although there are many excellent book-length treatments of factor analysis (e.g., Lawley & Maxwell, 1971; Gorsuch, 1983; Harmon, 1976), item factor analysis introduces its own special problems, for which highly specialized solutions have been provided.

Chapter 5, Factor Analysis for Items Scored in Two Categories. The introduction to chapter 5 provides a brief primer of factor analysis, with special attention to the relation of the factor analytic model with the internal structure of educational and psychological tests. Then we describe problems that may be associated with the application of commonly available factor analytic procedures to dichotomous data, such as item response data scored correct and incorrect.

Contemporary solutions to these problems that permit the useful factor analysis of item response data include *weighted least squares* factor analysis of *tetrachoric* correlations, and *full-information maximum likelihood* item factor analysis. The latter procedure is *multidimensional item response theory*, and, as such, is very closely related to our discussion of IRT in chapters 3 and 4; the former approach is best characterized, in the context of item response data, as an approximation method for the computationally demanding full-information approach. We describe these techniques, and illustrate their application with data from measures of educational achievement with dichotomously scored items.

As is generally true of material on factor analysis, in both chapters 5 and 6, the presentation of the material requires the use of matrix algebra for notational convenience. Extensive numerical examples are included to make the presentation more concrete.

Chapter 6, Factor Analysis for Items or Testlets Scored in More Than Two Categories. Factor analysis of *ordered, polytomous* response variables also involves its own special problems and solutions. Ordered, polytomous response variables are scored in two or more ordered categories, but the categories are generally too few and too discrete to justify the assumptions involved in the use of standard statistical procedures for factor analysis. Specifically, the assumption that the data arise from a multivariate normal distribution may not be plausible; that assumption forms the basis of factor analysis using maximum-likelihood estimation based on the observed covariance matrix.

Ordered, polytomous data may arise from the responses to educational and psychological tests in any of three ways: First, the responses may be scored in ordered categories to begin with, as is the case with rated performance assessments. Second, the responses may be associated with test-lets—combinations of closely related items that are analyzed as a unit. Third, the responses may be scores on *item parcels*—combinations of items that are scored as a unit to facilitate factor analysis, as a way to avoid the problems (described in chap. 5) with the factor analysis of dichotomous data.

In chapter 6, we describe two approaches to factor analysis that are useful for the examination of the structure of ordered, polytomous responses associated with educational and psychological tests. The first of these involves the computation of *polychoric* correlations among the responses, followed by weighted least squares estimation of the parameters of the factor analysis model; these procedures are implemented in the computer programs PRELIS and LISREL (Jöreskog & Sörbom, 1995a, 1995b), as well as in other software. The second approach is the generalization of full-information maximum-likelihood factor analysis for ordered, polytomous responses, as described by Muraki and Carlson (1995) and implemented in the computer program POLYFACT (Muraki, 1993).

We illustrate the use of these techniques to examine the degree to which multiple-choice and constructed-response items appear to measure the same construct on several assessments of educational achievement. Analyses such as these may form part of the basis for a decision about whether scores from different sections of a test are best reported separately, or whether some system for score combination may be appropriate for the use of the test. We also describe and illustrate some relatively recent results obtained by Yung, McLeod, and Thissen (1999) about the relationship between conventional factor analysis and *higher order* factor analysis—these results are very important in the interpretation of evidence from factor analysis about the dimensionality of tests with several components.

Score Combination

An increasing number of testing programs must report scores summarizing performance over a variety of item types. This presents problems that have not recently been extensively discussed in the psychometric literature in an integrated fashion, largely because in recent decades the problem has not frequently arisen.

Scores that are obtained by simply counting the number of correct responses are not easily applied to assessments that mix multiple-choice responses, which have item scores that are either correct or incorrect, with open-ended responses that are rated on some (numerically) arbitrary scale. The lack of a straightforward way to create a summary score makes it difficult to develop a norm-referenced score scale, such as the College Board's well-known 200–800 scale, or to develop conventional percentiles, because both of those are transformations of a number-correct scale. In addition, strictly norm-referenced scaling may not provide the information needed in assessment programs that are intended to provide scores referent to some set of standards.

Given these problems, one option is to report scores on open-ended assessments without combining; the National Assessment of Educational Progress (NAEP) did that in the early years of its operation (Education Commission of the States, 1970). However, in many cases this option is not compatible with some needs of the assessment program. If individual scores are required, single-item scores are usually not sufficiently generalizable. If the evaluation of change over time is required, alternate forms of the open-ended assessments are needed, and some superordinate score scale is necessary to compare responses to more and less difficult sets of items.

When most tests comprised only multiple-choice items, test constructors used either the "obvious" traditional solution (using the number of correct responses as the test score), or the more involved solution suggested by IRT, which uses an estimate of underlying proficiency as a scale score. Both of those test-scoring procedures are well documented for multiple-choice tests on which the individual items are scored correct or incorrect. However, only IRT scale scores for response patterns, as described in chapter 4, are widely documented as a solution for tests with mixed item types.

One of the goals of this book is to advance the psychometric state of the art with respect to score combination, and to present the state of the art in a way that is useful in the development of their assessment programs. In chapters 7 and 8, we use the basic principles of IRT (described in chapters 3 and 4) to develop novel methods to score tests with mixed item types.

Chapter 7, Item Response Theory Applied to Combinations of Multiple-Choice and Constructed-Response Items—Scale Scores for Patterns of Summed Scores. Scale scores based on IRT have been most often computed for each item response pattern; as we observe in chapters 3 and 4, that is the most efficient use of the data obtained with a test, but response-pattern scoring involves attendant practical difficulties in some contexts.

In chapters 3 and 4, we describe the computation of IRT scale scores based on summed scores as a practical alternative that may be useful in many applications. However, summed item scores may not form an attractive basis for test scoring when some of the items are of different types than others—this situation arises, for instance, when multiple-choice items, yielding one "point" per correct response, are mixed with open-ended items that are assigned some arbitrary number of "points" associated with scoring categories.

In chapter 7, we introduce a hybrid of response-pattern and summed-score IRT scale scores, specifically designed for scoring tests that combine item types: We use the IRT methods for summed scores described in chapters 3 and 4 to compute the likelihoods for the summed scores on each section (say, the multiple-choice section and the open-ended section); then we combine those likelihoods for each *pattern of summed scores* for the test as a whole. Conceptually the idea is straightforward: We simply follow the standard procedures of IRT, except that we use patterns of summed scores instead of patterns of item responses as the basis for assigning scale scores. The result is that the vexing "weighting problem" associated with mixed item types is implicitly solved, and a new system of (implicit) optimal weights is used to score the test. We illustrate the results obtained with this new scoring system using data from several tests that combine item types.

Chapter 8, Item Response Theory Applied to Combinations of Multiple-Choice and Constructed-Response Items—Approximation Methods for Scale Scores.   Although it can be said that the score-combination method we propose in chapter 7 "solves the weighting problem," it does so implicitly, and no scoring weights are visible in the solution. In chapter 8, we introduce a system that approximates the *pattern of summed scores* scale scores suggested in chapter 7 with weighted linear combinations of the scores on each component: If the test combines a multiple-choice section and an open-ended section, then each of those sections is given a score, and a weight; the two scores are then combined, using the weights, into the total score.

The approximation uses a combination of the basic principles of IRT (from chaps. 3 and 4) and some ideas from the traditional test theory (notably Kelley's equation from chap. 2). Using the approximation, we obtain a scoring system that may be simpler to implement, and that is certainly easier to explain to consumers, than the IRT system proposed in chapter 7. In addition, the approximation makes explicit the relative weights associated with various scores on the distinct sections of the test. We illustrate the use of the approximation with the some of the same data that are used in chapter 7, and examine the accuracy of the approximation and the IRT "weights" that follow from this application of the theory.

In the final sections of chapter 8, we extend the approximate method of score combination to develop a system for scoring multistage tests and computerized adaptive tests (CATs) comprising testlets. (Scoring methods for conventional, item-based CATs are described by Wainer & Mislevy, 1990, 2000). In these variations of adaptive testing, examinees respond to small fixed blocks of items, with the selection of the next block (or testlet) dependent on the responses those presented earlier. Because the data arising from such a testing situation are formally the same as those that arise from a multisection test, the same score-combination techniques can be used. In the context of the testlet scoring system, we present simulation results that illustrate the effectiveness of the system.

Subscore Augmentation

As assessments become more complex and time-consuming, there is increasing pressure on test developers to report scores on curriculum-specific parts of the test, or "subscores."[1] Because the scores from small numbers of items associated with any particular curricular objective on a test tend to be relatively unreliable, we consider scoring systems that augment the scores for parts of the test with information obtained from the rest of the test. We do this for tests that combine item types as well as for more traditional tests.

Chapter 9, Augmented Scores: "Borrowing Strength" to Compute Scores Based on Small Numbers of Items.
Although Kelley's (1927) development of regressed true score estimates predates the formal introduction of *empirical Bayes techniques* by several decades, Kelley's equation (as described in chap. 2) is now seen as an example of the general empirical Bayes approach to statistical estimation. In chapter 9, we introduce the general principles of empirical Bayes estimation, and then use those principles to develop the multivariate generalization of Kelley's (1927) regressed estimates of true scores. The goal of this development is the computation of reliable estimates of subscores.

A common context in which (usually, diagnostic) subscores are desirable, and problematic, involves a relatively long test that includes items in each of several relatively closely related subsets. Although some users of the test scores would like information about the performance of the examinees on each subset separately, the number of items associated with each subset may be too small to produce a reliable score on its own. The

---

[1]The nomenclature *subscore* must be taken generally here, because the methods we consider do not produce "subscores" that add up (in any obvious way) to be the total score on the test.

empirical Bayes approach to estimating subscores augments the information in the responses to the few items in any particular subset with the related information that can be gleaned from the rest of the test. In effect, it uses all of the item responses on the test to predict what the examinee's score would have been on a much longer test representing material that was actually covered by only a subset of the items.

Because this procedure is essentially multivariate, we use matrix algebra to express the solution. However, extensive numerical examples are provided that make the matrix expressions concrete and that illustrate the consequences of this approach to the estimation of subscores.

Score Reporting

Although any of a number of psychometrically sound scales may be used for some accountability purposes, the public nature of score reporting for many large-scale assessment programs requires that careful thought be given to the score scale. Often, multiple forms must be equated or linked; this mitigates against the use of the number-correct scale for any particular form. In addition, there is often a need to categorize scores according to some set of standards of achievement. Whether those standards are produced by a contrasting groups method (as they have been in North Carolina [Sanford, 1996] and elsewhere), or by an item-judgment method such as that recently used by the National Assessment Governing Board (National Academy of Education, 1993), the cutpoints for such standards must be placed on some scale. These technical considerations suggest the use of IRT scale scores at some level of test development and score reporting; thus, there is an emphasis throughout this volume on the use of IRT scale scores.

WHAT IS NOT INCLUDED?

Item Analysis and Calibration

Most of the systems for test scoring that are discussed here assume that the test has already been constructed, and often that the items have been calibrated using IRT. Although test development and item calibration are very complex subjects, there are a number of sources for that information readily available. For the use of traditional statistics, Gulliksen (1950/1987) and Lord and Novick (1968) are very useful. For item response theory, Lord (1980), Wainer and Mislevy (1990, 2000), Baker (1992), and van der Linden and Hambleton (1997) provide a great deal of useful information. In any event, much of the technology of item analysis and calibration has been embedded in computer software, with the result that its structure is of interest principally to a relatively small number of specialists.

The Bases for Final Decisions: The Uses of the Test Scores

There is no "one right way" to score a test. The value of any system of test scoring depends on the uses that are to be made of the scores. We make that point implicitly throughout this volume, when our illustrations use different scoring systems for the same test or set of items; in the real world, one would tend to use only one scoring system for a test. But there are many ways to use a collection of items and responses to form a test score. The goal of this volume is to offer and inform choices. It is then necessary for test constructors to evaluate their goals, and to select from among these and other alternatives test-scoring systems that best meet their needs.

ACKNOWLEDGMENTS

We thank Peter Behuniak, Jonathan Dings, Frank Evans, and Richard Hill for helpful comments on an earlier draft.

REFERENCES

American Psychological Association. (1985). *Standards for educational and psychological testing.* Washington, DC: Author.

Anastasi, A., & Urbina, S. (1997). *Psychological testing* (7th ed.). Upper Saddle River, NJ: Prentice Hall.

Baker, F. B. (1992). *Item response theory: Parameter estimation techniques.* New York: Marcel Dekker.

Bennett, R. E., Rock, D. A., & Wang, M. (1991). Equivalence of free-response and multiple-choice items. *Journal of Educational Measurement, 28,* 77–92.

Bock, R. D. (1972). Estimating item parameters and latent ability when responses are scored in two or more latent categories. *Psychometrika, 37,* 29–51.

Bock, R. D. (1975). *Multivariate statistical methods in behavioral research.* New York: McGraw-Hill.

Bock, R. D., Thissen, D., & Zimowski, M. F. (1996). *IRT domain score estimation.* Unpublished manuscript.

Bock, R. D., Thissen, D., & Zimowski, M. F. (1997). IRT estimation of domain scores. *Journal of Educational Measurement, 34,* 197–211.

Cattell, R. B. (1956). Validation and intensification of the Sixteen Personality Factor Questionnaire. *Journal of Clinical Psychology, 12,* 205–214.

Cattell, R. B. (1974). Radial parcel factoring versus item factoring in defining personality structure in questionnaires. *Australian Journal of Psychology, 26,* 103–119.

Cronbach, L. J. (1990). *Essentials of psychological testing* (5th ed.). New York: Harper Collins.

Education Commission of the States. (1970). *National Assessment of Educational Progress: 1969–1970 Science: National results and illustrations of groups comparisons.* Denver, CO: Author.

Gorsuch, R. L. (1983). *Factor analysis.* Hillsdale, NJ: Lawrence Erlbaum Associates.

Gulliksen, H. O. (1987). *Theory of mental tests.* Hillsdale, NJ: Lawrence Erlbaum Associates. (Original work published 1950)

Harmon, H. H. (1976). *Modern factor analysis* (3rd ed. rev.). Chicago: University of Chicago Press.

Hays, W. L. (1994). *Statistics* (5th ed.). Fort Worth, TX: Harcourt Brace.

Jöreskog, K. G., & Sörbom, D. (1995a). *LISREL 8 user's reference guide.* Chicago: Scientific Software, Inc.

Jöreskog, K. G., & Sörbom, D. (1995b). *PRELIS: A program for multivariate data screening and data summarization.* Chicago: Scientific Software, Inc.

Kelley, T. L. (1927). *The interpretation of educational measurements.* New York: World Book.

Kelley, T. L. (1947). *Fundamentals of statistics.* Cambridge, MA: Harvard University Press.

Koretz, D., McCaffrey, D., Klein, S., Bell, R., & Stecher, B. (1992). *The reliability of scores from the 1992 Vermont Portfolio Assessment Program.* Interim Technical Report. Santa Monica, CA: Rand Institute on Education and Training.

Lawley, D. N., & Maxwell, A. E. (1971). *Factor analysis as a statistical method.* New York: American Elsevier.

Leslie, L. A., & Funk, C. E. (1935). *25,000 Words spelled, divided, and accented.* New York: Funk & Wagnalls.

Lord, F. M. (1980). *Applications of item response theory to practical testing problems.* Hillsdale, NJ: Lawrence Erlbaum Associates.

Lord, F. M., & Novick, M. (1968). *Statistical theories of mental test scores.* Reading, MA: Addison Wesley.

Lunneborg, C. E., & Abbott, R. D. (1983). *Elementary multivariate analysis for the behavioral sciences.* New York: North-Holland.

Maxwell, A. E. (1977). *Multivariate analysis in behavioural research.* London: Chapman and Hall.

McDonald, R. P. (1985). *Factor analysis and related methods.* Hillsdale, NJ: Lawrence Erlbaum Associates.

Mislevy, R. J. (1986). Recent developments in the factor analysis of categorical variables. *Journal of Educational Statistics, 11,* 3–31.

Moore, D. S., & McCabe, G. P. (1993). *Introduction to the practice of statistics.* New York: W. H. Freeman.

Muraki, E. (1993). POLYFACT [Computer program]. Princeton, NJ: Educational Testing Service.

Muraki, E., & Carlson, J. E. (1995). Full-information factor analysis for polytomous item responses. *Applied Psychological Measurement, 19,* 73–90.

National Academy of Education. (1993). *The Trial State Assessment: Prospects and realities.* Stanford, CA: Author.

Nunnally, J. C., & Bernstein, I. H. (1994). *Psychometric theory* (3rd ed.). New York: McGraw-Hill.

Pedhazur, E. J. (1982). *Multiple regression in behavioral research* (2nd ed.). New York: Holt, Rinehart and Winston.

Samejima, F. (1969). Estimation of latent ability using a response pattern of graded scores. *Psychometric Monograph,* No. 17.

Sanford, E. E. (1996). *North Carolina end-of-grade tests.* Raleigh, NC: North Carolina Department of Public Instruction.

Shavelson, R. J. (1996). *Statistical reasoning for the behavioral sciences.* Boston: Allyn and Bacon.

Suen, H. K. (1990). *Principles of test theories*. Hillsdale, NJ: Lawrence Erlbaum Associates.

Tabachnick, B. G., & Fidell, L. S. (1996). *Using multivariate statistics* (3rd Edition). New York: Harper Collins.

Thissen, D., Wainer, H., & Wang, X. B. (1994). Are tests comprising both multiple-choice and free-response items necessarily less unidimensional than multiple-choice tests? An analysis of two tests. *Journal of Educational Measurement, 31*, 113–123.

van der Linden, W., & Hambleton, R. K. (1997). *Handbook of modern item response theory*. New York: Springer.

Wainer, H., & Mislevy, R. J. (1990). Item response theory, item calibration, and proficiency estimation. In H. Wainer, N. Dorans, R. Flaugher, B. Green, R. Mislevy, L. Steinberg, & D. Thissen, *Computerized adaptive testing: A primer* (pp. 65–102). Hillsdale, NJ: Lawrence Erlbaum Associates.

Wainer, H., & Mislevy, R. J. (2000). Item response theory, item calibration, and proficiency estimation. In H. Wainer, N. Dorans, D. Eignor, R. Flaugher, B. Green, R. Mislevy, L. Steinberg, & D. Thissen, *Computerized adaptive testing: A primer* (2nd ed., pp. 61–100). Hillsdale, NJ: Lawrence Erlbaum Associates.

Wainer, H., & Thissen, D. (1993). Combining multiple-choice and constructed response test scores: Toward a Marxist theory of test construction. *Applied Measurement in Education, 6*, 103–118.

Yung, Y. F., McLeod, L. D., & Thissen, D. (1999). On the relationship between the higher-order factor model and the hierarchical factor model. *Psychometrika, 64*, 113–128.

Part I

TRADITIONAL TEST THEORY AND ITEM RESPONSE THEORY

Chapter 2

True Score Theory:
The Traditional Method

Howard Wainer
Educational Testing Service

David Thissen
University of North Carolina at Chapel Hill

Test scores are used to help make decisions: decisions to hire or reject job applicants; decisions to award or withhold scholarships; decisions to pass or fail a course; decisions on the direction of further instruction. But how are these scores determined? What do they mean? How much can we count on them? Can we get more from them than we currently do?

This chapter describes some traditional ways to answer some of these questions. A key idea implicit throughout this chapter is that test scores are not merely data, but rather they provide information that is intended to serve as evidence for decisions. For test scores to provide meaningful evidence, the items from which the scores are derived must be carefully constructed. At this point it is important to make a distinction between an item and a question. An item has a surface similarity to a question, but *item* is a term with a very specific technical meaning. The term *question* encompasses any sort of interrogative:

Where's the bathroom?
What time is it?
Do you come here often?
What's your sign?

These are all questions, but they should not be confused with items. For a question to be called an item it needs an additional characteristic:

There must be a scoring rule.

In tests intended to measure academic proficiency, the basis for the scoring rule is usually that the question has some correct answer; however, the idea of a "correct answer" may be interpreted broadly—there may be many answers that are interpreted as correct. A scoring rule may be as narrow as "the answer πr^2 is worth one point, all other answers get zero points," or as broad as "score the essays holistically with 4 points to those essays you feel are excellent, 3 good, 2 fair, 1 poor, and 0 unacceptable."

Regardless of the interpretation that one gives to the requirement for a scoring rule, it is absolutely essential in any valid test that a specification of the score or code any answer is to receive is defined for every item. Making this explicit does not guarantee that an item will yield good measurement, but it does allow one to know exactly what the test comprises and, through various kinds of experiments, to measure the extent to which any item is useful for the measurement task of the test.

But what is the measurement task of a test? There are many possible tasks, but all are related to the goals of the early testers of the Han dynasty, who devised the first civil service examinations (DuBois, 1970; Hucker, 1975). The central idea of a test (as we noted in chap. 1) is that a relatively small sample of an individual's performance, measured under carefully controlled conditions, may yield an accurate picture of that individual's ability to perform under much broader conditions for a longer period of time. A test is used when it is impossible or impractical to have candidates do the actual task. When this is the case, a test is constructed that abstracts from the task elements that are thought essential or representative, and uses performance on those elements as a proxy for the actual task. The issues of this chapter are more easily understood if they can be referred to concrete examples.

The Driving Test: A Classic Performance Exercise.   In New Jersey, candidates drive a car around a special course with no other traffic. The examiner must infer from their performance on this very limited task whether they are able to drive safely on public roads. The hope is that the examiner's judgment is good enough, and the task is sufficiently similar to what is likely to be faced on the roads, that candidates who pass are relatively unlikely to endanger themselves or others.

How can we tell if the test works? One way is to set on the road some large number of untested drivers and keep track of their driving records (tickets, accidents, etc.) for, say, 5 years. Then compare their performance to a matched set of drivers (matched in terms of age, sex, and other physical characteristics) who have taken and passed the driving test whose efficacy we are trying to measure. The extent to which the tested group's performance exceeds that of the control group is a measure of the validity of the test. Of course, such a validity study would probably be unwise. But it is often useful to consider the ideal experiment before retreating to the possible.

A fallback position that is practical would be to examine the subsequent driving records of all people who pass the test and see if those who barely pass are any different from those who passed with flying colors. The vast distance between this practical validity study and the optimal experimental study typifies a fundamental problem in doing validity studies, more commonly noted in the context of college admissions tests than driving tests: To understand how well a college admissions test works in selecting students, one would have to admit some who are predicted to do very poorly. Because this is not ordinarily done, we must extrapolate from the usually narrow range of individuals who are admitted to the subjunctive case of what would have happened if admissions were carried out without the test.[1]

A second way to assess validity is through expert judgment. It seems plausible to believe that although it is surely necessary for potential drivers to know the rules of the road (which can be assessed well with a written test), such knowledge is not a sufficient demonstration of driving prowess to justify licensing that person to drive. For such a demonstration it would seem that getting the person behind the wheel in a controlled circum-

---

[1]If we wish to evaluate the validity of an admissions requirement, there is an alternative to admitting students who, on the basis of that requirement, are predicted to do poorly. This would be to further restrict admissions and see if those that are admitted under this more restrictive policy do better than was the case previously.

Such an experiment was done in 1986 when the NCAA passed proposition 48. This rule raised academic requirements for incoming freshmen on athletic scholarships, requiring a 2.0 high school grade point average in 11 core academic courses and a combined SAT mathematics and verbal score of at least 700. The results of this were dramatic, especially among African-American students. Specifically, there was a small decline in the percentage of athletic scholarships awarded to African-Americans (29% to 25%) but a large increase in both the percentage and number of African-Americans graduating. The details of this experiment are summarized in this table (from Klein & Bell, 1995):

2-Year Period	Percent of Scholarships to African-Americans	Percent Graduating	Number Graduating
Before proposition 48	29	36	2,593
After proposition 48	25	45	2,739
Change	−4	+9	+146

The higher admissions requirements yielded a population of African-American athletes who were better able to succeed in college. This is supporting evidence for the validity of the measures.

stance, where the potential damage from an incompetent candidate is minimized, is a sensible option.

Once the character of the test is settled on (a written part testing the rules of the road and a driving part that requires operating a motor vehicle), a number of operational details need attention. Principal among those details is the length of the test. Watching someone drive for 2 minutes tells us less than an exercise of 2 hours. Then there is the content: One minimal set for the test is a sample of driving tasks; a left turn, a right turn, a U-turn, and parallel parking, with short spurts of driving in between. Is this the only driving test that could be used? Of course not. One can imagine dozens, if not hundreds, of driving tests that are all different but are all of about equal difficulty. An examinee could fairly be given any one of these alternate test forms and we would still expect the same result. Such alternate forms, if they satisfy some simple conditions, are called *parallel test forms*. In addition, one might suspect that having the examinee do two or three of these parallel forms would yield a better sense of their driving ability than just one. This suspicion arises because it is natural to expect that the examiner might not reach the same conclusion on a second test. The performance observed the first time might be just good luck, or perhaps an unusually poor performance due to anxiety. Thus we would obtain a more accurate idea of driving ability if the test was repeated many times, although to get the examinee's absolutely true ability would require infinitely many such tests.

These heuristic ideas of what makes for a sensible, reliable test motivated psychometricians to develop a formal theory of mental tests called *true score theory*.

TRUE SCORE THEORY

The Concept of Reliability.   The fundamental idea of true score theory can be stated in a single simple equation:

$$\text{Observed score} = \text{true score} + \text{error} . \tag{1}$$

This equation explicitly states that the score on a test that we observe is composed of two components, the *true score* and an *error*. The term *true score* has a very specific technical meaning: It is not something mystical that can only be learned by delving deep into the soul of the examinee. It is the average score that we would expect to obtain if the examinee took parallel forms of the exam many, many times, and we averaged all of the scores. The *error* term characterizes the difference between the score observed on this particular test and what the unobserved average over many tests might have been, had we gone through the trouble to measure it. Such errors are defined to be random and hence unrelated to true score; in addition, we assume that the variation among the errors is about the same regardless of the size of the true score. This requires the errors to have an average of zero, and some constant variance.

Repeating this same discussion in mathematical terms yields an equation analogous to Eq. 1 for examinee j:

$$x_j = \tau_j + e_j \,, \tag{2}$$

where x_j is the observed score for examinee j, τ_j is examinee j's true score, and e_j is the error for examinee j. These quantities have the following definitional properties:

$$E(x_j) = \tau_j \,, \tag{3}$$

$$E(e_j) = 0 \,, \tag{4}$$

where $E(\cdot)$ is the expected value, or average, of the quantity in parentheses, and

$$\sigma_{\tau e} = 0 \,, \tag{5}$$

where $\sigma_{\tau e}$ is the covariance of τ and e.

In much of the discussion in the rest of this monograph it will be important to consider aggregating the scores over many examinees, with much consideration of the amount those scores vary. It is commonly assumed that the scores of any examinee are uncorrelated with any other examinee.[2] Using Eq. 2 and the definitions listed earlier, we can decompose the variance of the observed scores (σ_x^2) into two orthogonal components, true score variance (σ_τ^2) and error variance (σ_e^2). This yields:

$$\sigma_x^2 = \sigma_\tau^2 + \sigma_e^2 \,. \tag{6}$$

Equation 6 follows directly from the definitions of true score and error, but provides us with many tools to study test performance. Given that the total variance (σ_x^2) is the sum of true score variance (σ_τ^2) and error variance (σ_e^2), we obviously prefer tests whose error variance is small relative to observed score variance. A test with small error variance would measure an examinee's true score more reliably than a test with a large error vari-

---

[2]This assumption is false if one examinee copies from another, or perhaps if the examinees are nested within class, but under many credible testing situations it is plausible.

ance. We can characterize how reliably a test works by the ratio of error variance to observed score variance (σ_e^2/σ_x^2). If this ratio is sufficiently close to zero, the test is working well—the observed score involves very little error. If it is close to one the test is working poorly—the variation in observed score is mostly just error. This ratio is quite informative: When this quantity is rescaled so that it takes the value 1 when there is no error and 0 when there is only error, this index is the test's *reliability* $(\rho_{x\tau}^2)$.

Reliability is a very important concept, and it is worthwhile to briefly review its derivation: A definition of reliability is that it is the squared correlation between observed score (x) and the true score (τ):

$$\rho_{x\tau}^2 = \sigma_{x\tau}^2/\sigma_x^2\sigma_\tau^2.$$

The covariance $\sigma_{x\tau} = E(x\tau) - E(x)E(\tau)$, which, from Eq. 2, is

$$\sigma_{x\tau} = E[(\tau + e)\tau] - E(\tau + e)E(\tau)$$

$$= E(\tau^2) + E(\tau e) - E(\tau)^2 - E(e)E(\tau).$$

But from Eq. 4, $E(e) = 0$, and from Eq. 5, $E(\tau e) = 0$, so the expression for the covariance reduces to

$$\sigma_{x\tau} = E(\tau^2) - E(\tau)^2.$$

which is true score variance; thus

$$\sigma_{x\tau} = \sigma_\tau^2.$$

Substituting this result into the definition $\rho_{x\tau}^2 = \sigma_{x\tau}^2/\sigma_x^2\sigma_\tau^2$ yields another definitional form of reliability:

$$\rho_{x\tau}^2 = \sigma_\tau^2/\sigma_x^2 = 1 - (\sigma_e^2/\sigma_x^2). \tag{7}$$

So the reliability of a test is the fraction of observed score variance that is true score variance, or the proportion that is *not* error variance. These representations of reliability are intuitively appealing, but they are not in forms that can be directly computed from observed data; although we can observe σ_x^2, we cannot observe σ_e^2 or σ_τ^2. A slightly different conception, using the idea of parallel test forms, yields an observable quantity.

Before we use the idea of parallel test forms, we need a formal definition: Two forms of a test, form X and form X', having scores x and x' respectively, are parallel if

$$E(x) = E(x') = \tau \quad \text{and} \quad \sigma_x^2 = \sigma_{x'}^2, \tag{8}$$

for all subpopulations taking the test.[3]

The correlation of one parallel form with another, $\rho_{xx'}$, is

$$\rho_{xx'} = \frac{\sigma_{xx'}}{\sigma_x \sigma_{x'}}$$

$$= \frac{\sigma_{(\tau + e)(\tau + e')}}{\sigma_x \sigma_{x'}}$$

$$= \frac{\sigma_{\tau\tau} + \sigma_{\tau e} + \sigma_{\tau e'} + \sigma_{ee'}}{\sigma_x \sigma_{x'}}.$$

The last three terms in the numerator are zero, yielding

$$\frac{\sigma_{\tau\tau}}{\sigma_x \sigma_{x'}}.$$

But $\sigma_{\tau\tau} = \sigma_\tau^2$, and from Eq. 8, $\sigma_x = \sigma_{x'}$, so that $\sigma_x \sigma_{x'} = \sigma_x^2$. Combining these results we obtain

$$\rho_{xx'} = \sigma_\tau^2 / \sigma_x^2,$$

but because $\sigma_x^2 = \sigma_\tau^2 + \sigma_e^2$ (from Eq. 6), we can rewrite this as

$$\rho_{xx'} = 1 - (\sigma_e^2 / \sigma_x^2). \tag{9}$$

Comparing Eq. 9 with 7 yields the result that

$$\rho_{xx'} = \rho_{x\tau}^2. \tag{10}$$

This result is important because $\rho_{xx'}$ is directly estimable from data whereas $\rho_{x\tau}^2$ is not; in the rest of this book, we often use the simpler nota-

---

[3]Parallel test forms may be easy, or almost impossible, to construct, depending on the precision with which we can specify the domain the test is intended to measure. For easy, consider a spelling test: Alternate forms of a spelling test may be constructed by simple random sampling from an appropriate (long) word list; if such alternate forms are sufficiently long, they will be parallel by construction. For almost impossible, consider trying to develop parallel forms of a reading comprehension test to be administered to sighted and blind examinees, respectively, one printed and one in Braille. Even though the two forms may contain identical passages and questions, how would we ever determine if they were of equal difficulty, as required for parallel test forms?

tion ρ, instead of $\rho_{xx'}$, for reliability. Methods to estimate ρ accurately and efficiently have been the subject of a great deal of work that we only touch on here. One obvious way is to construct two parallel forms of a test, give them both to a reasonably large, appropriate sample of people, and calculate the correlation between the two scores. That correlation is an estimate of the reliability of the test. But making up a second form of a test that is truly parallel to the first is, at the very least, a lot of work.

An easier task is to take a single form, divide it randomly in half, consider each half a parallel form of the other, and correlate the scores obtained on the two halves. For obvious reasons, such a measure of test reliability is called *split-half reliability*. This would yield an estimate of reliability, except that each half is too short. The answer we would get would be the reliability for a test that is half as long as the test we actually gave. A second issue that must be resolved before using the split-half reliability operationally is to decide how to split the test. Certainly all splits will not yield the same estimate, and we would not want to base our estimate on an unfortunate division. Let us consider each of these issues in turn.

The Spearman–Brown "Prophecy" Formula. Suppose we take a test X, containing n items, and break it up into two half tests, say Y and Y', each with $n/2$ items. We can then calculate the correlation that exists between Y and Y' (call it $\rho_{yy'}$), but what we really want to know would have been the correlation between X and an imaginary parallel form X' ($\rho_{xx'}$). A formula (Eq. 11) for estimating this correlation was developed independently by Spearman (1910) and Brown (1910) and is named in their honor:

$$\rho_{xx'} = \frac{2\rho_{yy'}}{1+\rho_{yy'}}. \qquad (11)$$

A derivation of Eq. 11 follows directly from the characteristics of parallel tests and is given on pages 83–84 in Lord and Novick (1968). In the past, it has sometimes been called a "prophecy" formula because it appears to foretell the future: What would happen if the test was made twice as long? Of course, it is not prophecy; it is only algebra.

The relation of the effect of doubling test length on reliability, as it is related to the reliability one begins with, is shown in the Fig. 2.1. The curved line in Fig. 2.1 shows the estimated reliability of a test of double length. Note that when reliability of the original test is extreme (0 or 1), doubling its length has no effect. The greatest effect occurs in the middle; a test whose reliability is .50 attains a reliability of .67 when made twice as long.

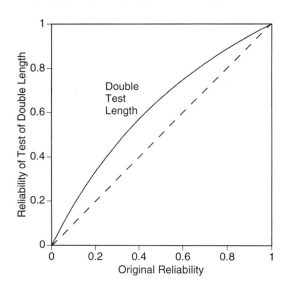

FIG. 2.1. Reliability of a test at doubled length as a function of reliability at unit length.

Equation 11 is an important result, because it allows us to calculate the split-half reliability as a correlation between two randomly parallel half tests and then analytically boost it to estimate the reliability of the entire test. As we show later, it is often useful to have a generalization of this equation to allow us to estimate the reliability of a test if it is lengthened (or shortened) by any amount. Such a generalization follows directly from the same derivation that gave the special case of the Spearman–Brown formula in Eq. 11.

Consider a test X, containing n items; it can be divided into m smaller parallel tests, say $Y_1, Y_2, \ldots, Y_m$, each with n/m items. We can then calculate the correlation between any pair of the subtests, say Y and Y', which we once again call $\rho_{yy'}$. Note that theoretically it doesn't matter which pair of subtests we choose to calculate $\rho_{yy'}$, because they are all parallel forms so all of the correlations are equal, at least in expectation. Once again, we really want to know the correlation between X and an imaginary parallel form X' ($\rho_{xx'}$). Equation 12 parallels Eq. 11 and is called the *generalized Spearman–Brown formula*:

$$\rho_{xx'} = \frac{m\rho_{yy'}}{1 + (m - 1)\rho_{yy'}}. \tag{12}$$

Note that if we divide the test in half ($m = 2$), Eq. 12 specializes to Eq. 11. The derivation of Eq. 12, although somewhat more complex than that required for Eq. 11, follows in the same spirit and is given on pages 85–90 in Lord and Novick (1968).

To recapitulate: After noting that because true score is not observable, the reliability of a test cannot be computed directly. This remains true in either of the two equivalent definitions, as the ratio of the true score variance to observed score variance, or as the squared correlation of the observed scores with the true scores. Instead, we showed that reliability is equivalent to the correlation between two parallel forms of the same test. This led us to estimate that correlation by dividing the test in half and correlating the scores on those two halves. This is a measure of reliability, but the reliability of a test that is only half as long as the test we were interested in. Happily, we are able to boost that reliability to what it would have been for a test that was twice as long using Eq. 11. For completeness, we described a useful generalization of Eq. 11, the *generalized Spearman–Brown formula* (Eq. 12).

The question that we address next completes the solution of the problem of how to compute test reliability, using only data from a single test. Specifically, how can we be sure that the particular split we chose is not unusual in some sense and yields an unfortunately unrepresentative value of the test's reliability?

Which Split Half? Cronbach's Coefficient α. There are many ways that we can split a test of n items in half (assuming that n is an even number). Specifically, there are

$$\frac{1}{2}\binom{n}{\frac{n}{2}} = \frac{n!}{2\left[\left(\frac{n}{2}\right)!\right]^2}$$

different ways that n items can be split in half; Table 2.1 shows these values for some short, and then some common, test lengths. With all of these possible ways to divide the test in half, it can be difficult to determine which one we should pick to best represent the reliability of the test. One obvious way around this problem is to calculate all of them and use their mean as our best estimate. But calculating all for any test of nontrivial length is impossible. For example, 50 items yields the possibility of more than 63 trillion split halves, and a 100-item test yields 5×10^{28} splits! Given that modern computers are very fast, is it possible to compute the correlations among all possible split halves? One hundred items is not an unusually long test, but if a computer could calculate correlations at 1 billion per second (which is at least a thousand times faster than current supercomputers) it would take almost 16 billion centuries to calculate them all!

TABLE 2.1
The Number of Ways That a Test of Various Lengths (Numbers of
Items) Can Be Divided in Half

Test Length	Number of Ways to Divide It in Half
2	1
4	3
6	10
8	35
10	126
12	462
14	1,716
16	6,435
18	24,310
20	92,378
30	77,558,760
40	68,923,264,410
50	63,205,303,218,876

What can we do? One option emerges if we remember that statistics can be thought of as the art of making inferences about a lot from a little. Perhaps we could judiciously choose a subset of the splits (say a thousand of them), calculate the mean of those, and use that as our estimate. This would probably work, but happily it isn't necessary. Cronbach (1951) derived a statistic that is a lower bound on the reliability of the test. It is equivalent to computing the mean for all possible splits, and using the Spearman–Brown formula to extend that to a reliability estimate for the test. Sixteen years later, Novick and Lewis (1967) provided the conditions under which Cronbach's statistic becomes equal to the reliability.[4] Cronbach's statistic is usually called *Cronbach's* α in his honor, and is shown as Eq. 13:

$$\rho_{xx'} \geq \frac{n}{n-1}\left[1 - \frac{\sum_{i=1}^{n}\sigma_{y_i}^2}{\sigma_x^2}\right] = \alpha.$$

(13)

(The special case of Eq. 13 for binary items was provided by Kuder and Richardson [1937]; the formula was equation number 20 in that article, so it came to be called "KR-20.")

---

[4]A necessary and sufficient condition for Cronbach's α to be equal to the test's reliability, and not just a lower bound, is that all of the components making up the score have the same true score. The technical name for this condition is that all components are τ-equivalent.

To calculate α, we conceive of the test score x as being composed of the sum of n items Y_i. We calculate the variance of each item's scores across all of the examinees who took that item and sum it up over all the items. Next we calculate the variance of the total score. The ratio of these two variances forms the core of Cronbach's α. Although other statistics have been proposed and are used for some purposes, this statistic is the most commonly used measure of test reliability. Among the others are Hoyt's (1941) analysis of variance (ANOVA) index and Armor's (1974) θ, but they can be shown to be either identical to α, or very similar (Li & Wainer, 1997). A tabulation by Feldt and Brennan (1989, p. 115) clarifies relations among a dozen formulas for reliability.

A Brief Summary. So far, we have described a simple linear model for test scores,

$$\text{Observed score} = \text{true score} + \text{error} ,$$

in which true score was defined as the expected score over many repeated parallel forms of the same test. The difference between observed score and true score is the error, which, for good measurement, we would like to be as small as possible. We described a measure of precision, test reliability, which is defined as the ratio of true score variance to observed score variance, or the squared correlation between observed score and true score; that was shown to be identical to the correlation between two observed scores on parallel test forms. This latter formulation allows us to compute this statistic from observable quantities. One way to do so requires that we split a test in half, correlate the scores on the two halves with one another, and then adjust this correlation with the Spearman–Brown formula to what the correlation would have been had the test been twice as long. This forms one basis for presenting Cronbach's α, which is the average reliability for all split halves and is a lower bound on the reliability of a test. All of these results are important in themselves, but in addition they contribute importantly to the next problem.

RELIABILITY FOR MORE COMPLEX SITUATIONS

Testlet Reliability. Thus far, we have developed the ideas involved in estimating reliability from internal consistency without much regard for the properties of the items themselves. Implicitly, we have assumed that the items on the test are *fungible* units—that is, any item may be used in place of any other item, so that the correlation between any two item scores is a reliability estimate, just like the correlation between scores on parallel forms of many items.

Feldt and Brennan (1989, p. 120) pointed out that if an average item level reliability is defined as the average of the covariances between pairs of items divided by the average item variances, as follows,

$$\bar{\rho}_{x_j x_{j'}} = \frac{\sum\limits_{\text{item pairs}} \sigma_{x_j x_{j'}}}{(n-1)\sum\limits_{\text{items}} \sigma_{x_j^2}}, \qquad (14)$$

then coefficient α may be defined as the Spearman–Brown extension of that average item-level reliability for an n-item test:

$$\alpha = \frac{n\bar{\rho} x_j x_{j'}}{1 + (n-1)\bar{\rho} x_j x_{j'}}. \qquad (15)$$

Although Feldt and Brennan's treatment of this material was more readily accessible, they noted that this algebraic version of coefficient α is due to Stanley (1957). Feldt and Brennan also noted that Cronbach (1951) demonstrated that α equals the average of all possible split-half coefficients (if one uses the right formula for split-half reliability). In fact, α equals the average of all possible reliability coefficients for any properly constructed subdivisions of the test.[5]

Feldt and Brennan (1989, p. 120) wrote that "This property of coefficient α could be viewed as a virtue or a flaw, depending on the nature of the test." If the items on the test are homogeneous, then any division of the items into subsets would produce an acceptable estimate of split-half reliability, because any division of the items would create two randomly equivalent (shorter) tests. In such a case, the fact that coefficient α is the average of the reliability estimates that would be obtained from all possible divisions is a good thing. On the other hand, if the test has some structure, then some divisions of the items into subsets would create tests that would not correspond to the structure of the original test. In the latter case, coefficient α may be an average of different reliabilities.

As we noted earlier, the goal in the use of internal consistency computations is to estimate parallel-form reliability without actually administering parallel forms. So the question is: How would a parallel form be related to the current form? If parallel forms could be constructed by selecting any

---

[5]For details, see Feldt and Brennan (1989, p. 120) and elsewhere for specific reliability formulas that need to be used to make this true.

random set of items from the same pool or domain—that is, if the items are the fungible units in test assembly—then coefficient α is the de facto standard for reporting reliability. Feldt and Brennan (1989) described several alternative formulas for reliability for such cases, but other formulations see little use in practice. Examples of tests for which the items are fairly clearly fungible are spelling tests, or multiple-choice vocabulary tests, or tests comprising simple arithmetic problems—in any of those cases, parallel forms could (either really, or hypothetically) be constructed by sampling individual items from a specifiable domain.

Other tests have more structure. The time-honored example is the reading comprehension test, in which a cluster of questions (multiple-choice or open-ended) are associated with some reading material (the *passage*).[6] Parallel forms of such a test cannot mix-and-match items in any random way—if a passage is included on the test, then some or all of the items associated with that passage are included. There have been many recommendations offered over the decades about how reliability should be computed for such tests. Feldt and Brennan (1989, p. 112) pointed out that the most common advice has been to keep the clusters intact when computing split-half reliability, or, by extension, any index of internal consistency; however, they observed that this practice may or may not give the desired answer. Feldt and Brennan used an example, a reading test, on which

> There might be a poem, a short essay, an excerpt from a novel, some dialogue from a play, a newspaper article, and so on. Typically, there is only one passage of each type. A parallel form also includes one passage of each type. In this setting, one may postulate four components of an observed score: (a) a component associated with general reading ability, (b) a component associated with materials of a given type, (c) a component associated with a specific example of a given type, and (d) a residual component encompassing other sources of variance including errors of measurement. (p. 112)

In this example, if split halves are created by assigning entire passages (with all of their questions) to one half or the other, all components of the score except the first are classified as error. However, the test specifications might require that any real parallel forms would have the same mix-

---

[6]Many other kinds of tests have passage analogs: Mathematics tests may have a series of questions about a particular graphic; problem-solving tests in virtually any content area may have a question with multiple parts that appear to be several questions. Some relatively new item types have even closer ties between or among sets of questions than do passage-based tests; as an example, consider mathematics questions that (in one question) ask for a solution to a problem, and in the next question ask for an explanation of the solution.

ture of types of passages, so that component (b) would not be error if an estimate of reliability were to be computed from actual parallel forms. On the other hand, if split halves divided the items following a particular passage, component (c) would be divided between the halves, and would contribute to true score rather than error variance, although component (c) would contribute entirely to error in an analysis of real parallel forms.

Feldt and Brennan (1989, p. 112) concluded that "treating passages as intact units tends to bias the resultant coefficient negatively. Splitting items within passages tends to bias the coefficient positively. Which of these is the more attractive, or the less unattractive, is a matter of opinion."

One possible way to develop an opinion about which strategy should be adopted for reliability reporting for tests comprising clusters of items is to extend our consideration of internal consistency to include the ways it may be related to validity for likely uses of the test scores. Elaborating on the example suggested by Feldt and Brennan, let us say that a reading comprehension test's specifications require that it shall always include clusters of questions based on passages that are "a poem, a short essay, an excerpt from a novel, some dialogue from a play, [and] a newspaper article." Parallel forms of this test would always include examples of those five passage types; this argument suggests that the best estimate derived from internal consistency data would be computed as "stratified reliability" or "the reliability of a composite test" (discussed in a subsequent section).

However, consider the likely use of scores on such a reading comprehension test: Inferences would probably be made about the level of comprehension that the examinee might exhibit after reading some material of some random type with some random content, where neither the type nor the content may have been represented on the particular form of the test on which the examinee was scored. If our use of reliability is intended to include the idea that the square root of reliability is the upper bound on validity (where validity is represented as the correlation between the test score and a hypothetical error-free validity criterion), then for this use of the test, more useful (albeit hypothetical) parallel forms would comprise several passages of entirely different types and with entirely different content. That is, we would want reliability to be an estimate of the correlation between form A and form B, where form A included a poem on flowers, a short essay on philosophy, an excerpt from a novel (make it a murder mystery), some dialogue from a play (Shakespeare), and a newspaper article on the economy, and an entirely hypothetical form B, which might include lyrics from a love song, a scientific research report, an excerpt from a biography, a political speech, and a legal contract. If we would like our estimate of reliability, derived from internal consistency, to be an estimate of the correlation between parallel forms such as those forms A and B, then the contributions of Feldt and Brennan's components (b), (c), and (d) are all clearly "error." Then, to compute split-half reliability, we would create halves of the test by placing all of the questions associated with each passage in one half or the other, because the true score that we are trying to estimate is what Feldt and Brennan called "a component associated with general reading ability"—general, that is, across passage type or content.

Coefficient α makes the computation of such a passage-level reliability straightforward: If one uses the summed score for the questions associated with each passage as the "item" scores in the computation of coefficient α, the result is the average of all of the split-half reliability estimates that could be computed by making up halves at the passage level. We have referred to the subunits of the test comprising a passage and its associated questions as a *testlet*. "A testlet is a group of items related to a single content area that is developed as a unit and contains a fixed number of predetermined paths that an examinee may follow" (Wainer & Kiely, 1987, p. 190). Often, the correlations between items within a testlet are higher than the correlations between items across testlet boundaries, due to the kinds of effects that Feldt and Brennan characterized as "component[s] associated with materials of a given type, [and] component[s] associated with a specific example of a given type." In cases in which we consider those components to be more specific than we intend to measure with the test, we refer to the "excess" interitem correlation due to those factors as *local dependence*.[7]

When tests are constructed of testlets, but the higher correlations observed for pairs of items within a testlet (as compared to pairs of items across testlet boundaries) are not due to components that we intend to measure explicitly with the test score, we have proposed that *testlet reliability* is appropriate: Compute coefficient α for the testlet scores. Sireci, Thissen, and Wainer (1991) reported that testlet α was about 10% lower than item-level α for two multiple-choice reading comprehension tests with 4 passages and 5–12 items associated with each passage. Wainer and Thissen (1996) elaborated on this theme, using as illustrations several forms of a state accountability multiple-choice reading test for which the difference between testlet α and item-level α was somewhat smaller (but always in the direction that testlet α was lower), and an analysis over several admissions tests that indicated that the more items are associated with each testlet, the greater is the reduction in testlet reliability relative to (apparent) item-level reliability. Lawrence (1995) compared item-level and section-level internal-consistency estimates of reliability with each other, and with test–retest estimates, for a number of passage-based SAT reading

---

[7]The term *local dependence* is not particularly well motivated within the context of the traditional test theory as discussed in this chapter; we return to this topic, and this term, in chapter 4, where we discuss the relations of testlets to item response theory.

comprehension forms, and found that the section-level estimates were consistently smaller than the item-level estimates (and test–retest estimates were lower than either).

When considered in association with many likely uses of test scores, item-level computation tends to overstate the reliability of testlet-based tests. This overstatement of reliability may lead test constructors to assemble tests that are really too short (and hence too inaccurate) for their intended purpose. This flaw is especially serious if the scores on the test are used to make high-stakes decisions, as is increasingly the case with large-scale accountability measures. Thus far, in practice, performance assessments appear to be even more likely to be constructed with testlets than are traditional multiple-choice tests. Given this, along with the relatively low reliability often associated with performance assessments (due to the fact that they often include substantially fewer items than traditional multiple choice tests), it is especially important that reliability computations for high-stakes performance assessments be done with the intended interpretations of the test scores in mind—and usually that means as testlet reliability.

The Difference Between Item and Testlet Reliability: The Multiple-Choice Sections of the Wisconsin Student Assessment System Reading and Language Tests. Table 2.2 shows coefficient α, computed for the item scores, and for the passage or testlet scores, for two forms (each) of the Wisconsin Student Assessment System reading and language tests. The parts of these tests considered here are 30-item multiple-choice tests. The Grade 8 reading test has between 5 and 9 comprehension items following each of five reading passages; the Grade 10 reading test has 9 to 11 items following each of three passages. For the language tests, the items are in blocks, which may involve (grammatical) sentence completion (9 or 10 items), correction of punctuation, capitalization, or word usage in a passage (5–6 items), identification of correctly-constructed sentences (10–11 items), or combining two sentences into one (3–5 items). For the reading test, testlet scores were computed as the number of questions answered

TABLE 2.2
Coefficient α, Computed for the Item Scores, and for the
Testlet Scores, for Two Forms (Each) of the Wisconsin
Student Assessment System Reading and Language Tests

	Item α	*Testlet* α
Grade 8 Reading	.78	.74
Grade 10 Reading	.81	.74
Grade 8 Language	.83	.76
Grade 10 Language	.80	.67

correctly after each passage; for the language test, testlet scores were the number correct within each section as defined by the four item types.

Table 2.2 shows, as we have found previously, that the reliability estimates computed using the item-level data on these structured tests are higher than those computed using the testlet scores. The difference between item-level and testlet-level reliability is larger for the Grade 10 tests, which tend to have larger numbers of items in each testlet than the Grade 8 tests. For the reading test, if we assume that a parallel form would be constructed for each of these tests by choosing several altogether different reading passages (this seems likely), then the reliability estimate based on the testlet scores is a better prediction of test–retest reliability than is the estimate based on item-level internal consistency. For the language test, it is less clear how a (conceptual) parallel form might be constructed. If an alternate language test was considered that had a different set of grammatical tasks, measuring the same language skills, then the testlet reliability estimate would be best. If, however, the set of grammatical tasks represented on the language test is taken as fixed, then neither of the estimates in Table 2.2 would be correct; instead, we should consider reliability for composite scores.

The Reliability of a Composite Score.   Scores for many tests are computed as a weighted sum of scores on two or more components; examples are the score on the Law School Admission Test (LSAT) that is a sum of scores on *Reading Comprehension, Analytical Reasoning,* and *Logical Reasoning* sections, and the score on the SAT II Writing Subject Test that is based on a weighted combination of scores on a multiple choice section and the rating of an essay. There are many ways to state what the weights are for such linear combinations. To avoid ambiguity, we define the composite score as

$$z_c = \sum w_v z_v, \tag{16}$$

where z_c is the composite score, w_v is the weight for component v, and z_v is the standardized score on component v. (The weights w for so-called "unweighted" sums of the summed scores of the components are actually the standard deviations of the component scores.)

The components of such a composite score may well "measure different things"; nevertheless, the idea of its reliability remains the same. Reliability is an estimate of the correlation we would obtain between these scores and those that would be obtained on a parallel form. In this case, the parallel form would have the same composite structure. The reliability of such composite scores is defined, in general, just as it is defined for simple summed scores in Eq. 7, as

$$\rho_c = 1 - \frac{\sigma_{e_z}^2}{\sigma_z^2} \tag{17}$$

where $\sigma_{e_z}^2$ is the error variance of the composite score (Feldt & Brennan, 1989, p. 116). In most practical applications, values of $\sigma_{e_z}^2$ and σ_z^2 can be obtained from sample data for a single administration of the components of the test; as a result, we can estimate ρ_c without actually administering parallel forms.

In general, Eq. 17 is

$$\rho_c = 1 - \frac{\sum_v w_v^2 \sigma_{e_v}^2}{\sum_v w_v^2 \sigma_{z_v}^2 + \sum_v \sum_{v'} w_v w_{v'} \sigma_{z_v} \sigma_{z_{v'}}}, \tag{18}$$

but with the convenience of standardized component scores, for which $(1 - \rho_v) = \sigma_{e_v}^2$, and the substitution of sample estimates r_v for the reliability of component v, and $r_{vv'}$ for the correlation between component v and component v', which becomes the estimate

$$r_c = 1 - \frac{\sum_v w_v^2 (1 - r_v)}{\sum_v w_v^2 + \sum_v \sum_{v'} w_v w_{v'} r_{vv'}}. \tag{19}$$

Various alternative forms of Eq. 19 are given by Feldt and Brennan (1989, pp. 116–118, where one form is also called "stratified α") and Lord and Novick (1968, pp. 203–204).

As a concrete example, consider a hypothetical test of writing skills that comprises a multiple-choice section that is allocated 40 minutes of testing time, for which coefficient α is .85, and an essay section that is allocated 20 minutes of testing time. The essay is written as a response to a single prompt, and scored by two raters, yielding a total score with alternate-form reliability estimated to be .60. The observed correlation between the multiple-choice scores and the essay scores is approximately .43. The total score on the test is a weighted combination of the standardized score on the multiple-choice part, weighted by 2, and the standardized score on the essay, weighted by 1. The 2:1 ratio of the weights was selected to represent the 2:1 ratio in testing time allotted to the two sections.[8]

A simplification of Eq. 19 for a test with two sections is

---

[8]Although these values for the reliabilities and correlation are hypothetical, the structure of this test is that of the SAT II Writing Subject Test, and the values of the reliabilities and the correlation between sections are similar to values obtained for that test.

$$r_c = 1 - \frac{w_1^2(1 - r_1) + w_2^2(1 - r_2)}{w_1^2 + w_2^2 + 2\,w_1 w_2 r_{12}}. \tag{20}$$

Substituting sample values for the writing test just described, we obtain

$$r_c = 1 - \frac{2^2(1 - 0.85) + 1^2(1 - 0.60)}{2^2 + 1^2 + 2 \times 2 \times 1 \times 0.43} \approx 0.851\,.$$

It is curious that the reliability of the composite score for this writing test is almost exactly the same as the reliability of the multiple-choice section alone. The use of the composite score, including the essay score, is usually justified by the developers of tests such as this one on the grounds that the essay score "measures the right thing," and even if it does so less reliably than the multiple-choice test that (allegedly) "measures the wrong thing," its score should be included. For examples such as this writing test, that argument is best supported by data concerning the relative validity (for some purpose) of the test with (and without) the essay section, because consideration of test reliability alone does not justify the additional effort involved in the essay section over and above the multiple-choice test.

What Should the Weights Be?   The formulas for the reliability of composite scores discussed in the preceding section assume that the weights w are known. But what if the problem is to choose the weights, or evaluate a set of proposed weights? It is universally acknowledged that the best way to select weights for a composite is to choose the weights that maximize the relation of the composite score with some reliable criterion chosen so that it represents validity for the purpose of the test. Regrettably, reliable data representing validity criteria are much more rare than the necessity to select weights. Absent a validity criterion, internal consistency may provide a basis for rational choice: How do the relative weights of the components of a composite score affect reliability?

Reconsider the hypothetical writing test used as an illustration in the preceding section—but now imagine that we do not know how we would like to weight the multiple-choice and essay sections in the composite. To make the problem a little more manageable, we rewrite Eq. 20 with the constraint that $w_1 + w_2 = 1$; therefore $w_2 = 1 - w_1$, and

$$r_c = 1 - \frac{w_1^2(1 - r_1) + (1 - w_1)^2(1 - r_2)}{w_1^2 + (1 - w_1)^2 + 2\,w_1(1 - w_1)r_{12}}. \tag{21}$$

Now we can reconsider the composite reliability for the writing test as a function of the (proportional) weight (w_1) given to the multiple-choice section:

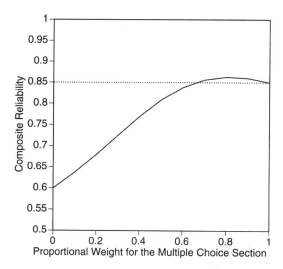

FIG. 2.2.   Composite reliability (r_c) plotted as a function of w_1 for the writing test example.

$$r_c = 1 - \frac{w_1^2(1-0.85) + (1-w_1)^2(1-0.60)}{w_1^2 + (1-w_1)^2 + 2\,w_1(1-w_1)0.43}.$$

Figure 2.2 shows composite reliability (r_c) plotted as a function of w_1. We note first the obvious: When $w_1 = 1$ (that is, the multiple-choice section is weighted 1 and the essay score is weighted zero), r_c is equal to the reliability of the multiple-choice section. When $w_1 = 0$ (that is, the multiple-choice section is weighted zero and the essay score is weighted 1), r_c is equal to the reliability of the essay score. A little less obviously, for values of $w_1 > 0.66$, the curve for ρ_c exceeds the reliability of the multiple-choice section (0.85), whereas for values of $w_1 < 0.66$, the curve drops fairly precipitously toward 0.6, the lower of the reliabilities of the two components.

The general form of Fig. 2.2 suggests a criterion that could be considered when weights are chosen for two unequally reliable parts of a composite score, such as the combination of an open-ended or performance assessment with a multiple-choice test. One might consider choosing the relative weights such that the reliability of the composite is *no less* than the reliability of the more reliable component.[9] If two components of a test are unequally reliable, with $r_1 > r_2$, then Eq. 21 can be solved for the lowest value of w_1 for which $r_c \geq r_1$; that value is w_H[10]:

---

[9] The commonly quoted summary of part of the Hippocratic Oath ("First do no harm") suggests the evocative *Hippocratic Criterion* for this rule. This eponymy is reflected in our notation w_H.

[10] We are grateful to A. Thissen-Roe for the algebraic development of the formula for w_H.

$$w_H = \frac{r_1 - r_2}{(r_1 - r_2) + 2r_{12}(1 - r_1)}.$$ (22)

For the writing test example,

$$w_H = \frac{0.85 - 0.60}{(0.85 - 0.60) + 2 \times 0.43(1 - 0.85)} \approx 0.66$$

and so we find that the 2:1 weights in use for that test (equivalent to $w_1 \approx$ 0.66) provide the lowest possible weight for the multiple-choice section for which the composite reliability of the test remains above that of the multiple-choice section alone. Using Eq. 22, if one is faced with the problem of choosing weights for two sections to be combined, and if one has estimates of the reliabilities of the two sections and their intercorrelation, the minimum (proportional) weight for the more reliable section can be computed that will yield a composite that is at least as reliable as its more reliable part. Common sense might suggest avoidance of weights below w_H.

For composites comprising more than two components, there is no simple computation (like that for w_H) that distinguishes good weighting schemes from those that are less good—many combinations of three or more weights may yield a reliability that is greater than the reliability of the most reliable component, and many others will not. However, weights that yield the maximum reliability for the composite (r_c) may be computed for any number of components.

If the components of a linearly combined composite are positively correlated, there is always some weighting scheme that yields maximum reliability for the composite (r_c). That is, there are some weights w_v that maximize Eq. 17. Unfortunately, the derivation of the procedure that may be used to compute the weights that give maximum composite reliability is somewhat more complex mathematically. Nevertheless, we reproduce a condensed version of the derivation here, with the result, so that those with access to appropriate computational facilities might make use of the weights that maximize ρ_c as guidance in the choice of weights.

The General Solution for Optimal Weights.[11]   Gulliksen (1950/1987, p. 346) credited Thomson (1940) with the first general solution to the problem, but it is the solution offered by Peel (1948) and refined by Green (1950) that yields the easiest computation using modern software for ma-

---

[11]This section relies on matrix algebra; see chapter 1, p. 5 for references to background material that may be useful.

trix manipulation. To approach the problem, it is useful to rewrite Eq. 17 in matrix format:

$$r_c = \frac{\mathbf{w'\,Cw}}{\mathbf{w'\,Rw}}.$$ (23)

In this matrix formulation, $\mathbf{w}$ is a vector of the weights for the components of the composite, $\mathbf{R}$ is the correlation matrix among those components, and $\mathbf{C}$ is identical to $\mathbf{R}$, except that $\mathbf{C}$ has the reliabilities of the components on its diagonal.[12]

With the constraint that

$$\mathbf{w'Rw} = 1,$$

standard results in matrix algebra (see Bock, 1975, pp. 91–92) give the result that the maximum value of r_c in Eq. 23 may be computed by solving the so-called "two-matrix eigen problem"

$$(\mathbf{C} - \lambda\mathbf{R})\mathbf{w} = 0.$$ (24)

There are as many solutions for Eq. 24 as there are components in the composite, but for the solution with the largest algebraic value of λ, $\lambda = r_c$, $\mathbf{w}$ contains weights that yield that composite reliability.

The two-matrix eigen problem is usually solved by converting the problem into a standard (one-matrix) eigen problem—and then solving that problem with one of the many standard procedures now implemented in computer software for that purpose. Green (1950) proposed that Eq. 24 be rewritten as

$$(\mathbf{DCD} - \lambda^*\mathbf{I})\mathbf{w}^* = 0,$$ (25)

in which $\mathbf{D}^{-2} = \mathbf{R} - \mathbf{C}$ (that is, the diagonal elements of the diagonal matrix $\mathbf{D}$ are $1/\sqrt{1 - r_v}$). After using standard procedures to solve Eq. 25 for the largest root (eigenvalue) λ^*, and the associated vector $\mathbf{w}^*$, one computes

$$r_c = \frac{\lambda^*}{1 + \lambda^*}$$ (26)

and

_____

[12]Li (1997) gave interesting formulas expanding alternative meanings of the maximum-of-linear-composite reliability formula. For a more recent treatment of constructing composites to maximize reliability, see Cliff and Caruso (1998).

$$\mathbf{w} = k \; \mathbf{Dw^*}. \tag{27}$$

The norming constant k in Eq. 27 may have any value; we use

$$k = \frac{1}{\mathbf{1'Dw^*}},$$

where $\mathbf{1}$ is a vector of ones, to obtain weights that are interpretable as proportions.

Turning again to the writing test example, we used Lisp-Stat (Tierney, 1990) to compute the maximum value of ρ_C and the associated weights; however, other statistical systems that support matrix operations, such as SAS IML (SAS Institute, Inc., 1988) or S (Becker & Chambers, 1984), could have been used as well. In matrix form, we have

$$\mathbf{R} = \begin{bmatrix} 1 & 0.43 \\ 0.43 & 1 \end{bmatrix},$$

because the correlation between the multiple-choice and essay sections is 0.43. Then

$$\mathbf{C} = \begin{bmatrix} 0.85 & 0.43 \\ 0.43 & 0.60 \end{bmatrix},$$

(inserting the reliabilities for the two sections on the diagonal), and

$$\mathbf{D} = \begin{bmatrix} 2.58 & 0 \\ 0 & 1.58 \end{bmatrix},$$

(the diagonal elements of $\mathbf{D}$ are $1/\sqrt{1-0.85}$ and $1/\sqrt{1-0.60}$). Then

$$\mathbf{DCD} = \begin{bmatrix} 5.667 & 1.755 \\ 1.755 & 1.5 \end{bmatrix},$$

and the largest eigenvalue (λ^*) of $\mathbf{DCD}$ is 6.308, so

$$r_c = \frac{6.308}{1+6.308} = 0.863,$$

and the weights, after normalization to sum to 1, are

$$w_1 = 0.82 \quad \text{and} \quad w_2 = 0.18.$$

Commentary on Optimal Weights. When these procedures were developed in the 1940s, tedious hand computation was required to solve even the simplified Eq. 25. That is one of the reasons that this procedure for determining optimal weights has seen little use. Another reason these procedures have been used relatively little is that influential writers, such as Gulliksen, advised (wisely) against their blind use. Gulliksen (1950/1987, pp. 350–351) warned that the optimal weights may well yield combinations other than those intended, depending on the composition of the composite score. Gulliksen (1950/1987, p. 351) recommended that "mathematical procedures are appropriately used when they serve to *guide* thought. If an attempt is made to utilize such routines as a *substitute* for thought, we may unwittingly arrive at and accept an absurd conclusion" (emphasis in the original).

Given modern computational machinery, and the problem of choosing weights for a composite score, we emphasize the usefulness of knowledge of the maximum reliability that can be obtained, and the weights that give that reliability, as a *guide* for choosing weights. Referring back to Figure 2.2, we note that for the writing test, the graph of r_c as a function of w_1 (the proportional weight for the multiple-choice section) is relatively flat in the general vicinity of its maximum value. However, below w_H, composite reliability drops sharply. This means that it would be wise to choose weights somewhere in the general vicinity of those that yield maximum composite reliability—or at least, one should be aware of how much less reliability than the maximum any particular set of weights might yield.

The finding that the optimal proportional weight for the multiple-choice section of the writing test is 0.82, combined with our earlier computation of $w_H = 0.66$ for these data, serves to provide numerical clarification of Figure 2.2, and a specification of where the weights "don't make no nevermind" (Wainer, 1976) and where the weights matter: For any (proportional) weight between 0.66 and 1 for the multiple choice section, composite reliability is between 0.85 and 0.863—that is the "flat" part of the curve in Figure 2.2; choice among weights in that region makes little difference for test reliability. For (proportional) weights below 0.66 for the multiple-choice section, composite reliability drops sharply toward the reliability of the essay scoring, 0.6, so any weight for the multiple-choice section below 66% of the total would result in sharply diminished reliability.

With respect to the writing test, we might consider two questions: If the essay portion of the test occupies half as much time as the multiple-choice section, why are the optimal weights (for reliability) in a ratio of 1:4? And what would need to be done to make a heavier weight for the essay section, which may be desirable for educational reasons, justifiable from a psychometric point of view—as a reduction in the error variance of the test scores? A nearly tautological answer to the first question is that the lower weight afforded to the essay section (in the optimal reliability computation) is due to the fact that the essay section is substantially less reliable than the multiple-choice section: 0.60 versus 0.85.

Why is the essay section less reliable? A naive answer is, "Because of the error inherent in the use of human judges to score the test." However, that answer is usually wrong for well-organized scoring systems for contemporary open-ended test responses. For instance, for the particular writing test on which we based our hypothetical example, the correlation between pairs of raters is about 0.6, which would suggest a reliability for the two-judge scoring of 0.75 if rater reliability was the crucial aspect of the system. The fact that alternate-forms reliability is 0.60 shows that is not the case.

So why is the essay section so unreliable? Probably because it is so short: It includes only one item. Writing samples have in common with many other kinds of performance assessments the property that person-by-task interactions (in the case of a writing test, person-by-prompt interactions) are often one of the largest variance components (Brennan & Johnson, 1995; Linn & Burton, 1994; Shavelson, Gao, & Baxter, 1993)—and those are "error." Translated from components of variance into English, this means what we all know: Some people can write better at a given moment in response to one prompt than in response to another. The random association between persons and the (one) prompt they happen to be given reduces the reliability of this one-item test. We must also remember how little material the raters are actually scoring: The writing samples (dare we call them essays at this length?) that obtain the maximum score for the test that inspired this example are about four paragraphs—about 250 words. Few of us write more in 20 minutes. Writing samples that obtain the minimum score appear often to be one paragraph—maybe 100 words. As a matter of fact, this paragraph and the preceding one (as a first draft, before we rewrote them several times for publication) are as much material as is rated in the writing sample. Given this paucity of information, it is surprising that the ratings of the writing samples can be as useful as they are.

Using reliability as an indication of the quality of measurement, what would it take to justify increasing the weight of the essay section (performance assessment) relative to the multiple-choice part (and incidentally increase the reliability of the composite from 0.85 to the value of 0.9, which is commonly expected of scores on high-stakes individual assessments)? The Spearman–Brown formula (Eq. 12), in combination with Eq. 21, gives us an answer: If the writing sample was quadrupled, to four essays, then the Spearman–Brown formula tells us that the reliability of the essay scoring would reach 0.857—almost exactly equal to the reliability of the multiple-choice section.[13] When the reliabilities of two sections to be combined into a composite are equal, there is no need to do complex computations to determine the optimal relative weights: They are equal. (Solution of the optimal weight problem for any two-section composite where the components have equal reliability gives equal weights as the answer, regardless of the value of the correlation between the components as long as that correlation is greater than zero.) Application of Eq. 21 gives us the result that an equally weighted combination of four essays and the multiple-choice section will have a composite reliability of 0.903. (If the essay section was only doubled, optimal reliability would increase to only 0.877; tripling the essay section yields 0.891.)

These values suggest that the amount of time spent on different kinds of testing may not be the best way to determine weights. Different kinds of testing yield different amounts of information per minute (Wainer & Thissen, 1993). The fact that twice as much time on the writing sample as on the multiple-choice section is necessary before the optimal-reliability system suggests equal weighting indicates that rating a writing sample produces about half as much information per minute of testing time as does answering well-crafted multiple-choice questions. If it is the case that the writing sample is a better indicator of the skills being measured for the purpose of the test, as advocates of performance assessment often propose, then the answer is simple: Give performance assessment enough time to provide high-quality information. Performance assessments, per se, do not necessarily have lower reliability than multiple-choice tests, nor must they always have lower weights in composites. The reliability of performance assessments only becomes a problem when they are expected to produce test scores that have the same psychometric qualities as multiple-choice tests that *take the same amount of time*—it appears that they do not do that, in practice, considering many kinds of performance assessments; writing is only one example.

(Apparent) Composites: Weights for Tests With Parts That Measure the Same Thing.

Many contemporary tests include sections with different item types that are intended to measure the same construct—or which do so, regardless of intention. Consider, for example, the high school end-of-course test in geometry that has recently been administered statewide in North Carolina, using four parallel forms. The geometry test included a 60-item multiple choice section, and open-ended responses to two problems that required geometric proof (the "proofs" section). The 60 multi-

---

[13]This Spearman–Brown-based estimate assumes that it is possible to set up the testing situation so that four essays may be obtained of equal quality to the first, by somehow avoiding fatigue effects.

ple-choice items differed for the four forms (H, I, J, and K). One of the proofs appeared on all four forms, and its solution was judged on a 0–4 scale by two raters; the other proof was form specific, and responses were judged by a single rater.

Summary statistics are tabulated in Table 2.3 for the four forms of the geometry test. For all four forms, coefficient α was .91 (to two decimal places) for the multiple-choice section. Coefficient α ranged from .62 to .67 for the proofs section. And the correlation between the multiple-choice score and the proofs score was always between .69 and .72. Table 2.3 also shows the "estimated true score correlation" computed by applying the classical "correction for attenuation" to the correlation between the multiple-choice score and the proofs score:

$$\text{"Estimated true score correlation"} = \frac{r}{\sqrt{\alpha_1 \alpha_2}}$$

where r is the correlation between the multiple-choice score and the proofs score, and α_1 and α_2 are the reliability estimates for the multiple-choice score and the proofs score, respectively. All four estimates of the true score correlation exceed 0.9, strongly suggesting that the proof ratings and the multiple-choice score "measure the same thing." One would reasonably expect that the estimate of the true score correlation between the multiple-choice score and the proofs score would be slightly less than 1.0, due to some small effect of the method of measurement. This would remain true even if the multiple-choice section and the proof section measure the same thing about individual differences in mathematics proficiency.

The complex eigenvalue-based procedure described in the previous section may be used to compute the maximum reliability, and corresponding optimal weights, to be used to combine the multiple-choice and proof

TABLE 2.3
For Four Forms of a North Carolina Geometry End-of-Course Test:
Coefficient α for the Multiple-Choice and Open-Ended ("Proofs")
Sections, the Correlation Between the Multiple-Choice and "Proofs"
Sections, and the Disattenuated Correlation Between the Sections
("the True Score Correlation")

Form	Multiple-Choice α	"Proofs" α	Section Correlation	True Score Correlation
I	.91	.65	.70	.91
J	.91	.67	.72	.92
K	.91	.63	.69	.91
L	.91	.62	.71	.95

scores for the geometry tests. But if one assumes that the two components measure the same true score, and thus that the correlation between the component scores is equal to the square root of the product of their reliabilities, the problem is more tractable: Truman Kelley (1927, pp. 211–213), above a footnote thanking Harold Hotelling for explaining to him how to solve the eigen problem, worked out the simple closed-form solution for the weights that give optimal composite reliability for several components that measure the same true score (more or less reliably). For this important special case, the weight for the standardized score for component v must be proportional to

$$\frac{\sqrt{\rho_v}}{1-\rho_v} . \tag{28}$$

Weights computed in this way are sometimes called "reliability weights," although that term is ambiguous, because over the decades different writers have proposed several slight variants, calling each "weighting according to reliability" (see Gulliksen, 1950/1987, pp. 331–334, where this answer is mixed with several other answers of less-clear origin).

For the geometry test, Eq. 28 gives optimal weights, normed to be proportional, of 0.82 for the standardized multiple-choice score and 0.18 for the standardized proof score, and a consequent composite reliability of 0.92, for form I. If one computes the optimal composite-reliability weights using the eigen solution described in the preceding section, the resulting proportional weights are 0.83 and 0.17. Across the four forms, the reliability weights vary from 0.81 to 0.83 for the multiple-choice section. After applying sensible rounding, it appears that a weighting system that would give excellent reliability for the geometry test would be 0.8 for the multiple-choice (standardized) score, and 0.2 for the proof (standardized) score—the same ratio of 4:1 that similar analysis suggested for the writing test that was discussed earlier.

It is of some interest to apply Eq. 28 to the values for the writing test example in the preceding section, although strictly speaking the writing example is inappropriate here, because the true-score ("corrected for attenuation") correlation between the writing multiple-choice score and the essay score is only 0.6 (= $0.43/\sqrt{0.85 \times 0.60}$). Eq. 28 gives relative weights (normalized to sum to one) of 0.76 and 0.24 for the multiple-choice and essay sections, respectively, while the general optimal composite reliability formula gave 0.82 and 0.18. The weights are not very different (although 0.76:0.24 would probably be expressed as 3:1 and 0.82:0.18 would probably be called 4:1). The fact is that for all of the difference in complexity involved in computing the two kinds of optimal weightings, "reliability weighting" using Eq. 28 *is* the solution to the general problem for finding weights for optimal composite reliability if the correlations between the parts equal the square root of the products of their reliabilities—that is, if the so-called "true score correlation" equals 1—and the weight computation is not particularly sensitive to the value of that correlation.

ESTIMATING TRUE SCORES

The results that emerge from theoretical considerations are usually obvious, but sometimes it takes some careful thought before we realize that they are. The estimation of true score is one such result. A naive approach to estimation would be to use the observed score as our estimate of true score. Such an estimate has the property that it is unbiased in that it equals, in expectation, the true score. But can we do better? It turns out we can, and in chapter 9 we use this improved estimation methodology to great advantage in estimating more accurate subscores.

Before we develop an estimator of true score, let us consider a heuristic argument that using the observed score is less than optimal. Suppose we observe a test score that is two standard deviations above the mean. If we interpret this as an estimate of the examinee's true score, we would have to conclude that the examinee is a rather rare individual: Under a Gaussian model for the distribution of proficiency, we would expect 97% of all examinees to score lower than this. Do we expect that if we gave this individual another version of the test he would do as well? Probably not, because the observed score has an error component, and, although errors can subtract from an examinee's score as easily as they can add, our suspicion about which occurred *after* we observe someone with a very high score is that the error added. Thus we must consider the probability that we are observing someone who has benefited from the error, and that the person's true score is at a lower, and hence more likely, level. Similarly, someone who scores at a very low level would probably not do so badly on a retest. Figure 2.3 shows the situation graphically. Someone who scores at level A most probably has a low true score, as well as some bad luck. A better estimate of his true score should nudge his score up a bit. In contrast, the observed score of someone at level C is probably higher than their true score. Last, someone whose observed score is right in the middle, at B, most likely has an observed score approximately equal to his true score—at least, we have no way to guess whether the error might have been positive or negative.

If we accept this heuristic argument, then we should "nudge" extreme scores inward toward the mean. But how big a nudge should we give the

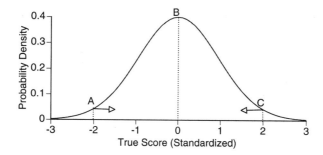

FIG. 2.3. A hypothetical distribution of test scores, with three individuals (A, B, and C) at different levels.

extreme scores? Obviously this depends on the accuracy of the test. If it is a very accurate test we shouldn't move them much at all. If the test is very inaccurate, the nudge becomes a kick. For example, if the test is so unreliable that it is all noise—each person's score is just a random number—the best estimate of each person's true score is the mean of the population. The test score itself provides no evidence at all to distinguish among the examinees.

Kelley's Equation.   The heuristic for estimating true score from observed score is now clear, and it requires three pieces of information: the observed score, the mean score over the population of examinees, and a measure of the test's accuracy. Truman Kelley, in 1927, used these three pieces to derive a linear estimator of true score that has become widely used (Kelley, 1927, p. 177; Kelley, 1947, p. 409). His derivation involved the direct estimation of the parameters of the linear equation that regresses true score on observed score. However, the same equation emerges even more directly if we try to predict what someone's score would be if the person took a second form of the test[14]—that is, if we regress the observed score from one test X onto the observed score from a parallel form X'. This regression, expressed in standardized units, is

$$\frac{\hat{x} - \mu}{\sigma} = \rho_{xx'}\left(\frac{x' - \mu}{\sigma}\right). \tag{29}$$

The slope of the regression, because these are standardized units, is merely $\rho_{xx'}$, the correlation between the two forms. Because the two forms

---

[14]This result parallels the fact that the correlation between the observed scores on two parallel forms is identical to the square of the correlation between observed score and true score.

are parallel, that is the reliability of the test. Also, because the two forms are parallel, they both have the same mean, μ, and the same standard deviation, σ.

Equation 29 can be simplified considerably, first by canceling the common denominator (σ), and next by moving μ from the left to the right side, yielding

$$\hat{x} = \rho_{xx'}(x' - \mu) + \mu ,\tag{30}$$

which after a little rearrangement is

$$\hat{x} = \rho_{xx'}x' + (1 - \rho_{xx'})\mu .\tag{31}$$

This is almost the final result, but before taking the last step it is worth considering Eq. 31 in some detail. It says that if we observe someone's score x' on test form X' and we wish to estimate what their score would be on a parallel form X, we regress it toward the mean of the population by an amount related to the test's reliability. If the test is perfectly reliable ($\rho_{xx'} = 1$), our estimate of the score on the parallel form is the same as that already observed. If the test is completely unreliable ($\rho_{xx'} = 0$), our estimate is the mean of the population from which the person came. Note also that for a given reliability, the amount of the adjustment depends on how far the observed score is from the mean. Thus Eq. 31 has all of the properties that we wanted for estimating true score. To estimate true score we merely substitute the right side of Eq. 2 into Eq. 31—substitute $\hat{\tau} + e$ for $\hat{x}$ on the left side—and remember that error, e, is unrelated to x', so its prediction reduces to zero. We obtain

$$\hat{\tau} = \hat{\rho}_{xx'}x' + (1 - \hat{\rho}_{xx'})\hat{\mu} .\tag{32}$$

Or, our estimate of true score, $\hat{\tau}$, results from the same regression that gave us $\hat{x}$. Equation 32 is the traditional form of what has come to be called Kelley's equation.[15]

An Alternative (Bayesian) Derivation of Kelley's Equation.   In this section, we present a derivation of Kelley's (Eq. 32) from a Bayesian perspective. This derivation is provided primarily because it may be used to relate Kelley's regressed estimates of the true score to similar ideas in item re-

---

[15]Understanding the consequences of Kelley's equation is important in the interpretation of results obtained using test scores, in addition to its use in test scoring. See Wainer (1999) for an examination of the consequences of the regression effect described by Kelley's equation as they apply to investigations of change over time, and Wainer (2000) for a demonstration of how easy it is to misunderstand the phenomenon described by this simple result.

sponse theory that are discussed in chapter 3. The derivation is "Bayesian" because, in this section, we make use of distributions that express our "degree of belief" about the location of unknown parameters (in this case, the true score). We assume that the distribution of true scores in the population is Gaussian, and also that the distribution of true scores given a specific observed score x is also Gaussian. We note that in the preceding section, no distributional assumptions were required for the regression derivation of Kelley's equation.

A graphical representation of this derivation is shown in Figure 2.4. In the top panel of Fig. 2.4 is a Gaussian distribution $h(\tau)$, with mean μ and variance $\sigma_\tau^2 = \rho_{xx'}\sigma_x^2$; that distribution represents our degree of be-

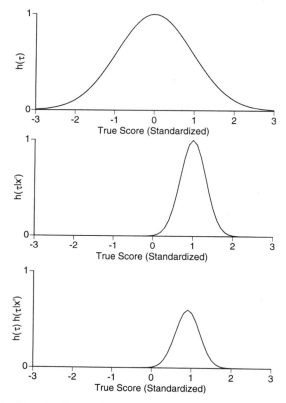

FIG. 2.4.   Top panel: Gaussian distribution $h(\tau)$, with mean μ and variance $\rho_{xx'}\sigma_x^2$—that distribution represents our degree of belief about the value of τ before administration of the test. Center panel: Gaussian distribution, $h(\tau|x')$, with mean x' and variance $(1 - \rho_{xx'})\sigma_x^2$—that distribution represents our degree of belief about the relative likelihood of various values of τ given that the test has been administered and a score x' obtained. Lower panel: The distribution that represents our belief that the examinee is a member of the population *and* obtained score x', proportional to $h(\tau)h(\tau|x')$.

lief about the value of τ before administration of the test, so, in Bayesian terminology, it is a *prior* distribution. In the second panel of Fig. 2.4 is another Gaussian distribution, $h(\tau|x')$, with mean x' and variance $\sigma_e^2 = (1 - \rho_{xx'})\sigma_x^2$; that distribution represents our degree of belief about the relative likelihood of various values of τ given that the test has been administered and a score x' obtained.

The two pieces of information represented by the distributions in the top and second panels of Fig. 2.4 are independent. The first represents the relative likelihood of each value of τ given that the examinee is a member of the population represented by the distribution in the top panel; the second represents the relative likelihood of each value of τ given that the examinee obtained score x'. Therefore, the distribution that represents our belief that the examinee is a member of the population *and* obtained score x' is proportional to $h(\tau)h(\tau|x')$; that product is shown in the lower panel of Figure 2.4. (The product is often referred to as the posterior distribution, because it is computed after the data, in this case, the test scores, are observed.) Because the two distributions that comprise the product $h(\tau)h(\tau|x')$ are Gaussian, we know that the product is a Gaussian distribution with mean $\bar{x}$ and variance $\sigma_{\bar{x}}^2$. We also know (see, e.g., Novick & Jackson, 1975, pp. 139–140) that the mean of $h(\tau)h(\tau|x')$, $\bar{x}$, is the weighted average of the means of the two component distributions, where the weights are the inverses of the variances:

$$\bar{x} = \frac{\dfrac{1}{(1-\rho_{xx'})\sigma_x^2} + \dfrac{1}{\rho_{xx'}\sigma_x^2}\mu}{\dfrac{1}{(1-\rho_{xx'})\sigma_x^2} + \dfrac{1}{\rho_{xx'}\sigma_x^2}}.$$

Canceling the σ_x^2, we obtain

$$\bar{x} = \frac{\dfrac{1}{(1-\rho_{xx'})}x' + \dfrac{1}{\rho_{xx'}}\mu}{\dfrac{1}{(1-\rho_{xx'})} + \dfrac{1}{\rho_{xx'}\sigma}};$$

and simplifying, we obtain

$$\bar{x} = \frac{\dfrac{\rho_{xx'}(1-\rho_{xx'})}{(1-\rho_{xx'})}x' + \dfrac{\rho_{xx'}(1-\rho_{xx'})}{\rho_{xx'}}\mu}{\dfrac{\rho_{xx'}(1-\rho_{xx'})}{(1-\rho_{xx'})} + \dfrac{\rho_{xx'}(1-\rho_{xx'})}{\rho_{xx'}\sigma}}$$

$$= \frac{\rho_{xx'} \, x' + (1 - \rho_{xx'})\mu}{\rho_{xx'} + (1 - \rho_{xx'})}$$

$$= \rho_{xx'} + (1 - \rho_{xx'})\mu.$$

That is Kelly's equation, identical to Eq. 32. The variance of the posterior distribution is, again by standard Gaussian theory,

$$\sigma_{\bar{x}}^2 = \frac{1}{\dfrac{1}{(1 - \rho_{xx'})\sigma_x^2} + \dfrac{1}{\rho_{xx'}\sigma_x^2}}$$
$$= \rho_{xx'}(1 - \rho_{xx'})\sigma_x^2,$$

which Lord and Novick (1968, pp. 67–68) called the variance *of estimation*.

These are the same results that were obtained in the preceding section; however, the graphical representation in Fig. 2.4 provides a link between this aspect of the traditional theory and the procedures that are used to compute test scores using item response theory, as described in chapter 3.

THREE MODELS FOR ERROR

The reliability coefficient provides us with one measure of the stability of the measurement. It is often useful to have another measure that is directly in the scale of the score. For example, we would usually like to be able to present the estimate of someone's true score with error bounds:

$$\hat{\tau} = 1.2 \pm 0.3$$

Such a statement raises two questions. The first is, "What does ± 0.3 mean?" The second is, "How did you get 0.3?"

There can be different answers to the first question depending on the situation. One common and reasonably useful answer is, "It means that two-thirds of the time for someone whose estimated value of $\hat{\tau}$ is this value, her true score is within 0.3 of this value."

The answer to the second question "How did we get it?" requires a little longer explanation. The explanation goes back to Eq. 2,

$$x = \tau + e.$$

The uncertainty in our estimates of true score is due to the variability of the error (e). To be able to provide a probability statement about the variability of the estimate we need to assume something about the distribution of the error. What sort of distribution we assume depends on the character of the scoring metric we use for the test. In this section we consider two different scoring metrics, summed scores and percent scores, each of which suggests a different error distribution. Happily, the two metrics yield parallel summary equations so that coefficient α, the Spearman–Brown formula, and Kelley's equation all work in either situation.

Summed Scores and the Normal Error Model. Suppose we give a test and score it by giving one point for each item answered correctly and no points for any item incorrectly answered. The score on the test might then be simply the sum of all the item scores. Stated more formally, let us define the score on item i for examinee j as

$$y_{ij} = \begin{cases} 1 & \text{if answered correctly} \\ 0 & \text{otherwise} \end{cases}$$

and the score on the test for examinee j as the number of items that were answered correctly, or

$$x_j = \sum_{i=1}^{n} y_{ij} \; .$$

There are many variations on this theme, for example:

1. The *proportion correct score*, in which the summed score is divided by the total number of items. That is, we define true score as the expected proportion correct,

$$\tau = E(x)/n \; .$$

Using proportion or percentage correct as the true score (instead of the summed score) can be done without loss of any generality.

2. The *formula summed score*, in which each correctly answered item is 1 point, each item omitted is 0 points, and each item answered incorrectly is $-\frac{1}{4}$ point (for five-alternative multiple-choice questions); this scoring method is thought to induce a psychological penalty for random guessing.

3. The *differentially weighted summed score*, in which some items might be worth 5 points, others 1 point, and still others 3 points. This method is common when test developers judge that some items are more important, take more time, or are more difficult than others.

If we suppose that there are many items on the test and that most people score in the middle range (e.g., there are 100 items and most people score about 50), and there are very few near either extreme (not many score above 85 or below 15) a plausible distribution of the error is the normal or Gaussian distribution. The normal model states that $h(x|\tau)$, the conditional distribution of the observed score given the true score, is Gaussian. Lord and Novick (1968, pp. 59–68) showed that the standard deviation of $h(x|\tau)$, called the *standard error of measurement*, is

$$\sigma_e = \sigma_x \sqrt{1 - \rho_{xx'}} \; ; \tag{33}$$

which is widely used as the standard error when the observed score is reported. If Kelley's regressed estimates of the true score are reported, the *standard error of estimation* is

$$\sigma_\varepsilon = \sigma_x \sqrt{\rho_{xx'}} \sqrt{1 - \rho_{xx'}} \; . \tag{34}$$

In either case, the average of $h(x|\tau)$ is the score (observed, or the estimated true score), and the estimates of the standard deviation given earlier are then sufficient to completely specify the normal distribution.

A key characteristic of the normal curve is its symmetry: An observed score is as likely to be too high as too low. Of course, when a test score is bounded, symmetry is limited for persons whose true scores are near an extreme. As an obvious example of a situation in which a normal error model fails, consider the case of examinees whose true scores are zero. Unless there is no variance in observed scores, the requirement expressed by Eq. 3 $[E(x) = \tau]$ is violated. A second characteristic of the normal error model is that the parameters of the distribution, the mean and the variance, must be independent of one another. This too is likely to be violated at the extremes where we would expect the variance to get smaller. As we move away from the extremes, as in the situation sketched earlier, a normal error model becomes more plausible.

This situation is illustrated for a test of 30 items in Fig. 2.5 [the notation $h(x|\tau)$ is used to denote the conditional distribution, which in this instance is normal]. Note that the observed score distributions for true scores between 10 and 20 (0.33 to 0.67, when expressed as proportions as they are in Fig. 2.5) behave perfectly reasonably, but that for extreme values of τ the normal error model predicts impossible observed scores with nonzero probability.

What is a plausible reference distribution for error when the conditions of the test suggest that the use of a normal distribution is not credible? There are a number of reasonable choices. In the next section we describe one rather general, yet easy to use, error distribution.

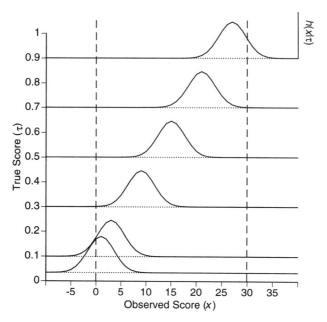

FIG. 2.5.   Normal conditional distributions of observed scores for various true scores for 30 items.

The Binomial (Negative Hypergeometric) Model.   The development provided here follows that given by Lord and Novick (1968, chap. 23), and assumes that the conditional distribution of observed score, given true score, is binomial. We do not, however, assume that the error distribution is independent of true score. Thus by maintaining the possibility that the error variance at the extremes of the distribution may be very small, we avoid some of the problems at the extremes that make the normal error model implausible.

Observed scores and true scores remain defined as they were previously; using proportion correct as the true score makes the binomial distribution more obviously applicable. All of the properties that were used previously remain true here, that is,

$$E(x/n \mid \tau) = \tau \tag{35}$$

and

$$E(e \mid \tau) = 0 . \tag{36}$$

We next assume that the conditional distribution of observed score x for a given true score τ is the binomial distribution $h(x \mid \tau)$,

$$h(x|\tau) = \binom{n}{x} \tau^x (1-\tau)^{n-x}, \quad x = 0, 1, \ldots, n .$$ (37)

If we use Eq. 37 to generate binomial conditional distributions, shown in Fig. 2.6, analogous to the normal distributions shown previously in Fig. 2.5, the anomalous predicted observed scores for extreme true scores have disappeared, but the observed score distributions for intermediate true scores look remarkably similar to those based on normal error.

The binomial model yields analogous measures for reliability and estimates of true score to those previously described. Under the assumption that the regression of true score on observed score is linear (an assumption underlying Kelley's equation, Eq. 32), we obtain a lower bound on reliability that is analogous to Cronbach's α (Eq. 13),

$$\alpha_{21} = \frac{n}{n-1}\left[1 - \frac{\mu_x(n-\mu_x)}{n\sigma_x^2}\right] .$$ (38)

This measure of reliability is sometimes called KR-21 after the Kuder and Richardson (1937) article in which it is equation 21. To use Eq. 38, one merely computes the sample mean and variance of the observed

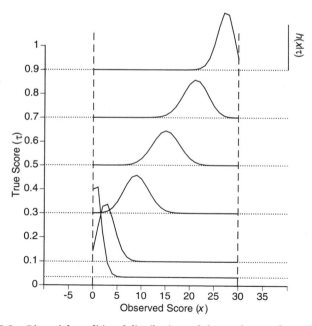

FIG. 2.6. Binomial conditional distributions of observed scores for various true scores for 30 items.

scores and substitutes them into equation 2.38 for μ_x and σ_x^2, respectively. One can substitute α_{21} directly into Eq. 32 to estimate true score. To estimate confidence bounds around observed scores requires a bit more work than merely looking up the appropriate bounds in a table of normal deviates, because, under the conditions specified (binomial errors and true score having a linear regression on observed score), the observed score has the negative hypergeometric distribution

$$h(x) \equiv \frac{b^{[n]}(-n)_x(a)_x}{(a+b)^{[n]}(-b)_x x!} \quad x = 0, 1, \ldots, n, \tag{39}$$

where

$$a = \left(\frac{1-\alpha_{21}}{\alpha_{21}}\right)\mu_x,$$

$$b = \left(\frac{n}{\alpha_{21}}\right) - (a+1),$$

$$(a)_x = a(a+1) \cdots (a+x-1),$$
$$b^{[n]} = b(b-1) \cdots (b-n+1), \text{ and}$$
$$(a)_0 = b^{[0]} = 1.$$

Combining Two Approaches: The Heteroscedastic Normal Model. So far, we have seen that the computation of standard errors and confidence bounds around observed scores is easiest when we can plausibly assume that errors are normally distributed. However, the assumption of normality becomes suspect toward the extremes of the true score distribution. When we are interested in accurate estimation of error in those extremes, an alternative model is required. We described one such alternative, the binomial. Careful study of the results of the binomial model that are shown in Fig. 2.6 supports our contention of the viability of this model. Comparing Fig. 2.6 with its normal counterpart shown in Fig. 2.5 also reveals enormous similarity between the two models in the middle of the true score range. Moreover, a glance at Eq. 39 and its associated definitions shows that although the computation of confidence bounds based on the hypergeometric distribution is not especially tedious, it is more difficult than just looking up the appropriate values in a normal table. In fairness, it should also be pointed out that this is the only place where this model causes an increase in the complexity of application; reliability and true score calculations are essentially identical with their counterparts in the normal case.

What is it about the binomial distribution that helps us fit the extremes that is not true for the normal? Because the normal distribution is often used as an easy to compute approximation for the binomial, it is not likely to be the shape. In fact, it isn't the distributional assumption at all, but rather the assumption that error is uncorrelated with true score. If we were to allow error variance to be a function of true score, could we obtain a model that fits as well as the binomial in the extremes but maintains the ease of computation of the normal model?

Let us define the conditional variance of observed scores to be a continuous function of true score

$$\sigma_{x|\tau} = n\tau(1-\tau) \tag{40}$$

and then assume that the conditional distribution of observed scores is normal with mean τ and variance as defined in Eq. 40. Such a model has many of the same characteristics as the binomial (the same formulas for reliability and true score would apply) and shares the ease of use of the normal. In Fig. 2.7 is a plot of the conditional distributions of observed scores based on this model. It bears a remarkable resemblance to the binomial plot in Fig. 2.6 and can be readily substituted for it.

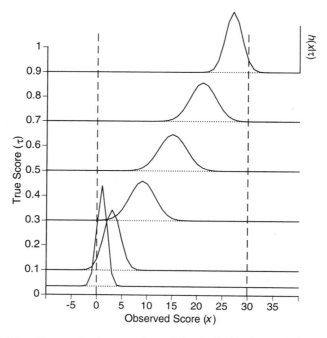

FIG. 2.7. Heterscedastic normal conditional distributions of observed scores for various true scores for 30 items.

Traditional Analysis: The North Carolina Test of Computer Skills—Word Processing/Editing.   To illustrate some of the ideas in this and subsequent chapters, we consider data obtained in an item tryout for the North Carolina Test of Computer Skills. This test as a whole comprises a 70-item multiple-choice section, as well as a performance section including four parts: Keyboarding Techniques (KB), Word Processing/Editing (ED), Database Use (DB), and Spreadsheet Use (SS). The test is intended for eighth-grade students, and was developed as part of a system to ensure basic computer proficiency for graduates of the North Carolina Public Schools. We consider scoring systems for the test as a whole in chapter 7, but we use parts of the test to illustrate concepts here, and in chapters 3 and 4.

The ED section, which we consider first here, is like the example shown in Fig. 2.8.[16] The student is presented with the instructions and copy-edited text shown, and uses a word processor to edit a file that opens with the text as shown in the right panel of Fig. 2.8. Subsequently, 10 items are scored; short names and scoring codes for the items are shown in Table 2.4. In this section we act as though the ED section was the entire test, to simplify the presentation.

A total of 3,104 students were tested in the item tryout for the North Carolina Test of Computer Skills, and provided sufficiently complete data to be included in the analysis. Table 2.5 shows the proportions (p_+) of students responding "correctly" (scored 1) for each of the items, the "corrected" correlation between the item score and the total (summed) score, and the value of coefficient α that would be obtained if each item was omitted from the test, as reported by the Reliability procedure in SPSS (Norušis, 1993). Coefficient α for this 10-item test is .84.

Considering the results from the perspective of the traditional theory, we note first of all that the test was relatively easy for this sample—the average summed score was 7.7 (out of 10), with a standard deviation of 2.6. All of the items are sufficiently easy that over half of the students responded correctly. The most difficult "item" was "move" (item 8). All 10 items exhibit relatively high item-total correlations, and no item performed sufficiently poorly to reduce internal consistency (i.e., coefficient α did not increase after deletion of any of the items).

Scores on large-scale standardized tests are usually reported on some scale that is a cosmetic linear transformation of the standard score (z-score) scale. The "College Board" (200–800) scale is a well-known ex-

---

[16]Figure 2.8 shows the "released form" of the North Carolina Test of Computer Skills Word Processing/Editing section. It is not identical to the form that was used to collect the data—specifically, the careful reader will note that not all of the scoring codes in Table 2.4 can be applied to this form. However, the released form is generally similar to the operational form.

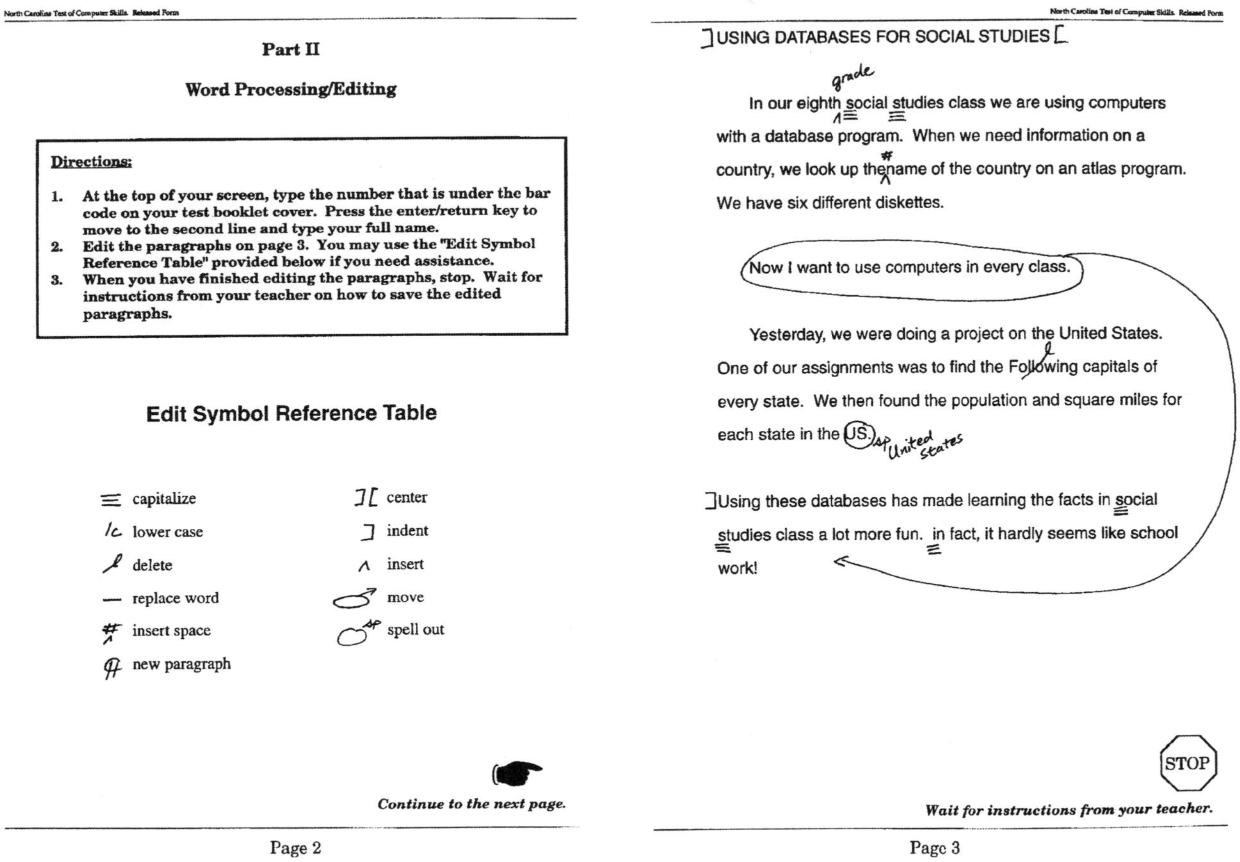

Part II

Word Processing/Editing

Directions:

1. At the top of your screen, type the number that is under the bar code on your test booklet cover. Press the enter/return key to move to the second line and type your full name.
2. Edit the paragraphs on page 3. You may use the "Edit Symbol Reference Table" provided below if you need assistance.
3. When you have finished editing the paragraphs, stop. Wait for instructions from your teacher on how to save the edited paragraphs.

Edit Symbol Reference Table

≡ capitalize		⫟⟍ center	
/c lower case		⟍ indent	
ℓ delete		∧ insert	
— replace word		⟋⟍ move	
# insert space		⟍ spell out	
⟋ new paragraph			

Continue to the next page.

Page 2

USING DATABASES FOR SOCIAL STUDIES

In our eighth grade social studies class we are using computers with a database program. When we need information on a country, we look up the name of the country on an atlas program. We have six different diskettes.

Now I want to use computers in every class.

Yesterday, we were doing a project on the United States. One of our assignments was to find the Following capitals of every state. We then found the population and square miles for each state in the US, United States.

Using these databases has made learning the facts in social studies class a lot more fun. in fact, it hardly seems like school work!

Wait for instructions from your teacher.

STOP

Page 3

FIG. 2.8. The Word Processing/Editing (ED) section of the North Carolina Test of Computer Skills. Reprinted with permission of the North Carolina Department of Public Instruction.

65

TABLE 2.4
Items and Scoring Codes for the North Carolina Test
of Computer Skills ED Section

	Scoring Codes	
Item	Not Acceptable	Acceptable
1. Center	0	1
2. Insert	0	1
3. Capitalize	0	1
4. Indent	0	1
5. Insert space	0	1
6. Lower case	0	1
7. Delete	0	1
8. Move	0	1
9. Spell out	0	1
	Other errors present	No additional errors
10. Other errors	0	1

TABLE 2.5
Item-Level Traditional Statistics for the North Carolina Test
of Computer Skills ED Section

		Computed With the Item Deleted	
Item	p_+	Item-Total r	Coefficient α
1. Center	.66	.46	.83
2. Insert	.73	.52	.82
3. Capitalize	.91	.54	.82
4. Indent	.76	.59	.81
5. Insert space	.90	.61	.82
6. Lower case	.89	.64	.81
7. Delete	.83	.57	.82
8. Move	.54	.49	.83
9. Spell out	.70	.57	.82
10. Other errors	.78	.43	.83

ample of such a scale, as is the T-score scale (20–80), with a mean of 50 and a standard deviation of 10. However, item analysis and test construction are usually done using scores on the z-score scale; the transformation to the more aesthetically pleasing reporting scales, with no negative numbers and no decimal points, is done later. Therefore, in this book we will usually discuss scores in the z-score scale, in order to maintain a single uniform scale when discussing tests from different sources, with different reporting scales. The standardized summed scores for the ED section of the North Carolina Test of Computer Skills are shown in Table 2.6, along with their standard errors of measurement; the latter are constant:

TABLE 2.6
Standardized Scores, Their Standard Errors of Measurement, Kelley
Regressed (Standardized) Scores, and Their Standard Errors of
Estimation, for the North Carolina Test of Computer Skills ED Section

Summed Score	Standard Score (z)	SE of Measurement	Kelley Regressed z	SE of Estimation
0	−3.00	0.41	−2.51	0.37
1	−2.61	0.41	−2.18	0.37
2	−2.22	0.41	−1.86	0.37
3	−1.83	0.41	−1.53	0.37
4	−1.44	0.41	−1.21	0.37
5	−1.05	0.41	−0.88	0.37
6	−0.67	0.41	−0.56	0.37
7	−0.28	0.41	−0.23	0.37
8	0.11	0.41	0.09	0.37
9	0.50	0.41	0.42	0.37
10	0.89	0.41	0.74	0.37

$0.41 = \sqrt{1 - 0.84} = \sqrt{1 - \alpha}$, as in Eq. 33. Table 2.6 also lists the values of the Kelley (1927) regressed estimates of the (standardized) true score, and their standard error of estimation, $0.37 = \sqrt{0.84} \sqrt{1 - 0.84} = \sqrt{\alpha} \sqrt{1 - \alpha}$ (see Eq. 34, and Lord & Novick, 1968, pp. 67–68). In this context, the Kelley regressed estimates are simply a rescaling of the standardized summed scores, and that rescaling would disappear with the linear transformation to any reporting scale. However, in subsequent chapters we have occasion to compare these scores to scores derived from item response theory that are more directly comparable to the Kelley regressed estimates than they are to the standard scores, so we include both here.

Traditional Analysis: The North Carolina Test of Computer Skills—Keyboarding Techniques. As a second illustration of some of the procedures described in this chapter, we consider data obtained in the item tryout for the North Carolina Test of Computer Skills Keyboarding Techniques (KB) section. The KB section is shown in Fig. 2.9.[17] The student is presented with the instructions and text shown, and uses a word processor to enter the text. Subsequently, three items are scored; short names and scoring codes for the items are shown in Table 2.7. To simplify the presentation, we continue with the practice begun in the description of the "Editing" portion of the test, now acting as though the KB section was the entire test.

---

[17]Figure 2.9 shows the "released form" of the North Carolina Test of Computer Skills Keyboarding Techniques section. It is not identical to the form that was used to collect the data, but it is generally similar to the operational form.

North Carolina Test of Computer Skills. Released Form

Part I

Keyboarding Techniques

Directions:

1. Key as accurately as possible the paragraphs below. Remember to use correct keyboarding techniques. Note: Do not worry about any differences in word wrap between what you type and how the paragraphs appear on this page.
2. When you have finished keying the paragraphs, stop. Wait for instructions from your teacher.

USING DATABASES IN THE SOCIAL STUDIES CLASS

In our eighth grade social studies class we are using computers with a database program. When we need information on a country, we look up the name of the country on an atlas program. We have six different diskettes.

Yesterday, we were doing a project on the United States of America. One of our assignments was to find the following
North Carolina
Utah
New Mexico
Vermont
Florida
Texas
We then found the population and area in square miles for each state.

Using these databases has made learning the facts in social studies a lot more fun. In fact, it hardly seems like school work!

Now I want to use computers in every class.   STOP

Wait for instructions from your teacher.

Page 1

FIG. 2.9. The Keyboarding Techniques (KB) section of the North Carolina Test of Computer Skills. Reprinted with permission of the North Carolina Department of Public Instruction.

A total of 3,104 students provided sufficiently complete data to be included in the analysis. Table 2.8 shows the proportions (p_k) of students responding in each of the four scoring categories for each of the items, the "corrected" correlation between the item score and the total (summed) score, and the value of coefficient α that would be obtained if each item was omitted from the test, as reported by the Reliability procedure in SPSS (Norušis, 1993). Coefficient α for this three-item test is .57.

TABLE 2.7
Items and Scoring Codes for the North Carolina
Test of Computer Skills KB Section

1. Typing accuracy (T): Spelling, punctuation, etc.
   Score
0	Not observed (blank)
1	Has five or more typing errors
2	Has up to five typing errors
3	Has only one or no typing errors
2. Spacing (S)
   Score
0	Not observed (blank)
1	Has three or more errors in spacing
2	Has one or two errors in spacing
3	Has no errors in spacing
3. Length (L)
   Score
0	Not observed (blank)
1	Has some portion of page typed
2	Has at least half of text typed (through first paragraph)
3	Has entire page typed

TABLE 2.8
Item-Level Traditional Statistics for the North Carolina Test
of Computer Skills KB Section

	Proportions for Scores				Computed With the Item Deleted	
Item	p_0	p_1	p_2	p_3	Item-Total r	Coefficient α
1. Typing	.02	.21	.47	.30	.38	.47
2. Spacing	.02	.35	.37	.26	.41	.43
3. Length	.02	.07	.53	.39	.36	.50

Like the ED section, this test was relatively easy for this sample—the average summed score was 6.2 (out of 10), with a standard deviation of 1.6. The modal response for all items was a 2 (on the 0–3 scale). The most difficult "item" was "Spacing" (item 2). All three items exhibit relatively high item-total correlations, and no item performed sufficiently poorly to reduce internal consistency (i.e., coefficient α did not increase after deletion of any of the items).

The standardized summed scores for the KB section of the North Carolina Test of Computer Skills are shown in Table 2.9, along with their standard errors of measurement; the latter are constant: $0.66 = \sqrt{1 - 0.57} = \sqrt{1 - \alpha}$, as in Eq. 33. Table 2.9 also lists the values of the Kelley (1927) regressed estimates of the (standardized) true score, and their standard error of estimation, $0.50 = \sqrt{0.57}\sqrt{1 - 0.57} = \sqrt{\alpha}\sqrt{1 - \alpha}$ (see Eq. 19 given earlier, and Lord

TABLE 2.9
Standardized Scores, Their Standard Errors of Measurement, Kelley
Regressed (Standardized) Scores, and Their Standard Errors of
Estimation, for the North Carolina Test of Computer Skills KB Section

Summed Score	Standard Score (z)	SE of Measurement	Kelley Regressed z	SE of Estimation
0	−3.80	0.66	−2.16	0.50
1	−3.20	0.66	−1.82	0.50
2	−2.59	0.66	−1.47	0.50
3	−1.98	0.66	−1.13	0.50
4	−1.37	0.66	−0.78	0.50
5	−0.76	0.66	−0.43	0.50
6	−0.15	0.66	−0.08	0.50
7	0.46	0.66	0.26	0.50
8	1.07	0.66	0.61	0.50
9	1.68	0.66	0.96	0.50

& Novick, 1968, pp. 67–68). We note that the best we can do with this three-item test, taken by itself, is to use the Kelley regressed estimates as the scores—and even then, the reported standard errors of 0.5 standard units are probably too large for most potential test uses.

SUMMARY

In this chapter we have described and illustrated the most rudimentary of all statistical theories of mental test scores, traditional true score theory. The model describes the scores we observe as just a simple linear combination of true score and error. From this formulation we derived a measure of a test's reliability and showed how this measure, Cronbach's α, is the mean of all split-half reliabilities of the test adjusted by the Spearman–Brown formula to be of full length. We also showed how the regression of true score on observed score provides us with a estimator of true score that tends to be more accurate than the naive use of the unadjusted observed score as the estimate of true score. Last, we showed that the assumption of normal errors falls short at the extremes of the conditional distribution of observed score, but that a strong true score theory based on the binomial distribution is an improvement. We also provided a normal approximation to the binomial that combines the ease of use of the normal theory with the better fit of the binomial.

ACKNOWLEDGMENTS

We thank Eric T. Bradlow, Jonathan Dings, Frank Evans, and Richard Hill for helpful comments on an earlier draft.

REFERENCES

Armor, D. J. (1974). Theta reliability and factor scaling. In H. L. Costner (Ed.), *Sociological methodology 1973–1974* (pp. 17–50). San Francisco: Jossey-Bass.

Becker, R. A., & Chambers, J. M. (1984). *S: An interactive environment for data analysis and graphics*. Monterey, CA: Wadsworth.

Bock, R. D. (1975). *Multivariate statistical methods in behavioral research*. New York: McGraw-Hill.

Brennan, R. L., & Johnson, E. G. (1995). Generalizability of performance assessments. *Educational Measurement: Issues and Practice, 14*, 9–27.

Brown, W. (1910). Some experimental results in the correlation of mental abilities. *British Journal of Psychology, 3*, 296–322.

Cliff, N., & Caruso, J. C. (1998). Reliable component analysis through maximizing composite reliability. *Psychological Methods, 3*, 291–308.

Cronbach, L. J. (1951). Coefficient alpha and the internal structure of tests. *Psychometrika, 16*, 297–334.

DuBois, P. H. (1970). *A history of psychological testing*. Boston: Allyn & Bacon.

Feldt, L. S., & Brennan, R. L. (1989). Reliability. In R. L. Linn (Ed.), *Educational Measurement* (3rd ed., pp. 105–146). New York: American Council on Education/Macmillan.

Green, B. F., Jr. (1950). A note on the calculation of weights for maximum battery reliability. *Psychometrika, 15*, 57–61.

Gulliksen, H. O. (1987). *Theory of mental tests*. Hillsdale, NJ: Lawrence Erlbaum Associates. (Original work published 1950)

Hoyt, C. (1941). Test reliability estimated by analysis of variance. *Psychometrika, 6*, 153–160.

Hucker, C. O. (1975). *China's imperial past: An introduction to Chinese history and culture*. Stanford, CA: Stanford University Press.

Kelley, T. L. (1927). *The interpretation of educational measurements*. New York: World Book.

Kelley, T. L. (1947). *Fundamentals of statistics*. Cambridge, MA: Harvard University Press.

Klein, S. P., & Bell, R. M. (1995). How will the NCAA's new standards affect minority student-athletes? *Chance, 8*(3), 18–21.

Kuder, G. F., & Richardson, M. W. (1937). The theory of the estimation of test reliability. *Psychometrika, 2*, 151–160.

Lawrence, I. (1995). *Estimating reliability for tests composed of item sets* (RR 95-18). Princeton, NJ: Educational Testing Service.

Li, H. (1997). A unifying expression for the maximal reliability of a linear composite. *Psychometrika, 62*, 245–249.

Li, H., & Wainer, H. (1997). Toward a coherent view of reliability in test theory. *Journal of Educational and Behavioral Statistics, 22*, 478–484.

Linn, R. L., & Burton, E. (1994). Performance-based assessment: Implications of task specificity. *Educational Measurement: Issues and Practice, 13*, 5–15.

Lord, F. M., & Novick, M. (1968). *Statistical theories of mental test scores*. Reading, MA: Addison-Wesley.

Norušis, M. J. (1993). *SPSS for Windows professional statistics release 6.0*. Chicago: SPSS, Inc.

Novick, M. R., & Jackson, P. H. (1975). *Statistical methods for educational and psychological research*. New York: McGraw-Hill.

Novick, M. R., & Lewis, C. (1967). Coefficient alpha and the reliability of composite measurements. *Psychometrika, 32*, 1–13.

Peel, E. A. (1948). Prediction of a complex criterion and battery reliability. *British Journal of Psychology, Statistical Section, 1*, 84–94.

SAS Institute, Inc. (1988). *SAS procedures guide, 6.03 edition*. Cary, NC: Author.

Shavelson, R. J., Gao, X., & Baxter, G. P. (1993). *Sampling variability of performance assessments* (CSE Tech. Rep. No. 361). Los Angeles, CA: National Center for Research on Evaluation, Standards, and Student Testing (CRESST), Graduate School of Education, University of California at Los Angeles.

Sireci, S. G., Thissen, D., & Wainer, H. (1991). On the reliability of testlet-based tests. *Journal of Educational Measurement, 28,* 237–247.

Spearman, C. (1910). Correlation calculated with faulty data. *British Journal of Psychology, 3,* 271–295.

Stanley, J. C. (1957). KR-20 as the stepped-up mean item intercorrelation. In *14th Yearbook of the National Council on Measurement in Education* (pp. 78–92). Washington, DC: American Council on Education.

Thomson, G. H. (1940). Weighting for battery reliability and prediction. *British Journal of Psychology, 30,* 357–366.

Tierney, L. (1990). *LISP-STAT: An object-oriented environment for statistical computing and dynamic graphics.* New York: Wiley.

Wainer, H. (1976). Estimating coefficients in linear models: It don't make no nevermind. *Psychological Bulletin, 83,* 213–217.

Wainer, H. (1999). Is the Akebono school failing its best students? A Hawaiian adventure in regression. *Educational Measurement: Issues and Practice, 18,* 26–35.

Wainer, H. (2000). Kelley's paradox. *Chance, 13,* 47–48.

Wainer, H., & Kiely, G. L. (1987). Item clusters and computerized adaptive testing: A case for testlets. *Journal of Educational Measurement, 24,* 185–201.

Wainer, H., & Thissen, D. (1993). Combining multiple-choice and constructed response test scores: Toward a Marxist theory of test construction. *Applied Measurement in Education, 6,* 103–118.

Wainer, H., & Thissen, D. (1996). How is reliability related to the quality of test scores? What is the effect of local dependence on reliability? *Educational Measurement: Issues and Practice, 15,* 22–29.

Chapter 3

Item Response Theory for Items Scored in Two Categories

David Thissen
University of North Carolina at Chapel Hill

Maria Orlando
RAND Corporation

Item response theory (IRT) is sometimes presented as an alternative to the traditional true score theory (some of which was described in the previous chapter). However, it is more realistic in applications involving large-scale test development and scoring to consider the traditional theory and IRT to be complementary: Practical test construction using IRT typically includes reference to traditional statistics as well as the item parameters and goodness-of-fit statistics of IRT. Both the traditional theory and IRT provide means to evaluate and report the precision of test scores, usually in the form of standard errors of measurement. In addition, although IRT need not make use of the summed score that is the central feature of the traditional theory, IRT's treatment of summed scores can be informative. In subsequent chapters, we mix and match aspects of the traditional theory and IRT rather freely.

IRT provides to a testing program many features that may be more difficult to obtain using extensions to the traditional theory. Most of these features accrue from the fact that IRT defines a scale for the underlying *latent* variable (often called *ability* or *proficiency*) that is measured by the test items. This aspect of IRT means that comparable scores may be computed for examinees who did not answer the same questions, without intermediate equating steps. As a result, an extremely large number of alternate forms of a test may be used. Computerized adaptive testing (CAT) based on IRT makes use of this feature, in some systems providing (almost) as many different test forms as there are examinees. Even in paper-and-pencil large-scale testing programs, the need to develop alternate forms scored on a common scale may provide sufficient motivation to use IRT.

This feature also makes it relatively easy to construct *vertically equated* tests, or *developmental scales*, in which completely nonoverlapping tests for disparate groups may be scored on the same scale (after a calibration step that involves some common items across groups).

Current applications of item response theory lean heavily on the use of logistic item response models. There are two lines of reasoning that have supported the historical development and continued use of these models. One is, essentially, that the models fit the data; the logistic models succinctly summarize the important aspects of many sets of item response data. A second line of reasoning is that, for sound theoretical reasons, item response data may be expected to follow these models. There are psychologically meaningful mathematical models of the item response process from which the logistic item response function may be derived, either on its own or as an approximation for the historically more interesting normal ogive model.

The items on a test may be analyzed using item response theory, and the item response model may also be used to provide scale scores. When we use item response theory to estimate scale scores, it is only loosely speaking that we say the test is "scored"; we do not simply count the positive responses, as the traditional test theory suggests. Instead, we estimate the scale score using the information in the item responses. Such estimates were suggested by Lazarsfeld (1950, p. 460), who called them the "trace line scores" of response patterns. Birnbaum (1968) investigated maximum likelihood estimation of scale scores for the logistic model, and Samejima (1977) studied both maximum likelihood and Bayes modal estimation for the normal and logistic models.

When working with such scale scores, we find that the concept of reliability, in the sense of classical test theory, can be improved upon. Test *information*, which is the inverse of the average error variance at each point on the scale, provides a description of the precision of measurement as a function of the scale scores. The concept of the information conveyed by the data about a parameter of a statistical model was introduced in connection with maximum likelihood estimation by R. A. Fisher in 1921. It was applied to mental tests by Birnbaum (1958a, 1958b); since Birnbaum's work appeared in Lord and Novick (1968), item and test information functions and plots have become a standard part of IRT.

LOGISTIC ITEM RESPONSE MODELS

The One-Parameter Logistic Model

The Rasch Model.   To develop his now widely known model, Rasch (1960/1980, pp. 74–75) specified that a person should be characterized by degree of ability ξ and an item should be characterized by a degree of difficulty δ. Both ξ and δ are assumed to be greater than zero. Then, following a metaphor with physical laws, Rasch specified that if a second person has twice the ability of the first, 2ξ, and a second item is twice as difficult as the first, 2δ, the second person should have the same probability of solving the second item as the first person has of solving the first item. This requires, to quote Rasch (1960/1980, p. 74), that "the probability is a function of the ratio, ξ/δ, between the degree of ability of the person and the degree of difficulty of the problem."

In his early work, Rasch turned to practical considerations to change the ratio ξ/δ into an item response model: a *trace line* (to use Lazarsfeld's 1950, p. 364, term for the curve that "traces" the probability of a correct resonse from zero to one as ability increases). Rasch (1960/1980, pp. 74–75) wrote, "The simplest function I know of, which increases from 0 to 1 as ζ goes from 0 to ∞, is $\dfrac{\zeta}{(1+\zeta)}$. If we insert $\zeta = \dfrac{\xi}{\delta}$ we get

$$\frac{\dfrac{\xi}{\delta}}{1+\dfrac{\xi}{\delta}} = \frac{\xi}{\xi+\delta}." \tag{1}$$

In later writing, Rasch (1966, 1977) developed epistemological reasons he considered compelling for the use of this model, arguing that certain consequences of its essentially multiplicative nature provided a kind of objectivity, called *specific objectivity*, not provided by other models. Because the probability of a correct response is a function of the ratio of the proficiency of the person to the difficulty of the item, the item parameters cancel for ratios of probability-correct for two persons, leaving an *item-free* comparison of their proficiencies. Thus, the model makes *objective* or *item-free* statements about the relative likelihood that two persons will respond correctly to an item or a set of items, without any reference to the items themselves. Some theorists regard this property of the model to be highly desirable (see Andrich, 1988, chap. 2, for advocacy of this position); others, including the authors, consider this property less important than other aspects of IRT models.[1]

A curious feature of the Rasch model is that this IRT model implies that all examinees with the same total summed score have the same IRT scale score (as described later in this chapter). This feature of the Rasch model is often called *summed score sufficiency*, because the summed score is a sufficient statistic for proficiency, when that is taken to be the parameter of in-

---

[1]We return to this discussion of the Rasch model at the end of the next section, after the introduction of the normal ogive model and its logistic approximation.

terest in the model. This is a consequence of the ratio-development of the model.

The One-Parameter Logistic Model, More Generally. The development of the Rasch (1960/1980) model has essentially nothing to do with the development of the normal ogive and two- and three-parameter logistic models that will be described in subsequent sections. However, matters become very confusing because the model in Eq. 1 is often reparameterized into a form that is very similar to those that will be developed for the two- and three-parameter logistic models: If we substitute exp θ for ξ and exp b for δ in Eq. 1, we have

$$\frac{\exp\theta}{\exp\theta + \exp b} = \frac{1}{1 + exp[-(\theta - b)]}.$$ (2)

We show later that Eq. 3.2 is simply a two-parameter logistic model without one of its item parameters (a); thus, it is sometimes called the *one-parameter logistic* (1PL) model. Indeed, the (now standard) form of the 1PL model given in Eq. 2 suggests that it is a special case of the two-parameter logistic in which the discrimination parameter (a) is unity. Actually, the one-parameter logistic model is *almost* that. When it is arranged to be maximally similar to the two parameter logistic, the model *has* a discrimination parameter; the requirement of the Rasch (1960/1980) derivation is simply that the discrimination parameter is *the same* for all items (see Thissen, 1982). So the model is sometimes written

$$T(u_i = 1|\theta) = \frac{1}{1 + exp[-a(\theta - b_i)]}.$$ (3)

in which a (lacking a subscript) takes the same value for all items, and b_i differs for each item i. [We begin here to use the notation $T(u_i = 1|\theta)$ for the curve that traces the conditional probability of an item response as a function of θ.]

When Eq. 2 is used as "the Rasch model" (as it is in many computer applications that are restricted to the Rasch family of models), the trace lines for more or less difficult items are as they appear in the bottom panel of Fig. 3.1: The logistic curves all appear as though Eq. 3 was used with $a = 1$. This, along with a location constraint (usually that $\sum b_i = 0$), "sets the scale" for proficiency (θ). Given this, the population distribution for proficiency, shown in the upper panel of Fig. 3.1, is not specified: It has some mean, relative to the average item difficulty, and some variance, relative to the unit slope of the trace lines. If conditional maximum likelihood (CML)

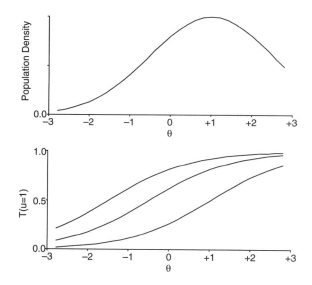

FIG. 3.1. Rasch model trace lines for three items of varying difficulty, with a not completely determined population distribution.

(Andersen, 1980) or the loglinear approach to maximum marginal likelihood (MML) (Kelderman, 1984) is used to estimate the item parameters, the shape of the population distribution is unknown; it is whatever shape it has to be to produce the observed score distribution. Cressie and Holland (1983) specified conditions that must be met by the model for this unspecified population distribution to be a possible distribution.

When the 1PL model is considered from the perspective that includes the two- and three-parameter logistic models, for purposes of item parameter estimation the population distribution of proficiency is usually specified to have mean zero and variance one (Thissen, 1982). Then, the difficulty parameters (b_i) are located relative to zero, which is average proficiency in the population, and the discrimination parameter (a) takes some value relative to the unit standard deviation of proficiency. This structure is shown in Fig. 3.2.

Thus, there is potential for confusion: In applications that follow the tradition of Rasch (1960/1980), the value of a is frequently fixed at unity and disappears from the model; it is actually absorbed in the scale of θ. In subsequent sections, when we consider the scale of the response process, we usually arbitrarily set the variance of θ to be one. That is the unit of measurement for the discrimination parameters of the two- and three-parameter models. When the 1PL model is used, if the variance of θ is set at one, the value of a in Eq. 3 is estimated. In many applications of the Rasch model, the form of the model in Eq. 2 is used, and the variance of θ

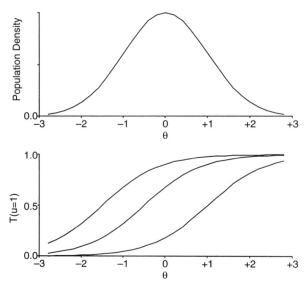

FIG. 3.2.   One-parameter logistic trace lines of varying difficulty ($a = 1.5$; $b = -1.5$, -0.5, 1.0), with $N(0,1)$ population distribution.

varies as a function of the data: If the items are what we could call highly discriminating, the variance of θ is large; if the items are less discriminating, the variance of θ is smaller. So, although applications of the theory of subsequent sections are almost always scaled so that the variance of θ is one, applications of the Rasch model frequently include unspecified variance for θ.

The Normal Ogive and Two-Parameter Logistic Models

The Normal Ogive Model: A Historical Aside.[2]   Item response theory is concerned with the measurement of such hypothetical constructs as *ability* or *proficiency*. Because such constructs have no concrete reality, their measurement is by analogy with some directly observable variable. In the historical development of psychometrics, the first example of such an observable variable was *age* as an indicator of the cognitive development of children. Apart from its background in psychophysics, psychometrics as we now know it was developed to measure the *mental age* of children. The concepts developed for that purpose were gradually extended to include individual differences in cognitive proficiency among adults, and finally to measures of aptitude, achievement, attitudes, and personality variables.

---

[2]For another brief history of IRT, see Bock (1997); an alternative view of history, emphasizing the Rasch model, is provided by Wright (1997).

The central concepts of IRT arise directly from Thurstone's (1925) efforts to improve and formalize the quantification of mental age. That concept originated with the construction of the Binet and Simon (1905) scale of intelligence. The central idea is that there are many tasks that more mature children can do, and less mature children cannot; that is, each task has some chronological age at which we begin to expect proficient performance. By observing whether children are ahead of, or behind, their expected performance for chronological age, we infer something about their mental age.

The Binet scales comprised a variety of items, including naming colors, coins, and months; repeating strings of numbers; and tasks that were almost psychophysics experiments, and that would certainly qualify as performance exercises today! An example of the latter was called "arranging five weights in order," described by Burt (1922, p. 51) as follows:

46.—Arranging Five Weights in Order

Materials. 5 boxes, identical in colour, shape, and size (about 1.5 × 2.5 × 3.5 cm., or 3/5 × 1 2/5 × 1 inches), and loaded with shot and cottonwool or candle wax to weigh, without rattling, 3, 6, 9, 12, and 15 grams . . .

Procedure. **"Do you see these boxes? They all look the same. But they don't weigh the same. Some are heavy and some are light. I want you to find the heaviest and put it here. Then find the one which is a little less heavy; then the one which is still less heavy; then the one which is lighter still; and, last, the one which is lightest here."** (Point in each case to the appropriate place.) . . .

Evaluation. The arrangement must be absolutely correct in **two out of three trials;** and the whole accomplished in **three minutes**.

Burt (1922, pp. 132–133) tabulated the percentages responding correctly to this item (along with the responses to 64 other items); the sample consisted of 2,764 London elementary school children. The proportions responding correctly for each age at which some, but not all, of the children succeeded are shown in Fig. 3.4.

Thurstone (1925) used these data, and others like them, to illustrate a (then) new method of scaling tests. Thurstone (1925, p. 436) wrote that

We assume the distribution of intelligence of children of any given age group to be approximately normal. Since test-intelligence is indicated by the correctness of answers to test questions, it is legitimate to designate the points on the scale of test-intelligence by means of the questions as landmarks. *Each test question is located at a point on the scale so chosen that the percentage of the distribution to the right of that point is equal to the percentage of right answers to the test question for children of the specified age.* [emphasis in the original]

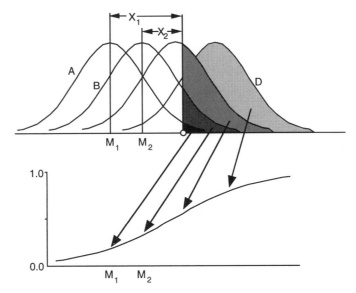

FIG. 3.3.   Distributions of ability for groups of examinees (A, B, C, and D), showing the proportions responding correctly to a test item located at the point marked by the small circle. See text for details.

Thurstone illustrated his conception of the relationship between the distributions of test-intelligence and item responses with a graphic containing the ideas shown in Fig. 3.3.[3]

Thurstone (1925, p. 437) described the ideas as follows:

> Let the frequency curve A represent the distribution of test ability for children of any specified age. Let the curve B represent the distribution for an older age group. The base line represents achievement, or relative difficulty of test questions, while the ordinates represent relative frequencies of children at each degree of achievement. The means of the two distributions are designated M_1 and M_2, respectively. . . .
>
> Let the small circle represent any particular test question. The shaded area in the B surface represents the proportion of the older age group who can answer the question correctly. The remaining unshaded part of the distribution represents the proportion who fail on that question. The same reasoning applies to the A distribution. There is a larger proportion of the older children who can answer the question, and that is reasonable because B represents children older than A.
>
> If we know the percentage of children of different ages who can answer

---

[3]Figure 3.3 is similar to Thurstone's (1925, p. 437) Fig. 2, which, in turn, is a relatively slight revision of Burt's (1922, p. 159) Fig. 23; Thurstone's crucial addition is the placement of the *item* on the same scale as ability.

each question, it is possible to locate the questions on an absolute scale, and it is also possible to locate the means of successive age groups on the same absolute scale. . . .

Let X_1 represent the deviation from the mean, M_1, of a particular question for children of a particular age. . . . In the same manner, let X_2 represent the deviation from the mean, M_2, of the same question for an older age group.

Thurstone (1925) provided a method, using statistical technology current in the 1920s, to combine several age-group means and items onto a common scale. His procedures have been replaced several times over in the intervening decades.[4] Thurstone's essential contribution was the idea that test items could be "located" on the same scale as proficiency. That concept is crucial to both the development of IRT, and the difference between IRT and classical test theory.

A consequence of Thurstone's (1925) description of the relationship between the distributions of ability and the locations of items is that, when plotted as a function of age, the proportion in each group, with average age M_i, responding correctly to a particular item should have the shape of the cumulative normal distribution, or *normal ogive*, as shown in the lower part of Fig. 3.3. That is, the proportion responding correctly to each item should be described by the curve of the normal integral:

$$\text{Proportion(correct)} = \frac{1}{\sqrt{2\pi}} \int_{(X - M_i)/s}^{\infty} e^{-z^2/2} \, dz. \qquad (4)$$

Equation 4 denotes the area of the "test-intelligence" distribution with mean M_i and standard deviation s that exceeds X—that is, the shaded areas of Fig. 3.3.

Thurstone's basic model remains largely unchanged today, with the exception of notation. It is now a widespread convention to denote the variable a test measures as θ in place of Thurstone's M. And the item is described in terms of the two parameters a and b, where $a = 1/s$ is commonly called the *discrimination parameter*, because large values of a are associated with items that discriminate sharply between different levels of θ, and $b = X$. The response for item i is usually assigned a binary variable, often $u_i = 1$ for correct and $u_i = 0$ for incorrect. One further sign-reversal gives the modern form of the normal ogive model:

---

[4]This process, now called item calibration, is discussed at length elsewhere and is not treated in this volume. The interested reader is referred to Wainer and Mislevy (1990) or Baker (1992).

$$T(u_i = 1|\theta) = \frac{1}{\sqrt{2\pi}} \int\limits_{-a_i(\theta - b_i)}^{\infty} e^{\frac{-z^2}{2}}\, dz \tag{5}$$

or, equivalently,

$$T(u_i = 1|\theta) = \Phi[-a_i(\theta - b_i)] \tag{6}$$

in which $u_i = 1$ indicates a correct response to item i, b_i is the age at which 50% of the children respond correctly, and a_i determines the rate of change of the proportion correct as a function of mental age (θ).

Figure 3.4 illustrates the best-fitting normal ogive for item 46 in Burt's data. It is clear that the normal ogive summarizes the shape of the curve fairly well: The curve is always within .03 of the observed proportion correct. The *location* of the item is at a (mental) age of 9.37 years, which is very near the value of 9.3 years reported by Thurstone (1925). Thurstone showed that, except for variation in location (b) and slope (a), the Binet items generally exhibited this form in Burt's (1922) data. Many other researchers have since reported similar results.

Curves such as the one illustrated in Fig. 3.4 are frequently called *item characteristic curves* (ICCs), because they summarize the essential characteristics of a test item; the phrase was attributed to Ledyard Tucker by Lord (1952). In the earlier literature of what has become IRT, these curves were called *trace lines* by Lazarsfeld (1950, p. 364), because they "trace" the probability of a particular item response (in this case, correct) as a function of an explanatory variable (in this case, age). The term *ICC* sees more widespread use in the recent IRT literature, because most discussion centers on items with binary responses, and the performance of such items is completely summarized by a single "characteristic" curve. When more than two responses are considered, as in chapter 4, each response has its

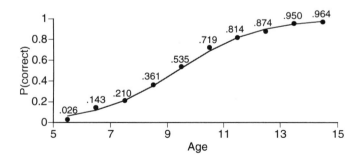

FIG. 3.4. Proportions correct on Burt's (1922) item 46, plotted against age, with a fitted normal ogive.

own curve and it is more convenient to refer to them as trace lines. We use both terms in the remainder of this book.

In the context of the mental age metaphor, it is clear that the two most obvious characteristics that differ among test items are captured by the ICC, or trace line. The first is the *location*; in this case that is the age at which children as a group have a 50–50 chance of responding correctly. Depending on the test item, that parameter (b) may vary from very young to never. The second characteristic of the curve is the *rate of change* of the curve as a function of age. There are some aspects of performance, or possible items, that change very rapidly as a function of age; an example would be "walking three steps or more" which goes from zero to almost 100% in a few months around age one. In contrast, several years are required for performance on item 46 (given earlier) to exhibit the same change. The slope parameter of the curve (a) indicates how well the item discriminates among children of different ages: Walking discriminates very well between children younger than 1 year and children older than 1 year; "arranging five weights in order" discriminates much less precisely between children under 9 and children over 9 years old.

The idea that mental growth is a function of age has remained in psychology since the times of Binet and Thurstone. It is not at all clear, however, that the *units* of mental growth are the same as the units of age (years). That is, while it is clear that a 12-year-old is 1 year older than an 11-year-old in the same sense as a 2-year-old is 1 year older than a 1-year-old, the parallel statement may well not be true for cognitive development. Bock (1983) attempted to identify the units of mental growth more realistically by fitting item-response curves to items on a recent version of the Stanford–Binet test, simultaneously rescaling age so that the units are determined, in part, from the form of the trace lines.[5] Here we make use of the data from a single item as another illustration of the form of item response data as a function of age.

Figure 3.5 shows the proportions of boys responding correctly and incorrectly to item 80 of a recent version of the Stanford–Binet test, in data provided by Mark Reckase (personal communication, 1979). The division into age groups is approximately every 10 months, and the average age in each group is tabulated on the x-axis. Figure 3.5 also shows the best-fitting normal ogive. For this item, $a = 0.3$ and $b = 9.7$ years. As before, the normal ogive describes the proportions correct quite well. The observed proportions deviate more from the fitted curve than those in Fig. 3.4 because the sample size for Fig. 3.5 is much smaller; thus, the observed proportions have more stochastic variation. For this particular item, the curve fits fairly well with the units of age taken to be years. However, when a large

---

[5]The choice of scale for developmental measures is a complex issue; see Yen (1986) for a thorough discussion.

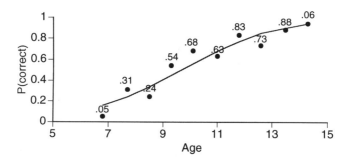

FIG. 3.5.   Proportions correct on Bock's (1983) item 80, plotted against
age, with a fitted normal ogive.

number of such items spanning the age range from 2 years to 15 years is
considered, there is substantial evidence that the units of mental growth
are not the same as the units of age. Mental growth is not linear in age.
This result may be used to compute and plot the form of the mental
growth curve (Bock, 1983).

The preceding discussion of the approximation of item-response data
by normal ogive and logistic models tends to be intuitively satisfying, but it
is less than precise from a statistical point of view. The early work with
item-response models itself tended to be much less than precise about *exactly* what it was that was assumed to be Gaussian, and what might not be. It
was also not very precise about which variables should be regarded as *fixed*
(the item parameters usually are), and which should be regarded as *random*, meaning that only their distribution, not a particular value, can be
known. The values of the latent variable (θ) are usually random variables.
Further, the distinction between observed (or, indeed, observable) quantities and unobservable (*latent*) variables has frequently been lost. Clarification of many of these issues appeared in the integrated summary provided
by Lord and Novick (1968).

Lord and Novick (1968, pp. 370–373) noted that the normal ogive
model "may be taken simply as a basic assumption, the utility of which can
be investigated with a given set of data. . . . Alternatively [it] can be inferred from other, possibly more plausible assumptions. We shall outline
one way of doing this, a way that some theorists find interesting and others
do not." The "outline" by Lord and Novick assumes for each item *i* the existence of an unobserved variable Y_i, linearly related to the latent variable
θ with some constant variance:

$$Y_i = \rho_i \theta + E_i \sqrt{1 - \rho_i^{\ 2}}. \tag{7}$$

Y, θ, and *E* (a random error component) are all unobserved random variables; therefore, they may be placed on any desired scale. It is most conve-

nient for statistical purposes to specify that they are standardized: All three variables (Y, θ, and E) have mean 0 and variance 1; then ρ_i is the correlation between Y_i and θ. Here, E is assumed to be normally distributed, and the distributions of Y and θ are unspecified.

The idea expressed by Eq. 7 is that the *response process* Y_i has correlation ρ_i with θ, and some random component E_i. The response process is a *number*; the name originated with Thurstone's (1927) treatment of psychophysical judgments, using early 20th-century language in which the *numerical outcome* of a "process of calculation" was called the "process." The name remains, although it is not compatible with the late 20th-century meanings of the term "process." The response process is a continuous variable that reflects an examinee's proficiency for *a particular item*; that is a combination of that examinee's proficiency in general (θ) and an error (unpredicted) component specific to item i. For instance, on a vocabulary test, examinees with large vocabularies have high values of θ, but a particular word on the test may or may not be one that the examinee knows. That random "may or may not" part of the examinee's knowledge of *a particular item* is included in E_i.

Conditional on θ, Y_i is normally distributed with mean

$$E(Y_i|\theta) = \mu_i|\theta = \rho_i\theta \tag{8}$$

and variance

$$\sigma^2|\theta = 1 - \rho_i^2 . \tag{9}$$

The item is assumed to be characterized by a constant γ_i, called the *threshold*, and:

- If $Y_i \geq \gamma_i$, the response is correct ($u_i = 1$).
- If $Y_i < \gamma_i$, the response is incorrect ($u_i = 0$).

Figure 3.6, like Fig. 16.6.1 of Lord and Novick (1968, p. 371), illustrates the relationships among θ, Y_i, γ_i, and the probability of a correct response $T(u_i = 1)$. Figure 3.6 is related to the ideas shown in Fig. 3.3: *Some distribution is divided at a threshold, with those above it responding correctly.* Unlike Fig. 3.3, however, in Fig. 3.6 the variable divided is explicitly hypothetical, representing an unobservable internal process. With the definitions already given, illustrated in Fig. 3.6, the probability of a correct response as a function of θ is

$$T(u_i = 1|\theta) = \Phi\left[\frac{\mu_i|\theta - \gamma_i}{\sigma_i|\theta}\right]. \tag{10}$$

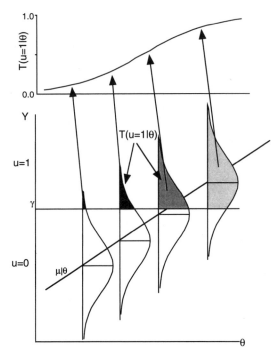

FIG. 3.6.   Illustration of the relationships involved in the normal ogive model (see text for explanation).

Substituting values from Eqs. 8 and 9, we have

$$T(u_i = 1|\theta) = \Phi\left[\frac{\rho_i\theta - \gamma_i}{\sqrt{1 - \rho_i^2}}\right] \tag{11}$$

which is

$$T(u_i = 1|\theta) = \Phi[a_i(\theta - b_i)] . \tag{12}$$

That is identical to Eq. 6, if

$$a_i = \frac{\rho_i}{\sqrt{1 - \rho_i^2}} \tag{13}$$

and

$$b_i = \frac{\gamma_i}{\rho_i} . \tag{14}$$

Lord and Novick (1968, p. 371) noted that "this derivation involves no assumptions about the frequency distribution of θ, or of Y_i, over the total group of examinees." The assumption of normality that yields the normal ogive concerns only the *random component* of the response process.

Because most item analysis in IRT is done in terms of the parameters a_i and b_i, it is convenient to be able to transform those values into ρ_i and γ_i if desired. To do that, Eqs. 13 and 14 are inverted, giving

$$\rho_i = \frac{a_i}{\sqrt{1 + a_i^2}} , \tag{15}$$

and

$$\gamma_i = \frac{a_i b_i}{\sqrt{1 + a_i^2}} . \tag{16}$$

The parameters a_i and b_i have interpretations in terms of the shape of the normal ogive, as shown in Fig. 3.7. The parameters ρ_i and γ_i have interpretations in terms of the display in Fig. 3.6, and are conceptually important in the response process description offered in this section. The parameter ρ_i is especially important in approaches to IRT from a factor analytic perspective, as described in chapter 5. In item factor analysis with a single common factor, ρ_i is the factor loading of item i. And the tetrachoric correlation between item i and (some other) item i' is

$$\rho_{ii'} = \rho_i \rho_{i'} .$$

Estimates of tetrachoric correlations obtained from the item-response data are sometimes used to provide estimates of ρ_i, and those, using Eq. 13, provide estimates of a_i.

The Logistic Substitution. By the 1960s, a second metaphor had appeared underlying item-response theory: an analogy between item-response curves and dose-response curves in bioassay. In bioassay, curves resembling those illustrated in Fig. 3.7 frequently appear, graphing the probability of some quantal response as a function of the dosage of some drug or chemical. In studies of the effectiveness of drugs, the binary response is usually improvement, or lack thereof, for subjects with some illness. In studies of the effectiveness of pesticides or the hazards associated

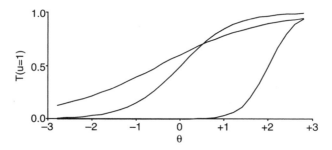

FIG. 3.7.   Normal ogive trace lines with different values of *a* and *b*; from left to right at the *T* = 0.5 level, *a* = 0.6, 0.9, and 1.2, and *b* = −0.5, 0.0, and 2.0.

with chemicals, the binary response is usually death. Increasing the dosage of the drug or chemical usually increases the probability of a positive response in a sigmoid fashion,[6] and the data are frequently fitted with normal ogives as a method of estimation of the parameter *b*. The parameter *b*, in the context of bioassay, is an estimate of the dosage at which one expects 50% positive responses; it is called the *LD50*, for "50% lethal dose," in pesticide research, or the *ED50*, for "50% effective dose," in drug research.

The metaphor was attractive: *The relationship between responding correctly to a test item and amount of proficiency is like the relationship between responding to a drug and the dose of the drug.* What was even more attractive was the fact that a great deal of statistical research had been done on the problem of fitting dose-response curves, and much of this could be transported into the item-response context. Finney (1952) had written a book summarizing *probit analysis*, as fitting normal ogives was called in bioassay. Finney (1952, p. 253) noted that the logistic function was preferred by some analysts over the normal for fitting dose-response curves, and Berkson (1944, 1953) strongly advocated the use of the logistic.

In chapters contributed to the Lord and Novick (1968) volume on test theory, Allen Birnbaum (1968) offered the suggestion that the normal ogive model be replaced with the logistic function for computational reasons. Birnbaum (1968, p. 399–400) noted that the logistic function

$$\Psi(x) = \frac{\exp[x]}{1 + \exp[x]} = \frac{1}{1 + \exp[-x]}$$

. . . differs by less than 0.01, uniformly in *x*, from the normal cdf with mean zero and standard deviation 1.7; that is

---

[6]In pesticide research, death is a "positive response." This is not as nasty as it sounds, because the subjects of the experiments are frequently relatively obnoxious insects.

$$|\Phi(x \mathbin{/} 1.7) - \Psi(x)| < 0.01 \quad \text{for all } x$$

or

$$|\Phi(x) - \Psi(1.7x)| < 0.01 \quad \text{for all } x$$

(Haley, 1952, p. 7). . . . We may view the logistic form for an item characteristic curve as a mathematically convenient, close approximation to the classical normal form, introduced to help solve or to avoid some mathematical or theoretical problems that arise with the normal model. Or we may view it as the form of a test model that is of equal intrinsic interest and of very similar mathematical form.

[Although Haley's (1952) work, cited by Birnbaum, is now largely unavailable due to the obscure nature of its publication, Camilli (1994) recently reconstructed Haley's development.]

It is very difficult to distinguish between the normal ogive and logistic curves on any reasonable scale. Therefore, it is easy to see why it makes little difference if the logistic is substituted for the normal ogive. The computational advantage of the logistic is, of course, that it is not an integral. Fitting item-response curves means estimating the parameters of the trace line function; usually this is done with an algorithm that requires repeated computations of the item-response function. Using conventional computers, it takes a good deal more time to compute the value of the normal ogive than it does to compute the value of the logistic function. Therefore, practical (fast) computer programs for the most part use the logistic function $\Psi(x)$.

Here, the logistic item response model

$$T(u_i = 1|\theta) = \frac{1}{1 + \exp[-1.7a_i(\theta - b_i)]} \tag{17}$$

is justified on the grounds of its similarity to the (more fundamental) normal ogive model. The numerical values of the parameters a_i and b_i are essentially the same for either model. Estimates of the trace line parameters obtained with the logistic model may be used to provide estimates of ρ_j and γ_i, to be interpreted as already described.

Of course, the only observed variable in this entire theoretical collection is the item response, u_i. Fortunately, with several item responses and modern software such as BILOG (Mislevy & Bock, 1990) and MULTILOG (Thissen, 1991), it is possible to estimate values for some of the unobserved quantities and test the goodness of fit of the model.

Philosophical Differences Underlying the Different Approaches Represented by the Rasch Model and the 2PL.   As a conclusion to his presidential address to the Psychometric Society, subsequently published in *Science*, L. L. Thurstone (1937; reprinted in Thurstone, 1959, p. 11) said:

> In encouraging students to help us build an integrated interpretation of mental phenomena on an experimental foundation, let us remember that a psychological theory is not good simply because it is cleverly mathematical, that an experiment is not good just because it involves ingenious apparatus, and that statistics are merely the means for checking theory with experiment.

(In the 1930s, any data collection was referred to as an "experiment," so that term should be read broadly.)

Historically there have been two approaches to model building in IRT. The approach that led to the normal ogive model and its logistic approximation arose from a series of attempts to develop a model for the item-response *process*. IRT models developed following this approach are oriented primarily toward item analysis: The idea is that the model should reflect the properties of item-response data sufficiently accurately that the behavior of the item is summarized by the item parameters. Then item analysis is based on parameter estimates. Item analysis based on parameters has advantages in the simplicity of its summary of the data and the ready availability of statistical tests of significance.

However, it is essential in this approach that the item-response model accurately capture all aspects of the trace lines; model misspecification may cause erroneous estimation of the entire set of parameters. The properties of the model for measurement are consequences of the observed item-response data, as summarized by the parametric model: Items are assumed to measure as they *do*, not as they should. This is the philosophical position of the authors of this book. This is not an atheoretical position— but the purpose of a theory in this approach is to explain the data. The theory underlying the normal ogive model, completed by Lord and Novick (1968) but with its roots in the ideas of Thurstone (1925), is an elegant example.

Another approach to the development of IRT models, discussed previously and following a tradition established by Rasch (1960/1980), is to develop the item-response model to obtain specific measurement properties. In this approach, optimal measurement is defined mathematically, and then the class of item response models that yields such measurement is derived. The item-response model is then used as a Procrustean bed that the item-response data must fit, or the item is discarded. Item analysis in this approach consists primarily of analysis of residuals from the model.

The existence of these two approaches to model construction, within IRT, has led to continuing disagreement in the literature of test theory about the best way to do item analysis and test scoring. This disagreement is not based on any misunderstanding; advocates of the Rasch position agree with us about the philosophical nature of the basis of the disagreement. For example, in his defense of the Rasch model during an invited debate on this issue at the 1992 annual meeting of the American Educational Research Association, Wright (1994, p. 197) pointed out that "The Birnbaum model is designed to imitate data. . . . Quite different from that is the Rasch model which is not designed to fit any data, but instead is derived to define measurement." Where the Rasch theorists and those of us writing this book part company is on the relative evaluation of these two approaches: We consider "imitating" (that is, fitting) the data to be the primary goal of model building in psychology, whereas some among the Rasch theorists write that what is done with the 2PL model, and other models we introduce in this volume in subsequent sections and chapters, "is not measurement" (Wright, 1996, p. 481).

Following Stevens (1951, p. 1; see also Bock & Jones, 1968, p. 7), we define measurement as "the assignment of numerals to objects or events according to rules." Using this definition, the procedures described in this book provide measurement. The reader should be cautioned that when others write that what we are doing here is "not measurement," that statement is based on the use of a different definition of the word.

We cannot pretend not to take sides on this issue; one cannot write a book on measurement without a definition of measurement. This book follows the traditions of Thurstone (1937), Stevens (1951), Bock and Jones (1968), and many others in setting as the primary goal of the modeling enterprise: to accurately characterize the data with a mathematical function—in short, to fit the data. In the rare cases in which the Rasch (1960/1980) model fits a set of item-response data, that model provides a level of elegant simplicity in the item analysis and test scoring that is unequaled by any alternative. In subsequent chapters, we illustrate the virtues of the model. However, we do not follow Rasch (1966) and others to the extent that we consider *only* data that the Rasch model fits. We apply the Rasch model when it is useful, and the more traditional normal ogive or "1.7 logistic" when their greater complexity corresponds to the complexity of the data.[7]

---

[7]When the logistic is used as a proxy for the normal ogive, the scale factor 1.7 is often included in the exponent so that the parameters have approximately the same values as they would if the normal ogive had been used. Because the derivation of the Rasch (1960/1980) model has nothing whatever to do with the normal ogive, there was never any reason in that tradition to include the 1.7 in the model. So about half of the literature on logistic models includes the 1.7 in the model and about half does not.

The Three-Parameter Normal Ogive and Logistic Models

Birnbaum's (1968) Development.   In this section, we consider the application of the theory to multiple-choice items that may elicit guessing. We continue to assume that the item response depends on the value of the same unobservable response process Y_i. The response to a multiple choice item is determined only in part by the relationship of Y_i to the threshold γ_i; it is also influenced by the probability g_i that the examinees respond correctly even if they do not know the answer:

- If $Y_i \geq \gamma_i$, the response is correct ($u_i = 1$).
- If $Y_i < \gamma_i$, $u_i = 1$ with probability g_i, and $u_i = 0$ with probability $1 - g_i$.

For values of the response process greater than γ_i, the item response is correct, as in the preceding description; for values of the response process less than γ_i, the item response is correct with probability g_i.

Then the trace line of a positive response may be expressed in two parts (as it was by Lord [1953b]):

$$T(u_i = 1|\theta = g_i T(Y_i < \gamma_i|\theta) + T(Y_i \geq \gamma_i|\theta)$$

$$= g_i \left(1 - \Phi \left[\frac{\mu_i|\theta - \gamma_i}{\sigma_i|\theta} \right] \right) + \Phi \left[\frac{\mu_i|\theta - \gamma_i}{\sigma_i|\theta} \right]$$

where the first term represents the probability that the response process is below, or to the left of, the threshold, and the examinee guesses correctly, and the second term represents the probability that the response process exceeds the threshold, and the examinee knows the correct response.

The model is usually rewritten to become

$$\begin{aligned}
T(u_i = 1|\theta) &= g_i (1 - \Phi[a_i(\theta - b_i)]) + \Phi[a_i(\theta - b_i)] \\
&= g_i - g_i \Phi[a_i(\theta - b_i)] + \Phi[a_i(\theta - b_i)] \\
&= g_i + (1 - g_i)\Phi[a_i(\theta - b_i)]
\end{aligned}$$

in which the normal ogive appears with parameters a_i and b_i, and the model has a constant lower asymptote on the left plus the ogive. It is conceptually useful to remember, however, that the final form of the model is a simplifying rearrangement of terms, and the model is derived from the idea that the probability of *really knowing* the correct answer is a function of θ represented by the normal ogive. The constant lower asymptote g_i is really a sum of the increasing probability of really knowing the answer $\Phi[a_i(\theta - b_i)]$ and g_i times the decreasing probability of *not* knowing, $1 - \Phi[a_i(\theta - b_i)]$.

In the context of dose-response relationships, especially for the effects of pesticides, the three-parameter normal ogive model was discussed by Finney (1952, chap. 8). In that context, where the sigmoid curve is used to fit the proportion of test subjects killed by varying doses of the pesticide, the lower asymptote was used to represent natural mortality. Especially in cases in which the test subjects are insects with short life spans, one may expect a considerable proportion of dead subjects at the end of the experiment, even in the groups receiving the lowest doses of pesticides. These insects die for the wrong reason (any reason other than the pesticide being tested). Thus, the probability of natural mortality has to be added to the probability that they die from the pesticide, to give the total death rate.

Our conception of the item-response process for multiple-choice items is different only in that it is less morbid. In place of death, the psychometric models have correct item responses. Examinees may make such correct responses because they really know the answer; this is analogous to death really induced by the pesticide in an experiment. Examinees may also guess, or "select the right response for some wrong reason." This aspect of the data can only be modeled as some proportion of the responses.

Birnbaum (1968, pp. 404–405) introduced the three-parameter normal ogive and logistic models as item-response functions essentially simultaneously; the three-parameter logistic is the model that has seen extensive practical use. The three-parameter logistic (3PL) is usually written in a form parallel to the final form of the normal ogive model:

$$T(u_i = 1|\theta) = g_i + \frac{1 - g_i}{1 + \exp[-1.7a_i(\theta - b_i)]} \tag{18}$$

in which the item parameters are essentially interchangeable with those of the normal ogive model.

Note that when $g_i = 0$ the three-parameter model becomes identical to the two-parameter version. Also note that when $g_i > 0$ the meanings of the other parameters change from those associated with the two parameter models. For instance, in the two-parameter models, ρ_i may be estimated by the tetrachoric correlations among the observed item responses. In the three-parameter models, the cross-classifications (2×2 tables) of correct and incorrect responses for pairs of items include the effects of guessing; they are not simply a realization of the division of the underlying response processes into four quadrants. Therefore, the tetrachoric correlations *cannot* be used to estimate ρ_i, and then a_i, for multiple-choice items. In the two-parameter models, the parameter b_i is the value of θ at which respondents have a 50% chance of responding correctly; in the three parameter models, the proportion responding correctly at b_i is $0.5 + 0.5g_i$.

The Three-Parameter Logistic Model and Data.   The geometry problem shown in Fig. 3.8 appeared as item 3 on one of the 1991 forms of the North Carolina Test of Geometry, an end-of-course test for high school students. Item 3 was surprisingly difficult; only 57% of the examinees responded correctly.

Using data from 11,850 students who were administered this form of the test, we fitted the 3PL model to all 60 items using MULTILOG

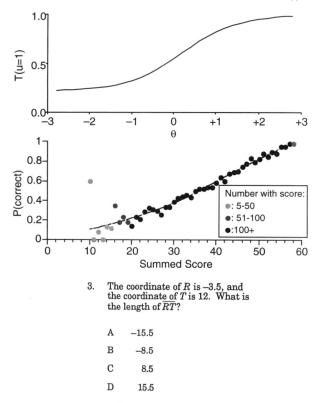

3. The coordinate of R is -3.5, and
    the coordinate of T is 12. What is
    the length of $\overline{RT}$?

    A -15.5

    B -8.5

    C   8.5

    D   15.5

FIG. 3.8.   Top panel: The fitted 3PL curve for item 3 of the North Carolina Test of Geometry; $a = 0.9$, $b = 0.2$, and $c = 0.22$. Middle panel: The observed proportion correct for item 3 plotted against the summed score for the 60-item test; the probability of a correct response computed using the IRT model is shown as a series of horizontal lines, and the observed proportions are shown as dots (that are more lightly shaded for score groups with small samples). Bottom panel: Item 3 of the North Carolina Test of Geometry; alternative D is correct. Reprinted with permission.

(Thissen, 1991). The fitted trace line for the correct response to item 3 is shown at the top of Fig. 3.8; the item parameters are $a = 0.9$, $b = 0.2$, and $c = 0.22$. In many respects, this is a representative multiple-choice item: Its difficulty parameter ($b = 0.2$) is very near the average proficiency of the population (0.0), its discrimination parameter is about the value commonly found for high-quality achievement test items, and the guessing level is just less than the value of 0.25 that would be obtained if guessing had been uniformly distributed among the four alternatives. A goodness-of-fit statistic ($S\text{-}X^2$) developed by Orlando (1997; Orlando & Thissen, 2000) indicates that the 3PL model fits the data satisfactorily for this item ($S\text{-}X^2(45) = 55.6$, $p = .13$); this value of the goodness-of-fit statistic is representative of the average of the goodness of fit among the 60 items of this test.[8]

It is a complex matter to examine the goodness of fit of, say, a logistic trace line to data under the assumptions of an IRT model. As a heuristic argument, in our discussion of Figs. 3.4 and 3.5, we plotted the proportion correct as a function of age, and showed that relation to be very similar in form to the normal ogive. However, that heuristic is not accurate in mathematical detail. IRT assumes that the normal ogive, or logistic, describes the relation of the probability of a correct response with the latent variable θ—which is, in principle, unobservable. Therefore, there is no (accurate) way to add data points to the trace line plot in the top panel of Fig. 3.8 to compare to the modeled curve, because we do not know the values of θ for the examinees.[9]

The proportions correct for examinees obtaining each summed score on all 60 items is, of course, observable; that is plotted in the middle panel of Fig. 3.8. The summed score is not the same as θ (although the two are monotonically related in expectation). Therefore, the plot of proportion correct as a function of summed score should not be the same as the trace line. However, the IRT model does yield an estimate of the probability of a correct response among examinees with each summed score; these probabilities may be computed using an algorithm described in the final section of this chapter. Those IRT-modeled probabilities (correct, for each summed score) are plotted as a series of horizontal lines in the middle panel of Fig. 3.8, and it is on those probabilities that the computation of $S\text{-}X^2$ is based.

---

[8]The statistic $S\text{-}X^2$ compares observed and expected frequencies correct and incorrect for the groups that obtain each summed score on the test; its values are distributed approximately as χ^2 if the model fits the data.

[9]Procedures have been proposed (i.e., by Bock, 1972, and Yen, 1981) that attempt to construct "observed" proportions to compare to the probability plotted as the trace line. Those procedures do not yield goodness of fit statistics that perform well (Orlando, 1997).

Examination of the middle panel of Fig. 3.8 shows that the observed proportions correct across the score groups closely correspond with the probabilities predicted using the IRT model. (For a few score groups, concentrated near the lower end of the range, there are very few examinees; those points use lighter shades of gray in Fig. 3.8. The fact that the observed proportions for some of those differ from the modeled probabilities is attributable to the larger sampling error associated with the very small sample sizes.) We conclude that the 3PL model represents the performance of item 3 very well.

As a matter of fact, the 3PL model fits all of the items on this 60-item test fairly well. The worst-fitting item, as measured by $S\text{-}X^2$, is item 47, shown in the bottom panel of Fig. 3.9. Item 47 was extremely easy: 92% of the examinees responded correctly. The fitted trace line for the correct response to item 47 is shown at the top of Fig. 3.9; the item parameters are $a = 0.8$, $b = -2.0$, and $c = 0.30$. The goodness-of-fit statistic indicates that the 3PL model fits the data poorly (in a statistical sense): $S\text{-}X^2(44) = 98.2$, $p < .0001$. At first glance, it appears that the IRT-modeled score-group probabilities for the correct response differ no more from the observed proportions (in the middle panel of Fig. 3.9) than they did for item 3 (in the middle panel of Fig. 3.8). Closer examination of the data underlying Fig. 3.9 shows that, although the modeled probabilities and observed proportions are similar, there is a pattern to the differences between them: For low score groups, the observed proportions tend to lie below the fitted probabilities; for score groups around 30, the observed proportions are (slightly) higher than the model probabilities; and then for very high score groups the observed proportions are again (slightly) too low. Thus, considered in great detail, and with a very large sample, the 3PL model does not fit the data for this item in the sense that the shape of the fitted curve is not quite correct. However, from any practical point of view, the approximation of the data by the 3PL model is excellent, as shown by the fact that the deviations just described are not clearly visible in the middle panel of Fig. 3.9.

Recalling that item 47 is the worst fitting item on the entire 60-item test, we conclude that the 3PL model represents the trace lines for these items very well. Other similar graphical analyses derived from very large samples (i.e., by Wainer, 1983; Wainer, Wadkins, & Rogers, 1984, and Lord, 1965; also reproduced by Lord & Novick, 1968, p. 364)[10] show that the form of the regression of the proportions correct for multiple-choice

---

[10]Other published plots of the regression of the correct item response on the total test score used a test score that omitted the item in question. This slight modification tends to make the item-test regression appear to be somewhat more similar to the 3PL form than the displays in Figs. 3.8 and 3.9, especially for very low scores.

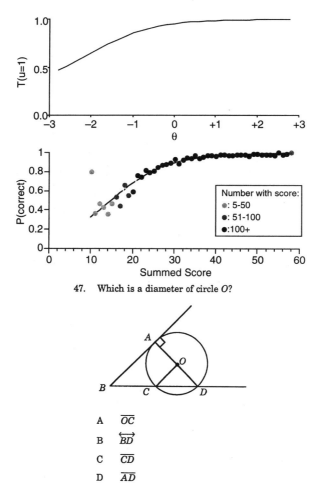

47. Which is a diameter of circle O?

A $\overline{OC}$

B $\overleftrightarrow{BD}$

C $\overline{CD}$

D $\overline{AD}$

FIG. 3.9. Top panel: The fitted 3PL curve for item 47 of the North Carolina Test of Geometry; $a = 0.8$, $b = -2.0$, and $c = 0.30$. Middle panel: The observed proportion correct for item 47 plotted against the summed score for the 60-item test; the probability of a correct response computed using the IRT model is shown as a series of horizontal lines, and the observed proportions are shown as dots (that are more lightly shaded for score groups with small samples). Bottom panel: Item 47 of the North Carolina Test of Geometry; alternative D is correct. Reprinted with permission.

items on the total test score is generally similar to those that are produced by the 3PL model.

We have shown only four illustrations of the close approximation of item response data by the normal ogive and logistic models; we could have shown hundreds, or even thousands. The point has been that the normal ogive model, and its logistic approximation, capture the essential features of the relationship between the probability of a correct item response and some variable that underlies that response.

The logistic and normal ogive models are not the only IRT models; however, they are in most widespread use. Alternatives have been proposed: Ramsay (1989) compared two differently-constructed trace line models (both based on logistic functions) with the Rasch model; Ramsay and Abrahamowicz (1989) and Ramsay and Winsberg (1991) considered the use of spline functions as trace lines; and Ramsay (1991) described the use of kernel smoothing techniques to obtain item response functions. The kernel smoothing approach has been implemented in the computer program TESTGRAF (Ramsay, 1995). Each of these procedures offers different strengths, and has different weaknesses, as item analysis. However, each yields a functional representation of the trace line, and trace lines form the basis of all of the approaches to the computation of scale scores that are discussed in the remainder of this chapter. Thus, either the widely used logistic or normal ogive models, or other less widely used alternatives are fully compatible with the computation of scale scores based on IRT.

SCALE SCORES

Estimates of Proficiency Based on Response Patterns

The Simplest Case: Two Items.   In a useful binary test item, the relationship between the probability of a positive response and proficiency (θ) is usually more or less like the function in the top panel of Fig. 3.10. Proficiency (θ) is frequently arbitrarily placed on the standard z-scale; thus, θ values may range roughly from −3 to +3. Item response theory is used to convert item responses into a scaled estimate of θ, as well as to calibrate items and examine their properties as in the preceding section.

For item 1, in the upper panel of Fig. 3.10, the probability of a positive response, $T(u = 1)$, is plotted against θ. The curve in the top panel of Fig. 3.10 is a logistic, as are all of the trace lines in this section. For the moment, let us assume that we know that the location parameter of item 1 is $b = 0$ and its slope is $a = 1$ (in real applications, these numbers are obtained from observed data during item calibration). The trace line for item 2, in the center panel of Fig. 3.10, describing an incorrect response, is for an item with a higher slope ($a = 2$) than item 1; the location of item 2 is also higher, at $b = 1$.

Although it is not of great practical value to consider the computation of scale scores for two items, it is useful to do so in a presentation of the concepts involved. Because the trace lines for items 1 and 2 are known, as functions of their parameters, the information conveyed by the trace lines

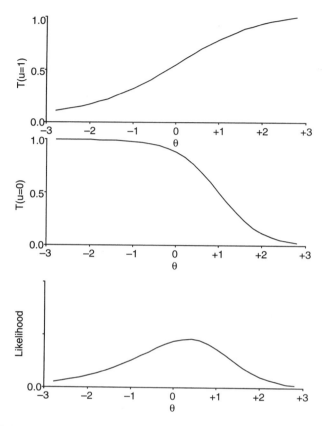

FIG. 3.10. Top panel: Trace line for a positive response, $T_1(1)$, for an item with parameters $a = 1$ and $b = 0$. Middle panel: Trace line for a negative response, $T_2(0)$, for an item with parameters $a = 2$ and $b = 1$. Bottom panel: The product of the trace lines in the upper two panels, $L = T_1(1)T_2(0)$.

may be used to estimate θ for an examinee who responds positively to item 1 and negatively to item 2.

Consider first the method of estimating θ based on the principle of *maximum likelihood* (ML). Because IRT models assume that the probabilities of each of the item responses are independent given a particular value of θ, the joint likelihood of the sequence {right, wrong} at any value of θ is the product of the item 1 and item 2 probability values at that level of θ. That product is labeled "Likelihood" at the bottom of Fig. 3.10. The likelihood is low for low values of θ because it is unlikely that a person there would respond positively to item 1, and it is low for high values of θ, because it is unlikely that a person there would respond negatively to item 2. The likelihood of the sequence {right, wrong} for these two items is highest at about $\theta = 0.3$, so that is the maximum-likelihood estimate (MLE) for

TABLE 3.1
Newton–Raphson Computation of the Mode of the
Likelihood for the Illustration in Fig. 3.10

$\hat{\theta}$	l	$\dfrac{\partial l}{\partial \theta}$	$\dfrac{\partial^2 l}{\partial \theta^2}$	$\dfrac{\partial l / \partial \theta}{\partial^2 l / \partial \theta^2}$	Next $\hat{\theta}$
0.0	−.3562	0.2616	−0.6700	−0.3905	0.3905
0.3905	−.3369	−0.0526	−0.9450	0.0556	0.3348
0.3384	−.3363	−0.0011	−0.9046	0.0012	0.3336
0.3336	−.3363	−0.0000	−0.9037	0.0000	0.3336

θ, called $\hat{\theta}$ or MLE[θ].[11] So a person who responds {right, wrong} might be assigned a trait value of 0.3 as a "test score" or measurement.

Although it is possible, and conceptually useful, to locate the mode of the joint likelihood of the item responses graphically, that process is excessively tedious and cannot be used to estimate scale scores for large numbers of examinees and/or large numbers of items. In practice, numerical methods are used to compute MLE[θ]. The most commonly used method for computing the maximum of the likelihood is the Newton–Raphson procedure, which we describe briefly here and illustrate in Table 3.1.

Calculating MLE [θ] for Two Items. In general, an equation describing the joint likelihood of binary item responses as a function of θ is

$$L = \prod_{i=1}^{\text{nitems}} T_i(u_i|\theta) . \tag{19}$$

In the case of the two items of Fig. 3.10, the product may be written out:

$$L = T_1(u_1|\theta)T_2(u_2|\theta) .$$

However, when there are more items, the notation of Eq. 19 is more convenient.

The maximum of the likelihood is the value of θ at which the function described by Eq. 19 has its maximum value. The Newton–Raphson procedure is a simple algorithm that locates the maximum value of such a function in a finite number of trials, or iterations.

---

[11]Lazarsfeld (1950, p. 464) called such a modal estimate a "maximum probability score (MPS)." Later writers universally refer to such estimates as MLEs. The replacement of the word "probability" with "likelihood" in such contexts is due to Fisher (1925, p. 10 [in the 1954 reprint]), who used the term *likelihood* to refer to a "mathematical quantity which appears to be appropriate for measuring our order of preference among" different values of θ in this case. Notice that the value of this likelihood, even at the maximum, may be an extremely small number because it is the product of as many probabilities as there are items on the test.

It is more convenient to locate the maximum of the log of the likelihood,

$$l = \sum_{i=1}^{\text{nitems}} \log T_i(u_i|\theta) .$$ (20)

Both the log (Eq. 20) and the original likelihood (Eq. 19) have their maximum at the same value of θ. To locate the modal value of θ, we choose an arbitrary starting value θ_0, and evaluate the first and second derivatives of Eq. 20 at θ_0. Then we use the Newton–Raphson iteration

$$\theta_h = \theta_{h-1} - \frac{\partial l / \partial\theta}{\partial^2 l / \partial\theta^2}$$ (21)

to find a new value θ_h (in this case, $h = 1$). Then we recompute the derivatives and reapply Eq. 21 until the sequential values of θ stop changing between successive iterations h and $h + 1$.

For the two parameter logistic model,[12]

$$\frac{\partial l}{\partial\theta} = \sum_{i=1}^{\text{nitems}} \frac{1}{T_i(u_i)} \frac{\partial T_i(u_i)}{\partial\theta}$$

$$= \sum_{i=1}^{\text{nitems}} [-1]^{(1-x_i)} \frac{a_i T_i(u_i)[1 - T_i(x_i)]}{T_i(x_i)}$$

$$= \sum_{i=1}^{\text{nitems}} [-1]^{(1-x_i)} a_i [1 - T_i(u_i)]$$

and

$$\frac{\partial^2 l}{\partial\theta^2} = \sum_{i=1}^{\text{nitems}} a_i^2 T_i(x_i)[1 - T_i(u_i)] .$$

Illustrative computations for the two items in Fig. 3.10 are shown in Table 3.1, starting with $\hat{\theta}_0 = 0.0$. In the example, beginning with an arbitrary initial estimate, $\hat{\theta}_0 = 0.0$, we compute the first and second derivatives of the loglikelihood (0.2616 and −0.67, respectively). The ratio of those derivatives, −0.3905, is the so-called correction; that is subtracted from the initial

---

[12] We include the partial derivatives for the 2PL model here to make this discussion more concrete. We do not include such detail for the 3PL model, or for the more elaborate models discussed in chapter 4; the interested reader is referred to Lord's (1980) volume or Baker's (1992) text—both include all of the equations necessary for 3PL estimation, and the latter includes those for the multiple-category models as well.

estimate to obtain a new estimate, $\hat{\theta}_1 = 0.3905$. The values of the derivatives and the correction are then recomputed and used to obtain the next estimate, until repetition of the process results in no change. These computations are, of course, normally embedded in computer programs. Although such programs usually use the Newton–Raphson procedure described here, it is frequently modified in minor ways to make its convergence speedier and more reliable.

The MLE, or the mode of the likelihood in Fig. 3.10, is a point estimate of location that provides a very limited summary of the total likelihood. An estimate of the width or spread of the total likelihood may be used to specify the precision with which MLE[θ] estimates θ. Because the form of the distribution of total likelihood is generally roughly Gaussian, an estimate of the standard deviation of that distribution is a useful and widely comprehensible index of spread. If the item parameters are taken to be fixed and known and the only parameter to be estimated is the value of θ for a particular examinee, the curve representing the product of the trace lines for the observed item responses is the distribution of θ for examinees giving that response pattern, and its standard deviation is the standard error (SE) of MLE[θ].

It is possible to employ any of a variety of methods to describe the spread of distributions such as the likelihood in Fig. 3.10. One method that is extremely convenient in the context of ML estimation makes use of the fact (Fisher, 1921; Kendall & Stuart, 1967, p. 35) that the negative inverse of the expected value of the second derivative of the loglikelihood is approximately equal to the variance of the estimate:

$$SE^2[\theta] = -\frac{1}{E\left(\dfrac{\partial^2 l}{\partial \theta^2}\right)}.$$

That value is a routine by-product of ML estimation and is frequently used as the estimated SE, describing the spread of the total likelihood in terms that are interpretable in a roughly Gaussian sense, i.e. a 95% confidence interval is MLE[θ] ± 2 SE From the last line in Table 3.1, we note that $\partial^2 l/\partial \theta^2 = -.9037$; therefore the estimate of the error variance associated with MLE[θ] is $1/0.9037 \approx 1.1066$ and the standard error is $\sqrt{1.1066} \approx 1.05$. Examination of Fig. 3.10 reveals that, although the total likelihood is not strictly Gaussian, the inflection points are very nearly at $0.33 - 1.05 = -.72$ and $0.33 + 1.05 = 1.38$, as would be expected if the distribution was Gaussian and 1.05 was the standard deviation.

The use of the mode as the scale score for examinees with the response pattern {right, wrong} described by the curves in Fig. 3.10 has two advantages. The first is that it is conceptually straightforward: The mode is the

MLE, or the value of θ for which that particular response pattern is most likely. The second advantage is that, given an efficient algorithm like the Newton–Raphson procedure described earlier and suitable computing machinery, the mode is very easy to locate.

The mode is, however, not the only obvious way to assign a scale score to the likelihood of the item responses shown in Fig. 3.10. The mean of the likelihood is a clear alternative. In his original description of the use of what he called "trace line scores," Lazarsfeld (1950, p. 464) also suggested the mean, which he called the "expected value score (EVS)."[13]

Calculating the Mean of the Likelihood [θ] for Two Items.   Computation of the mean of a theoretical function such as the likelihood in Fig. 3.10 is slightly different from the computation of an average with observed data. For data, the mean is the sum of each observed value multiplied by the proportion of the observations that take that value. In a theoretical function, all values (in this case, of θ) have some likelihood, and the mean is the ratio of two integrals:

$$\text{EVS}[\theta] = \frac{\int_{-\infty}^{\infty} \prod_{i=1}^{\text{nitems}} T_i(u_i)\theta \, d\theta}{\int_{-\infty}^{\infty} \prod_{i=1}^{\text{nitems}} T_i(u_i) \, d\theta} . \tag{22}$$

In practice, the values of the integrals in Eq. 22 must be approximated numerically. Fortunately, relatively crude approximations using summation are frequently sufficiently accurate for practical use. Straightforward rectangular quadrature involves evaluating the ordinates of the function under the integrals in the numerator and denominator of Eq. 22 at some set of q points, called **quadrature points**. Then each of the integrals are evaluated as sums of those q points:

$$\text{EVS}[\theta] \approx \frac{\sum_{1}^{q} \prod_{i=1}^{\text{nitems}} T_{iq}(u_i)\theta_q \, d\theta}{\sum_{1}^{q} \prod_{i=1}^{\text{nitems}} T_{iq}(u_i) \, d\theta} . \tag{23}$$

---

[13]Actually, Lazarsfeld (1950) considered expected value scores only in the context of a particular population distribution of θ; such scores are called EAP[θ] and are discussed in a subsequent section. Unlike the mode, the mean of the likelihood may be undefined for some combinations of trace lines. Thus, this scale score is rarely used in practice.

The numerator of Eq. 23 is the weighted sum of the θ terms, and the denominator is the sum of the weights; the ratio is the mean. To determine the value of q, the number of quadrature points, Mislevy and Bock (1990) suggest $2\sqrt{I}$ (for I items) as a rule of thumb for large numbers of items. We generally use 46 points, equally spaced between −4.5 and 4.5, as a simple general-purpose computational solution. However, in the tables presenting examples in this chapter, we use arbitrary numbers of quadrature points chosen to illustrate the concepts with the particular data at hand.

In Table 3.2 we show the values of the ordinates of the trace lines and their product, and the product normalized such that the sum is unity, at 29 evenly spaced points along the θ axis, and Fig. 3.11 illustrates the approximation of the likelihood by the corresponding collection of histobars. The sum of the product of the rightmost column times the first column of Table 3.2 is −0.098. Therefore, for the likelihood in the bottom

TABLE 3.2
Values Used in the Numerical Approximation of the Mean
of the Likelihood Illustrated in Figs. 3.10 and 3.11

θ	$T_i(u_i = 1)$	$T_2(u_2 = 0)$	$\prod\limits_{i=1}^{nitems} T_{iq}(u_i)\, d\theta$	$\dfrac{\prod\limits_{i=1}^{nitems} T_{iq}(u_i)}{\sum\limits_{1}^{q} \prod\limits_{i=1}^{nitems} T_{iq}(u_i)}$
−11.0	0.00002	0.99999	0.00002	0.00001
−10.0	0.00005	0.99999	0.00005	0.00003
−9.0	0.00012	0.99999	0.00012	0.00009
−8.0	0.00034	0.99999	0.00034	0.00024
−7.0	0.00091	0.99999	0.00091	0.00066
−6.0	0.00247	0.99999	0.00247	0.00178
−5.0	0.00669	0.99999	0.00669	0.00482
−4.0	0.01799	0.99995	0.01799	0.01294
−3.0	0.04743	0.99966	0.04741	0.03411
−2.0	0.11920	0.99753	0.11891	0.08555
−1.0	0.26894	0.98201	0.26410	0.19002
0.0	0.50000	0.88080	0.44040	0.31686
1.0	0.73106	0.50000	0.36553	0.26299
2.0	0.88080	0.11920	0.10499	0.07554
3.0	0.95257	0.01799	0.01713	0.01233
4.0	0.98201	0.00247	0.00243	0.00175
5.0	0.99331	0.00034	0.00033	0.00024
6.0	0.99753	0.00005	0.00005	0.00003
7.0	0.99909	0.00001	0.00001	0.00000
8.0	0.99966	0.00000	0.00000	0.00000
9.0	0.99988	0.00000	0.00000	0.00000
10.0	0.99995	0.00000	0.00000	0.00000
11.0	0.99998	0.00000	0.00000	0.00000

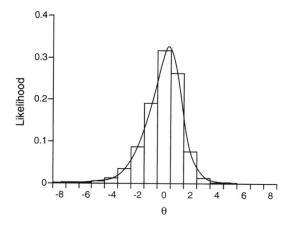

FIG. 3.11. Approximation of the likelihood from the lower panel of Fig. 3.10 by rectangular blocks, using the values in Table 3.4.

panel of Fig. 3.10, the mean is about −0.1. The density is somewhat negatively skewed, so the mean is lower than the mode.

(In this example, we use rectangular quadrature, or the "repeated midpoint formula" [Stroud, 1974, p. 120], to compute the values of the integrals. Stroud described a number of alternative methods for numerical evaluation of such integrals. Some of the more complicated methods, like Gauss–Hermite quadrature, have often been used in IRT. Stroud [1974, p. 187] noted that although "often a Gauss formula will be superior to any other formula with the same number of points . . . it is not true, however, that a Gauss formula is always best." For the integration of functions that depend on a large number of unknown parameters like those considered here, Stroud recommended that various quadrature methods be compared over a wide range of possible values of the parameter set to determine which method might be best. If such a comparison were to be done, it would be very useful for many other applications of IRT, as well as that discussed here.)

The estimate of the standard deviation of the joint likelihood used in connection with EVS[θ] is the standard deviation of the likelihood:

$$SD[\theta] = \left(\frac{\int_{-\infty}^{\infty} \prod_{i=1}^{nitems} T_i(u_i)(\theta - EVS[\theta])^2 \, d\theta}{\int_{-\infty}^{\infty} \prod_{i=1}^{nitems} T_i(u_i) \, d\theta} \right)^{1/2}.$$

Again, the integral is approximated numerically by a sum,

$$SD[\theta] \approx \left(\frac{\sum\limits_{1}^{q} \prod\limits_{i=1}^{\text{nitems}} T_i(u_i)(\theta_q - \text{EVS}[\theta])^2)\, d\theta}{\sum\limits_{1}^{q} \prod\limits_{i=1}^{\text{nitems}} T_i(u_i)\, d\theta} \right)^{1/2}.$$

For the trace lines and joint likelihood in Fig. 3.10, the standard deviation is 1.41, which differs somewhat from the standard error of 1.05 determined from the ML solution. The standard deviation of the likelihood is more sensitive to the relatively heavy, and not particularly Gaussian, tails of the likelihood in Fig. 3.10—thus, the larger value.

Figure 3.12 shows the trace lines and joint likelihood for the other response pattern with one correct response, {wrong, right}, for the same

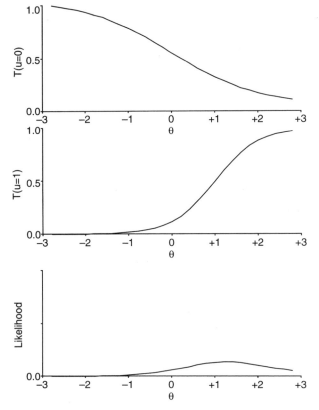

FIG. 3.12. Top panel: Trace line for a negative response, $T_1(0)$, for an item with parameters $a = 1$ and $b = 0$. Middle panel: Trace line for a positive response, $T_2(1)$, for an item with parameters $a = 2$ and $b = 1$. Bottom panel: The product of the trace lines in the upper two panels, $L = T_1(0)T_2(1)$.

items used in Fig. 3.10. The slopes of these two items are unequal. The response to the item with the higher slope (item 2) has a larger effect on the joint likelihood, and therefore on the estimated scale scores: MLE[θ] is 1.2 and EVS[θ] is 1.5; both are higher than the corresponding scale scores for the other response pattern with the same summed score (1). Except in the special case of the Rasch model, the estimated scale scores differ for different response patterns with the same summed scores. This is due to the fact that, under the theory from which the scores are derived, the joint likelihoods differ for each response pattern, as Fig. 3.12 differs from Fig. 3.10. In this case, item 2 is more strongly related to the trait being measured than is item 1, so the response to item 2 is a stronger determinant of the scale score than is the response to item 1.

Figure 3.13 shows the trace lines and joint likelihood for the same two items, for the case of two positive responses. The likelihood increases monotonically, with the result that MLE[θ] has the value $+\infty$, and EVS[θ] is

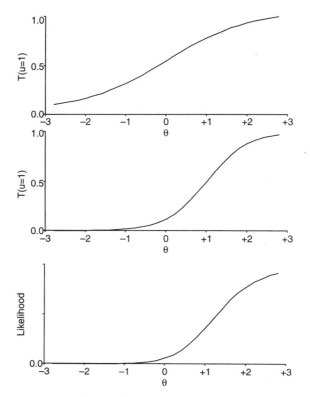

FIG. 3.13.   Top panel: Trace line for a positive response, $T_1(1)$, for an item with parameters $a = 1$ and $b = 0$. Middle panel: Trace line for a positive response, $T_2(1)$, for an item with parameters $a = 2$ and $b = 1$. Bottom panel: The product of the trace lines in the upper two panels, $L = T_1(1)T_2(1)$.

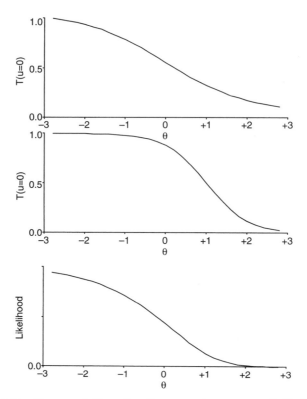

FIG. 3.14. Top panel: Trace line for a negative response, $T_1(0)$, for an item with parameters $a = 1$ and $b = 0$. Middle panel: Trace line for a negative response, $T_2(0)$, for an item with parameters $a = 2$ and $b = 1$. Bottom panel: The product of the trace lines in the upper two panels, $L = T_1(0)T_2(0)$.

undefined because both the numerator and denominator of Eq. 23 are infinite. Figure 3.14 is a similar illustration for the case of two negative responses; the mode is $-\infty$ and the mean is similarly undefined.

There are two ways to look at $+\infty$ and "undefined" as scale scores. The first is that there is a sense in which those are reasonable scores: When the examinee responds positively to all (in this case, both) of the items, all we really know is that the examinee's proficiency exceeds the difficulty of the items on the test. We don't know by how much; it may as well be infinite. A similar argument applies to "scores" of $-\infty$, or negative and undefined.

Some thought, however, indicates that such an argument must be silly: No person has infinite proficiency, or an infinite attitude, or any other infinite θ. We know that before we give the test. People vary on the attributes denoted by θ, but that variation is always describable by some distribution. Inclusion of information about the population distribution of θ results in a more reasonable set of scale scores, including finite scores for all response patterns.

Two Items and a Population Distribution. Frequently, information is available or can be assumed about the distribution of θ in the population of persons responding to a test. This information is equivalent to another test item to which all of the members of the population respond identically, but to which members of some other population may respond differently. For instance, the assumption that the examinees are drawn from a standard normal distribution over θ is equivalent to a trace line for a Gaussian distribution. It is not necessary that the population distribution of θ be Gaussian, or that it be assumed to be Gaussian. However, for the sake of simplicity we use Gaussian population distributions in the examples in this chapter. The curve marked "Population Density" in Fig. 3.15 is such a Gaussian density. Information of this sort may be combined with the item responses just as though it represented an item on the test.

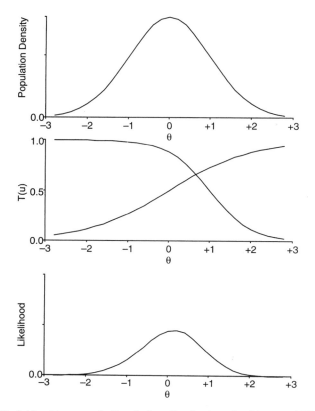

FIG. 3.15. Top panel: Population distribution, in this case $N(0,1)$. Middle panel: Trace lines for two items with positive and negative responses, from the top two panels of Fig. 3.10. Bottom panel: The product of the population distribution and the trace lines in the upper two panels, $L = T_1(1)T_2(0)\phi(\theta)$.

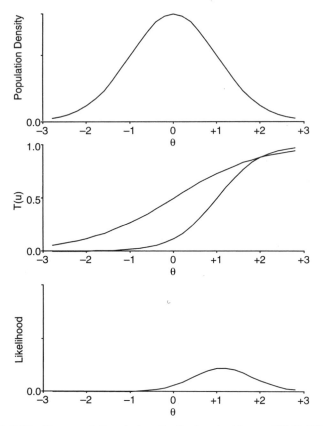

FIG. 3.16.   Top panel: Population distribution, in this case $N(0,1)$. Middle panel: Trace lines for two items with positive responses, from the top two panels of Fig. 3.13. Bottom panel: The product of the population distribution and the trace lines in the upper two panels, $L = T_1(1)T_2(1)\phi(\theta)$.

The population density is sometimes referred to as *prior* information, because it is available (in principle) before the examinee responds to the items. The trace lines for the items (and their *likelihood*) come later. Then, the joint likelihood that is the product of the population density and item trace lines is sometimes called a *posterior* density (after it is renormalized so that its integral is 1). Using this language, the mode of the posterior density is called the *maximum a posteriori* estimate, or MAP[θ]. The graphics in Figs. 3.15 and 3.16 show the joint likelihood, not the posterior; however, the mode (and the mean) is the same in either case.

Calculations for Two Items and a Population Distribution.   Including the population distribution, the product likelihood in the lower panel of Fig. 3.15 is

$$L = \prod_{i=1}^{\text{nitems}} T_i(u_i|\theta)\phi(\theta) \tag{24}$$

which is the same as Eq. 19 with the addition of the term $\phi(\theta)$, which represents the population distribution of θ. The log of the product of the joint item likelihood and the population distribution is

$$l = \sum_{i=1}^{\text{nitems}} \log T_i(u_i|\theta) + \log \phi(\theta) \tag{25}$$

which is the same as Eq. 20, with the addition of a term representing the log of the population density. For the two-parameter logistic model and $\phi(\theta)$ assumed to be $N(0,1)$,

$$\frac{\partial l}{\partial \theta} = \sum_{i=1}^{\text{nitems}} \frac{1}{T_i(u_i)} \frac{\partial T_i(u_i)}{\partial \theta} + \frac{\partial \log \phi(\theta)}{\partial \theta}$$

$$= \sum_{i=1}^{\text{nitems}} (-1)^{(1-x_i)} \frac{a_i T_i(u_i)[1-T_i(u_i)]}{T_i(u_i)} - \theta$$

$$= \sum_{i=1}^{\text{nitems}} (-1)^{(1-x_i)} a_i [1-T_i(u_i)] - \theta$$

and

$$\frac{\partial^2 l}{\partial \theta^2} = \sum_{i=1}^{\text{nitems}} a_i^2 \, T_i(u)[1-T_i(u_i)] - 1.$$

MAP[θ] may be computed with the same algorithm previously described for MLE[θ]. The Newton–Raphson computations are illustrated in Table 3.3; in this example, the value of MAP[θ] is 0.15, and the corresponding standard error is $\sqrt{1/1.7725} \approx 0.75$.

TABLE 3.3
Newton–Raphson Computation of the MAP
for the Illustration in Fig. 3.15

MAP[θ]	l	$\dfrac{\partial l}{\partial \theta}$	$\dfrac{\partial^2 l}{\partial \theta^2}$	$\dfrac{\partial l / \partial \theta}{\partial^2 l / \partial \theta^2}$	Next MAP[θ]
0.0	−0.3562	0.2616	−1.6700	−0.1566	0.1566
0.1566	−0.3544	−0.0081	−1.7757	0.0046	0.1521
0.1521	−0.3540	−0.0000	−1.7725	0.0000	0.1521

The mean of a posterior density (which is proportional to Eq. 24 and the bottom panel of Fig. 3.15) is called the *expected a posteriori* or EAP[θ] estimate (Bock & Mislevy, 1982); this is really what Lazarsfeld (1950) called EVS. The definition of EAP[θ] is the same as Eq. 22, except for the addition of the population distribution terms:

$$EAP[\theta] = \frac{\int_{-\infty}^{\infty} \prod_{i=1}^{nitems} T_i(u_i)\phi(\theta)\theta \, d\theta}{\int_{-\infty}^{\infty} \prod_{i=1}^{nitems} T_i(u_i)\phi(\theta) \, d\theta} . \tag{26}$$

Numerical integration is used to compute such estimates. The integral is approximated by

$$EAP[\theta] \approx \frac{\sum_{1}^{q} \prod_{i=1}^{nitems} T_{iq}(u_i)\phi(\theta_q)\theta_q \, d\theta_q}{\sum_{1}^{q} \prod_{i=1}^{nitems} T_{iq}(u_i)\phi(\theta_q) \, d\theta} . \tag{27}$$

EAP[θ] for the joint likelihood in the lower panel of Fig. 3.15, computed using the values in Table 3.4, is 0.06.

The standard deviation is numerically approximated by

$$SD[\theta] \approx \left(\frac{\sum_{1}^{q} \prod_{i=1}^{nitems} T_i(u_i)\phi(\theta_q)(\theta_q - EAP[\theta])^2 \, d\theta_q}{\sum_{1}^{q} \prod_{i=1}^{nitems} T_i(u_i)\phi(\theta_q) \, d\theta} \right)^{1/2} .$$

For the values in Table 3.6, $SD[\theta] \approx 0.77$. Among other things, the use of the population distribution makes the posterior more Gaussian than the likelihood was, so EAP[θ] is more similar to MAP[θ] and $SD[\theta]$ is more similar to $SE[\theta]$.

Figure 3.16 shows an $N(0,1)$ population distribution with the trace lines for positive responses to the same two items, as well as the joint likelihood including the population distribution. Note that, unlike the likelihood in Fig. 3.13, in which the two positive responses were considered without reference to a population distribution for θ, the joint likelihood in the bottom panel of Fig. 3.16 has both a finite mode (1.1) and a finite mean (1.2). This is more reasonable than the result obtained without consideration of the population distribution. We know that examinees with two positive re-

TABLE 3.4
Values Used in the Numerical Approximation of the
Mean of the Joint Likelihood Illustrated in Fig. 3.15

θ	$T_i(u_i = 1)$	$T_2(u_2 = 0)$	$\prod\limits_{i=1}^{nitems} T_{iq}(u_i)\phi(\theta)\, d\theta$	$\dfrac{\prod\limits_{i=1}^{nitems} T_{iq}(u_i)\phi(\theta)}{\sum\limits_{1}^{q}\prod\limits_{i=1}^{nitems} T_{iq}(u_i)\phi(\theta_q)}$
−3.5	0.02931	0.99988	0.00006	0.00004
−3	0.04743	0.99966	0.00053	0.00031
−2.5	0.07586	0.99909	0.00331	0.00195
−2	0.11920	0.99753	0.01609	0.00942
−1.5	0.18243	0.99331	0.05883	0.03445
−1	0.26894	0.98201	0.16019	0.09380
−0.5	0.37754	0.95257	0.31738	0.18584
0.0	0.50000	0.88080	0.44040	0.25787
0.5	0.62246	0.73106	0.40158	0.23514
1	0.73106	0.50000	0.22170	0.12982
1.5	0.81757	0.26894	0.07138	0.04180
2	0.88080	0.11920	0.01421	0.00832
2.5	0.92414	0.04743	0.00193	0.00113
3	0.95257	0.01799	0.00019	0.00011
3.5	0.97069	0.00669	0.00001	0.00001

sponses probably have high values of θ; however, we also know that they are sampled from the same distribution as the others, so their values of θ are not indefinitely (or infinitely) high. The MAP and EAP estimates include information obtained both from population membership and from the item responses in the computation of the scale scores.

The values for MAP[θ] and EAP[θ] for the four response patterns to the two items considered so far in this chapter are shown in Table 3.5 with the values of MLE[θ] and EVS[θ]. Note that all four values for both estimates that include the population distribution are finite, and all are closer to zero than the corresponding values of MLE[θ]. The effect of consideration of the population distribution is to shrink the estimates toward zero. This is shown graphically in the similarity of Fig. 2.4 to Figs. 3.15 and 3.16: MAP and EAP estimates are *regressed* estimates, analogous to Kelley's estimated true score.

Computer programs such as BILOG (Mislevy & Bock, 1990) and MULTILOG (Thissen, 1991) routinely include information from the population distribution in the computation of scale scores; that is, they normally compute MAP and/or EAP estimates of θ. Some commonly used computer programs do not consider population information, and use ad hoc procedures to avoid attempts to compute infinite estimates for the all-positive and all-negative response patterns. An old, but widely used, ver-

TABLE 3.5
Four Estimates of θ for Each of the Four Response Patterns
for Two Items with {a,b} equal to {1,0} and {2,1}

			Population	
Pattern	MLE	EVS	MAP	EAP
00	−∞	?	−0.5	−0.6
10	0.3	−0.1	0.2	0.1
01	1.2	1.5	0.7	0.6
11	+∞	?	1.1	1.2

sion of LOGIST (Wingersky, Barton, & Lord, 1982) computes MLEs, but limits the estimates to the range from −7 to +3, where −7 usually means −∞ and +3 really means +∞. BIGSTEPS (Linacre & Wright, 1995), widely used to compute Rasch-model estimates, computes MLEs with an extrapolation system used to augment the estimates with finite values for the zero and perfect scores. The use of information from the population distribution continues to be a subject of contention among researchers in item response theory. Although some advocate procedures that ignore the existence of the population distribution, it is not clear how the theory works without it.

More Items and a Population Distribution. These procedures are easily extended to more items. We illustrate with an example:

IRT Analysis: The North Carolina Test of Computer Skills—Word Processing/Editing. To illustrate the ideas involved in using the IRT logistic models, we return to our analysis of the 10-item North Carolina Test of Computer Skills ED section introduced in chapter 2. Using the item response data from the 3104 students who completed the item tryout forms, we fitted the 2PL model with the computer program MULTILOG (Thissen, 1991); the item parameter estimates are listed in Table 3.6. The 10 trace lines for the correct responses are shown in Figure 3.17.

One could contemplate the use of the 1PL model for these data; however, the goodness-of-fit statistic indicates that may not be a very good representation of the data. When we fitted the 1PL model, the value of −2loglikelihood for the MML estimates of the item parameters was 312 higher than for the 2PL model. Under standard likelihood theory, that difference is distributed as χ^2 with 9 degrees of freedom, and a value of 312 represents a very unlikely event ($p < .0001$). (The χ^2 is a [joint] test of the significance of the differences among the slope parameters, the a terms, for the 10 items.) We conclude that some items (those with higher values of a) measure editing skill more precisely than other items. Spe-

TABLE 3.6
2PL Item Parameters for the North Carolina Test
of Computer Skills ED Section

	Item Parameters	
Item	a	b
1. Center	1.45	−0.60
2. Insert	1.84	−0.82
3. Capitalize	2.55	−1.60
4. Indent	2.27	−0.87
5. Insert space	3.68	−1.41
6. Lower case	4.07	−1.33
7. Delete	2.26	−1.16
8. Move	1.87	−0.11
9. Spell out	2.19	−0.64
10. Other errors	1.33	−1.23

Note. The computer program MULTILOG (Thissen, 1991) does not use the "1.7" in its parameterization of the 2PL model, so the values of a in the table are not to be multiplied by 1.7 in the logistic function.

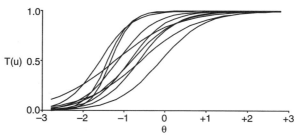

FIG. 3.17. The 10 2PL trace lines for the correct responses for the North Carolina Test of Computer Skills ED section.

cifically, items 5 and 6 appear to be most discriminating, and the "catch-all" item 10 is least discriminating, probably because it is just that, a "catch-all" item that includes many different responses.

IRT scale scores (EAP[θ]) for some of the response patterns, using the 2PL item parameters in Table 3.6, are shown in Table 3.7. There is a total of 1024 possible response patterns for the 10-item test, so in principle there are 1024 different scale scores. However, only 312 of those response patterns were actually observed in the data. Table 3.7 shows the scale scores for the 48 most common response patterns, all of which had frequencies greater than 10. Note that the scale scores vary for different response patterns that have the same total score, and also that the standard errors vary, unlike the constant estimate derived from the traditional test theory and shown in Table 2.6. Also note that a consequence of the fact that this is an easy, short test is that almost one third of the examinees

TABLE 3.7
Some EAP[θ] Response-Pattern Scale Scores, and Their
Corresponding Standard Deviations (*SD*), Using the 2PL Model for the
North Carolina Test of Computer Skills ED Section

Response Pattern	Summed Score	EAP[θ]	SD[θ]	Frequency
0000000000	0	−2.26	0.47	81
0000000001	1	−2.01	0.39	37
0000001000	1	−1.88	0.36	10
0010000000	1	−1.84	0.35	11
0010100000	2	−1.48	0.29	13
0010111000	4	−0.98	0.29	12
0010111001	5	−0.86	0.31	17
1010111000	5	−0.85	0.31	10
0110111000	5	−0.81	0.31	11
0010111010	5	−0.77	0.32	10
0011111000	6	−0.77	0.32	13
1010111001	6	−0.71	0.33	11
0010111101	6	−0.67	0.33	11
0110111001	6	−0.67	0.33	18
0010111011	6	−0.63	0.34	10
0011111001	6	−0.62	0.34	16
1011111000	6	−0.61	0.34	20
0110111010	6	−0.57	0.35	12
1010111011	7	−0.45	0.37	10
1011111001	7	−0.44	0.37	23
0110111011	7	−0.40	0.38	22
0111111001	7	−0.39	0.38	22
0011111101	7	−0.38	0.38	15
1110111010	7	−0.38	0.38	12
1111111000	7	−0.37	0.38	11
0011111011	7	−0.34	0.39	19
1011111010	7	−0.32	0.39	10
0111111010	7	−0.26	0.40	23
1110111011	8	−0.17	0.42	30
1111110011	8	−0.17	0.42	14
1111111001	8	−0.16	0.42	44
1011111101	8	−0.15	0.42	35
0110111111	8	−0.10	0.43	24
1011111011	8	−0.09	0.43	36
0111111101	8	−0.08	0.43	32
1110111110	8	−0.08	0.44	14
0111111011	8	−0.02	0.45	71
0011111111	8	−0.01	0.45	24
1111111010	8	0.00	0.45	42
0111111110	8	0.09	0.47	17
1110111111	9	0.21	0.50	41

(*Continued*)

TABLE 3.7
(Continued)

Response Pattern	Summed Score	EAP[θ]	SD[θ]	Frequency
1111110111	9	0.22	0.50	41
1111111101	9	0.23	0.50	84
1111111011	9	0.32	0.52	280
1011111111	9	0.33	0.52	65
0111111111	9	0.44	0.55	155
1111111110	9	0.47	0.56	66
1111111111	10	0.97	0.67	866

Note. Scores for response patterns that occurred with frequency >10 in the tryout sample of 3104 are tabulated, with the frequency in the rightmost column.

(866 of 3104) responded correctly to all 10 items. Thus, in any scoring system, all of those students are given the same score.

Information. IRT standard errors usually vary for different response patterns for the same test. The likelihoods may be broad or narrow, depending on the relative locations of θ for the individual and the item parameters; then the *SE* or *SD* varies because it describes the width of those likelihoods. With some exceptions, there is a pattern to the standard errors: They are small for θ locations near clusters of discriminating items and large far away, usually at the edges of the range of the test. This variation is at odds with the classical concept of reliability (ρ), which is based on a model in which all the estimates have the same error of estimate, which is equal to $\sqrt{1-\rho}$ for tests scored on the standard scale.

No single number characterizes the precision of the entire set of IRT scale scores from a test. So reliability is frequently not a useful characteristic of an IRT scale-scored test. Instead, the pattern of precision over the range of the test may be plotted. A plot of the standard error against θ would serve this purpose, but the variable conventionally plotted is *information*, which is approximately equal to $1/SE^2$. This definition, due to Fisher (1921) and therefore sometimes called Fisher's information, uses the word *information* in an intuitively obvious way: If SE^2 reflects our lack of knowledge about the parameter, then its inverse is information. Information is used primarily because it is additive: Each test item provides a fixed quantity of information at each level of θ; the information function for a test is simply the sum of the item information functions. This allows easy computation of information functions for tests of varying compositions.

The test information curve for the Computer Skills ED section (using the 2PL model) is shown in Fig. 3.18. In contrast to the traditional analysis of these data in chapter 2, the test information curve shows clearly the

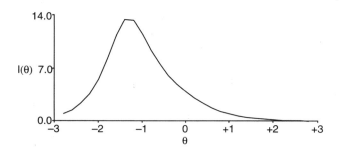

FIG. 3.18.   The test information function for the 10 2PL trace lines for the correct responses for the North Carolina Test of Computer Skills ED section.

consequences for measurement of the fact that this is a very easy test. Information is very high for examinees in the lower half of the (standardized) score range, so standard errors of measurement will be correspondingly low there. However, information is very low for the top half of the score range.

The population distribution contributes information as well. If the population distribution is Gaussian with $\sigma^2 = 1$, then the information contributed by the population distribution has the constant value $1/\sigma^2 = 1$. If we add 1.0 to the ordinate of the test information curve in Fig. 3.18, we obtain a curve with height between 8 and 15 for most values of $\theta < 0$; we will use 10 as a representative value. Then $\sqrt{\frac{1}{10}} \approx 0.3$ is approximately equal to the standard error associated with MAP[θ] or the standard deviation associated with EAP[θ].

The estimates of the width of the posteriors in Table 3.7 correspond closely to the information curve in Fig. 3.18, if we remember to add 1.0 to the ordinate of the curve for the contribution of the population distribution. That is, for negative values of θ, the information curve is about 10 (with the population distribution), so most of the standard errors for negative θ in Table 3.9 are about 0.3. At the right, the test information curve drops to about 2, and the *SD* for the highest value of θ (for response pattern {1111111111}) is $\sqrt{\frac{1}{2}} \approx 0.7$.

Information functions characterize tests more completely than reliability. They provide estimates of the standard errors of measurement of the test, and a description of the pattern of those standard errors over the range of the test. This facilitates the construction of tests with flat information curves to measure a broad range of persons equally well, or tests with peaked information functions for use in contexts in which some decision is required about whether the examinee exceeds some arbitrary point on the θ scale. Test and item information curves can be extremely useful to the test constructor. Their computation is a by-product of the process involved in scaling the items.

For situations in which it is desirable to present a single number that summarizes test precision for tests constructed using IRT, *marginal reliability* was suggested by Green, Bock, Humphreys, Linn, and Reckase (1984). The calculation of marginal reliability is analogous to that for traditional reliability, after an average error variance,

$$\overline{SE}^2[\theta] = \int \overline{SE}^2[\theta]\phi(\theta)\,d\theta,$$

is computed, weighting the value of SE^2 at each level of θ by the population density, $\phi(\theta)$. Then *marginal reliability* is computed as

$$\overline{\rho} = \frac{\text{Variance}[\theta] - \overline{SE}^2[\theta]}{\text{Variance}[\theta]}$$

in general, or, for standardized θ,

$$\overline{\rho} = 1 - \overline{SE}^2[\theta].$$

Estimates of Proficiency Based on Summed Scores

Summed Scores From the Perspective of IRT. In applied measurement contexts, it is often desirable, for various reasons, to consider the implications of the IRT analysis for summed scores, rather than response patterns, even if the IRT model used is not part of the Rasch family. For example, in a large-scale testing program it may be desirable to tabulate the IRT scaled scores associated with each summed score on operational forms, using item parameter estimates obtained from item tryout data, before the operational forms are administered. Or a testing program may require both some special features most easily obtained using IRT, and a scoring system based on the simple summed score. An example is the North Carolina end-of-grade testing program, which uses developmental scales based on IRT for the Grade 3–8 reading and mathematics tests (Williams, Pommerich, & Thissen, 1998), but which also requires a decentralized scoring system based on number correct on many alternative forms. The North Carolina testing program has also used scoring based on the combination of summed scores and IRT in a linkage of one of its tests with the corresponding measure in the National Assessment of Educational Progress (NAEP; see Williams, Rosa, McLeod, Thissen, & Sanford, 1998).

It may also be useful to compute model-based estimates of the summed score distribution—for example, to create percentile tables for use as an interpretive aid for score reporting. Model-based estimates of the summed-score distribution may also have value as a statistical diagnostic of the goodness of fit of the IRT model, including the validity of the assumed underlying population distribution.

For any IRT model for items indexed by i with item scores $u = 0,1$, the likelihood for any summed score $x = \sum u_i$ is

$$L_x(\theta) = \sum_{(u_i) = x} L(\mathbf{u}|\theta) ,$$

where the summation is over all of the response patterns that contain x correct responses. That is, for all values of θ the likelihood of a summed score is obtained as the sum of the likelihoods of all of the response patterns that have that summed score. The joint likelihood for each response pattern is

$$L(\mathbf{u}|\theta) = \prod_i T_{u_i}(\theta)\phi(\theta) ,$$

where $T_{u_i}(\theta)$ is the trace line for response u to item i (this more compact notation is convenient here), and $\phi(\theta)$ is the population density. Thus, the likelihood for each score is

$$L_x(\theta) = \sum_{(u_i) = x} \prod_i T_{u_i}(\theta)\phi(\theta) ,$$

and so the probability of each score x is

$$P_x = \int L_x(\theta)\, d\theta ,$$

or

$$P_x = \int \sum_{(u_i) = x} L(\mathbf{u}|\theta)\, d\theta ,$$

or, most intimidatingly,

$$P_x = \int \sum_{(u_i) = x} \prod_i T_{u_i}(\theta)\phi(\theta)\, d\theta . \tag{28}$$

Given an algorithm to compute the integrand in Eq. 28, it is straightforward to compute the average value of θ associated with each score,

$$\mathrm{EAP}[\theta | x = \sum u_i] = \frac{\int \theta L_x(\theta)\, d\theta}{P_x}, \tag{29}$$

and the corresponding standard deviation,

$$SD[\theta | x = \sum u_i] = \left(\frac{\int [\theta - \mathrm{EAP}(\theta | \sum u_i)]^2 L_x(\theta)\, d\theta}{P_x} \right)^{1/2}. \tag{30}$$

The values computed using Eq. 29 may be tabulated and used as the IRT scaled-score transformation of the raw scores, and the values of Eq. 30 may be used as a standard description of the uncertainty associated with those scaled scores.

The score histogram created using the values of Eq. 28 may be used to construct summed-score percentile tables; if the IRT model fits the data, this can be done using only the item parameters, for any group with a known population density. Thus, percentile tables for summed scores can be constructed using item tryout data, before the operational test is administered. This same histogram may also prove useful as a diagnostic statistic for the goodness of fit of the model, by comparing the modeled representation of the score distribution to the observed data.

Algorithms for Computing $L_x(\theta)$. Lord (1953a) used heuristic procedures to describe the difference between the distribution of summed scores, $L_x(\theta)$, and the underlying distribution of θ, $\phi(\theta)$ (see also Lord & Novick, 1968, pp. 387–392). However, practical calculation of the summed-score distribution implied by an IRT model has awaited both contemporary computational power and solutions to the apparently intractable computational problem.

Brute force evaluation of Eq. 28, requiring the computation of 2^I likelihoods for I items, is easy for a few items, but it is inconceivable for many items. Lord and Novick (1968, p. 525) stated that "approximations appear inevitable," and suggested the use of an approximation to the compound binomial, attributed to Walsh (1963), to compute the likelihood of a summed score for binary items as a function of θ. For I items, this Taylor-series expansion has I terms; however, in practice the first two terms suffice for acceptable accuracy.

Yen (1984) used this approximation to develop an algorithm to compute the mode of

$$\sum_{(u_i) = x} \prod_i T_{u_i}(\theta)$$

(the MLE, given x) for use as a scale score for examinees with summed score x on a multiple-choice test using the three-parameter logistic model. She reported that the two-term Taylor expansion produced noticeably better results than the one-term solution, which is simply an inverse transformation of the test characteristic curve; however, additional terms did not appear to add useful precision.

A better solution to the computational problem is provided by an alternative procedure briefly described by Lord and Wingersky (1984). Abandoning the contention of Lord and Novick (1968, p. 525) that "approximation is inevitable," Lord and Wingersky described a simple recursive algorithm for the computation of

$$\sum_{(u_i) = x} \prod_i T_{u_i}(\theta)$$

for items with binary responses. The algorithm is based on the distributive law, and generalizes readily to items with any number of response categories.

We use the notation $i = 0, 1, \ldots, I$ for the items,[14] $u = 0, 1$ for the responses for item i, and $T_{u_i}(\theta)$ for the trace line for response u to item i. In addition, the summed scores for a set of items $[0 \ldots I^*]$ are $x = 0, 1, \ldots, I^*$ and the likelihood for summed score x for a set of items $[0 \ldots I^*]$ is $L_x^{I^*}(\theta)$. The recursive algorithm is:

$$\text{Set } I^* = 0$$

$$L_x^{I^*}(\theta) = T_{x_{I^*}}(\theta) \quad \text{for } x = 0, 1$$

Repeat:

For item $I^* + 1$, compute

$$L_0^{I^* + 1}(\theta) = L_0^{I^*}(\theta)\, T_{0_{I^*+1}}(\theta)$$

and for scores $x = 1, \ldots, I^*$

$$L_{x+1}^{I^* + 1}(\theta) = L_x^{I^*}(\theta)\, T_{0_{I^*+1}}(\theta) + L_{x-1}^{I^*}(\theta) T_{1_{I^*+1}}(\theta)$$

---

[14]It is somewhat unusual to index the items from 0 to I for $I + 1$ items. However, in this case the correspondence of that system with the usual practice of indexing the scores from zero, and the common practice of indexing the item response categories from zero, simplifies both the notation and the software implementation.

and

$$L_{x+1}^{I*+1}(\theta) = L_x^{I*}(\theta)\, T_{1_{I*+1}}(\theta)$$

Set $I* = I* + 1$

until $I* = I$.

For a sample from a population with distribution $\phi(\theta)$, the likelihood for score x is

$$L_x(\theta) = L_x^{I}(\theta)\phi(\theta)$$

and $EAP[\theta\,|\,x = \sum u_i]$, $SD[\theta\,|\,x = \sum u_i]$, and P_x can be computed by integrating $L_x(\theta)$.

A Numerical Example. Consider three binary items with $a_0 = 0.5$, $b_0 = -1.0$, $a_1 = 1.0$, $b_1 = 0.0$, $a_2 = 1.5$, $b_2 = 1.0$. For this illustration, we use only seven quadrature points at θ values $-3, -2, -1, 0, 1, 2,$ and 3. Numerical representations of the trace lines, and a number of intermediate results, are shown in Table 3.8. The uppermost block of the table shows the values of the trace lines at the seven values of θ, $-3, -2, -1, 0, 1, 2,$ and 3. For $I* = 0$, there are only two possible scores, 0 and 1, and $L_x^0(\theta)$ is equal to $T_{x0}(\theta)$. Then, as $I*$ increases and each successive item is used, the likelihood for a score is the sum of the two terms: the product of the likelihood for that score on the preceding items and $T_{0I*}(\theta)$, and the product of the likelihood for that score less one on the preceding items and $T_{1I*}(\theta)$ (except, of course, for the summed scores of 0 and $I*$, which involve only a single product).

For tests with more than the four score categories illustrated here, 7-point rectangular quadrature is not adequate; we usually use 30–50 points. However, the relative robustness of the method to quadrature is illustrated by the fact that if quadrature in the example in Table 3.8 is increased, from the 7 points at unit intervals shown in the table to 46 points between -4.5 and 4.5 with an interval of 0.2, the precision improves only slightly: The final values of the proportion in each score group differ by less than 0.0001, and the values of the EAP terms differ by less than 0.01. Of course, it is necessary to carry the computations to more decimal places than are illustrated in Table 3.8.

IRT Scale Scores for Summed Scores: The North Carolina Test of Computer Skills—Word Processing/Editing. To illustrate the ideas presented in this section, we revisit the 10-item North Carolina Test of Computer Skills ED section introduced in chapter 2, and fitted with the 2PL model in the preceding section. Using the item parameter estimates listed in Table

TABLE 3.8
A Numerical Example of the Computation of
Summed-Score IRT Likelihoods for Three Binary Items

			List of ordinates, at $\theta = -3, -2, -1, 0, 1, 2, 3$						
	i	x	Initialization: Trace line ordinates						
$T_{xi}(\theta)$	0	0	0.73	0.62	0.50	0.38	0.27	0.18	0.12
		1	0.27	0.38	0.50	0.62	0.73	0.82	0.88
	1	0	0.95	0.88	0.73	0.50	0.27	0.12	0.05
		1	0.05	0.12	0.27	0.50	0.73	0.88	0.95
	2	0	0.99	0.99	0.95	0.82	0.50	0.18	0.05
		1	0.00	0.01	0.05	0.18	0.50	0.82	0.95
		x	Initialization: For $I^* = 0$						
$L_0^0(\theta) = T_{00}(\theta)$		0	0.73	0.62	0.50	0.38	0.27	0.18	0.12
$L_1^0(\theta) = T_{10}(\theta)$		1	0.27	0.38	0.50	0.62	0.73	0.82	0.88
		x	For $I^* = 1$						
$L_0^1(\theta) = L_0^0(\theta)T_{01}(\theta)$		0	0.70	0.55	0.37	0.19	0.07	0.02	0.01
$L_1^1(\theta) = L_1^0(\theta)T_{01}(\theta) + L_0^0(\theta)T_{11}(\theta)$		1	0.29	0.41	0.50	0.50	0.39	0.27	0.15
$L_2^1(\theta) = L_1^0(\theta)T_{11}(\theta)$		2	0.01	0.04	0.13	0.31	0.54	0.72	0.84
		x	For $I^* = 2$						
$L_0^2(\theta) = L_0^1(\theta)T_{02}(\theta)$		0	0.70	0.54	0.35	0.15	0.04	0.00	0.00
$L_1^2(\theta) = L_1^1(\theta)T_{02}(\theta) + L_0^1(\theta)T_{12}(\theta)$		1	0.29	0.41	0.49	0.44	0.23	0.07	0.01
$L_2^2(\theta) = L_2^1(\theta)T_{02}(\theta) + L_1^1(\theta)T_{12}(\theta)$		2	0.01	0.05	0.15	0.35	0.46	0.34	0.19
$L_3^2(\theta) = L_2^1(\theta)T_{12}(\theta)$		3	0.00	0.00	0.01	0.06	0.27	0.59	0.80

3.6, as well as the 1PL item parameter estimates, we have computed EAP[θ] for each summed score, and tabulated those values with the Kelly regressed standard scores (from Table 2.6) in Table 3.9. For this test, although the 1PL model did not fit the data, the 1PL scale score estimates are very similar to the 2PL scale score estimates for the summed scores. Both sets of scale score estimates are curvilinearly related to the Kelley regressed standard scores, as shown in Fig. 3.19.

Table 3.10 compares the 2PL summed-score scale scores to the 2PL response-pattern scale scores for the 48 response patterns tabulated in Table 3.9. The relation between the two sets of scores is shown graphically in Fig. 3.20, for all 312 response patterns observed in these data. For most examinees, the scale scores associated with each summed score are within about 0.2 standard units of the response-pattern scale scores.

Of course, there is some loss of information involved in using only the total summed score, as opposed to the response pattern, as the basis for the IRT inference about proficiency (unless the 1PL model is used, in

TABLE 3.9
EAP[θ] Scale Scores Associated With Each Summed Score,
and Their Corresponding Standard Deviations (*SD*), Using the
2PL Model for the North Carolina Test of Computer Skills ED Section,
as Well as the 1PL Model Scores and SDs, and the Kelley
Regressed Standard Scores From Table 2.6

| | Summed Scores | | 2PL IRT Model | | 1PL IRT Model | |
Sum	Kelley Regressed z	SE of Estimation	EAP[θ]	SD[θ]	EAP[θ]	SD[θ]
0	−2.51	0.37	−2.26	0.47	−2.33	0.49
1	−2.18	0.37	−1.89	0.38	−1.92	0.41
2	−1.86	0.37	−1.60	0.32	−1.62	0.37
3	−1.53	0.37	−1.36	0.30	−1.36	0.34
4	−1.21	0.37	−1.14	0.31	−1.12	0.33
5	−0.88	0.37	−0.92	0.32	−0.89	0.33
6	−0.56	0.37	−0.68	0.35	−0.65	0.34
7	−0.23	0.37	−0.41	0.39	−0.39	0.36
8	0.09	0.37	−0.09	0.44	−0.09	0.41
9	0.42	0.37	0.34	0.53	0.32	0.49
10	0.74	0.37	0.97	0.67	0.98	0.65

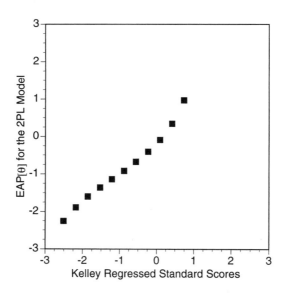

FIG. 3.19.   2PL scale score estimates plotted against the Kelley regressed
standard scores for the North Carolina Test of Computer Skills ED section.

TABLE 3.10
Some EAP[θ] Response-Pattern Scale Scores, and Their
Corresponding Standard Deviations (*SD*), Using the 2PL Model for the
North Carolina Test of Computer Skills ED Section

Response Pattern	Summed Score	For Summed Scores		For Response Patterns	
		EAP[θ]	SD[θ]	EAP[θ]	SD[θ]
0000000000	0	−2.26	0.47	−2.26	0.47
0000000001	1	−1.89	0.38	−2.01	0.39
0000001000	1	−1.89	0.38	−1.88	0.36
0010000000	1	−1.89	0.38	−1.84	0.35
0010100000	2	−1.60	0.32	−1.48	0.29
0010111000	4	−1.14	0.31	−0.98	0.29
0010111001	5	−0.92	0.32	−0.86	0.31
1010111000	5	−0.92	0.32	−0.85	0.31
0110111000	5	−0.92	0.32	−0.81	0.31
0010111010	5	−0.92	0.32	−0.77	0.32
0011111000	6	−0.68	0.35	−0.77	0.32
1010111001	6	−0.68	0.35	−0.71	0.33
0010111101	6	−0.68	0.35	−0.67	0.33
0110111001	6	−0.68	0.35	−0.67	0.33
0010111011	6	−0.68	0.35	−0.63	0.34
0011111001	6	−0.68	0.35	−0.62	0.34
1011111000	6	−0.68	0.35	−0.61	0.34
0110111010	6	−0.68	0.35	−0.57	0.35
1010111011	7	−0.41	0.39	−0.45	0.37
1011111001	7	−0.41	0.39	−0.44	0.37
0110111011	7	−0.41	0.39	−0.40	0.38
0111111001	7	−0.41	0.39	−0.39	0.38
0011111101	7	−0.41	0.39	−0.38	0.38
1110111010	7	−0.41	0.39	−0.38	0.38
1111111000	7	−0.41	0.39	−0.37	0.38
0011111011	7	−0.41	0.39	−0.34	0.39
1011111010	7	−0.41	0.39	−0.32	0.39
0111111010	7	−0.41	0.39	−0.26	0.40
1110111011	8	−0.09	0.44	−0.17	0.42
1111110011	8	−0.09	0.44	−0.17	0.42
1111111001	8	−0.09	0.44	−0.16	0.42
1011111101	8	−0.09	0.44	−0.15	0.42
0110111111	8	−0.09	0.44	−0.10	0.43
1011111011	8	−0.09	0.44	−0.09	0.43
0111111101	8	−0.09	0.44	−0.08	0.43
1110111110	8	−0.09	0.44	−0.08	0.44
0111111011	8	−0.09	0.44	−0.02	0.45
0011111111	8	−0.09	0.44	−0.01	0.45
1111111010	8	−0.09	0.44	0.00	0.45
0111111110	8	−0.09	0.44	0.09	0.47
1110111111	9	0.34	0.53	0.21	0.50

(Continued)

TABLE 3.10
(Continued)

Response Pattern	Summed Score	For Summed Scores		For Response Patterns	
		EAP[θ]	SD[θ]	EAP[θ]	SD[θ]
1111110111	9	0.34	0.53	0.22	0.50
1111111101	9	0.34	0.53	0.23	0.50
1111111011	9	0.34	0.53	0.32	0.52
1011111111	9	0.34	0.53	0.33	0.52
0111111111	9	0.34	0.53	0.44	0.55
1111111110	9	0.34	0.53	0.47	0.56
1111111111	10	0.97	0.67	0.97	0.67

Scores for response patterns that occurred with frequency >10 in the tryout sample of 3104 are tabulated.

which case all response patterns with the same summed score yield the same characterization of proficiency). Figure 3.21 shows the posterior standard deviations, which would be reported as the standard errors of the scale scores, for the EAP[θ] terms based on the response patterns, and for those based on the summed scores. Except for the extreme score groups, for which pattern and summed-score estimates are identical for any model, the standard deviations for the summed-score estimates are slightly larger than the standard deviations for most of the response pattern estimates. But the difference is small for tests with something like the

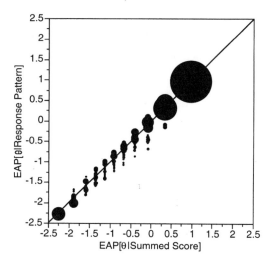

FIG. 3.20. 2PL response-pattern scale scores plotted against the summed-score scale scores for all 312 response patterns observed in the data for the North Carolina Test of Computer Skills ED section.

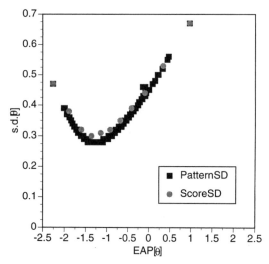

FIG. 3.21. The posterior standard deviations, which would be reported as the standard errors of the scale scores, for the EAP(θ)s based on the response patterns, and for those based on the summed scores, for the North Carolina Test of Computer Skills ED section.

amount of variation in the *a* parameters listed in Table 3.6: Use of the summed-score estimates does not produce standard errors more than 10% larger than those for pattern estimates near the same proficiency.

Table 3.11 lists the observed frequencies (and the associated proportions), and the model-computed frequencies and probabilities for each of the 11 score groups for the Computer Skills ED section using the 1PL and

TABLE 3.11
Approximation of the Summed-Score Distribution,
Using the 2PL Model, as Well as the 1PL Model, for the
North Carolina Test of Computer Skills ED Section

	Observed		*2PL IRT Model*		*1PL IRT Model*	
Sum	*Frequency*	*Proportion*	*Frequency*	*Probability*	*Frequency*	*Probability*
0	81	.03	52	.02	38	.01
1	71	.02	69	.02	62	.02
2	55	.02	80	.03	87	.03
3	89	.03	95	.03	115	.04
4	79	.02	121	.04	146	.05
5	142	.05	162	.05	183	.06
6	213	.07	222	.07	230	.07
7	293	.09	309	.10	296	.10
8	465	.15	438	.14	398	.13
9	751	.24	640	.20	581	.19
10	866	.28	916	.30	968	.31

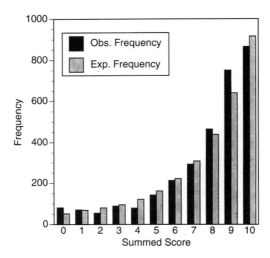

FIG. 3.22. The observed and (2PL) estimated score distributions for the North Carolina Test of Computer Skills ED section as histograms.

2PL models and a Gaussian population distribution for θ. Figure 3.22 shows the observed and estimated score distributions as histograms. The modeled probabilities from the 2PL model are in close agreement with the observed frequencies. Note that this is true even though the score distribution is extremely skewed, and the population distribution for θ is Gaussian; this illustrates the point first made by Lord (1953a) that the summed score distribution is a function of both the population distribution and the properties of the items.

As Yen (1984) noted, and as illustrated in this example, IRT scaled scores can be effectively computed for each observed summed score on a test, providing the usefulness of the IRT score scale without the problems associated with response-pattern scoring. Although some loss of information follows from the simplification of scoring from response patterns to summed scores, that loss of information is small from some points of view—the corresponding change in the reported standard error would often not result in a visible change in the number of decimals usually reported. The loss may be counterbalanced by more practical or socially acceptable score reporting.

In addition, when the population distribution is included in the IRT model, computation of the observed score distribution itself is straightforward. The expected distribution can be used to provide smoothed percentile tables for the current form of the test, or preoperational percentile tables for tests assembled with IRT, using the item parameters and the parameters of the population distribution.

If the population distribution assumed in the IRT model does not, as a matter of fact, well represent the distribution of θ for the examinees, then the inferred score distribution will depart from the observed score distribution. This is a combination of good news and bad news. The good news is that such a departure should be useful as a diagnostic suggesting misspecification of the population distribution. The bad news is that the inferred score distribution will not be accurate as a source of preoperational percentile tables or for other similar uses. The extent to which the inferred score distribution might be sensitive to misspecification of the population distribution has not yet been examined. In all cases in which it has been used thus far with operational testing programs, the assumption of a normal population distribution for θ has produced score distributions very much like the observed score distributions.

IRT Scale Scores for Summed Scores: Wisconsin Third-Grade Reading Field Test. As another illustration of IRT scale scores associated with summed scores, we consider data obtained from 522 examinees who participated in a field test of a form including 16 multiple-choice items being developed for Wisconsin's third-grade reading test.[15] The 16 items are four-alternative reading comprehension questions, all following a single reading passage. We fitted the 3PL model to these items using MULTILOG (Thissen, 1991); although a sample size of 522 is often considered on the small side for use of the 3PL model, the use of a mild Bayesian prior distribution[16] for the guessing parameter (g) was sufficient to produce stable item parameter estimates. In addition, we consider scores computed using the Rasch model, as implemented in the computer program BIGSTEPS (Linacre & Wright, 1995).

Two sets of scale scores associated with the summed scores are shown in Table 3.12. The values of EAP[θ] and SD[θ], as well as the probability for each score predicted from the 3PL model, were computed using the algorithm described in the previous section. For the 3PL item calibration, the population distribution of θ was assumed to be $N(0,1)$, so the values of EAP[θ] and SD[θ] are "naturally" on a standard (z-score) scale.

When the Rasch model is used, there is no difference between response-pattern scoring and calculating scale scores associated with each summed score, because the response-pattern scale scores for all response patterns that have the same summed score are identical. The implementation of Rasch model procedures in BIGSTEPS (Linacre & Wright, 1995)

---

[15]We thank Frank Evans of the Wisconsin Department of Public Instruction for kindly providing both these data and parts of the analyses presented here.

[16]The prior distribution used for the lower asymptote parameter for the four-alternative multiple-choice items was $N(-1.1, 0.5)$ for logit(g); that distribution has a mode of 0.25 for g.

TABLE 3.12
Scale Scores Associated With Each Summed Score for the Multiple-
Choice Section of the Wisconsin Third-Grade Reading Field Test

	3PL			Rasch	
Sum	EAP[θ]	SD[θ]	Probability	MLE[θ]	SE[θ]
0	−2.28	0.49	.0002	−3.16	0.85
1	−2.17	0.49	.0015	−2.73	0.61
2	−2.05	0.50	.0048	−2.26	0.45
3	−1.91	0.49	.0107	−1.96	0.38
4	−1.75	0.49	.0183	−1.73	0.35
5	−1.58	0.47	.0260	−1.53	0.32
6	−1.39	0.44	.0327	−1.36	0.31
7	−1.21	0.41	.0383	−1.19	0.31
8	−1.03	0.37	.0428	−1.03	0.30
9	−0.85	0.35	.0469	−0.86	0.31
10	−0.68	0.33	.0513	−0.70	0.31
11	−0.50	0.32	.0576	−0.53	0.32
12	−0.30	0.33	.0678	−0.33	0.34
13	−0.08	0.36	.0855	−0.11	0.38
14	0.20	0.41	.1166	0.19	0.45
15	0.57	0.51	.1694	0.65	0.61
16	1.10	0.64	.2298	1.07	0.84

Note. EAP[θ] and SD[θ] are shown, as computed with the 3PL model, as well as MLE[θ] and SE[θ], computed using the Rasch model. The probability for each score, as predicted by the 3PL model for the population from which the sample was drawn, is also shown.

computes modal estimates of MLE[θ] for each summed score. No popula-tion distribution is assumed a priori in the Rasch item calibration, and the scale for the scale scores is arbitrary, set so that the slope of the trace lines is 1.0 and the average of the difficulty parameters is 0.0. For these data, that means that the Rasch scale scores as originally computed had a mean of 1.8 and a standard deviation of 1.5; because those values are somewhat inconvenient, we have linearly transformed the Rasch MLEs to have a mean of 0 and the same standard deviation as the 3PL estimates in Table 3.12. (Finite scale scores are tabulated in Table 3.12 for the Rasch model for scores of 0 and 16; the BIGSTEPS software computes the scale scores that correspond with expected summed scores a fraction of a point above 0 and below 16, and reports those values.)

Figure 3.23 shows both the 3PL EAP[θ]s and the (rescaled) Rasch MLE[θ]s plotted against the summed score. The scale scores computed us-ing the two models are very similar for most scores, except for summed scores less than 3. For the latter scores, "below chance" for 16 four-alternative multiple-choice items, the Rasch model scale scores are (in-creasingly) lower than the 3PL scale scores. Because the Rasch model makes no theoretical provision for guessing, the Rasch model "says" that

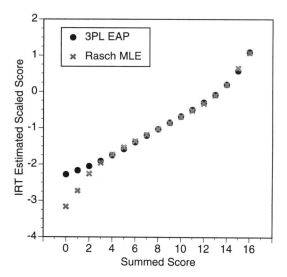

FIG. 3.23. The 3PL EAP[θ]s and the (rescaled) Rasch MLE[θ]s plotted against the summed score for the 16 multiple-choice items of the Wisconsin third-grade reading field test.

examinees who responded correctly to fewer questions (below the chance level) are less proficient (to anthropomorphize the model). In contrast, the 3PL model "says" that, for scores below chance, as those scores decrease there is less evidence that the examinees are less proficient, and more evidence that they may have made unlucky guesses.

Does this difference between the scale scores make any practical difference? That would depend on the use that was made of the scores. Overall, the 3PL model predicts that fewer than 1% of the examinees would obtain scores of 0, 1, or 2. So only a relatively small number of examinees would obtain very different scale scores depending on whether the 3PL model or the Rasch model was used. However, that small percentage could be a large number, if the test was administered to a large population. Or, that 1% of the examinees could be concentrated in units of analysis (such as classes or schools) about which the test scores were used to make inferences; if that happened, comparisons between those units could be different depending on the scale scores used.

Comparing the estimates of uncertainty, $SD[θ]$ for the 3PL model and $SE[θ]$ for the Rasch model, for the scale scores in Table 3.14, we find that they are very similar for central scores (from about 10 to 13), and more different at both extremes. Two differences between the models are concatenated to produce the differences in the standard errors: The 3PL estimates include the information provided by the population distribution; that has the general tendency to make all of the 3PL uncertainty estimates smaller than those for the Rasch model. On the other hand, the 3PL's model for guessing tends to increase the uncertainty associated with relatively low scores—on this very easy test, the result is that the 3PL standard deviations are larger than the Rasch model standard errors for scores between 2 and 10.

The reader considering Figs. 3.19 and 3.23 might well ask, why use scale scores at all? Why not just report the summed scores? The scale scores appear to be nearly linearly related to the summed scores, except at the extremes.

There are two reasons to use scale scores for reporting: The first is linked to subsequent data analysis that may make use of the scores, whereas the second is involved with large-scale test construction.

If the scores will be subject to subsequent data analysis—for instance, to compare demographic groups or to examine the relation of the test scores with other variables—then the scale scores may yield results with fewer artifacts than would be obtained if the summed score scale had been used. Theoretically, the scale scores are linearly related to other variables (if proficiency is linearly related to those other variables), whereas the summed scores are not. In practice, much of the difference between summed scores and scale scores in this respect derive from the ceiling effect on high summed scores and the randomness that may be involved in low summed scores; both these artifactual phenomena are reduced on IRT's scale.

IRT Scale Scores for Summed Scores: The North Carolina Test of Computer Skills—Multiple-Choice Sections. The main motivation for the use of IRT proficiency estimates as scores in large-scale testing arises from the ease with which comparable scores can be computed for alternate forms. Most large-scale testing programs require alternate forms, either for simultaneous administration or for repeated (often annual) assessment. Because it is obvious that one form may be "easier" than another, some adjustment to the summed scores must be made so that the alternate forms yield comparable scores. Traditional test theory uses *equating* to produce comparable scores on some arbitrary scale (see Holland & Rubin, 1982, for a thorough treatment of many equating methods). But the procedures described in this chapter produce comparable scores from alternate forms without any intermediate equating steps.

As an illustration, Table 3.13 shows the scoring tables for two alternate forms of the North Carolina Test of Computer Skills multiple-choice section, a 70-item test associated with the performance sections of this test previously discussed. The scale scores (EAP[θ]) tabulated in Table 3.13 have been linearly transformed from the *z*-score scale to be reported as integers, with a mean value of 50 and a standard deviation of 10; most large-

TABLE 3.13
Scale Scores Associated With Each Summed Score for the Multiple-Choice Sections of Two Forms of the North Carolina Test of Computer Skills, as Computed Using the 3PL Model

Sum	Form 1		Form 2	
	EAP[θ]	*SD[θ]*	*EAP[θ]*	*SD[θ]*
0	21	4	20	4
1	21	4	20	5
2	21	4	21	5
3	22	5	21	5
4	22	5	22	5
5	22	5	22	5
6	23	5	23	5
7	23	5	23	5
8	24	5	24	5
9	24	5	24	5
10	25	5	25	5
11	26	5	26	5
12	26	5	26	5
13	27	5	27	5
14	28	5	28	5
15	29	5	29	5
16	29	5	29	5
17	30	5	30	5
18	31	5	31	5
19	32	5	32	5
20	33	5	33	5
21	34	4	34	4
22	35	4	35	4
23	36	4	36	4
24	37	4	37	4
25	38	4	38	4
26	38	4	38	4
27	39	4	39	4
28	40	3	40	3
29	41	3	41	3
30	42	3	42	3
31	42	3	42	3
32	43	3	43	3
33	44	3	44	3
34	45	3	45	3
35	45	3	45	3
36	46	3	46	3
37	47	3	47	3
38	47	3	48	3
39	48	3	48	3
40	49	2	49	3
41	49	2	50	3
42	50	2	51	3

(Continued)

TABLE 3.13
(Continued)

	Form 1		Form 2	
Sum	EAP[θ]	SD[θ]	EAP[θ]	SD[θ]
43	51	2	51	3
44	51	2	52	3
45	52	2	53	3
46	53	2	54	3
47	53	2	54	3
48	54	2	55	3
49	55	2	56	3
50	55	2	57	3
51	56	2	58	3
52	57	2	59	3
53	57	2	60	3
54	58	2	61	3
55	59	2	62	3
56	60	3	63	3
57	61	3	64	3
58	62	3	65	3
59	62	3	66	3
60	63	3	67	3
61	64	3	68	3
62	66	3	70	3
63	67	3	71	3
64	68	3	72	3
65	69	3	74	3
66	71	3	76	4
67	73	4	77	4
68	75	4	79	4
69	77	4	81	4
70	79	5	83	4

Note.   The scores are transformed for integer reporting, with a mean of 50 and a standard deviation of 10.

scale testing programs use some such transformation for scale scores. Because the two test forms are very similar, for most of the summed scores both forms have nearly the same scaled estimate of proficiency. However, Form 2 is somewhat more difficult than Form 1, so for relatively high scores the scale scores for Form 2 are higher: For example, for a summed score of 60, the scale score for Form 1 is 63 (1.3 standard deviations above the mean), whereas the scale score for Form 2 is 67 (1.7 standard deviations above the mean); this difference is larger than the standard error associated with the scale scores, and must be taken into account to make the reported scores on the two forms comparable.

The convenience of IRT scale scores for alternate-form linking becomes much more salient in chapter 4, when we consider alternate forms for assessments comprising open-ended questions or performance exercises. Variability between forms for performance exercises tends to be much larger than for well-constructed multiple-choice tests. Scale scores will appear much more desirable in chapters 7 and 8, when we consider tests that combine different item types—and "points" in the summed score lose all meaning.

ADDITIONAL CONSIDERATIONS

The examples in this chapter, which (except the last) use very few items for purposes of explication, do not illustrate all of the complexity of scale score estimation. The computation of $MAP[\theta]$ is not particularly affected by the number of items on the test. However, the numerical integration involved in $EAP[\theta]$ is substantially affected by an increase in the number of items. For tests involving many items, the likelihood is not nearly as wide as the two-item joint likelihood illustrated in Fig. 3.15; in fact, for tests involving dozens of items the likelihood may become narrower than a single one of the histobars used in Fig. 3.15 to numerically evaluate the integral. Thus, as the number of items increases the number of quadrature points must also increase and the spacing between the quadrature points must decrease. As we observed earlier, Mislevy and Bock (1990) suggested $2\sqrt{I}$ (for I items) as a good value for the number of quadrature points for large numbers of items. We generally use 46 points, equally spaced between −4.5 and 4.5, as a simple general-purpose computational solution. This suggestion assumes that the slope parameters for the items fall within the commonly observed range; if the items are very highly discriminating, the likelihoods may be quite narrow for very few items, and more quadrature points are required.

For the three-parameter models, some item-response patterns may have bimodal likelihoods (Bradlow, 1996; Yen, Burket, & Sykes, 1991); this introduces problems in both the computation and interpretation of $MLE[\theta]$ or $MAP[\theta]$. Iterative algorithms for locating the mode, such as the Newton–Raphson procedure, generally locate the mode that happens to be nearest the starting value. If there is more than one mode, the one located first may not be the "correct" value (the global maximum of the likelihood). This problem does not arise with the 1PL and 2PL models, for which the likelihoods are always unimodal, but it represents an excellent reason for the use of $EAP[\theta]$ in conjunction with the three-parameter models.

There are many alternative procedures for computing scale scores; Wainer and Thissen (1987) described a Monte Carlo evaluation of 10 distinct estimators, including EAP[θ] and MAP[θ], as well as several "robustified" competitors, crossed with models: 1PL, 2PL, and 3PL. The data were simulated using a complex model, which included guessing, as well as anomalies that are not modeled even with the 3PL. In general, EAP[θ] with the 3PL model performed better than the competition. One of the robust estimators, the so-called "Biweight" estimator (Mislevy & Bock, 1982), also performed fairly well if the absolute scale of the estimates is not a matter of concern. It is likely, however, that EAP[θ] is the best choice among the scale score estimates that have been developed, considered, and made widely available in software.

In the simulation described by Wainer and Thissen (1987), 1PL model estimates did not fare well (in terms of mean squared error) for realistically simulated multiple-choice responses. The poor handling of guessing by the 1PL model, illustrated earlier in the data from the Wisconsin Reading test, probably accounts for most of that poor performance. In general, theory and what simulations have been done suggest that the best scale score is EAP[θ], computed using item-response models appropriate for the item types and data at hand.

ACKNOWLEDGMENTS

We thank Jonathan Dings, Frank Evans, Richard Hill, James Ramsay, and Howard Wainer for helpful comments on an earlier draft.

REFERENCES

Andersen, E. B. (1980). *Discrete statistical models with social science applications*. Amsterdam: North Holland.

Andrich, D. (1988). *Rasch models for measurement*. Newbury Park, CA: Sage.

Baker, F. B. (1992). *Item response theory: Parameter estimation techniques*. New York: Marcel Dekker.

Berkson, J. (1944). Application of the logistic function to bio-assay. *Journal of the American Statistical Association, 39*, 357–375.

Berkson, J. (1953). A statistically precise and relatively simple method of estimating the bioassay with quantal response, based on the logistic function. *Journal of the American Statistical Association, 48*, 565–599.

Binet, A., & Simon, T. (1905). Methodes nouvelles pour le diagnostic du niveau intellectuel des anormaux. *Année Psychologique, 11*, 191–244.

Birnbaum, A. (1958a). *On the estimation of mental ability* (Series Rep. No. 15, Project No. 7755-23). Randolph Air Force Base, TX: USAF School of Aviation Medicine.

Birnbaum, A. (1958b). *Further considerations of efficiency in tests of mental ability* (Series Rep. No. 17, Project No. 7755-23). Randolph Air Force Base, TX: USAF School of Aviation Medicine.

Birnbaum, A. (1968). Some latent trait models and their use in inferring an examinee's ability. In F. M. Lord & M. R. Novick (Eds.), *Statistical theories of mental test scores* (pp. 395–479). Reading, MA: Addison-Wesley.

Bock, R. D. (1972). Estimating item parameters and latent ability when responses are scored in two or more latent categories. *Psychometrika, 37,* 29–51.

Bock, R. D. (1983). The mental growth curve reexamined. In D. J. Weiss (Ed.), *New horizons in testing* (pp. 205–219). New York: Academic Press.

Bock, R. D. (1997). A brief history of item response theory. *Educational Measurement: Issues and Practice, 16,* 21–33.

Bock, R. D., & Jones, L. V. (1968). *The measurement and prediction of judgment and choice*. San Francisco: Holden-Day.

Bock, R. D., & Mislevy, R. J. (1982). Adaptive EAP estimation of ability in a microcomputer environment. *Applied Psychological Measurement, 6,* 431–444.

Bradlow, E. T. (1996). Negative information and the three-parameter logistic model. *Journal of Educational and Behavioral Statistics, 21,* 179–185.

Burt, C. (1922). *Mental and scholastic tests*. London: P. S. King.

Camilli, G. (1994). Origin of the scaling constant $d = 1.7$ in item response theory. *Journal of Educational and Behavioral Statistics, 19,* 293–295.

Cressie, N., & Holland, P. W. (1983). Characterizing the manifest probabilities of latent trait models. *Psychometrika, 48,* 129–141.

Finney, D. J. (1952). *Probit analysis: A statistical treatment of the sigmoid response curve*. London: Cambridge University Press.

Fisher, R. A. (1921). On the mathematical foundations of theoretical statistics. *Philosophical Transactions* A, *222,* 309–368.

Fisher, R. A. (1925). *Statistical methods for research workers*. Edinburgh: Oliver and Boyd.

Green, B. F., Bock, R. D., Humphreys, L. G., Linn, R. B., & Reckase, M. D. (1984). Technical guidelines for assessing computerized adaptive tests. *Journal of Educational Measurement, 21,* 347–360.

Haley, D. C. (1952). *Estimation of the dosage mortality relationship when the dose is subject to error* (Tech. Rep. No. 15). Stanford, CA: Applied Mathematics and Statistics Laboratory, Stanford University.

Holland, P. W., & Rubin, D. B. (Eds.). (1982). *Test equating*. New York: Academic Press.

Kelderman, H. (1984). Loglinear Rasch model tests. *Psychometrika, 49,* 223–245.

Kendall, M. G., & Stuart, A. (1967). *The advanced theory of statistics, Vol. II: Inference and relationship* (2nd ed.). New York: Hafner.

Lazarsfeld, P. F. (1950). The logical and mathematical foundation of latent structure analysis. In S. A. Stouffer, L. Guttman, E. A. Suchman, P. F. Lazarsfeld, S. A. Star, & J. A. Clausen (Eds.), *Measurement and prediction* (pp. 362–412). New York: Wiley.

Linacre, J. M., & Wright, B. D. (1995). *A user's guide to BIGSTEPS*. Chicago: MESA Press.

Lord, F. M. (1952). A theory of test scores. *Psychometric Monographs, 7.*

Lord, F. M. (1953a). The relation of test score to the trait underlying the test. *Educational and Psychological Measurement, 13,* 517–548.

Lord, F. M. (1953b). An application of confidence intervals and of maximum likelihood to the estimation of an examinee's ability. *Psychometrika, 18,* 57–76.

Lord, F. M. (1965). An empirical study of item-test regression. *Psychometrika, 30,* 373–376.

Lord, F. M. (1980). *Applications of item response theory to practical testing problems*. Hillsdale, NJ: Lawrence Erlbaum Associates.

Lord, F. M., & Novick, M. (1968). *Statistical theories of mental test scores*. Reading, MA: Addison-Wesley.

Lord, F. M., & Wingersky, M. S. (1984). Comparison of IRT true-score and equipercentile observed-score "equatings." *Applied Psychological Measurement, 8,* 453–461.

Mislevy, R. J., & Bock, R. D. (1982). Biweight estimates of latent ability. *Educational and Psychological Measurement, 42,* 725–737.

Mislevy, R. J., & Bock, R. D. (1990). *BILOG 3: Item analysis and test scoring with binary logistic models.* Chicago: Scientific Software.

Orlando, M. (1997). *Item fit in the context of item response theory.* Unpublished doctoral dissertation, University of North Carolina at Chapel Hill.

Orlando, M., & Thissen, D. (2000). New item fit indices for dichotomous item response theory models. *Applied Psychological Measurement, 24,* 50–64.

Ramsay, J. O. (1989). A comparison of three simple test theory models. *Psychometrika, 54,* 487–499.

Ramsay, J. O. (1991). Kernel smoothing approaches to nonparametric item characteristic curve estimation. *Psychometrika, 56,* 611–630.

Ramsay, J. O. (1995). *TESTGRAF: A program for the graphical analysis of multiple-choice test and questionnaire data.* Unpublished manuscript, McGill University, Montreal.

Ramsay, J. O., & Abrahmowicz, M. (1989). Binomial regression with monotone splines: A psychometric application. *Journal of the American Statistical Association, 84,* 906–915.

Ramsay, J. O., & Winsberg, S. (1991). Maximum marginal likelihood estimation for semiparametric item analysis. *Psychometrika, 56,* 365–379.

Rasch, G. (1966). An item analysis which takes individual differences into account. *British Journal of Mathematical and Statistical Psychology, 19,* 49–57.

Rasch, G. (1977). On specific objectivity: An attempt at formalizing the request for generality and validity of scientific statements. In M. Blegvad (Ed.), *The Danish yearbook of philosophy* (pp. 58–94). Copenhagen: Munksgaard.

Rasch, G. (1980). *Probabilistic models for some intelligence and attainment tests.* Chicago: University of Chicago Press. (Original work published 1960)

Samejima, F. (1977). The use of the information function in tailored testing. *Applied Psychological Measurement, 1,* 233–247.

Stevens, S. S. (1951). Mathematics, measurement, and psychophysics. In S. S. Stevens (Ed.), *Handbook of experimental psychology* (pp. 1–49). New York: John Wiley & Sons.

Stroud, A. H. (1974). *Numerical quadrature and solution of ordinary differential equations.* New York: Springer-Verlag.

Thissen, D. (1982). Marginal maximum likelihood estimation for the one-parameter logistic model. *Psychometrika, 47,* 175–186.

Thissen, D. (1991). *MULTILOG user's guide: Multiple, categorical item analysis and test scoring using item response theory.* Chicago: Scientific Software.

Thurstone, L. L. (1925). A method of scaling psychological and educational tests. *Journal of Educational Psychology, 16,* 433–449.

Thurstone, L. L. (1927). A law of comparative judgment. *Psychological Review, 34,* 278–286.

Thurstone, L. L. (1937). Psychology as a quantitative rational science. *Science, 85,* 228–232.

Thurstone, L. L. (1959). *The measurement of values.* Chicago: University of Chicago Press.

Wainer, H. (1983). Pyramid power: Searching for an error in test scoring with 830,000 helpers. *American Statistician, 37,* 87–91.

Wainer, H., & Mislevy, R. J. (1990). Item response theory, item calibration, and proficiency estimation. In H. Wainer, N. Dorans, R. Flaugher, B. Green, R. Mislevy, L. Steinberg, & D. Thissen (Eds.), *Computerized adaptive testing: A primer* (pp. 65–102). Hillsdale, NJ: Lawrence Erlbaum Associates.

Wainer, H., & Thissen, D. (1987). Estimating ability with the wrong model. *Journal of Educational Statistics, 12,* 339–368.

Wainer, H., Wadkins, J. R. J., & Rogers, A. (1984). Was there one distractor too many? *Journal of Educational Statistics, 9,* 5–24.

Walsh, J. E. (1963). Corrections to two papers concerned with binomial events. *Sankhyā Ser. A, 25*, 427.

Williams, V. S. L., Pommerich, M., & Thissen, D. (1998). A comparison of developmental scales based on Thurstone methods and item response theory. *Journal of Educational Measurement, 35*, 93–107.

Williams, V. S. L., Rosa, K. R., McLeod, L. D., Thissen, D., & Sanford, E. (1998). Projecting to the NAEP scale: Results from the North Carolina End-of-Grade testing program. *Journal of Educational Measurement, 35*, 277–296.

Wingersky, M. S., Barton, M. A., & Lord, F. M. (1982). *LOGIST user's guide*. Princeton, NJ: Educational Testing Service.

Wright, B. D. (1994). IRT in the 1990s: Which models work best? *Rasch Measurement Transactions, 6*, 196–200.

Wright, B. D. (1996). Construct problems with descriptive IRT. *Rasch Measurement Transactions, 10*, 481.

Wright, B. D. (1997). A history of social science measurement. *Educational Measurement: Issues and Practice, 16*, 33–52.

Yen, W. M. (1981). Using simulation results to choose a latent trait model. *Applied Psychological Measurement, 5*, 245–262.

Yen, W. M. (1984). Obtaining maximum likelihood trait estimates from number-correct scores for the three-parameter logistic model. *Journal of Educational Measurement, 21*, 93–111.

Yen, W. M. (1986). The choice of scale for educational measurement: An IRT perspective. *Journal of Educational Measurement, 23*, 299–325.

Yen, W. M., Burket, G. R., & Sykes, R. C. (1991). Nonunique solutions to the likelihood equation for the three-parameter logistic model. *Psychometrika, 56*, 39–54.

Chapter 4

Item Response Theory for Items Scored in More Than Two Categories

David Thissen
Lauren Nelson
Kathleen Rosa
University of North Carolina at Chapel Hill

Lori D. McLeod
Research Triangle Institute

Many contemporary tests include constructed-response items, for which the item scores are ordered categorical ratings provided by judges. When the judges' ratings use only two categories, the models described and illustrated with such data in chapter 3 may be used. However, in most cases, responses to *extended constructed-response items* or *performance exercises* are relatively long, and their scoring rubrics specify several graded categories of performance. The use of IRT with data from these kinds of items requires generalizations of the models described in chapter 3, to accommodate the larger number of responses.

Alternatively, the responses to individual items on modern tests may not be locally independent, as required by the computations that produce IRT scale scores. There are many reasons for *local dependence*: Several items may be based on a common stimulus; examples include the questions following a passage on a reading comprehension test, logical reasoning questions following a vignette, and mathematics questions based on some common graphic or illustration. Constructed-response items may be divided into parts that appear to be items; as examples, a mathematics problem may be followed by a second item that asks for an explanation of the answer, or an examinee may be asked to make a drawing and then provide some written commentary on their art. Although the parts of these kinds of items may be scored separately, the item scores are likely to be correlated due to immediate associations having to do with the common stimulus or common aspects of the responses. Combining the parts of these locally dependent items into a larger unit, called a *testlet* (Wainer & Kiely, 1987), permits the use of the valuable machinery of IRT for item analysis and test scoring. Testlets, by nature, are large items that produce scores in more than two categories; these may use the same extensions of IRT as have been developed for large items rated by judges in several scoring categories.

In some cases, the constructed-response items or may comprise the entire test; in other cases, there are multiple-choice items as well. In either case, some total score is often required, combining the judged ratings or testlet category scores, and the binary item scores on the multiple-choice items, if any are present. Simple summed scores may not be very useful in the latter context, because of the problems associated with the selection of relative weights for the different items and item types, and in any event because the constructed-response items are often on forms of widely varying difficulty. If the collection of items is sufficiently well represented by a unidimensional IRT model, scale scores may be a viable scoring alternative.

An example for which this idea proved useful was the California Learning Assessment System (CLAS) 1992 field test for Grade 4 mathematics. For those CLAS data, Wilson and Wang (1995) found that a projection-based system that added information from a multiple-choice section to the measurement of the latent variable defined by a performance section did not produce scores different from those of straightforward joint calibration of the multiple-choice and performance sections, such as we illustrate here. Wilson and Wang correctly noted that this result may well vary from test to test, but it serves as an illustration of the potential workability of the simplest IRT approach.

Wholly performance assessments may include so-called *integrated* items that measure, say, mathematics achievement in the context of science achievement; the Maryland School Performance Assessment Program (MSPAP) uses such items (Ercikan, Schwarz, Weber, Ferrara, & Michaels, 1997). In scoring, the responses to the integrated items, usually scored in multiple categories, are combined with a similarly scored set of non-integrated items to establish the content-area scores that are commonly required.

One of the great advances of item response theory over traditional approaches to educational and psychological measurement is the facility with which IRT handles items that are scored in more than two categories. Indeed, in the transition from dichotomously scored items to polytomously scored items, the only changes in IRT are the trace line models themselves. In this and subsequent chapters, we consider the application of item response models to data in which the items have multiple (that is, more than two) possible scores.

LOGISTIC RESPONSE MODELS FOR ITEMS WITH MORE THAN TWO SCORING CATEGORIES

Samejima's (1969) Graded Model

An Item With Three Scoring Categories. A model for items with three or more *graded* or ordered scoring categories was proposed by Samejima (1969, 1997), in what may be the earliest extension of IRT to items with multiple categorical responses. Samejima's motivation for her model involved the idea of partial credit on multiple-choice tests of cognitive proficiency; however, better models for that purpose have since been proposed (Samejima, 1979; Thissen & Steinberg, 1984, 1997; Thissen, Steinberg, & Fitzpatrick, 1989). In this and subsequent chapters, we consider the application of Samejima's (1969) model to data arising from judge-scoring of constructed-response items and performance assessments—an application for which this model appears to be ideally suited.

We first describe Samejima's graded model as it may be applied to one of the items of the North Carolina Test of Computer Skills "Keyboarding Techniques" section introduced in chapter 2. We consider item 2, "Spacing," which was originally scored in four categories; we combine two of the original scoring categories here to obtain:

0   Not observed (blank),[1] or has three or more errors in spacing.

1   Has one or two errors in spacing.

2   Has no errors in spacing.

Samejima used the normal ogive and logistic models described in chapter 3 as building blocks in her now widely known model for graded responses. We consider only the logistic version of the model here, because most software implementations use that rather than the normal ogive. The binary models trace, for each response category k, "the probability of a response in category k or above," which may be called $T_i^*(k \mid \theta)$ for item i. For an item with three response categories, this graded model yields two trace lines giving the probabilities that a respondent at any particular level of θ is predicted to respond in that scoring category *or one of the higher*

---

[1]"Not observed (blank)" was originally a distinct judgment category for all three items on the KB section, as described in chapter 2. However, if any of the three items are coded "blank," then all must be. This artifactual consistency in the coding of "0" would cause difficulties when the IRT trace line model was fitted to the data. To avoid those difficulties, the scoring category for "blank" has been combined with the lowest scoring category here. This solution is not perfect, but the fact is that there is no perfect general solution for the problem of missing data (Mislevy & Wu, 1996). This particular solution is the same as the common practice of considering omitted multiple-choice items to be answered incorrectly.

numbered ones. Here, θ represents a subset of computer skills—"keyboarding"—from low proficiency at the left to high proficiency at the right.

Given that there is a response, the probability that the response to item i is observed to be in category 0 or higher is clearly

$$T_i^*(0|\theta) = T_i^* \text{ (Category 0 or higher}|\theta) = 1 \, .$$

That is, in our example, the probability that the response is in category 0 or higher (that is, in category 0 or 1 or 2 or 3) is unity—we are certain that the response is in one of the three categories!

The probability that an item response is observed to be in category 1 or higher (in category 1 or 2) is the same logistic function of θ used for binary item responses in chapter 3:

$$T_i^*(1|\theta) = T_i^* \text{ (Category 1 or higher}|\theta) = \frac{1}{1 + \exp[-a_i(\theta - b_{i1})]} \, ,$$

except we note that the location parameter, b_{i1}, now has two subscripts: i for the item, and 1 because it is the first of three threshold parameters that will be used for this item. The probability that an item response is observed to be in category 2 or higher (in this case, there is no higher) is similarly:

$$T_i^*(2|\theta) = T_i^* \text{ (Category 2 or higher}|\theta) = \frac{1}{1 + \exp[-a_i(\theta - b_{i2})]} \, .$$

A second threshold parameter, b_{i2}, is introduced: If θ exceeds b_{i2}, the probability that the response is scored 2 exceeds 50%.

The top panel of Fig. 4.1 shows the logistic curve for $T_i^*(k|\theta)$ for $k = 1$ and 2. The idea is straightforward: This single three-category item appears as two binary items—the leftmost curve is "Has the material been typed, with two or fewer errors in spacing?" and the rightmost curve is "Has it been typed with no errors in spacing?"

This is all very sensible, but we don't have what we want—trace lines for the observed responses themselves. However, if we add the notational convenience that $T_i^*(3|\theta) = 0$ for an item response with 3 categories [for 3 responses, numbered 0–2, this is T_i^* (Category 3 or higher$|\theta) = 0$], we can use these equations to give curves tracing the probability of observing each graded response as a function of θ. These curves are the trace lines, with the same meaning as those for the binary item responses:

$$T_i[\text{Category } k|\theta] = T_i^*(k|\theta) - T_i^*(k + 1|\theta) \, .$$

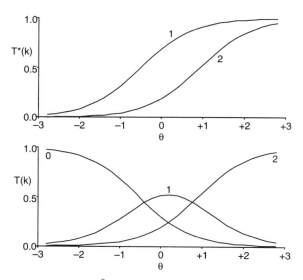

FIG. 4.1.   Upper panel: $T_i^*(k|\theta)$ for $k = 1$ and 2. Lower panel: Trace lines for item 2, "Spacing," for the KB section of the North Carolina Test of Computer Skills.

That is, the probability of an observation in category k is the probability of observing category k *or higher* minus the probability it is higher. In the taxonomy of item response models (Thissen & Steinberg, 1984), we call this the "difference model" approach because the probability of a response in category k is a difference: $T_i^*(k|\theta) - T_i^*(k + 1|\theta)$.[2]

Written out completely for three responses, $u = k$, $k = 0$, 1, or 2, the logistic form of Samejima's (1969) graded model is:

$$T_i(u = 0|\theta) = 1 - \frac{1}{1 + \exp[-a_i(\theta - b_{i1})]},$$

$$T_i(u = 1|\theta) = \frac{1}{1 + \exp[-a_i(\theta - b_{i1})]} - \frac{1}{1 + \exp[-a_i(\theta - b_{i2})]},$$

and

$$T_i(u = 2|\theta) = \frac{1}{1 + \exp[-a_i(\theta - b_{i2})]}.$$

---

[2]The "difference model" approach is not the only way to construct a model for such data; in a subsequent section we introduce an alternative.

The lower panel of Fig. 4.1 shows the trace lines for item 2, "Spacing," for the North Carolina Test of Computer Skills. The curves tell us that item score 1 (blank, or three or more errors) is the most likely response for students with $\theta < -0.5$ (in standard units); score category 1 (one or two errors) is most likely among students with proficiency between -0.5 and about $+0.7$; and score category 3 (no errors) is most likely for the more proficient students.

Samejima's (1969) Graded Model, in General. A general statement of Samejima's (1969) graded model, for ordered responses $u = k$, $k = 0, 1, 2, \ldots, m - 1$, where response $m - 1$ reflects highest θ value, is:

$$T(u = k) = \frac{1}{1 + \exp[-a_i(\theta - b_{ik})]} - \frac{1}{1 + \exp[-a_i(\theta - b_{i\,k+1})]}, \quad (1)$$

$$= T^*(k) - T^*(k + 1)$$

in which a_i is the slope and b_{ik} is threshold(k). $T^*(k)$ is the trace line describing the probability that a response is in category k or higher, for each value of θ. For completeness of the model definition, we note that $T^*(0) = 1$ and $T^*(m) = 0$. The value of b_{ik} is the point on the θ axis at which the probability passes 50% that the response is in category k or higher. The properties of the model are extensively described by Samejima (1969). (Note that when $m = 2$, this graded model is the 2PL model.)

If $T^*(k|\theta)$ is a logistic function, as it has been in this chapter, or a normal ogive, it is necessary that the slope parameters be equal for all of the elemental trace lines that make up the trace lines that define the probability of a particular categorical response. This is true because normal ogives or logistics with different slopes always cross each other somewhere; where they did, the differences would become negative and the system would collapse. It is possible to consider the use of other binary trace lines that are not necessarily parallel in the "difference" conception; the only requirement is that the differences between successive $T^*(k|\theta)$ terms be nonnegative. Samejima (1995, 1997) greatly expanded this class of models. Nevertheless, the original graded model as described earlier remains the most widely used.

Bock's (1972) Nominal Model

The Nominal Model, in General. Shortly after the publication of Samejima's (1969) monograph, Bock (1972) proposed an alternative model to provide trace lines for each of the alternatives of a multiple-choice item—

the so-called *nominal model*. As was the case with the graded model, the nominal model has proven not to be entirely adequate for multiple-choice items, but various versions of it are very useful for judged ratings, as well as for testlet analysis.

Although there are several theoretical developments that lead to the nominal model, the most straightforward is based on a different decomposition of a model for several response alternatives into a set of binary models: If one assumes that the trace line for a particular response, say k, given that the response is either k or k', is a 2PL logistic function, then the multivariate logistic equation that is the nominal model follows, yielding trace lines of all of the alternatives. Unlike the graded model, in its unconstrained form, the nominal model does not require any a priori specification of the order of the responses with respect to θ.

The nominal model trace line for score $u = 0, 1, \ldots, m_i - 1$, for item i is

$$T_{iu}(\theta) = \frac{\exp[a_{iu}\theta + c_{iu}]}{\sum\limits_{k=0}^{m-1} \exp[a_{ik}\theta + c_{ik}]} , \qquad (2)$$

where the $\{a_k, c_k\}_i$, $k = 0, 1, \ldots, m_i - 1$, are the item category parameters that characterize the shape of the individual response trace lines. The a_k terms are analogous to discriminations; the c_k terms are analogous to intercepts. The model is not fully identified, so we need to impose some additional constraints. It is convenient to insist that the sum of each of the sets of parameters equal zero, that is,

$$\sum\limits_{k=0}^{m-1} a_{ik} = \sum\limits_{k=0}^{m-1} c_{ik} = 0 . \qquad (3)$$

When we use the nominal model for responses that are suspected, a priori, to have some known order with respect to θ, we often reparameterize the model using centered polynomials of the associated scores to represent the category-to-category change in a_k terms and the c_k terms:

$$a_{ik} = \sum\limits_{p=1}^{P} \alpha_{ip}\left(k - \frac{m_i - 1}{2}\right)^p \qquad (4)$$

and

$$c_{ik} = \sum\limits_{p=1}^{P} \gamma_{ip}\left(k - \frac{m_i - 1}{2}\right)^p , \qquad (5)$$

where the parameters $\{\alpha_p, \gamma_p\}_i$, $p = 1, 2, \ldots, P$, for $P \leq m_i - 1$ are the free parameters to be estimated from the data. The polynomial representation often provides more efficient estimation with no significant loss of accuracy. It also provides a check on the fit of the model when the categories are ordered.

The Generalized Partial Credit Model. Although the nominal model was developed for data with no particular order specified for the response alternatives, it can be used for ordered categories. If the categories are ordered, the a terms must be monotonically ordered (Samejima, 1972); a guaranteed-ordered model arises if the a terms are a linear function of the response-category sequence numbers—that is, if $P = 1$ in Eq. 4 (Thissen & Steinberg, 1986). Muraki (1992, 1997) described this model, using the nomenclature *generalized partial credit* (GPC) model, in reference to its relation to the *partial credit* (PC) model described in the next section. The same model was also proposed by Yen (1993) under the name *two-parameter partial credit model*, as a part of a solution strategy for problems with local dependence.[3] The generalized partial credit model is now widely used for constructed-response items in several large-scale testing programs, most notably the National Assessment of Educational Progress (NAEP; see Allen et al., 1995) and the Maryland School Performance Assessment Program (MSPAP; see Yen & Ferrara, 1997).

The Partial Credit Model. Masters (1982) developed the *partial credit* model entirely within the Rasch-model tradition: He assumed that the trace line for a particular response, say k, given that the response is either k or $k - 1$, is a 1PL logistic function, and developed the consequent model for all of the response alternatives. The result is a Rasch-family model, with the familiar property of models in that family: The simple sum of the response codes is a sufficient statistic for proficiency. The partial credit model, as originally formulated, was derived and parameterized very differently from the nominal model; as a result, although it was immediately obvious that the partial credit model was related to earlier developments in the Rasch model family (by Andersen, 1973, and Andrich, 1978a, 1978b), its relation to the nominal model was not as clear. However, further investigation showed that the partial credit model is, indeed, a constrained version of the nominal model in which not only are the a terms constrained to be linear functions of the category codes (as per Eq. 4, with $P = 1$), but all of those linear functions are constrained to have the same slope ($\alpha_{i1} = \alpha$ for all i).

---

[3]Mellenbergh (1995) developed another set of alternative procedures to relate Bock's (1972) model to ordered categories.

The Rating Scale Model. Andrich (1978a, 1978b) proposed a model that is now most succinctly described as a version of the partial credit model in which the "category boundaries" (e.g., the boundaries between the judged ratings of 0 and 1, and between 1 and 2) are identically spaced across all of the items. This idea is most often motivated with reference to Likert-type, or *rating scale*, responses, such as "agree," "neutral," and "disagree." One might theorize that the two boundaries (between "agree" and "neutral," and between "neutral" and "disagree") dividing the latent scale into three categories should be associated with the response scale, and remain invariantly spaced across items.[4] The boundaries may be shifted left or right, depending on the content of the item itself, but their relative spacing must remain the same. The original development of this model was related to earlier work by Rasch (1961) and Andersen (1977). Thissen and Steinberg (1986) showed that this model may also be developed as a constrained parameterization of Bock's (1972) nominal model.

ITEM PARAMETER ESTIMATION FOR MODELS WITH MORE THAN TWO RESPONSE CATEGORIES

Contemporary approaches to item parameter estimation for the models discussed in this chapter are beyond the scope of this book; Baker (1992) provided an extensive treatment of this subject. In addition, several chapters of van der Linden and Hambleton's (1997) *Handbook of Modern Item Response Theory* described estimation procedures for these models: Samejima (1997) discussed both the version of the graded model described here and some of her subsequent generalizations of that model, Bock (1997) considered the nominal model, and Muraki (1997) developed the generalized partial credit model; all three describe the maximum marginal likelihood (MML) approach to item parameter estimation. Masters and Wright (1997) and Andersen (1997) presented the partial credit model and the rating scale model, and considered both MML and conditional maximum likelihood (CML) approaches to item parameter estimation.

Item parameter estimation for all of these models is usually accomplished using data from a calibration sample, and one of several special-purpose computer programs. The computer program MULTILOG (Thissen, 1991) is designed to estimate the parameters for Samejima's (1969) graded model and for any of the variations of Bock's (1972) nominal

---

[4]In practice, this theory appears rarely, if ever, to correspond with data. Even for the prototypical Likert-type items, usually the interaction between the semantics of the stem statement and the response labels appears to change the meanings of the responses ("agree" etc.).

model described earlier, in any combination. PARSCALE (Muraki & Bock, 1991) was developed specifically to estimate the parameters of the generalized partial credit model and Samejima's graded model. For the Rasch-family models, the computer programs BIGSTEPS (Wright & Linacre, 1992) and QUEST (Adams & Khoo, 1992) are widely used.

SCALE SCORES FOR ITEMS WITH MORE THAN TWO RESPONSE CATEGORIES

Estimates of Proficiency Based on Response Patterns

This section is abbreviated, because the principles underlying the computation of scale scores using any of the polytomous models are identical to those described at length in chapter 3. The joint likelihood for any response pattern $\mathbf{u} = \{u_1, u_2, u_3, \ldots\}$ is

$$L = \prod_{i=1}^{\text{nitems}} T_i(u_i | \theta)\phi(\theta) .$$

(6)

This is identical to Eq. 24 in chapter 3, regardless of whether the u terms represent dichotomous or polytomous response categories. The latent variable (proficiency) is denoted θ, and $\phi(\theta)$ is the population distribution [assumed to be $N(0,1)$ in all of the examples in this chapter]. The only new point to be raised here is that the trace lines, $T_i(u_i | \theta)$, describing the probability of a response in category u_i for item i as a function of θ, may take different functional forms for the different item types and response formats: It does not matter if the trace lines arise from the one-, two-, or three-parameter logistic, or from the graded model, or from the nominal model or any of its specializations. MAP[θ] and EAP[θ] may still be computed exactly as described in chapter 3.

IRT Analysis: The North Carolina Test of Computer Skills—Keyboarding Techniques. To illustrate the ideas involved in using the IRT models for graded responses, we return to our analysis of the 10-item North Carolina Test of Computer Skills KB section introduced in chapter 2. Using the item response data from the 3104 students who completed the item tryout forms, we fitted the graded model, the generalized partial credit model, and the partial credit model, with the computer program MULTILOG (Thissen, 1991), all with a Gaussian population distribution for θ. The item parameter estimates for the graded model are listed in Table 4.1, and those for the generalized partial credit model are in Table

TABLE 4.1
Graded Model Item Parameters for the
North Carolina Test of Computer Skills KB Section

Item	Item Parameters		
	a	b_1	b_2
1. Typing	1.05	−1.40	0.97
2. Spacing	1.59	−0.52	0.92
3. Length	0.93	−2.97	0.55

TABLE 4.2
Generalized Partial Credit Model Item Parameters for the
North Carolina Test of Computer Skills KB Section

Item	Item Parameters					
	a_1	a_2	a_3	c_1	c_2	c_3
1. Typing	−0.84	0.0	0.84	−0.47	0.57	−0.10
2. Spacing	−1.19	0.0	1.19	0.04	0.42	−0.46
3. Length	−0.81	0.0	0.81	−1.40	0.90	0.50

4.2. For these data, the graded model fits better than the generalized partial credit model: Both models use the same number of parameters, and −2loglikelihood is 105 for the graded model and 119 for the generalized partial credit model (here, smaller is better). Because these models are not hierarchically nested, there is no straightforward way to associate a probability statement with the fact that the graded model provides a better fit; nevertheless, that is the fact.[5] The partial credit model (constraining all the item discrimination parameters to be equal) is testable, because it is hierarchically nested within the generalized partial credit model; the test of the null hypothesis that the slopes are equal is rejected: $G^2(2) = 7$, $p = .03$.

The trace lines for the graded and generalized partial credit models are shown in Fig. 4.2. We note that the trace lines for the two models are very similar. The small differences in the shapes of the curves account for the difference between the goodness-of-fit of the two models, but have only a little consequence for scoring. Table 4.3 shows the values of EAP[θ] and SD[θ] for the 27 response patterns, using the graded and generalized partial credit models, respectively. For the most part, scale scores for the same response pattern from either of the two models differ by less than

---

[5]In our experience, fitting hundreds of data sets over two decades, it has almost always been the case that the graded model fits rating data better than does the generalized partial credit model. The difference is usually small, as it is in this case.

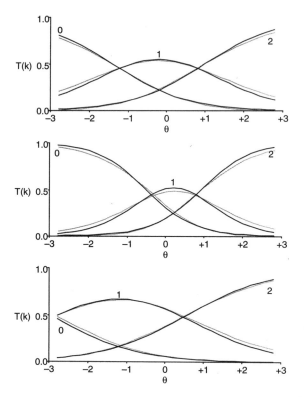

FIG. 4.2. Trace lines for the graded (black) and generalized partial credit (gray) models for the North Carolina Test of Computer Skills KB items. Top, "Typing Accuracy"; middle, "Spacing"; bottom, "Length."

0.1 standard units. Exceptions are response patterns that involve some points for items 1 and 2, but 0 for item 3 (010, 110, and 220); those relatively rare patterns have scale scores that are 0.1 to 0.2 standard units different for the generalized partial credit model than for the graded model.

Test information curves for this three-item test, as computed using both the graded and the generalized partial credit models, are shown in Fig. 4.3. As one would expect, given the similarity of the trace lines, the two information curves in Fig. 4.3 are very similar to each other. The striking feature of the two curves is that they are both very flat, across a wide range of θ. This is IRT's display of the primary advantage of multiple-category scoring: Each item provides information at two (in this case) or more (in general) levels of proficiency. By adjusting the definitions of the scoring categories, it is reasonably easy to construct a test that measures proficiency almost equally accurately over a wide range of proficiency. For most values of θ near the middle of the scale, the value of test information is about 2.0; therefore, following the same procedures we described in

TABLE 4.3
EAP[θ] Response-Pattern Scale Scores, and Their Corresponding
Standard Deviations (*SD*), Using the Graded and Generalized Partial
Credit (GPC) Models for the North Carolina Test of Computer Skills
KB Section, With the Frequency in the Rightmost Column

Response Pattern	Summed Score	Graded Model		GPC Model		Frequency
		EAP[θ]	SD[θ]	EAP[θ]	SD[θ]	
000	0	−1.55	0.76	−1.53	0.75	64
001	1	−1.12	0.72	−1.09	0.72	236
100	1	−1.03	0.72	−1.07	0.72	25
010	1	−0.74	0.70	−0.89	0.71	31
002	2	−0.71	0.73	−0.67	0.70	96
101	2	−0.68	0.69	−0.66	0.70	337
200	2	−0.67	0.76	−0.65	0.70	17
011	2	−0.43	0.67	−0.49	0.69	142
110	2	−0.34	0.67	−0.48	0.69	58
020	2	−0.30	0.80	−0.31	0.69	8
201	3	−0.31	0.72	−0.27	0.69	137
102	3	−0.28	0.70	−0.26	0.69	138
111	3	−0.08	0.64	−0.10	0.69	340
012	3	−0.04	0.67	−0.09	0.68	57
210	3	0.03	0.69	−0.08	0.68	27
021	3	0.05	0.75	0.07	0.68	37
120	3	0.15	0.74	0.08	0.68	11
202	4	0.15	0.74	0.13	0.68	76
211	4	0.27	0.66	0.29	0.69	167
112	4	0.27	0.64	0.30	0.69	212
121	4	0.42	0.70	0.45	0.69	138
022	4	0.54	0.75	0.47	0.69	36
220	4	0.65	0.76	0.48	0.69	14
212	5	0.66	0.67	0.69	0.70	126
122	5	0.85	0.70	0.86	0.71	196
221	5	0.87	0.71	0.88	0.71	97
222	6	1.34	0.73	1.30	0.74	281

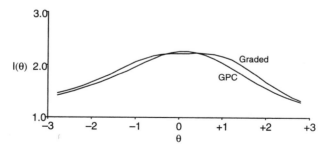

FIG. 4.3. Test information curves for the North Carolina Test of Computer Skills KB section, as computed using both the graded and the generalized partial credit (GPC) models.

153

chapter 3 to interpret information curves, we expect the standard errors of the scale scores to be about $\sqrt{\dfrac{1}{2}} \approx 0.7$, as they are in Table 4.3.

Estimates of Proficiency Based on Summed Scores

A straightforward generalization of the results obtained for summed scores using dichotomous IRT in chapter 3 provides the parallel results for summed scores for items with more than two response alternatives (Thissen, Pommerich, Billeaud, & Williams, 1995). For any IRT model for items indexed by i with ordered item scores u that may take values $k = 0, \ldots, K_i$, the likelihood for any summed score $x = \sum u_i$ is

$$L_x(\theta) = \sum_{(u_i) = x} L(\mathbf{u}|\theta) \, ,$$

where the summation is over all of the response patterns for which the total number of points is x. That is, the posterior for each score is proportional to

$$L_x(\theta) \approx \sum_{(u_i) = x} \prod_i T_{k_i}(\theta)\phi(\theta) \, . \tag{7}$$

using the notation $T_{k_i}(\theta)$ for the trace line for category k of item i.

The generalization of the recursive algorithm described in chapter 3 for any number of item response categories, to compute the likelihood for any summed score, follows. We use the notation $i = 0, 1, \ldots, I$ for the items, $k = 0, 1, \ldots, K_i$ for the response categories for item i, and $T_{k_i}(\theta)$ for the trace line for category k of item i. In addition, the summed scores for a set of items $[0 \ldots I^*]$ are $x = 0, 1, \ldots, \sum_{I^*} K_i$ and the likelihood for summed score x for a set of items $[0 \ldots I^*]$ is $L_x^{I^*}(\theta)$.

The generalized recursive algorithm is:

Set $I^* = 0$.

$$L_x^{I^*}(\theta) = T_{x_{I^*}}(\theta) \quad \text{for } x = 0, 1, \ldots, K_{I^*}$$

Repeat:
For item $I^* + 1$ and scores $x = 0, 1, \ldots, \sum_{I^*} K_i$, compute:

$$L_{x+k}^{I^*+1}(\theta) = \sum_{k_{I^*+1}} L_x^{I^*}(\theta) T_{k_{I^*+1}}(\theta) \quad \text{for } 0 \le x + k \le \sum_{k_{I^*+1}} K_i \, .$$

Then set $I^* = I^* + 1$, until $I^* = I$.

For a sample from a population with distribution $\phi(\theta)$, the posterior for score x is proportional to

$$L_x(\theta) \approx L_x^I(\theta)\phi(\theta) ,$$

and the expected value of θ for summed-score x, $EAP[\theta \,|\, x = \sum k_i]$, the standard deviation of θ for summed-score x, $SD[\theta \,|\, x = \sum k_i]$, and the modeled probability for summed-score x, $P_x(\theta)$, can be computed by integrating $L_x(\theta)$, in a way that is parallel to that described in chapter 3.

Again, no particular parametric form for the trace lines is assumed in the formulation of the recursive algorithm. In principle, any trace lines could be used, such as the nonparametric kernel smoothes described by Ramsay (1991). The algorithm would produce accurate, if nonsensical, results if it were used with items for which the responses are *not* ordered. The results would be useless because the response patterns included in any particular summed score would not tend to have likelihoods concentrated near the same values of θ, so such summed-score likelihoods would tend to be very flat with very large standard deviations.

IRT Scale Scores for Summed Scores: The North Carolina Test of Computer Skills—Keyboarding Techniques.

To illustrate the ideas presented in this section, we revisit the three-item North Carolina Test of Computer Skills KB section introduced in chapter 2, and fitted with the graded, generalized partial credit, and partial credit models in a preceding section. Using the item parameter estimates listed in Tables 4.1 and 4.2, as well as the parameters for the partial credit model, we have computed $EAP[\theta]$ for each summed score, and tabulated those values in Table 4.4. For this test, the three sets of scale scores for the summed scores are all very similar.

TABLE 4.4
EAP[θ] Scale Scores Associated With Each Summed Score, and Their
Corresponding Standard Deviations (*SD*), Using the Graded,
Generalized Partial Credit (GPC), and Partial Credit (PC) Models
for the North Carolina Test of Computer Skills KB Section

Sum	Graded Model		GPC Model		PC Model	
	EAP[θ]	*SD[θ]*	*EAP[θ]*	*SD[θ]*	*EAP[θ]*	*SD[θ]*
0	−1.55	0.76	−1.53	0.75	−1.57	0.75
1	−1.08	0.73	−1.07	0.73	−1.07	0.72
2	−0.60	0.70	−0.61	0.70	−0.59	0.71
3	−0.14	0.69	−0.14	0.69	−0.13	0.70
4	−0.31	0.69	−0.33	0.69	−0.32	0.70
5	−0.79	0.70	−0.81	0.71	−0.79	0.72
6	1.34	0.73	1.30	0.74	1.29	0.75

Table 4.5 compares the graded summed-score scale scores to the graded response-pattern scale scores for the 27 response patterns tabulated in Table 4.3. The relation between the two sets of scores is shown graphically in Fig. 4.4; the graphic makes it clear that there is relatively little difference, for this set of items, between using the response-pattern and summed-score scale scores.

As was the case with binary items, there is some loss of information involved in using only the total summed score, as opposed to the response pattern, as the basis for the IRT inference about proficiency (unless a Rasch family model is used, in which case all response patterns with the same summed score yield the same characterization of proficiency). Figure 4.5 shows the posterior standard deviations, which would be reported

TABLE 4.5
EAP[θ] Summed-Score and Response-Pattern Scale Scores,
and Their Corresponding Standard Deviations (SD), Using the Graded
Model for the North Carolina Test of Computer Skills KB Section

Response Pattern	Summed Score	For Summed Scores		For Response Patterns	
		EAP[θ]	SD[θ]	EAP[θ]	SD[θ]
000	0	−1.55	0.76	−1.55	0.76
001	1	−1.08	0.73	−1.12	0.72
100	1	−1.08	0.73	−1.03	0.72
010	1	−1.08	0.73	−0.74	0.70
002	2	−0.60	0.70	−0.71	0.73
101	2	−0.60	0.70	−0.68	0.69
200	2	−0.60	0.70	−0.67	0.76
011	2	−0.60	0.70	−0.43	0.67
110	2	−0.60	0.70	−0.34	0.67
020	2	−0.60	0.70	−0.30	0.80
201	3	−0.14	0.69	−0.31	0.72
102	3	−0.14	0.69	−0.28	0.70
111	3	−0.14	0.69	−0.08	0.64
012	3	−0.14	0.69	−0.04	0.67
210	3	−0.14	0.69	0.03	0.69
021	3	−0.14	0.69	0.05	0.75
120	3	−0.14	0.69	0.15	0.74
202	4	0.31	0.69	0.15	0.74
211	4	0.31	0.69	0.27	0.66
112	4	0.31	0.69	0.27	0.64
121	4	0.31	0.69	0.42	0.70
022	4	0.31	0.69	0.54	0.75
220	4	0.31	0.69	0.65	0.76
212	5	0.79	0.70	0.66	0.67
122	5	0.79	0.70	0.85	0.70
221	5	0.79	0.70	0.87	0.71
222	6	1.34	0.73	1.34	0.73

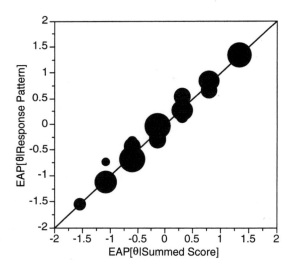

FIG. 4.4. Graded response-pattern scale scores plotted against the summed-score scale scores for all 27 response patterns for the North Carolina Test of Computer Skills KB section; the areas of the plotted bubbles are proportional to the relative frequency for each response pattern.

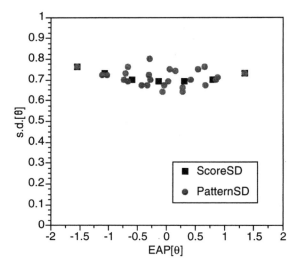

FIG. 4.5. The posterior standard deviations, which would be reported as the standard errors of the scale scores, for the graded EAP[θ]s based on the response patterns, and for those based on the summed scores, for the North Carolina Test of Computer Skills KB section.

as the standard errors of the scale scores, for the EAP[θ]s based on the response patterns, and for those based on the summed scores. Except for
the extreme score groups, for which pattern and summed-score estimates
are identical, the standard deviations for the summed-score estimates
tend to be slightly larger than the standard deviations for the response
pattern estimates. Some of the response-pattern estimates have larger
standard errors—those are associated with inconsistent responses, like
020. However, in either direction, the difference is small, for the amount of
variation in the a parameters listed in Table 4.1; use of the summed-score
estimates does not produce standard errors more than about 10% larger or
smaller than those for pattern estimates near the same proficiency.

Table 4.6 shows the approximation of the summed-score distribution
by the graded and generalized partial credit models. Both models fit the
observed-score distribution closely; under some circumstances, this means
that these models may be used to construct norming (percentile) tables,
possibly after item tryout and before the test is operationally administered. However, as we show in a subsequent example, this use of the theory
is subject to more problems when it is used with large open-ended items
than when it is (commonly) used for multiple-choice tests.

***Using IRT Scale Scores for Summed Scores to Link Alternate Forms: The
1993 North Carolina Open-Ended End-of-Grade Tests—Eighth-Grade
Mathematics.*** Large-scale testing often requires the use of alternate
forms that must be scored comparably, on the same scale. There are a
large number of methods for *test equating* that may be used to adjust score
scales to a common metric (see Holland & Rubin, 1982, for an extensive
treatment of this topic). However, many of the standard equating methods, especially those based on various forms of matching of the summed-
score distributions, are stymied by data that often arise with performance

TABLE 4.6
Approximation of the Summed-Score Distribution, Using the Graded
Model, as Well as the Generalized Partial Credit (GPC) Model,
for the North Carolina Test of Computer Skills KB Section

	Observed		Graded Model		GPC Model	
Sum	Frequency	Proportion	Frequency	Probability	Frequency	Probability
0	64	.02	67	.02	69	.02
1	292	.09	328	.11	328	.11
2	658	.21	597	.19	600	.19
3	747	.24	719	.23	713	.23
4	643	.21	667	.22	668	.22
5	419	.14	484	.16	495	.16
6	281	.09	242	.08	230	.07

assessments. Compared to multiple-choice tests, few extended con-structed-response items may appear on any given form, and each of those may be scored in only a few categories. The result is that an entire test form may have only 10 or so possible scores, and the score distributions can be very difficult to rationally match across forms.

IRT provides an alternative to raw-score equating, in what is often called *test linking* or joint *calibration* (Linn, 1993; Mislevy, 1992). Using any of a number of designs, data are collected that are sufficient to permit the simultaneous estimation of the parameters of the IRT models to be used for the items comprising all of the forms. Then, scale scores for each examinee are computed using their item responses and the jointly cali-brated item parameters in the IRT models; the resulting scores are said to be "on the same scale."[6]

As an example, here we consider data from the 1993 administration of three forms (A, B, and C) of the North Carolina Open-Ended End-of-Grade Test of Mathematics. Form A included three items, two rated 0–3 and the third rated 0–2, so the sum score range was 0–8; form B had four items, two scored 0–2, one scored 0–3, and the fourth scored 0–4, so the sum score range was 0–11; and form C included three items, two rated 0–3 and the third rated 0–4, so the sum score range was 0–10. Thus, on the surface, the summed scores of the ratings across forms are obviously not comparable, because there were different numbers of "points" obtainable on each of the three forms. Something simple, like conversion of the summed ratings to percentages of the maximum number of points for the form, may or may not make scores on such forms comparable. Here, we consider IRT analysis in an effort to convert scores on all three forms into scale scores that are comparable.

The forms were spiraled during the operational administration, so we may assume that the samples who responded to the three forms represent three random samples from a common population—that is, we may as-sume that the three form samples have the same distribution of mathe-matics proficiency (θ). Using item response data from approximately 22,000 students for each form, we fitted the graded model to each of the items.

Consideration of the test characteristic curves (TCCs) for the three forms is an easy way to examine the relation of the summed scores with θ; the TCC is a graph of the expected summed score as a function of θ,

---

[6]IRT calibration usually does not meet the strict requirements of equating; for two forms of an assessment, X and Y, to be called equated, "Any question that could be addressed using X scores can be addressed in exactly the same way using Y scores, and vice versa" (Mislevy, 1992, p. 21). However, IRT calibrated scores are estimates of proficiency on the same scale, and that is sufficient for the uses of scores in many large-scale testing contexts.

$$\text{TCC} = \sum_{i=1}^{I} \sum_{k=0}^{K-1} kT_{ik}(\theta) \ .$$

The TCCs for the three forms of the eighth grade mathematics test are shown in Fig. 4.6. The forms clearly differ markedly in both difficulty and discrimination: Considering the raw score, form B is easiest, and form C is very difficult, with form A between. Form A is highly discriminating over a narrow range of proficiency near the average value ($\theta = 0$), whereas forms B and C are less discriminating, but cover a wider range. Conversion of the rated "points" to proportions of the maximum score would reduce the apparent differences between the forms, but would not eliminate them.

It is not at all uncommon for alternate forms that include extended constructed-response items to differ in difficulty to this degree—indeed, it is a difficult situation to avoid. When one must assemble test forms using only three or four items, the test constructor does not have nearly as much freedom to match difficulty across forms as is the case when assembling multiple-choice forms with 60 or 80 items. Some extended constructed-response items are simply more (empirically) difficult than others; a test form that includes one or more such items is simply more difficult (like form C, here).

In addition, the summed-score distributions for tests comprising a few extended-response items may be very different; Fig. 4.7 shows the observed (and IRT model expected) score distributions for forms A and C. It would be extremely difficult to use such distribution-matching procedures as equipercentile equating to obtain acceptable scoring tables for those two forms, because the distributions differ so markedly in shape. [We also note that even in the case of the fairly pathological distribution for form A, the IRT model fits the observed-score distribution very well, again making the point that the assumption that proficiency (θ) follows a Gaussian distri-

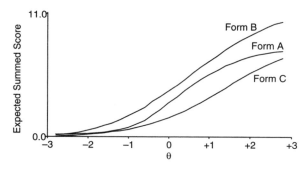

FIG. 4.6.   Test characteristics curves (TCCs) for forms A, B, and C of the 1993 North Carolina Test Open-Ended End-of-Grade Mathematics Test for the eighth grade.

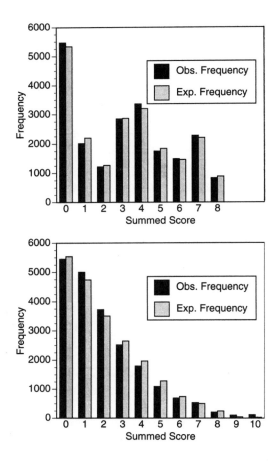

FIG. 4.7. Summed-score distributions for forms A (upper panel) and C (lower panel) of the 1993 North Carolina Test Open-Ended End-of-Grade Mathematics Test for the eighth grade.

bution can be associated with very non-Gaussian summed-score distributions.]

IRT scale scores for the three forms are one way to provide comparable scores. Scale scores based on response patterns could be used for this purpose, but in many large-scale testing programs it is preferable to have a summed score-to-scale score conversion table, both for practical operational reasons and because such tables are easier to present to some of the users of the test scores. Table 4.7 includes the summed-score-to-scale-score conversion tables for these three test forms, using EAP[θ|summed score] as the scale score and SD[θ|summed score] as the measure of precision, both in standard units. From the table, for example, we see that summed scores of 5 on form A, 7 on form B, and 4 on form C are roughly

TABLE 4.7
Scale Scores Associated With Summed Scores for Three Forms of the
1993 North Carolina End-of-Grade Open-Ended Mathematics Test

Sum Score	Form A		Form B		Form C	
	$EAP[\theta]$	SD	$EAP[\theta]$	SD	$EAP[\theta]$	SD
0	−1.08	0.65	−1.35	0.71	−0.81	0.79
1	−0.42	0.53	−0.86	0.65	−0.30	0.74
2	−0.20	0.53	−0.55	0.65	0.10	0.71
3	−0.16	0.54	−0.26	0.64	0.35	0.74
4	0.32	0.51	−0.01	0.65	0.62	0.73
5	0.62	0.51	0.23	0.64	0.92	0.71
6	0.78	0.54	0.46	0.64	1.21	0.69
7	1.14	0.54	0.71	0.63	1.50	0.72
8	1.81	0.61	0.96	0.63	1.77	0.73
9			1.25	0.63	1.77	0.71
10			1.59	0.64	2.01	0.72
11			2.05	0.66		

comparable, with scale scores of 0.62, 0.71, and 0.62, respectively. For reporting purposes, most testing programs would (linearly) convert these scores to some nice numbers, for example, by using a mean of 50 and a standard deviation of 10, and rounding.

With appropriate data collection, it is also possible to use this same procedure to produce comparable scores on forms that may be administered at different times, for instance at the end of different years. The calibration data must include some data from some administration that links at least some of the forms that are being calibrated. However, large-scale testing programs can use scale scores from tests calibrated in this way to assess change over time.

Using IRT Scale Scores for Summed Scores to Construct Scoring Tables Preoperationally: The 1996 North Carolina Open-Ended Reading and Mathematics Tests. One could hope that the use of IRT models would permit performance exercises to be calibrated in an item tryout, and then that the item parameters could be used to provide scale scores and predict the score distribution of the test when it is administered operationally. This sequence is commonly used with multiple-choice tests. It allows the construction of alternative forms with specified score distributions, and immediate scoring, because score-translation tables can be constructed before the test is administered.

However, a problem arises with this scenario that appears to be much more severe with tests comprising relatively large performance exercises than it is for multiple choice tests: The (empirical) difficulty of performance exercises appears to change, often unpredictably, between an item tryout administration and operational administration. McLeod (1996) collected retrospective data on a large number of open-ended items from the North Carolina End-of-Grade Testing Program that were included in item tryout forms in 1991–1993 and subsequently operationally administered in 1994. Simultaneous IRT analysis of the item tryout and operational data for each item provides an estimate of the change in (apparent) difficulty[7]—and that change varied widely. Although most items appeared to become easier when administered operationally than they had been at item tryout, the magnitude of the change varied from as much as one standard unit, on the IRT score scale, to less than zero (the latter for items that appeared to become more difficult when the test was administered operationally).

Of course, there are many reasons that apparent difficulty might be expected to change between item tryout and operational administration: One might expect the students to be more motivated during the operational administration, or one might believe that there were changes in instructional practices in the intervening period. The IRT model can easily be used to adjust for some (known) constant change in the apparent difficulty of the items between tryout and operational use; the change can simply be subtracted from the difficulty parameters (or, equivalently, added to the mean of the population distribution) when scale scores and the predicted score distribution are computed. However, when the change in apparent difficulty varies from item to item, and no available aspects of the data can be found that predict that variation, problems arise. (McLeod, 1996, searched the available data for any variable that might be related to the variation in the shift in apparent difficulty between tryout and operational use, and found none.)

Nevertheless, in 1996 we attempted to construct scale scores, and predict the score distribution, for a new North Carolina End-of-Grade Open-Ended Testing Program, with mathematics and reading tests administered in the fifth and eighth grades. We simultaneously calibrated a large set of potential items that were included in three item tryout administrations, in November 1995, and March and April 1996. The open-ended item responses were rated on scales with two to four scoring categories; all items were fitted with the graded model,[8] and the changes in proficiency for different times of administration during the academic year were esti-

---

[7]The change in apparent difficulty may be conceptualized either as a change in difficulty of the item (possibly because the item's content was taught more effectively between the item tryout and operational administration), or a change in the proficiency of the students being tested. The IRT model cannot distinguish between those two alternatives; item difficulty is always relative to average examinee proficiency, or vice versa. For ease of language use, we refer in the text to the change as one of difficulty.

[8]For two categories, of course, the graded model is the 2PL model.

mated using the means of the proficiency distributions for the different item tryouts. After the operational forms were constructed by selecting a subset of items from the tryout forms, we constructed summed-score to scale score conversion tables using EAP[θ|summed score], computed with the item tryout parameters, as the scale score. In addition, we computed predictions of the summed-score distributions using the IRT model.

Prediction of the summed-score distributions required some estimate of the change in apparent difficulty of the items between item tryout and operational use. We knew from McLeod's (1996) results that prediction might be poor; however, we used the average values for similar items that were obtained in that study. (McLeod's average shifts in apparent difficulty were about 0.4 standard units for mathematics items and 0.75 standard units for reading items.) The scale scores were linearly transformed to a reporting metric that was intended to have an average of 50 and a standard deviation of 10 for all four tests (reading and mathematics, at the fifth and eighth grades). All of the operational forms included five items, with summed scores that ranged from 0–15 to 0–18.

After the tests were administered to approximately 90,000 examinees in November 1996 and scored, we obtained the operational observed-score distributions shown in Figs. 4.8 (for the fifth-grade tests) and 4.9 (for the eighth-grade tests). Especially for the two reading tests, the observed-score distributions are not nearly as closely approximated by the IRT model as are the score distributions when the items are calibrated using the operational data (compare, e.g., Fig. 4.7). The shapes of the IRT-predicted distributions are approximately correct. And for the two mathematics tests, the average and standard deviation are also approximately as they should be: For the fifth grade, the operational average scale score was 49.9, with a standard deviation of 8.8, and for the eighth grade the average was 50, with a standard deviation of 10.3—both close to the expected values of 50 and 10. However, for the reading tests, for the fifth grade the operational average scale score was 45.2, with a standard deviation of 11.6, and for the eighth grade the average was 46.8, with a standard deviation of 10.0. In other words, both reading tests were more (empirically) difficult than the preoperational computations had led us to expect.

These results, although disappointing, correspond to the results McLeod (1996) obtained with the earlier North Carolina End-of-Grade Open-Ended Testing Program. The fact that the 1996 reading tests were nearly a half standard unit more difficult than the preoperational data had led us to expect is entirely within the range of variation observed in McLeod's (1996) analysis. These results suggested that changes should be made in the testing program so that scaling is not preoperational: In subsequent years, the new open-ended forms are scaled after the operational administration, using the operational data and linking to previous years'

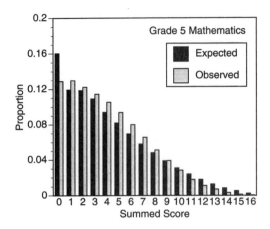

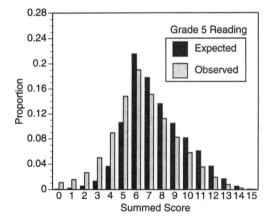

FIG. 4.8 Observed and expected summed-score distributions for the 1996 North Carolina Open-Ended mathematics (upper panel) and reading (lower panel) tests for Grade 5.

forms using spiraled readministration of earlier items. This approach (postoperational IRT scaling) is also used in the National Assessment of Educational Progress (NAEP), another test that has a large constructed-response component, for the same reasons: It appears not to be feasible, at this stage in our understanding of the behavior of large items, to use item tryout data to predict operational performance of a test with sufficient accuracy to link forms or establish percentiles.

Using IRT Scale Scores for Response Patterns to Score Tests Combining Multiple-Choice and Constructed-Response Sections: Wisconsin Third-Grade Reading Field Test.   To illustrate the use of IRT scale scores associ-

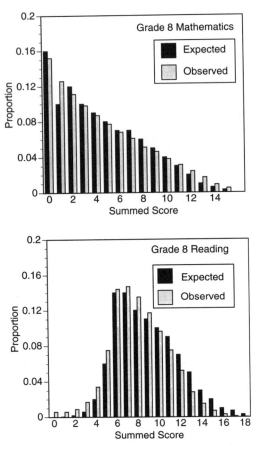

FIG. 4.9. Observed and expected summed-score distributions for the 1996 North Carolina Open-Ended mathematics (upper panel) and reading (lower panel) tests for Grade 8.

ated with response patterns to score tests comprising both multiple-choice and constructed-response sections, we return to the field test of a form of Wisconsin's third-grade reading test that we first considered in chapter 3. The data were obtained from 522 examinees; here we use the responses to the 16 multiple-choice items that we used in the example in chapter 3, as well as the responses to 4 constructed-response items. All 20 items followed a single reading passage. The multiple-choice items were in a conventional four-alternative format; the constructed-response items were open-ended questions that required a response on a few lines. The open-ended items were rated on a 4-point scale (0–3). We simultaneously fitted the 3PL model to the multiple-choice items and the graded model to the open-ended items using MULTILOG (Thissen, 1991) and the same mild

TABLE 4.8
3PL and Graded Model Item Parameter Estimates
for the Wisconsin Third-Grade Reading Test

3PL Model Multiple-Choice Items		
a	b	g
0.60	−0.71	0.20
1.27	−1.38	0.31
1.35	−1.19	0.22
0.86	−0.93	0.23
1.35	−0.40	0.23
2.12	−0.51	0.19
1.21	−0.55	0.23
1.53	−1.29	0.28
0.86	−0.93	0.20
1.62	−0.61	0.18
1.11	−0.98	0.22
1.34	−0.37	0.28
0.86	−0.76	0.20
2.29	−0.46	0.25
0.92	−0.09	0.26
0.95	−1.25	0.21

Graded Model Constructed–Response Items			
a	b_1	b_2	b_3
0.87	−4.96	−2.87	1.17
0.93	−4.46	−1.43	1.14
1.31	−3.41	−1.76	−0.52
0.73	−5.53	−1.73	2.22

Bayesian prior distribution[9] for the guessing parameter of the 3PL model (g) that we used in chapter 3. The parameter estimates are shown in Table 4.8.

Figure 4.10 illustrates the computation of the IRT scale score for an individual examinee for this 20-item test. This examinee responded correctly to 12 of the 16 multiple-choice items, and obtained scores of 2 on 2 of the open-ended items and 3 on the other 2, for a total score (if one sums the "points") of 22. IRT response-pattern scoring ignores the summed score, and instead multiplies the trace lines shown in Fig. 4.10: The top panel shows the trace lines for this examinee's responses to the multiple-choice items (12 increasing curves, and 4 decreasing curves, for the 12 cor-

---

[9]The prior distribution used for the lower asymptote parameter for the four-alternative multiple-choice items was $N(-1.1, 0.5)$ for logit(g); that distribution has a mode of 0.25 for g.

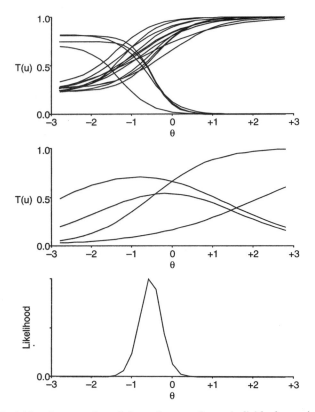

FIG. 4.10.   Computation of the scale score for an individual examinee on
the Wisconsin third-grade reading test: The top panel shows the 3PL trace
lines for this examinee's responses to the multiple choice items. The middle
panel shows the graded model trace lines associated with the open-ended
responses. The lower panel shows the product of the 20 curves in the other
two panels, along with the $N(0,1)$ population distribution curve.

rect and 4 incorrect item responses); the middle panel shows the trace
lines associated with the open-ended responses—the 2 nonmonotonic
curves are the graded trace lines for the 2s, and the 2 increasing trace lines
are those for the 3s. The lower panel of Fig. 4.10 is the product of the 20
curves in the other two panels [along with the $N(0,1)$ population distribution curve]. The mode of the curve in the lower panel is MAP[θ], which
takes a value of -0.54 (with $SE = 0.27$)—that is the IRT scale score in z-
score units for this examinee.

IRT scale scores computed as illustrated in Fig. 4.10 for each examinee
provide a solution to the weighting problem for tests, such as this one, that
combine multiple-choice and open-ended items. Many would question the
use of summed "points" to score a test such as this one, asking why one of

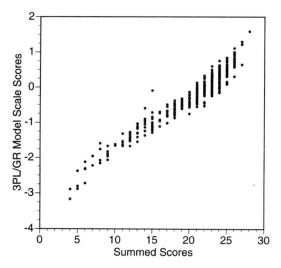

FIG. 4.11. Scatter plot of the scale scores for the combined 3PL and graded (GR) model, plotted against the summed scores for the Wisconsin third-grade reading test.

the rated "points" for the open-ended responses should be equal to the value of a correct multiple-choice response. However, the IRT scale scoring process neatly finesses the issue: All of the item responses (open-ended and multiple-choice) are implicitly weighted; indeed, the effect of each item response on the examinee's score depends on the other item responses. Each response pattern is scored in a way that best uses the information about proficiency that the entire response pattern provides, assuming that the model summarizes the data accurately.

IRT scale scores computed in this way may vary a good deal for examinees with the same summed score. Figure 4.11 shows a scatter plot of the scale scores for the combined 3PL and graded model, plotted against the summed score computed taking the number of open-ended rated "points" literally.[10] For some summed scores, the range of IRT scale scores is as much as a standard unit. A good deal of this range is attributable, in this case, to the differential treatment by the IRT model of the open-ended responses: As shown in Fig. 4.10, the slopes of the trace lines[11] for the open-ended responses is substantially less than the slopes of the 3PL trace lines in the vicinity of this examinee's score. As a result, the

---

[10]Examinees with missing responses are omitted from Fig. 4.11, because it is not clear how to compute their summed scores in a way that is comparable to those of the other examinees.

[11]Here, *slope* is best taken generally, to mean the rate of change of the response probability as a function of θ.

3PL responses count more in the score, and the open-ended responses count relatively less. For examinees other than the one shown in Fig. 4.10, who also obtained a summed score of 22, the IRT scale score is higher, because they responded correctly to more of the highly discriminating multiple-choice items, even though they obtained fewer points for their open-ended responses.

Assuming that the combined 3PL and graded model accurately represents the data, the IRT scale scores simultaneously provide more accurate estimates of each examinee's proficiency, and avoid any need for explicit consideration of the relative weights of the different kinds of "points."

However, not all IRT models include differential item weighting; models in the "Rasch family" (Masters & Wright, 1984) do not. For comparison, we fitted these same data with the 1PL model for the multiple-choice responses and the partial credit model for the open-ended responses, again using MULTILOG (Thissen, 1991).[12] Figure 4.12 shows the 1PL and partial credit trace lines for the same data that were used to make Fig. 4.10. The 1PL trace lines in the upper panel of Fig. 4.12 have generally lower slopes than the corresponding trace lines in Fig. 4.10, and the partial credit model trace lines in the middle panel of Fig. 4.12 have generally higher slopes than the graded trace lines in Fig. 4.10. Because the 1PL/partial credit model must use the same slope parameter for all of the items and the rating categories for the open-ended items, that slope must be a compromise between the higher values the previous analysis gave to the multiple-choice items and the lower values for the open-ended responses. For the examinee with the trace lines shown in Fig. 4.12, the IRT scale score, which is the mode of the likelihood in the lower panel of the figure, is −0.05, with an SE of 0.41.

The 1PL/partial credit model yields a single scale score for each summed score, where the sum in this case treats each "point" for the ratings of the open-ended responses the same as a correct multiple-choice re-

---

[12] We use estimates of the 1PL/partial credit model combination here computed with MULTILOG to facilitate direct comparison with the estimates for the 3PL/graded model. Fitting the 1PL/partial credit combination model with MULTILOG is not exactly the same in some respects as a Rasch-model analysis might be done by others, say, using the computer program BIGSTEPS (Wright & Linacre, 1992). The MULTILOG model fitting includes an $N(0,1)$ population distribution that a BIGSTEPS analysis would not, and the MULTILOG parameter estimation is done using maximum marginal likelihood, whereas BIGSTEPS uses a joint maximum likelihood algorithm. However, after all of that is said, the correlation between the MULTILOG and BIGSTEPS MAP[θ]s for these data is 0.996—it is less than 1.0 due to a very slight curvilinearity in the relationship induced by the shrinkage toward the mean of the population distribution in the MULTILOG estimates and the lack thereof in the BIGSTEPS estimates. This latter point is difficult to evaluate, because the BIGSTEPS estimates for zero and perfect scores are arbitrarily placed, at values a fraction of a "point" above zero and below the maximum score.

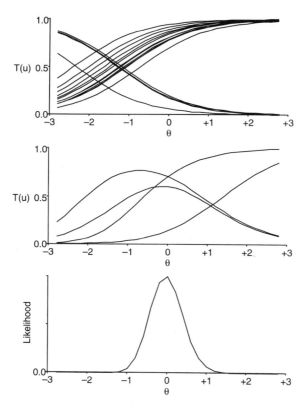

FIG. 4.12. Another computation of a scale score for an individual examinee on the Wisconsin third-grade reading test: The top panel shows the 1PL trace lines for this examinee's responses to the multiple-choice items; the middle panel shows the partial credit model trace lines associated with the open-ended responses. The lower panel shows the product of the 20 curves in the other two panels, along with the $N(0,1)$ population distribution curve.

sponse. The 1PL/partial credit scale scores are shown, plotted against the summed scores, in Fig. 4.13.[13] Unlike the 3PL/graded scale scores shown in Fig. 4.11, the 1PL/partial credit scale scores are only a curvilinear transformation of the summed scores—it does not matter what combination of item responses yields a summed score of, say, 22; that is always associated with the same scale score.

For the examinee with the trace lines shown in Figs. 4.10 and 4.12, the estimate from the Rasch family of models is nearly a half standard unit higher than the estimate computed for the 3PL/graded model; for other

---

[13]Figure 4.13 shows only those scores actually observed in the data; no one obtained a score less than four.

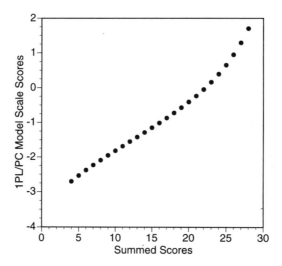

FIG. 4.13. Scatter plot of the scale scores for the combined 1PL and partial credit (PC) model, plotted against the summed scores for the Wisconsin third-grade reading test.

examinees the Rasch family estimate is lower. Figure 4.14 shows a scatter plot of the 3PL/graded scale scores plotted against the 1PL/partial credit scale scores for all 522 examinees with data for this item tryout form. Although the 1PL/partial credit and 3PL/graded analyses are both based on IRT, it is clear from Fig. 4.14 that the resulting scale scores are very different for many examinees. Indeed, the only difference between Fig. 4.14 and Fig. 4.11 (plotting the 3PL/graded scale scores against the summed scores) is that the relation in Fig. 4.14 lacks some of the slight curvilinearity apparent in Fig. 4.11. The fact that the 3PL/graded model weights some of the responses (in this case, mostly the open-ended responses) somewhat less than others (mostly the multiple-choice responses) creates different scores.

Which scores are better? If the 3PL/graded model is a better representation of the process underlying the item responses, then those scale scores should be better. The only evidence we can obtain about this from these item tryout data is the goodness of fit of the models to the data; in this case, the 3PL/graded model fits the data substantially better than the 1PL/partial credit model. Similarly, in a more extensive comparison of item fit, using data from the Maryland School Performance Assessment Program (MSPAP) and the Maryland Writing Test (MWT), Fitzpatrick et al. (1996) found that the more general 3PL/generalized partial credit combination consistently fitted mixed multiple-choice and constructed-response items better than the 1PL/partial credit combination. However,

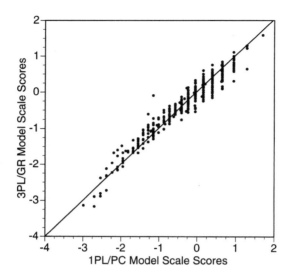

FIG. 4.14. Scatter plot of the scale scores for the combined 3PL and graded (GR) model, plotted against the combined 1PL and partial credit model, for the Wisconsin third-grade reading test.

the best test of the relative value of the two scoring procedures would be to consider the validity of the scores with respect to some criterion external to the test.

THE TESTLET CONCEPT

The concept of the testlet was introduced to the literature by Wainer and Kiely (1987, p. 190): "A testlet is a group of items related to a single content area that is developed as a unit and contains a fixed number of predetermined paths that an examinee may follow." Wainer and Kiely proposed the use of testlets as the units of construction and analysis for computerized adaptive tests (CATs); however, the testlet concept is now viewed as a general-purpose solution to the problem of *local dependence* (Yen, 1993). If a pair or cluster of items exhibits local dependence, with respect to the construct being measured by the test as a whole, then that pair or cluster of items may be aggregated into a single unit—a testlet. The testlet then yields locally independent responses in the context of the other items comprising the measure. Testlets and individual items can then be included in an IRT model for item analysis and test scoring.

By definition, a testlet is a kind of (super) test item that yields more than two responses; further, the relative ordering of those responses with respect to the construct being measured may or may not be known a priori. Although traditional approaches to item analysis and test assembly may be stymied by the presence of items with multiple, purely nominal responses, Bock's (1972) IRT model for responses in several nominal categories may be used to provide straightforward item analysis and test scoring. Analysis using the nominal model can also be used to determine if the responses are, as a matter of empirical fact, ordered; if they are, then a constrained version of the nominal model, like the generalized partial credit or partial credit model, or Samejima's (1969) graded model, may be effectively used.

Our first illustration of the testlet idea (Thissen, 1993; Thissen & Steinberg, 1988) used data reported by Bergan and Stone (1985) involving the responses to four items measuring the numerical knowledge of a sample of preschool children, and the nominal IRT model. This example represents what we now call *response-pattern testlets*, in which every pattern of responses to the items comprising the testlet becomes a response category for the testlet as a whole. An extensive theoretical treatment of processes that may be represented by fitting the nominal model to response-pattern testlets was recently provided by Hoskens and De Boeck (1997), who reanalyzed the Bergan and Stone example and contributed others.

There is no loss of information involved in the construction of response-pattern testlets; the data are merely redefined. However, given current technology, response-pattern testlets may include only a few items (two, three, or perhaps four), and only a few responses for each item. The number of response categories for the testlet is the product of the numbers of response categories for the items, and that cannot become larger than, say, 16 and still permit any reasonable amount of data to be used to calibrate the nominal model.

As discussed in chapter 2, when several items follow a common stimulus, it may be better to view the summed score on the test as the sum of the number-correct scores for the subsets of items associated with each of the common stimuli (often passages in reading comprehension tests). Both the nominal model and the graded model have been used for the analysis of passage-based tests (Thissen, Steinberg, & Mooney, 1989; Wainer, Sireci, & Thissen, 1991); Wilson and Adams (1995) also proposed the use of their multinomial logit model, which is closely related to the nominal model. To implement this idea, a test with, say, 10 questions following each of four reading passages is treated as a four-testlet test, and the graded model or (some version of) the nominal model is fitted to the 11 response categories that represent each possible number-correct score. In this case, there is some loss of information relative to full response-pattern analysis of the test data; however, the loss of information is usually small and is more than compensated by the fact that the testlet analysis is a proper analysis of locally independent responses, while the response-pattern analysis may be distorted by the local dependence induced by the passages. For this reason, testlet-based IRT analysis yields a more accurate description of the reliability and scale score standard errors for such tests (see also Sireci, Thissen, & Wainer, 1991).[14]

The reason that pairs or clusters of items should be treated as testlets is sometimes obvious, as in the case of clustered tasks (e.g., the pairs of questions on the preschool numerical knowledge test), or the questions following a passage on a reading comprehension test. On the other hand, local dependence may also be an unexpected or even surprising empirical phenomenon. Yen (1993) and her colleagues at CTB/McGraw-Hill successfully used empirical procedures to detect local dependence on recently constructed performance-based educational assessments; they used a statistic called Q_3, proposed by Yen (1984), to identify local dependence. However, Q_3 may exhibit unpredictable behavior under some circumstances (Chen & Thissen, 1997; Reese, 1995). For binary test items, we use the *LD-index* described in detail by Chen and Thissen (1997). The LD-index provides a straightforward analysis of the residuals from the IRT model for each pair of items: If the items are locally independent, then the residuals from the fitted model for each pair of items are statistically independent, and the χ^2-distributed statistic is expected to be about 1. If the items are locally dependent, the LD-index is large. When substantial local dependence is detected, say by the LD-index, or expected, because the test was deliberately constructed with related items, we combine those items into testlets and use the same IRT machinery for test scoring that we use with any test that has items with several response categories.

Using the Nominal Model for Items Combined Into Response-Pattern Testlets: An Example from the North Carolina End-of-Course Geometry Test. A pair of items that exhibit relatively extreme local dependence is shown in Fig. 4.15. On a 1991 test form of the North Carolina End-of-Course Geometry test, these two items were numbers 14 and 15, and physically adjacent, as shown in the figure; such physical proximity often exacerbates local dependence when it may exist. Using data from 2,739 examinees, we calibrated the 60-item test and computed the LD-index for each pair of items. The value of the LD-index for this pair of items was 180; for a statistic that is distributed approximately as a χ^2 with 1 df in the

---

[14]Bradlow, Wainer, and Wang (1999) approached the relation of IRT models with testlets differently than we do here, to solve the problem that was raised first in chapter 2, that the existence of local dependence may produce erroneous estimates of reliability and test score precision. Bradlow et al. developed an IRT model that specifically modeled local dependence within testlets using a correlation-like parametric structure, in such a way that the effects of local dependence could be removed from the parameter estimates of the main IRT model.

14.   Which term describes ∠1 and ∠2?

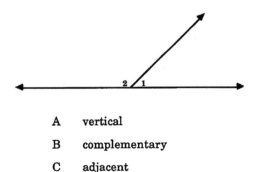

A   vertical

B   complementary

C   adjacent

D   congruent

15.   If $m\angle A = 60$, what is the measure
of the supplement of $\angle A$?

A   120

B   90

C   40

D   30

FIG. 4.15.   Two items (14 and 15) from the 1991 North Carolina End-of-Course Test of Geometry that exhibit substantial local dependence.

null case, that is remarkable. Many more examinees than the IRT model predicts respond correctly to both items, or incorrectly to both items.

Examining the items, it is easy to see why. Indeed, there are several ways to describe the probable reasons for the local dependence. A succinct description is to say that the two items are both vocabulary items on a geometry test, and that students whose teachers emphasized the memorization of vocabulary would do better on both. A somewhat more elaborate chain of reasoning explains that item 14 could serve to give away the answer to item 15, even for students with limited knowledge: If we assume that, among the three terms *adjacent, complementary*, and *supplementary*, the first is the easiest to remember, then we may assume that item 14 is easy to answer correctly (by selecting *adjacent*). However, the picture clearly shows that the angles in item 14 sum to 180°; that implies that *complementary*, as an incorrect distractor for item 14, cannot be the word that means "sums to 180°." Now, when we turn to item 15, if we remember that *supplementary* is "one of those words" and means either "sums to 180°" or "sums to 90°," we eliminate alternatives B and C—and then (correctly) choose alternative A, because *supplementary* has to be "sums to 180°" if (from item 14) *complementary* is not.

In any event, the empirical fact is that the responses to the two items are not locally independent. The solution proposed by Yen (1993) for this kind of local dependence is to combine the two items into a single testlet, and redo the IRT analysis—this serves to eliminate the local dependence and keep the IRT model and its usefulness for scale scoring. The alternatives are to keep the local dependence and eliminate the unidimensional IRT model, or complicate the model; neither of those ideas was attractive. In this case, we rescored these two items as a single testlet with four response categories: 0 for response pattern {00}, 1 for response pattern {01}, 2 for response pattern {10}, and 3 for response pattern {11}. Then we recalibrated the test using the 3PL model for the remaining 58 items and the nominal model for the testlet.

The nominal model trace lines for the four response patterns to items 14 and 15 are shown in the lower panel of Fig. 4.16. The trace lines for {00}, {01}, and {10} are all monotonically decreasing (and nearly proportional to each other) over the useful range of θ. Of course, the trace line for {11} is monotonically increasing. This differs from any pattern that can be obtained by combining two 3PL trace lines, for which the likelihoods of the four response patterns must be ordered, with {11} associated with higher values of θ, {01} and {10} associated with some intermediate values of θ, and {00} lowest. The 3PL trace lines for items 14 and 15 are shown in the upper panel of Fig. 4.16, and the products of those two curves (and their complements) are shown in the middle panel of the figure. In an attempt to fit the data, as accurately described by the nominal in the lower panel, the 3PL model has extremely high values of g (the lower asymptote) for both items—they are 0.43 and 0.48, respectively. Nevertheless, the 3PL model must imply that the likelihoods for the response patterns {01} and {10} are associated with relatively higher values of θ than {00}; this causes the misfit with the data that is detected by the LD-index.

If the 3PL trace lines were used to compute IRT scale scores, the effect would be that examinees who responded correctly to either one of the two items would receive higher scale scores than those who responded correctly to neither. However, trace lines from the nominal model for the testlet have different consequences for scale scoring: Effectively, the examinee "gets credit" (the scale score increases) for response pattern {11}, but the scale score tends to decrease (slightly) for any of the patterns that include an incorrect response. That is, the testlet combination and subsequent nominal model analysis has created a scoring rule for this pair of items that, to anthropomorphize, basically says "this pair is a single

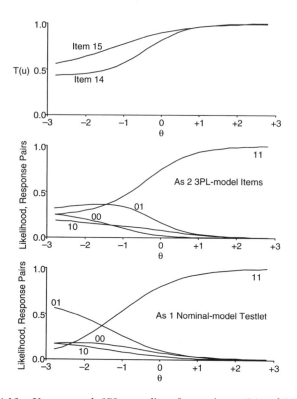

FIG. 4.16.   Upper panel: 3PL trace lines for two items (14 and 15) from the 1991 North Carolina End-of-Course Test of Geometry that exhibit substantial local dependence. Middle panel: Likelihoods for the four possible response patterns for items 14 and 15, computed as products of the trace lines in the upper panel and their complements. Lower panel: Trace lines for the four possible response patterns for items 14 and 15, treated as the four responses to a testlet and fitted using the nominal model.

item; you get one point if you respond correctly to both questions, and zero points if you miss either." The IRT analysis indicates that using this scoring rule makes this pair of items a better indicator of proficiency in geometry than any that would be obtained treating the two items separately.

We have described response-pattern testlet modeling and scoring as an a posteriori "fix" for observed local dependence, and the procedure is used that way. However, as Hoskens and De Boeck (1997) and others pointed out, the availability of this kind of analysis makes it possible for the test constructor to plan or intend to construct item combinations as testlets. An example could be the mathematics item format that asks for the solution to a problem and then follows up with what appears to be a second question, "Explain your answer." After the solution is scored, possibly as correct or incorrect, and the explanation is rated by judges following some rubric, perhaps on a three-point scale, all of the patterns of {solution score, explanation score} can be treated as the response alternatives for a single testlet, fitted with the nominal model.[15]

Another example that illustrates this possibility is suggested by the Wisconsin Third-Grade Reading item tryout form that was the subject of previous examples in this chapter and in chapter 3. On that test form, in addition to the 16 multiple-choice items, and the 4 open-ended items that required verbal responses, which we analyzed earlier in this chapter, there was one additional item: Based on the reading passage, the examinees were asked to draw a picture, and the quality of the drawing was scored by raters, using a 5-point scale. The fourth open-ended response was, then, based on a question *about the picture*.

Local dependence (rather than local independence) is an obvious assumption about those two responses, the rating of the picture and the rating of the open-ended (verbal) response to the item about the picture. Unfortunately, testlet analysis was not planned when the scoring rubrics were designed, and casting those two responses as a single response-pattern testlet would generate $4 \times 5 = 20$ response categories. That, combined with only 522 examinees in the item tryout, would yield an average of only about 26 examinees per response category; that is not sufficient data to fit the nominal model. (Actually, many of the response categories were empty, or nearly so.) In principle, however, such a combination could be handled with the combination of testlet and nominal model technology, permitting the use of both such innovative question formats and the useful features of IRT for score scaling and reporting.

Using the Graded Model for Items Combined Into Summed-Scored Testlets, Combined With Open-Ended Ratings: The Wisconsin Eighth-Grade Reading Test.   As we observed in chapter 2, passage-based tests, as illustrated by the conventional reading comprehension format, often include a component of variation that is attributable to the passages. That component of variation induces local dependence among the items that follow each passage. Thissen et al. (1989) suggested that a solution to this type of problem is to compute testlet scores, the summed scores that are the number of correct responses associated with each of the several passages on the test, and then use an IRT model for multiple responses with the testlet scores treated as the "items." This approach is the IRT analog of the computation of coefficient α using the passage summed scores, which is what we suggested in chapter 2.

---

[15]Some testing programs use ordered versions of the nominal model, such as the generalized partial credit model, for this purpose. That may be effective, but we would recommend that the unconstrained nominal model be fitted, or some other analysis performed, to check that the empirical order of the testlet categories corresponds to the order assumed in fitting an ordered item response model.

We illustrate that idea here, using data from 6,499 examinees who took the Wisconsin Student Assessment System eighth-grade reading comprehension test in 1995.[16] The test included six reading passages; the first five passages were each followed by five to nine four-alternative multiple-choice questions, whereas the sixth passage formed the basis for three relatively short constructed-response questions that were each subsequently rated 0–3.[17] One could score such a test simply by summing the "points" (number correct [of 30] on the multiple-choice items plus the ratings of the open-ended responses), but this would invite questions such as, "What would have happened to the scores if the open-ended responses had been scored on a 0–6 scale instead of 0–3?"

Such questions are avoided by the use of IRT scale scores that (implicitly) weight the responses associated with each passage according to their relation to the proficiency that underlies responses to the test as a whole. To compute such scale scores, using the testlet concept to construct locally independent responses for the model, we first compute the summed scores for the items following each passage. That yields six passage scores: The first five are counted correct multiple-choice responses, and the sixth is the sum of the ratings of the three open-ended items that were associated with the final reading passage. Then we fitted the graded model to this six-"item" test, and computed the values of MAP[θ], using MULTILOG (Thissen, 1991).

The graded trace lines, one set for each passage, are shown in Figs. 4.17 and 4.18; they are computed using the graded model item parameter estimates in Table 4.9. The score for Passage 1 (upper panel, Fig. 4.17) is least discriminating; that is interesting, because passage 1 on this test is a little unusual: The passage is an advertisement, and the questions are about the content and meaning of the ad. Passage 2 is the most discriminating of the set; that is a conventional narrative story. The scores for passages 3, 4, and 5 are all about equally discriminating, and their trace lines differ very little from those for the final passage, even though in the latter case the trace lines are associated with the sum of ratings of open-ended responses.

To compute the values of MAP[θ] for each examinee, one selects the trace line corresponding to that examinee's summed score for each of the six passages, and then forms their product with the $N(0,1)$ population distribution, to yield the joint likelihood. The mode of that likelihood is MAP[θ], just as described in chapter 3. Figure 4.19 shows the values of MAP[θ] for 650 of the examinees (a 10% random sample of the total, to re-

---

[16] We thank Frank Evans of the Wisconsin Department of Public Instruction for kindly providing these data.

[17] In chapter 6, we describe the results of factor analysis of these data; after the test is redefined as six testlet scores, it may be considered essentially unidimensional, especially when the constructed-response questions are combined into a single testlet score as they are here.

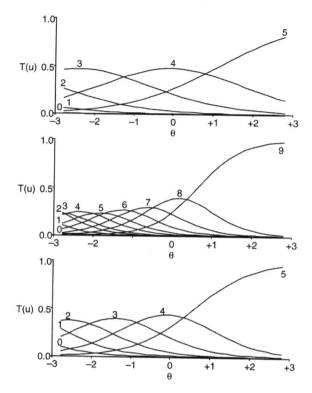

FIG. 4.17.   Graded trace lines for the number-correct score following passages 1 (upper panel), 2 (middle panel), and 3 (lower panel) of the Wisconsin eighth-grade reading test.

duce the density), plotted against the summed score—the number correct plus number of rating points on the open-ended questions. For this test, the general relation between the IRT scale scores and the summed score is remarkably linear. As is always the case with IRT models outside the Rasch family, there is some variation among the scale scores for examinees with the same summed score, due to the fact that different response patterns are associated with higher or lower proficiency. Because they make use of this information, the IRT scale scores are somewhat more efficient than the summed scores. However, that effect is fairly small here, and the most compelling reasons to use IRT scale scores for this test would arise from a desire to link alternate forms, or construct, say, a developmental scale that connected different forms administered in different grades.

We have presented this illustration to make the point that, by using the testlet concept and multiple-category IRT models, IRT scale scores may be straightforwardly computed even in the presence of fairly obvious local dependence among the (original, apparent) items on the test. In addition,

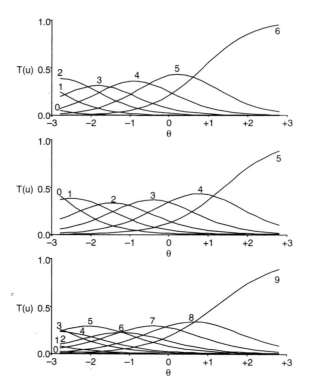

FIG. 4.18. The graded trace lines for the number-correct score following Passage 4 (upper panel), Passage 5 (middle panel), and for the total of the rating points for the open-ended questions following Passage 6 (lower panel) of the Wisconsin eighth-grade reading test.

TABLE 4.9
Graded Model Item Parameter Estimates for the Wisconsin
Eighth-Grade Reading Test, With the Summed Score Associated
With Each of the Five Passages as a Testlet Score

	Passage 1	Passage 2	Passage 3	Passage 4	Passage 5
a	0.89	1.82	1.35	1.52	1.42
b_1	−8.56	−5.03	−4.45	−4.70	−3.06
b_2	−5.67	−3.90	−3.18	−3.35	−1.94
b_3	−3.54	−3.14	−2.02	−2.26	−0.97
b_4	−1.24	−2.63	−0.79	−1.39	0.10
b_5	1.11	−2.08	0.59	−0.38	1.39
b_6		−1.56		0.84	
b_7		−0.96			
b_8		−0.29			
b_9		0.62			

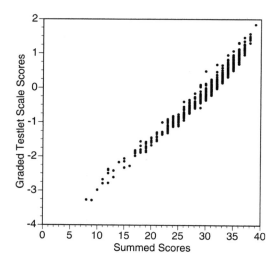

FIG. 4.19.   MAP[θ] for 650 of the Wisconsin eighth-grade reading test examinees plotted against the summed score (number correct plus number of rating points on the open-ended questions).

this analysis has provided a rational solution to the weighting problem that arises in combining the ratings of the open-ended responses with the multiple-choice items.

CONCLUSION

IRT models for items with responses scored in more than two categories provide a useful way to compute scale scores for the otherwise difficult data that arise in the context of performance assessments. Although the rating categories used by judges to provide the item-level scores for constructed-response items are often arbitrary, the IRT models provide a mechanism to combine those ratings into scores on a useful scale. Weighting problems, once the province of guesswork or committees, are naturally handled in the process of the computation of IRT scale scores; each item is implicitly weighted according to its relation with the aspect proficiency that is common to all of the items (θ).

The computation of IRT scale scores requires that the item responses must be locally independent, because that justifies the multiplication of the trace lines for those responses to compute the likelihood that is the basis of the scale scores. Although this requirement may seem, at first blush, restrictive in the context of performance assessment, as we have seen, the testlet concept may be used to combine items that may be locally dependent into testlets, in such a way that the testlet responses are locally independent. Then, IRT models for responses in more than two categories, such as those we have discussed in this chapter, may be used to gain all of the advantages of IRT—a well-defined scale with well-defined standard errors, form linking, and even adaptive testing.

IRT scale scores may always be computed using the full response pattern, and, if the model is well chosen for the data, that yields the most (statistically) efficient scores. In some contexts, IRT scale scores may usefully be computed for each summed score—that is often more practical in large-scale testing programs, but it is not so useful when the items being considered are of very different kinds. In chapters 7 and 8, we consider elaborations of the concepts of IRT scale scoring that are explicitly designed for tests that combine different item types—after a more explicit treatment of the topics of dimensionality and factor analysis, as they relate to tests and items, in chapters 5 and 6.

REFERENCES

Adams, R. J., & Khoo, S. T. (1992). QUEST: The interactive test analysis system [Computer software]. Melbourne, Victoria: Australian Council for Educational Research.

Allen, N. L., Mazzeo, J., Ip, S., Swinton, S., Isham, S. P., & Worthington, L. H. (1995). Data analysis and scaling for the 1994 Trial State Assessment in reading. In J. Mazzeo, N. L. Allen, & D. L. Kline (Eds.), *Technical report of the NAEP 1994 Trial State Assessment program in reading* (pp. 169–219). Washington, DC: Office of Educational Research and Improvement, U.S. Department of Education.

Andersen, E. B. (1973). Conditional inference for multiple choice questionnaires. *British Journal of Mathematical and Statistical Psychology, 26*, 42–54.

Andersen, E. B. (1977). Sufficient statistics and latent trait models. *Psychometrika, 42*, 69–81.

Andersen, E. B. (1997). The rating scale model. In W. van der Linden & R. K. Hambleton (Eds.), *Handbook of modern item response theory* (pp. 67–84). New York: Springer.

Andrich, D. (1978a). A rating formulation for ordered response categories. *Psychometrika, 43*, 561–573.

Andrich, D. (1978b). Application of a psychometric rating model to ordered categories which are scored with successive integers. *Applied Psychological Measurement, 2*, 581–594.

Baker, F. B. (1992). *Item response theory: Parameter estimation techniques*. New York: Marcel Dekker.

Bergan, J. R., & Stone, C. A. (1985). Latent class models for knowledge domains. *Psychological Bulletin, 98*, 166–184.

Bock, R. D. (1972). Estimating item parameters and latent ability when responses are scored in two or more latent categories. *Psychometrika, 37*, 29–51.

Bock, R. D. (1997). The nominal categories model. In W. van der Linden & R. K. Hambleton (Eds.), *Handbook of modern item response theory* (pp. 33–50). New York: Springer.

Bradlow, E. T., Wainer, H., & Wang, X. (1999). A Bayesian random effects model for testlets. *Psychometrika, 64*, 153–168.

Chen, W. H., & Thissen, D. (1997). Local dependence indices for item pairs using item response theory. *Journal of Educational and Behavioral Statistics, 22*, 265–289.

Ercikan, K., Schwarz, R., Weber, M., Ferrara, S., & Michaels, H. (1997, April). *The effect of integrated items on the validity and reliability of tests: Sciences and mathematics integration in a state-*

wide performance assessment. Paper presented at the Annual Meeting of the National Council on Measurement in Education, Chicago.

Fitzpatrick, A. R., Link, V. B., Yen, W. M., Burket, G. R., Ito, K., & Sykes, R. C. (1996). Scaling performance assessments: A comparison of one-parameter and two-parameter partial credit models. *Journal of Educational Measurement, 33,* 291–314.

Holland, P. W., & Rubin, D. B. (1982). *Test equating.* New York: Academic Press.

Hoskens, M., & De Boeck, P. (1997). A parametric model for local dependence among test items. *Psychological Methods, 2,* 261–277.

Linn, R. L. (1993). Linking results of distinct assessments. *Applied Measurement in Education, 6,* 83–102.

Masters, G. N. (1982). A Rasch model for partial credit scoring. *Psychometrika, 47,* 149–174.

Masters, G. N., & Wright, B. D. (1984). The essential process in a family of measurement models. *Psychometrika, 49,* 529–544.

Masters, G. N., & Wright, B. D. (1997). The partial credit model. In W. van der Linden & R. K. Hambleton (Eds.), *Handbook of modern item response theory* (pp. 101–122). New York: Springer.

McLeod, L. D. (1996). *Exploration of the use of the graded item response model in open-ended test assembly.* Unpublished master's thesis, University of North Carolina at Chapel Hill, Chapel Hill, NC.

Mellenbergh, G. J. (1995). Conceptual notes on models for discrete polytomous item responses. *Applied Psychological Measurement, 19,* 91–100.

Mislevy, R. J. (1992). *Linking educational assessments: Concepts, issues, methods, and prospects.* Princeton, NJ: Educational Testing Service.

Mislevy, R. J., & Wu, P. K. (1996). *Missing responses and IRT estimation: Omits, choice, time limits, and adaptive testing* (RR-96-30-ONR). Princeton, NJ: Educational Testing Service.

Muraki, E. (1992). A generalized partial credit model: Application of an EM algorithm. *Applied Psychological Measurement, 16,* 159–176.

Muraki, E. (1997). A generalized partial credit model. In W. van der Linden & R. K. Hambleton (Eds.), *Handbook of modern item response theory* (pp. 153–164). New York: Springer.

Muraki, E., & Bock, R. D. (1991). PARSCALE: Parameter scaling of rating data [Computer software]. Chicago: Scientific Software, Inc.

Ramsay, J. O. (1991). Kernel smoothing approaches to nonparametric item characteristic curve estimation. *Psychometrika, 56,* 611–630.

Rasch, G. (1961). On general laws and the meaning of measurement in psychology. *Proceedings of the Fourth Berkeley Symposium on Mathematical Statistics and Probability* (pp. 321–333). Berkeley: University of California Press.

Reese, L. M. (1995). *The impact of local dependencies on some LSAT outcomes.* LSAC Research Report Series. Newtown, PA: Law School Admission Council.

Samejima, F. (1969). Estimation of latent ability using a response pattern of graded scores. *Psychometric Monograph, 17.*

Samejima, F. (1972). A general model for free-response data. *Psychometric Monograph, 18.*

Samejima, F. (1979). *A new family of models for the multiple choice item* (Research Rep. No. 79-4). Knoxville, TN: Department of Psychology, University of Tennessee.

Samejima, F. (1995). Acceleration model in the heterogeneous case of the general graded response model. *Psychometrika, 60,* 549–572.

Samejima, F. (1997). Graded response model. In W. van der Linden & R. K. Hambleton (Eds.), *Handbook of modern item response theory* (pp. 85–100). New York: Springer.

Sireci, S. G., Thissen, D., & Wainer, H. (1991). On the reliability of testlet-based tests. *Journal of Educational Measurement, 28,* 237–247.

Thissen, D. (1991). MULTILOG user's guide—Version 6 [Computer software]. Chicago: Scientific Software, Inc.

Thissen, D. (1993). Repealing rules that no longer apply to psychological measurement. In N. Frederiksen, R. J. Mislevy, & I. Bejar (Eds.), *Test theory for a new generation of tests* (pp. 79–97). Hillsdale, NJ: Lawrence Erlbaum Associates.

Thissen, D., Pommerich, M., Billeaud, K., & Williams, V. S. L. (1995). Item response theory for scores on tests including polytomous items with ordered responses. *Applied Psychological Measurement, 19*, 39–49.

Thissen, D., & Steinberg, L. (1984). A response model for multiple-choice items. *Psychometrika, 49*, 501–519.

Thissen, D., & Steinberg, L. (1986). A taxonomy of item response models. *Psychometrika, 51*, 567–577.

Thissen, D., & Steinberg, L. (1988). Data analysis using item response theory. *Psychological Bulletin, 104*, 385–395.

Thissen, D., & Steinberg, L. (1997). A response model for multiple choice items. In W. J. van der Linden & R. K. Hambleton (Eds.), *Handbook of item response theory* (pp. 51–65). New York: Springer-Verlag.

Thissen, D., Steinberg, L., & Fitzpatrick, A. R. (1989). Multiple choice models: The distractors are also part of the item. *Journal of Educational Measurement, 26*, 161–176.

Thissen, D., Steinberg, L., & Mooney, J. A. (1989). Trace lines for testlets: A use of multiple-categorical-response models. *Journal of Educational Measurement, 26*, 247–260.

van der Linden, W. J., & Hambleton, R. K. (Eds.). (1997). *Handbook of modern item response theory*. New York: Springer-Verlag.

Wainer, H., & Kiely, G. L. (1987). Item clusters and computerized adaptive testing: A case for testlets. *Journal of Educational Measurement, 24*, 185–201.

Wainer, H., Sireci, S. G., & Thissen, D. (1991). Differential testlet functioning: Definitions and detection. *Journal of Educational Measurement, 28*, 197–219.

Wilson, M., & Adams, R. J. (1995). Rasch models for item bundles. *Psychometrika, 60*, 181–198.

Wilson, M., & Wang, W.-C. (1995). Complex composites: Issues that arise in combining different modes of assessment. *Applied Psychological Measurement, 19*, 51–71.

Wright, B. D., & Linacre, J. M. (1992). BIGSTEPS Rasch analysis [Computer software]. Chicago: MESA Press.

Yen, W. M. (1984). Effect of local item dependence on the fit and equating performance of the three-parameter logistic model. *Applied Psychological Measurement, 8*, 125–145.

Yen, W. M. (1993). Scaling performance assessments: Strategies for managing local item dependence. *Journal of Educational Measurement, 30*, 187–214.

Yen, W. M., & Ferrara, S. (1997). The Maryland School Performance Assessment Program: Performance assessment with psychometric quality suitable for high stakes usage. *Educational and Psychological Measurement, 57*, 60–84.

Part II

FACTOR ANALYTIC THEORY

Chapter 5

Factor Analysis for Items Scored in Two Categories

Lori D. McLeod
Research Triangle Institute

Kimberly A. Swygert
Law School Admission Council

David Thissen
University of North Carolina at Chapel Hill

The process of test development includes checks of validity, reliability, and internal consistency for a set of items selected to measure a desired construct. Factor analysis may provide evidence that a set of test items really measures the one (or more) proficiency (or proficiencies) for which the items were designed, by providing a description of the underlying structure of the test.

Factor analysis suggests the constructs (or factors) that a group of items have in common by finding patterns in the covariation among the item scores. These patterns are then used to judge the extent of internal consistency for a group of items. For example, if items in a set measure the same aspects of proficiency, then all of the covariation within a group of student responses should be explained by the students' scores on this one proficiency factor. Then, if all of the items are found to measure one construct, a single score may be given to represent a student's ability level. Otherwise, if more than one factor is needed to explain the covariation among the items, alternative scoring (such as might be obtained by constructing subscales) must be considered.

The Relation of Factor Analysis to Curricular Objectives. Curriculum specialists often decide, based on the item content, which items are more appropriate for a test of academic achievement and which items do not belong. For example, a test designed to measure knowledge of mathematics should not include a verbal item because the verbal item does not measure the same aspects of proficiency as the group of mathematics items. However, an item may appear to measure the same proficiency, yet it may not belong with the others due to subtle differences that are only detected using item response data. For example, a mathematics test may include the following item: "What is the sum of twenty-two and ninety-five?" The remaining items may be given in the following format: "35 + 67 = _____." At a superficial level, a curriculum specialist may argue that the item containing text belongs, and that the text interpretation is another aspect of mathematics the students should know. However, this item may be measuring a student's reading proficiency more than his or her mathematics proficiency, and thus cannot be considered solely a mathematics item. If there were other relatively verbal items as well, a factor analysis might show that this item loads on a second factor that may be considered a reading factor.

Curriculum specialists also need to know which items weakly measure the construct and which items are performing better, and the extent to which items measure the same or different constructs. These distinctions among items may not be readily made from simple descriptive statistics or using subjective judgment; item discrimination indices may indicate the strength of each item's relation with a single construct, but those statistics cannot point to multiple factors. To analyze whether the items are indeed measuring the same knowledge, or different kinds of knowledge, and to estimate the strength of the relationships among a set of items, an empirical procedure should be used. Factor analysis is an appropriate tool for this task.

TRADITIONAL FACTOR ANALYSIS

There are many book-length treatments of factor analysis (examples are texts by Gorsuch, 1983, Harman, 1976, and McDonald, 1985). In addition, there are many developments and technical critiques involving the use of item factor analysis (e.g., Bock, Gibbons, & Muraki, 1988; Mislevy, 1986). There are very few nontechnical articles on procedures for doing item factor analysis. (For exceptions, see the readable introduction and overview of traditional factor analysis and its relation to classical test theory and item response theory in the text by McDonald [1985, chaps. 1 and 7], and McDonald's [1999, chap. 14] treatment of multidimensional item response models.) Nevertheless, item factor analysis is something that those who score tests that combine subject matter areas or item types very much want to do. Factor analysis is also used to examine the relationship of new item types with existing tests (see, e.g., Bridgeman & Rock, 1993). Therefore, before we introduce specialized methods to produce scores for combined item types (in chaps. 7 and 8), we discuss item factor analysis. The goal of this chapter (and chap. 6) is to describe some recently developed techniques that may permit useful item factor analysis. Before describing these new techniques, we briefly review traditional factor analysis.

Factor analysis is capable of revealing subtle aspects of data. To illustrate one possible collection of procedures and the outcomes, and set factor analysis in its traditional context, in this section we step back briefly away from item factor analysis to describe the factor analysis of two sets of hypothetical tests. The first set of tests is best described by a one-factor model and the second set of tests is best described by a two-factor model.

The first data set is composed of four tests, each designed to measure knowledge of mathematics. In factor analysis, the data are described with a regression model, in which the test scores are hypothesized to be made of two parts. The first part is the construct component (in our case, the construct is the latent variable that is common among the tests) and the second part is unique to each test. The unique part represents the uncorrelated component that remains when the mathematics component is removed from the test scores—the variances of the unique parts are associated with what were originally called *unique factors*, which are factors represented by only one variable. The model may be stated as

$$z_j = \lambda f_j + \varepsilon, \tag{1}$$

where z_j represents the observed standardized test score (with a mean of zero and a standard deviation of one) for person j, λ is the regression coefficient (loading) for the mathematics factor (or latent variable) for each test, f_j is the mathematics factor score, and ε is the unique or error component that is not correlated with the mathematics factor. The factor score f is an unobserved, or latent, variable, just as is θ in the IRT models introduced in chapters 3 and 4; it is merely a notational convention to use f for the factor score and θ for the IRT latent variable.

For a set of test scores, the regression model in Eq. 1 implies the values of the correlations among the tests. In matrix notation, the one-factor model may be stated as

$$\mathbf{R} = \mathbf{\Lambda}\mathbf{\Phi}\mathbf{\Lambda}' + \mathbf{\Delta} \tag{2}$$

where $\mathbf{R}$ is the correlation matrix among the test scores, $\mathbf{\Lambda}$ is a matrix (actually, a vector, for the one-factor model) that contains the factor loadings,

$\mathbf{\Phi}$ is $E(ff')$, which may be taken as the factor correlation matrix, and $\mathbf{\Delta}$ is $E(\varepsilon\varepsilon')$, a diagonal matrix containing the unique variances.

For the first hypothetical data set, the matrix of test score correlations, $\mathbf{R}$ is

$$
\begin{bmatrix}
1 & & & \\
0.64 & 1 & & \\
0.64 & 0.64 & 1 & \\
0.64 & 0.64 & 0.64 & 1
\end{bmatrix}
$$

and the solution of $\mathbf{R} = \mathbf{\Lambda\Phi\Lambda'} + \mathbf{\Delta}$ is

$$
\mathbf{\Lambda} =
\begin{bmatrix}
0.8 \\
0.8 \\
0.8 \\
0.8
\end{bmatrix},
$$

$\mathbf{\Phi} = 1$, and

$$
\mathbf{\Delta} =
\begin{bmatrix}
0.36 & & & \\
0.00 & 0.36 & & \\
0.00 & 0.00 & 0.36 & \\
0.00 & 0.00 & 0.00 & 0.36
\end{bmatrix}.
$$

For this data set, all four tests are associated with factor 1 with loadings (which are also the regression coefficients in Eq. 1) of 0.8. This factor accounts for all of the covariation between the tests; therefore, we can conclude that this dataset is unidimensional—it represents a set of tests that all measure the same thing (factor 1). The unique part of the variance for all tests is 36% $(1 - 0.8^2)$.

Now consider a second hypothetical data set that is also composed of four tests. However, the first two tests include mathematics questions and the other two are made up of verbal questions. A two-factor linear model for these data may be written as

$$
z_j = \lambda_1 f_{j1} + \lambda_2 f_{j2} + \varepsilon \tag{3}
$$

where the z_j terms are the observed standardized test scores, f_{j1} is the mathematics factor score, λ_1 is the coefficient for the mathematics factor for each test, f_{j2} is the verbal factor score, λ_2 is the coefficient for the verbal factor for each test, and ε is the error or unique variance not explained by these two factors.

For our second hypothetical data set, the matrix of test score correlations is

$$\begin{bmatrix} 1.00 & & & \\ 0.64 & 1.00 & & \\ 0.36 & 0.36 & 1.00 & \\ 0.36 & 0.36 & 0.64 & 1.00 \end{bmatrix}$$

and a (possible) set of solution matrices is

$$\Lambda = \begin{bmatrix} 0.71 & 0.37 \\ 0.71 & 0.37 \\ 0.71 & -0.37 \\ 0.71 & -0.37 \end{bmatrix}$$

$$\Phi = \begin{bmatrix} 1 & 0 \\ 0 & 1 \end{bmatrix}$$

and

$$\Delta = \begin{bmatrix} 0.36 & & & \\ 0.00 & 0.36 & & \\ 0.00 & 0.00 & 0.36 & \\ 0.00 & 0.00 & 0.00 & 0.36 \end{bmatrix}.$$

This solution is (essentially) the *principal-axis* orientation of a factor model that fits this data set. The principal-axis solution for a two-factor model is arranged so that the first factor contributes the most variance possible, and the second factor contributes the greatest additional variance independent of, or orthogonal to, the first factor. The factors are constrained to be uncorrelated with each other.

When a factor model contains more than one factor, the solution is not unique because any linear combination of the factors fits the data equally well. Thus, the solution may be transformed (or rotated) into many identical solutions. This is a special kind of indeterminacy that affects factor analysis. One way to visualize the indeterminacy is to think about the tests

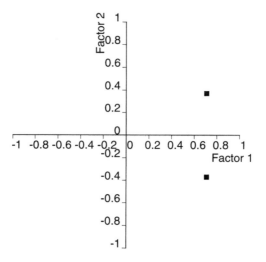

FIG. 5.1.   Principal-axis orientation of factor loadings for the hypothetical data described in the text.

graphically as forming a space based on their loadings.[1] The loadings are the coordinates on the axes that define the space. The graphs are useful for describing the rotations and the orthogonality (or lack of it) of the factors (axes). Figure 5.1 represents the principal-axis orientation for these data. Note that the axes are orthogonal.

One can change the axes without changing the relationships among the clusters of tests. For example, the solution matrices for our second example may also be:

$$\Lambda = \begin{bmatrix} 0.24 & 0.76 \\ 0.24 & 0.76 \\ 0.76 & 0.24 \\ 0.76 & 0.24 \end{bmatrix}$$

$$\Phi = \begin{bmatrix} 1 & 0 \\ 0 & 1 \end{bmatrix}$$

---

[1]Graphical rotation, as shown in Figs. 5.1–5.3, is of largely historical interest. The kinds of graphics shown in Figs. 5.1–5.3 were used before the widespread availability of digital computers to carry out transformations of factor structures—hence the name *rotation*. Since most of the computations involved in factor analysis have been computerized, analytical solutions that yield results similar to graphically aided rotation have replaced the use of such graphics in practice. However, the name *rotation* remains.

and

$$\Delta = \begin{bmatrix} 0.36 & & & \\ 0.00 & 0.36 & & \\ 0.00 & 0.00 & 0.36 & \\ 0.00 & 0.00 & 0.00 & 0.36 \end{bmatrix}.$$

This solution is (essentially) the orthogonal simple structure or *varimax* (Kaiser, 1958) orientation. When the factor solution is transformed using a varimax approach, the new factors are uncorrelated, as they were for the principal-axis factors. The varimax algorithm is intended to rotate the solution to "simple structure" (Thurstone, 1947, p. 181ff), to increase the interpretability of the factor solution. The requirements for simple structure state that the factor loadings should be relatively large and relatively small in value without any medium value loadings. Figure 5.2 shows the varimax orientation for the second example; note that Fig. 5.2 may be obtained by rotating (pivoting) the axes in Fig. 5.1 approximately 45° clockwise.

The solution matrices for the example may also be:

$$\Lambda = \begin{bmatrix} 0.8 & 0.0 \\ 0.8 & 0.0 \\ 0.0 & 0.8 \\ 0.0 & 0.8 \end{bmatrix}$$

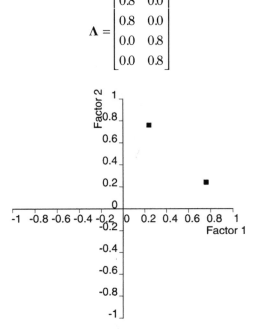

FIG. 5.2. Varimax orientation of factor loadings for the hypothetical data described in the text.

$$\Phi = \begin{bmatrix} 1 & 0.56 \\ 0.56 & 1 \end{bmatrix}$$

and

$$\Delta = \begin{bmatrix} 0.36 & & & \\ 0.00 & 0.36 & & \\ 0.00 & 0.00 & 0.36 & \\ 0.00 & 0.00 & 0.00 & 0.36 \end{bmatrix}.$$

This solution is an *oblique* simple-structure orientation, which is another transformation of the original solution. However, the new factors are not constrained to be orthogonal to each other. Instead, the factors are allowed to correlate in order to construct a more simple structure. In this way, Thurstone's (1947) principle of simple structure may yield more meaningful factors. The third figure for these data, Fig. 5.3, shows the oblique solution. Note that the angle between the factors is less than 90°—specifically, the angle is arccos(0.56), because 0.56 is the correlation between the factors. (Figure 5.3 shows a ghosted image of the axes of Fig. 5.2, to indicate how each has been rotated separately into the oblique reference system.)

These examples show that factor analysis reduces the group of tests into the factor (or factors) they have in common. These factors are the underlying constructs which the tests as a group indicate or measure. Factor anal-

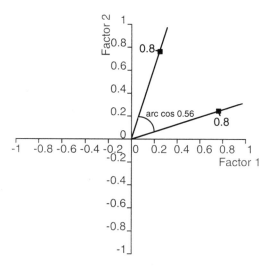

FIG. 5.3.   Oblique rotation of factor loadings for the hypothetical data described in the text. Note that the axes are not orthogonal.

ysis may be used to explore the interrelationships among tests through these underlying dimensions. Versions of traditional factor analysis procedures may be found in many software packages, such as LISREL (Jöreskog & Sörbom, 1995) or SAS procedures FACTOR and CALIS (SAS Institute, Inc., 1989).

ITEM FACTOR ANALYSIS

In the same spirit, item factor analysis may be used to explore the interrelationships among items through these underlying dimensions. By examining the magnitude of the item loadings for a factor, the value of retaining an item on a test may be investigated. In addition, the magnitude of the item loadings across factors may be used to assess the dimensionality of a test. Weak loadings for all items on a factor may represent error and not the verification of an additional underlying construct.

In many computerized statistical applications, the default steps for performing traditional factor analysis begin with the Pearson product–moment correlations, or the covariances, among the variables. Some caution should be observed, however, when applying traditional techniques for factor analysis to item-level data. The factor analysis model was designed for continuous data, not categorical item-level data. Carroll (1945) observed that the Pearson product–moment coefficient tends to decrease as the items analyzed become less similar in difficulty. Therefore, traditional factor analysis on the matrix of Pearson coefficients may produce spurious difficulty factors for the items (Carroll, 1945; McDonald & Ahlawat, 1974).

Some have suggested using tetrachoric correlations instead of Pearson correlations when factor analyzing dichotomous item-level data. These correlations are appropriate for categorical data that may be assumed to reflect underlying variables that are normally distributed. However, tetrachoric matrices for item-level data are often not positive definite, a property needed for many modern factor analysis procedures; in addition, when correlation values approach ± 1, estimates of the tetrachoric correlation become difficult to compute. Various corrections have been developed to overcome some of these problems, but they restrict the number of items analyzed (Bock et al., 1988). Furthermore, linear factor analyses using tetrachoric correlations have been found to indicate more factors than are actually present in the data (Hambleton & Rovinelli, 1986; Nandakumar, 1994). Solutions to the tetrachoric-based factor analysis problem do exist for short tests (Christoffersson, 1975; Muthén, 1978), but become computationally more difficult as the number of items analyzed increases. For the most part, those solutions do not include any specific model component for the guessing that occurs with multiple-choice items.

A New Approach Using Item Response Theory: Full-Information Factor Analysis for Dichotomous Items

A relatively new method of factor analysis proposed by Bock et al. (1988), full-information item factor analysis, avoids spurious difficulty factors and other problems associated with factor analysis of correlation coefficients. As a matter of fact, it does not use the interitem correlations, except for the possible use of the tetrachoric correlation matrix (smoothed to be positive definite) to compute starting values for the iterative estimation procedure. Instead, it uses the item response data directly. Thurstone's multiple-factor model is fitted by maximum marginal likelihood estimation in current implementations. Then the IRT parameter estimates are translated into factor analytic notation. The remainder of this chapter contains a description of full-information factor analysis and an example in which the method is used to study test structure.

A Multidimensional IRT (MIRT) Model for Dichotomous Items. Thurstone's multiple-factor model to item response data uses the observed item responses to describe an underlying process that produce the observed responses. The underlying response process may reflect many dimensions. In more detail, an underlying response process Y_i, for item i, is linearly related to several latent variable(s) $\theta_1, \theta_2, \ldots, \theta_M$:

$$Y_i = \lambda_{i1}\theta_1 + \lambda_{i2}\theta_2 + \cdots + \lambda_{iM}\theta_M + \varepsilon_i; \qquad (4)$$

Y and θ are usually assumed to be normally distributed and standardized across persons. θ_m represents the proficiency on dimension m; because of its roots in IRT, we follow IRT conventions in this section and refer to the latent variables with the IRT notation θ in place of the factor analytic notation f. The λ_{im} terms represent each item's regression coefficient, or weight attributed to the mth dimension for that item.

Bock and Aitkin (1981) adapted this model for dichotomously scored items, using the same theory described in chapter 3. Each item is assumed to be characterized by a constant γ_i, called the *threshold*, and:

- If $Y_i \geq \gamma_i$, the response is correct ($u_i = 1$).
- If $Y_i < \gamma_i$, the response is incorrect ($u_i = 0$).

If ε is normally distributed, it follows that the probability of a correct response as a function of θ is

$$T(u_i = 1|\theta) = \Phi\left[\frac{\lambda_{i1}\theta + \lambda_{i2}\theta + \cdots + \lambda_{iM}\theta - \gamma_i}{\sigma_i}\right] \qquad (5)$$

where $\sigma_i^2 = 1 - \sum \lambda^2$; an alternative expression is

$$T(u_i = 1|\theta) = \Phi[a_{i1}\theta_1 + a_{i2}\theta_2 + \cdots + a_{iM}\theta_M + d_i]. \tag{6}$$

Equation 6 is a version of Eq. 12 in chapter 3 for more than one θ; note that there are as many a terms (slopes) as there are dimensions, but there is only one difficulty parameter d_i for item i. The combination rule for levels of the latent variables expressed in Eq. 6 is linear, so having less proficiency on one dimension can be compensated by higher proficiency on another dimension. The addition of a guessing parameter for multiple-choice items gives

$$T(u_i = 1|\theta) = g_i + (1 - g_i)\Phi[a_{i1}\theta_1 + a_{i2}\theta_2 + \cdots + a_{iM}\theta_M + d_i]. \tag{7}$$

The logistic version of the multidimensional two-parameter logistic model is:

$$T(u_i = 1|\theta) = \frac{1}{1 + \exp[-1.7(a_{i1}\theta_1 + a_{i2}\theta_2 + \cdots + a_{iM}\theta_M + d_i)]}. \tag{8}$$

Although both the normal and logistic version of the model have virtues, many current implementations of MIRT use the normal ogive model. The factor analysis parameters are easily translated into their MIRT analogs using the equations in Table 5.1.

Summary Statistics. Some useful statistics for the MIRT model have been cataloged by Reckase (1985, 1997) and Reckase and McKinley (1991). These statistics are useful for evaluating a set of items for proficiency dimensionality and good discrimination. The first statistic meas-

TABLE 5.1
Translation Formulas Between MIRT Model
Parameters and Traditional Factor Analytic Notation

MIRT Model Parameters	Factor Analysis Parameters
$a = \dfrac{\lambda}{\sigma}$	$\lambda = \dfrac{a}{\sqrt{1 + \sum a^2}}$
$d = -\dfrac{\gamma}{\sigma}$	
where	
$\sigma = \sqrt{1 - \sum \lambda^2}$	$\gamma = \dfrac{-d}{\sqrt{1 + \sum a^2}}$

ures the multidimensional discrimination (MDISC) for a given item. Its formula is

$$\text{MDISC} = \sqrt{\sum a^2} \,. \tag{9}$$

MDISC is an item's maximum discrimination in a particular direction of the proficiency space. It is also useful to know in what direction an item is most discriminating; another index reflects that. This index is the cosine of the angle of the direction of highest discrimination with axis θ_m:

$$\cos \alpha_m = \frac{a_m}{\text{MDISC}} \,. \tag{10}$$

The angle α_m is the angle of maximum discrimination with respect to an axis θ. It follows that the mth coordinate of the point of highest discrimination in θ–-space is defined by:

$$\frac{d}{\text{MDISC}} \cos \alpha_m \,. \tag{11}$$

Full-Information Item Factor Analysis: Wisconsin Eighth-Grade Mathematics Test. Here we use the MIRT analog of the three-parameter normal ogive model suggested by Bock et al. (1988),

$$T(u_i = 1|\theta) = g_i + (1 - g_i)\Phi[a_{i1}\theta_1 + a_{i2}\theta_2 + \cdots + a_{iM}\theta_M + d_i] \,. \tag{12}$$

The maximum marginal likelihood (MML) method is used to estimate the a terms and d for each item. A version of the procedure is implemented for multiple-choice items in TESTFACT (Wilson, Wood, & Gibbons, 1991) that requires the item response data and g parameter values as input. The g parameters are treated as constants by TESTFACT and must be supplied by the user. These may be computed prior to running TESTFACT using such programs as BILOG (Mislevy & Bock, 1990) or MULTILOG (Thissen, 1991). For the factor analytic solution, the a terms are translated to λ terms using the formulas given in Table 5.1.

The data are the responses of 5,205 students who completed a Wisconsin Student Assessment System eighth-grade test of Mathematics. This test is made up of 30 multiple-choice and 3 open-ended items. The multiple-choice items test the student's knowledge of general arithmetic, algebra, fractions and percentages, table and graph interpretation, and some simple geometry. The multiple-choice items are graded as binary items (0, incorrect; 1, correct). The three open-ended items are word problems that assess knowledge of probability and algebra. These items, which require students to show their work and explain their reasoning, are scored from 0 to 3.

In this example we consider only the multiple-choice items (in chap. 6 we discuss the items scored in more than two categories.) The MIRT model was fitted to the set of 30 items using TESTFACT. The MIRT parameters are translated into factor loadings for a two dimensional solution. Table 5.2 shows the factor-loading tables for one-, two-, and three-factor analyses of the Wisconsin eighth-grade math data. For the two- and three-factor solutions, the default TESTFACT promax rotation to oblique simple structure is shown in Table 5.2. The contrast between the boldface and roman-printed loadings for the two-factor oblique solution in Table 5.2 shows that the two (correlated) factors are best represented by items 1–18 and 19–30, respectively. The (two) bold entries in the three-factor solution indicate that the third factor, although statistically significant, represents a doublet—local dependence.

Item 10 from this test provides the scale of a hypothetical map (1 inch represents 100 miles) and asks for the number of miles represented by $2\frac{3}{4}$ inches. Figure 5.4 shows the *trace surface* for Item 10. This surface (and the associated a parameters, or the factor loadings shown in Table 5.2) shows that the item discriminates more for Factor 1 than for Factor 2. Graphics like Fig. 5.4 are two-dimensional analogs of graphics like the top panel of Fig. 3.8. In a wire-grid plot like Fig. 5.4, each line in the grid is a trace line across one of the θ terms, conditional on some specified value of the other θ. (The orthogonal axes from the varimax rotation are used in the wire-grid plots, not the oblique axes of the promax-rotated loadings in Table 5.2.)

Item 28 includes an illustration of a rectangular box with specified dimensions, and asks the examinee to compute the volume. The correct response for this item has the response surface represented in Fig. 5.5. This item discriminates more equally for the two dimensions; note that the plot rises almost equally as values of either θ_1 or θ_2 increase.

The multidimensional IRT summary statistics may be used to describe the items graphically in the test's multidimensional θ-space using vectors in an arrow plot (Reckase, 1997). MDISC is used as the length of a vector, so that reflects the item's maximum discrimination, and α_m is used as the angle for the direction of the vector, showing the direction of maximum discrimination. Figure 5.6 shows the arrow plot for the 30 items plotted in the Wisconsin eighth-grade math test's two-dimensional θ-space. The two tightly bundled groups of arrows indicate the two dimensions covered by the test. For the most part, the first 18 items are algebraic in character, like Item 10, while the final 12, like Item 28, use more geometry; Fig. 5.6, or, equivalently, the loadings for the two-factor solution in Table 5.2 show

TABLE 5.2
Factor Loadings for the One-, Two-, and Three-Factor Models for the
Multiple-Choice Items of the Wisconsin Eighth-Grade Mathematics Test

		Two-Factor		Three-Factor		
Item	λ	λ_1	λ_2	λ_1	λ_2	λ_3
1	.5	**.5**	.0	.5	.1	.0
2	.4	**.4**	.0	.4	.0	.0
3	.4	**.5**	−.0	.4	.0	−.0
4	.7	**.7**	−.0	.7	−.0	.0
5	.7	**.7**	−.0	.7	−.0	.0
6	.7	**.6**	.1	.7	−.0	.1
7	.7	**.8**	.0	.8	−.0	.0
8	.6	**.7**	−.1	.7	−.0	−.0
9	.4	**.3**	.1	.3	.1	−.0
10	.8	**.8**	.0	.8	.0	.0
11	.7	**.8**	−.1	.8	−.0	−.0
12	.6	**.7**	−.0	.6	.1	−.1
13	.4	**.4**	−.0	.4	.0	−.0
14	.5	**.5**	.0	.4	.2	−.1
15	.7	**.6**	.1	.6	.2	.0
16	.6	**.6**	.0	.6	.1	.0
17	.4	**.3**	.1	.3	.2	−.0
18	.7	**.4**	.3	.3	.4	−.1
19	.5	.0	**.5**	−.1	.7	−.2
20	.5	.2	**.3**	.1	.4	−.1
21	.6	.1	**.5**	−.0	.7	−.1
22	.7	.1	**.7**	.0	.7	.1
23	.6	.1	**.6**	−.0	.7	−.0
24	.7	.0	**.7**	−.0	.7	.1
25	.7	.2	**.6**	.2	.5	.1
26	.6	.1	**.6**	−.1	.8	−.0
27	.8	−.0	**.9**	.2	.1	**.8**
28	.8	−.1	**.9**	.1	.2	**.8**
29	.7	.2	**.5**	.2	.5	.1
30	.7	.1	**.7**	.1	.5	.2
		Factor *r*		Factor **R**		
		1.0		1.0		
		0.8	1.0	0.8	1.0	
				0.5	0.6	1.0

Note. Contrast between boldface and roman-printed loadings shows that the two correlated factors are best represented by items 1–18 and 19–30, respectively.

that there are two highly correlated dimensions of proficiency measured
by this test.

It is probably best to stop the factor analysis of these data with the two-
factor solution. Although the extraction of a third factor yields a statistically significant improvement in fit, the values of the loadings in Table 5.2
make it clear that the third factor is a "doublet" (Thurstone, 1947, p. 182):

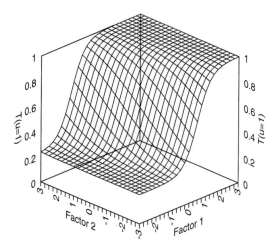

FIG. 5.4.   Trace surface fitted to the responses to item 10 from the Wisconsin Eighth-Grade Mathematics Test.

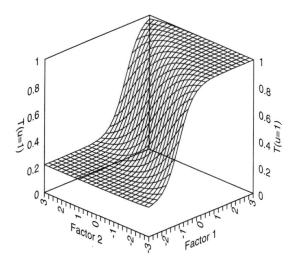

FIG. 5.5.   Trace surface fitted to the responses to Item 28 from the Wisconsin Eighth-Grade Mathematics Test.

"a factor which is involved in the variance of only two" items. This is an example of the kind of multidimensionality we refer to in chapter 4 as *local dependence*. The two items involved are Item 28, which involves the computation of the volume of a rectangular solid, and Item 27, which requires computation of the area of a rectangle given its dimensions. Clearly, the factor in common for those two items (and, it happens, only those two

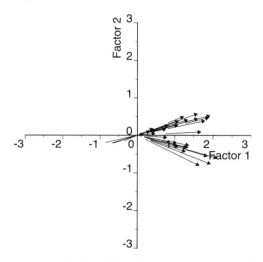

FIG. 5.6.   An arrow plot, in which each arrow represents an item on the
Wisconsin Eighth-Grade Mathematics Test; the origin of each vector is at
the point of maximum discrimination of the trace surface for the item
(computed using Eq. 11), the direction of the vector is the direction of maximum discrimination, and the length is proportional to the discrimination
index (MDISC).

items!) is a very narrow aspect of mathematics involving the application of
the formulas for area and volume. That and the adjacency of the two items
on the test form have the result that responses to these two items are more
highly correlated with their relation with the (other) common factors
would lead us to expect. However, the factor involved probably carries no
further explanatory power than that, and might better be considered correlated error of measurement. Thus, we concentrate on the two-factor solution that ignores the doublet.[2]

***An Aside: The Relation Between Higher Order and Hierarchical Factor
Models.***   An unresolved issue in item factor analysis has centered around
whether it might be best to use a simple-structure rotation (or a higher order factor structure with a simple-structure rotation at the first level), versus a hierarchical structure. Both structures have been applied to composite tests that may include different item types, or cover different content

---

[2]The appearance of doublets and triplets is a kind of nemesis of item factor analysis using
sophisticated procedures such as are described in this chapter and chapter 6. The procedures are very powerful and sensitive, and often detect the small disturbances in the data that
are induced by small amounts of local dependence between pairs or among triples of items.
In exploratory factor analysis, great care is required to avoid overfactoring before rotation;
otherwise, too many factors might be rotated with poor results.

areas. The higher order model describes the composites as multidimensional, but then accounts for observed correlation among the dimensions with one or more higher order, more general factors. The hierarchical model describes the tests as combinations of a general factor and several content- or item type-specific factors. McDonald (1999, pp. 188–191, 314ff) emphasized the usefulness of hierarchical models in item factor analysis.

Yung, Thissen, and McLeod (1999) proved an extension of the Schmid and Leiman (1957) result relating higher-order factor solutions with hierarchical (bifactor) solutions; Yung et al. showed how the two models are identical. Their result can be used to produce more easily-interpretable item factor analysis. Figure 5.7 illustrates the Yung et al. result graphically, using the conventions of path diagrams.

The left panel of Fig. 5.7 shows a path diagram representation of a modified second-order factor structure for seven items in two classes (A and B). Factors $\mathcal{A}$ and $\mathcal{B}$ account for the covariation among the items in classes A and B respectively, and factor $\mathcal{G}$ accounts for the covariation between factors $\mathcal{A}$ and $\mathcal{B}$. The paths labeled g (from the general factor $\mathcal{G}$ to the observed variables) are not normally included in a second-order factor

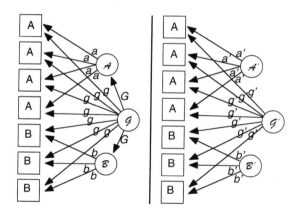

FIG. 5.7.   Left panel: Path diagram representation of a modified second-order factor structure for seven items in two classes (A and B). Factors $\mathcal{A}$ and $\mathcal{B}$ account for the covariation among the items in classes A and B respectively, and factor $\mathcal{G}$ accounts for the covariation between factors $\mathcal{A}$ and $\mathcal{B}$. (The paths labeled g [from the general factor $\mathcal{G}$ to the observed variables] are not normally included in a second-order factor model.) Right panel: Path diagram representation of a hierarchical factor structure for seven items in two classes (A and B). Factor $\mathcal{G}'$ accounts for the covariation that is in common to all items in both classes, whereas factors $\mathcal{A}'$ and $\mathcal{B}'$ account for the covariation that is unique within classes A and B, respectively. The three factors are orthogonal.

TABLE 5.3
Factor Loadings Corresponding to the Paths in the Left Panel of
Fig. 5.7 for the Observed Variables (Items Designated A and B) on the
General Second-Order Factor $\mathcal{G}$, and the First-Order Factors $\mathcal{A}$ and $\mathcal{B}$

Items/Testlets	$\mathcal{G}$	$\mathcal{A}$	$\mathcal{B}$
A	g	a	0
A	g	a	0
A	g	a	0
A	g	a	0
B	g	0	b
B	g	0	b
B	g	0	b

model.[3] Table 5.3 shows a way in which the path diagram in the left panel
of Fig. 5.7 might be displayed as a table of factor loadings—in the diagram, the lower-case a, b, and g terms represent loadings. The zeros in Table 5.3 are fixed in advance, and represent arrows that are not present in
Fig. 5.7. The methods of confirmatory factor analysis and structural equation modeling (discussed in chap. 6) can be used to fit the factor model
with such constraints; indeed, those methods can be used to fit the second-
order model as it is shown in the left panel of Fig. 5.7.

The conventional interpretation of the second-order factor model
shown in the left panel of Fig. 5.7, and represented schematically in Table
5.3, is that the item set is multidimensional, with factors $\mathcal{A}$ and $\mathcal{B}$. Those
factors, in turn, are correlated, and that correlation is due to the dependence of both factors on the higher order factor $\mathcal{G}$. The left panel of Fig. 5.7
adds to the usual second-order factor model so-called *direct effects* between
the general factor $\mathcal{G}$ and the observed variables (the items)—those are represented by the loadings g. Although this model is difficult to fit to data, it
makes a great deal of sense as a model for item response data, with a
superordinate general factor (or latent variable) accounting for covariation among all of the items, which, in turn, may be in clusters.

The right panel of Fig. 5.7 shows a path diagram representation of a hierarchical factor structure for the same seven items in two classes (A and
B). In the hierarchical solution, the factor $\mathcal{G}'$ accounts for the covariation
that is in common to all items in both classes, whereas factors $\mathcal{A}'$ and $\mathcal{B}'$ account for the covariation that is unique within classes A and B, respec-

---

[3]Figure 5.7 lacks some of the details that are usually included in such path models; specifically, the unique variance terms are omitted. In addition, the model in the left panel of Fig.
5.7 is not identified without the imposition of (somewhat arbitrary) constraints; see Yung et
al. (1999) for details.

TABLE 5.4

Factor Loadings Corresponding to the Paths in the Right Panel of
Fig. 5.7 for the Observed Variables (Items Designated A and B) on the
General Factor $\mathcal{G}'$, and the Orthogonal Group Factors $\mathcal{A}'$ and $\mathcal{B}'$

Items/Testlets	$\mathcal{G}'$	$\mathcal{A}'$	$\mathcal{B}'$
A	g'	a'	0
A	g'	a'	0
A	g'	a'	0
A	g'	a'	0
B	g'	0	b'
B	g'	0	b'
B	g'	0	b'

tively. Table 5.4 shows the loadings in the path diagram in the right panel of Fig. 5.7 as they might be displayed in tabular form. The three factors are orthogonal; this is sometimes called a bifactor solution, because each item has a nonzero loading on two, and only two, factors. It is important to note in comparing the two panels of Fig. 5.7, or Table 5.3 with Table 5.4, that the factor loadings g' are not the same as g; similarly, the loadings a' are not the same as a, and the values of b' are not the same as b.

The hierarchical structure in the right panel of Fig. 5.7, and in Table 5.4, also has straightforward interpretation for item factor analysis: If the loadings on the general factor (g') are relatively larger than the loadings on the Factors $\mathcal{A}'$ and $\mathcal{B}'$ (a' and b'), we conclude that the set of items is primarily unidimensional with smaller clustering of subsets of the items that may or may not be problematic for unidimensional models, depending on its magnitude.

Yung et al. (1999) showed that the models in the two panels of Fig. 5.7 (or the models represented by Tables 5.3 and 5.4) are identical—one is a transformation of the other. Specifically, the model in the right panel of Fig. 5.7 represents an orthogonalized version of the model in the left panel—so that in the right panel, all of the overall covariance among the items is accounted for by the general factor, and only covariance unique within subsets of items is included in that accounted for by factors $\mathcal{A}'$ and $\mathcal{B}'$.

Because the models are actually the same, and because the model in the right panel of Fig. 5.7 is, generally speaking, easier to fit to data than the higher order model, it is usually advantageous to fit the hierarchical model. The interpretation of the model may take advantage of either structure shown in Fig. 5.7; Yung et al. showed how to transform the loadings for one model into the values that would be obtained if the other form had been used.

Full-Information Item Factor Analysis: Wisconsin Eighth-Grade Mathematics Test—Target Rotation to (Near) Hierarchical Form. To return to the Wisconsin eighth-grade reading test data, Table 5.5 shows the loadings from the two-factor solution (in Table 5.2) rotated to most closely approximate a hierarchical factor solution in which there is a general factor common to all of the items, and a factor with nonzero loadings for items 19–30 (largely, geometry items). This model is a subset of the full hierarchical factor model, which would also include an orthogonal third factor with nonzero loadings for items 1–18; we are assuming that those loadings are uniformly zero, and that all of the covariation among items 1–18 is accounted for by the general factor.

TABLE 5.5
Target-Rotated Factor Loadings for the Two-Factor Model for the
Multiple-Choice Items of the Wisconsin Eighth-Grade Mathematics Test

Item	λ_1	λ_2
1	**.6**	.0
2	**.4**	−.0
3	**.4**	−.0
4	**.7**	−.0
5	**.7**	−.0
6	**.7**	.0
7	**.8**	−.0
8	**.6**	−.1
9	**.4**	.0
10	**.8**	.0
11	**.8**	−.1
12	**.6**	−.0
13	**.4**	−.0
14	**.5**	.0
15	**.7**	.0
16	**.6**	.0
17	**.4**	.1
18	**.7**	.1
19	**.4**	**.3**
20	**.4**	**.2**
21	**.5**	**.3**
22	**.7**	**.4**
23	**.6**	**.3**
24	**.6**	**.4**
25	**.6**	**.3**
26	**.6**	**.3**
27	**.7**	**.5**
28	**.6**	**.6**
29	**.6**	**.3**
30	**.7**	**.4**

Note. Boldface loadings are those rotated to non-zero target values, while the target value for roman-printed loadings was zero.

To compute the loadings shown in Table 5.5, we used the computer program CEFA (Browne, Cudeck, Tateneni, & Mels, 1998), which implements Browne's (1972) procedure permitting the rotation of a matrix of factor loadings to a partially specified target. We specified that the loadings on the second factor for items 1–18 should be zero, and then transformed the entire set of loadings so that criterion is most nearly met. The result is the set of loadings in Table 5.5, in which all of the loadings for items 1–18 on the second factor are 0.0 or ±0.1; the loadings of all of the items on the first (general) factor range from 0.4 to 0.7, and the loadings of items 19–30 on the second factor are smaller, ranging from 0.2 to 0.6. This rotational solution is probably the most easily interpretable result for the exploratory analysis of these data: It shows a strong general factor (so the test is nearly unidimensional), with a weaker factor indicating a slight contribution from a second dimension for the geometry items. That is the same conclusion we reach on examination of Fig. 5.6.

Full-Information Item Factor Analysis: Wisconsin Eighth-Grade Mathematics Test—Bi-factor Analysis. Hierarchical factor models of the form shown schematically in Table 5.4 and the right panel of Fig. 5.7 are called "bi-factor" models because each item has nonzero loadings on exactly two factors: the general factor (which has nonzero loadings for all items) and one group factor.[4] Gibbons and Hedeker (1992) showed that if full-information item factor analysis is specialized for the bi-factor model, the computational load is greatly reduced over that for a general analysis with the same number of factors; the savings are due to the fact that only two dimensions are involved in the computations for each item, regardless of the total number of factors. TESTFACT 3.0 (Bock et al., 2000) implemented the Gibbons–Hedeker algorithm for full-information bi-factor analysis, as well as general full-information item factor analysis.

In the application of confirmatory full-information bi-factor analysis to the data from the Wisconsin eighth-grade mathematics test, we use a priori information about the items—the facts that items 1–18 are largely algebraic and items 19–30 are predominantly geometric—as well as information gleaned from the exploratory factor analyses of these items described previously. We fitted a two-factor bi-factor model with one group factor for the geometric items, and a three-factor bi-factor model with two group factors, one for the geometric items and one for the algebraic items, and a four-factor bi-factor model, which added a factor for the items 27–28 doublet we observed in the exploratory analysis. The factor loadings for those three models are shown in Table 5.6.

---

[4]In a bi-factor model, an item may have a nonzero loading only on the general factor, in which case that item has only one nonzero loading, not the definitional two—but such a model is the exception that proves the rule.

TABLE 5.6
Factor Loadings for the Two-, Three-, and Four-Factor
Bifactor Models for the Multiple-Choice Items of the
Wisconsin Eighth-Grade Mathematics Test

Item	Two-Factor		Three-Factor			Four-Factor			
	λ_1	λ_2	λ_1	λ_2	λ_3	λ_1	λ_2	λ_3	λ_4
1	.6		.5		.2	.5		.3	
2	.4		.4		.2	.4		.2	
3	.4		.4		.2	.4		.2	
4	.7		.6		.4	.6		.4	
5	.7		.6		.4	.6		.4	
6	.7		.7		.3	.7		.3	
7	.8		.7		.4	.7		.4	
8	.6		.5		.4	.5		.4	
9	.4		.4		.1	.4		.1	
10	.8		.8		.4	.8		.4	
11	.8		.7		.4	.7		.4	
12	.6		.6		.3	.6		.3	
13	.4		.3		.2	.3		.2	
14	.5		.5		.2	.5		.2	
15	.7		.7		.3	.7		.3	
16	.7		.6		.3	.6		.3	
17	.4		.4		.1	.4		.1	
18	.7		.7		.1	.7		.1	
19	.5	.2	.5	−.0		.5	.2		
20	.5	.2	.5	−.0		.5	.1		
21	.5	.3	.6	.0		.6	.2		
22	.7	.4	.8	.2		.7	.3		
23	.6	.3	.7	.1		.6	.3		
24	.6	.4	.7	.2		.7	.3		
25	.7	.3	.7	.1		.7	.2		
26	.6	.3	.7	.1		.6	.4		
27	.7	.5	.7	.6		.8			.6
28	.7	.6	.7	.6		.8			.6
29	.6	.3	.7	.1		.7	.1		
30	.7	.4	.7	.2		.7	.1		

The two-factor bi-factor analysis gives loadings (tabulated in the left section of Table 5.6) that are nearly identical to those obtained with target rotation of the exploratory two-factor solution (in Table 5.5). A difference is that the bi-factor results in Table 5.6 are truly confirmatory: Instead of the near-zero loadings on the second (geometric) factor for the algebraic items (1–18) shown in Table 5.5, the blank spaces for those loadings in Table 5.6 indicate that their values are fixed at exactly 0.0.

As was the case with the exploratory three-factor solution, the doublet comprising items 27 and 28 produces surprising results in the three-factor bi-factor solution, with estimated loadings shown in the central part of Table 5.6. In that analysis, factor 2 was intended to be a group factor for the geometric items, but only items 27 and 28 have loadings much different from zero; in a sense, that factor has been "stolen" to fit the covariation involved in the doublet. Factor 3 has the nonzero, but small, loadings we expect for the algebraic cluster of items.

The four-factor bi-factor solution shown in the right section of Table 5.6 includes a factor for the geometric subset of items, a factor for the algebraic subset of items, and a factor for the doublet. This final analysis shows the bi-factor procedure in its best light: Although it may be very difficult to obtain a stable four-factor solution in an exploratory factor analysis of data like these, it is easy to obtain this bi-factor solution, and likely it will have interpretable results. It is would have been difficult to obtain an exploratory four-factor solution because so many of the $4 \times 30 = 120$ factor loadings would have had ill-defined values near zero; those are difficult to estimate precisely. On the other hand, the three-factor and four-factor bi-factor solutions in Table 5.6 have *exactly the same number* of estimated factor loadings, 60, so the solutions are equally easy to compute.

Looking at the loadings in Table 5.6 for the four-factor solution, we see that removing the doublet (items 27 and 28) from the geometric factor has permitted that factor (for items 19–26, and 29–30) to resolve into a group factor with loadings similar in magnitude to those for the algebraic items (1–18). We note again that the loadings for the items on the general factor are substantially larger, in general, than the loadings on the group factors, suggesting that the test is largely unidimensional, although two group factors and a clearly locally dependent doublet exist. The bi-factor model, like the Bradlow, Wainer, and Wang (1999) model for testlets, provides an estimate of the percentage of total variance associated with each factor; for this analysis, 37% of the variance is associated with the first (general) factor, 2% is associated with the geometric factor and with the items 27–28 doublet, and 5% is associated with the group factor for the algebraic items. The remaining 54% of the variance is unique to the items.

Both the bi-factor model implemented in TESTFACT 3.0 and the closely related Bradlow et al. (1999) testlet model permit estimation of standard errors for IRT scale scores on the general factor of a test such as this to be computed in ways that correct for the fact that the test is not entirely unidimensional. As increasing emphasis is placed on the accuracy of test scores, and increasingly high stakes come to be associated with those scores, it is likely that testing programs may begin to use such subtle, but important, corrections to statements about the precision of measurement.

To conclude the example: TESTFACT integrates IRT and factor analysis, but future improvements are desirable; it would be useful to be able to do more general confirmatory models (see chap. 6) in this multidimensional IRT context, and additional rotation alternatives would also be helpful for exploratory analyses.

OTHER APPROACHES TO DIMENSIONALITY ASSESSMENT

This chapter has not been an exhaustive summary of the new approaches to dimensionality analysis for items scored in two categories. Roussos, Stout, and Marden (1998, p. 3) observed that

> test dimensionality assessment methods can generally be organized into a two-by-two classification scheme. First, the methods can be categorized as either parametric or nonparametric. . . . Secondly, the methods either attempt full dimensionality estimation (number of dimensions and which items measure which dimensions) or merely attempt to estimate or detect the lack of unidimensionality.

In this chapter and chapter 6, we concentrate on various approaches to item factor analysis, which are parametric methods (they assume a particular parametric model for the item response function, or trace surface), and which attempt "full dimensionality estimation." The methods of item factor analysis are straightforward multidimensional generalizations of the item response theory that we introduced in chapters 3 and 4, and that we use in the methods of chapters 7, 8, and 9, so they fit very well with the flow of reasoning we develop in this volume.

However, for many purposes alternate approaches to the assessment of dimensionality may be useful. Chief among recent developments in the nonparametric class are DIMTEST (Nandakumar & Stout, 1993; Stout, 1987) and DETECT (Kim, 1994; Zhang & Stout, 1999a, 1999b). The nonparametric methods answer many of the same broad questions that are answered by item factor analysis, such as whether a test is unidimensional, how many dimensions the test measures, and which items tend to measure which dimensions. However, the development of nonparametric methods has not yet evolved to the point of providing the more detailed results that are part of item factor analysis, such as estimates of the degree to which an item measures a dimension.

Strictly speaking, the DIMTEST method is not a factor-analytic technique; it is a procedure that uses a statistic T for a nonparametric test of unidimensionality. The purpose of the DIMTEST procedure is to test the IRT assumption of local independence for a set of items. The null hypothesis that T is testing is that the "essential dimensionality" (Stout, 1987) of a set of items is 1. The statistic T can be applied in either an exploratory or confirmatory way with the DIMTEST method. The DIMTEST method is useful because it makes no assumptions about the shape of the item response function, other than to assume a monotone, increasing function—that is to say, high scores mean more knowledge of a construct than low scores.

As an example, assume a test composed of 40 items that is meant to measure a unidimensional mathematics skill. The DIMTEST procedure requires that the 40 items be separated into a core set of items, called the assessment subtest, and the partitioning subtest, which places items in subgroups for further stratified analyses. If local independence holds for the entire math test, both the assessment and partitioning subtests will be unidimensional; if not, the assessment subtest items will load on at least one other dimension than the main math skill. These analyses can be performed in an exploratory fashion; if the researcher has no information about the supposed dimensionality of the 40 math items, the DIMTEST procedure suggests using the tetrachoric correlations to perform a principal components analysis that will identify items for the assessment subtest. On the other hand, the researcher may suspect a priori that 10 of the 40 items represent a dimension other than the main construct. Then the researcher can use the confirmatory approach, setting these 10 items aside as the assessment subtest and using T to see if these items actually represent a second dimension.

This has been a very simplified description of the DIMTEST procedure; for further information, see Nandakumar and Stout (1993) and Stout (1987), along with Stout et al. (1996), for a comparison of the DIMTEST procedure to other nonparametric tests of unidimensionality. A full assessment of the performance of the statistic is given in Hattie, Krakowski, Rogers, and Swaminathan (1996). The DIMTEST and DETECT procedures provide indications of whether some parts of a test exhibit multidimensionality relative to other parts; such statistical analysis may be sufficient for many purposes, but it does not provide the direct relations with unidimensional IRT that we seek here.

Nonlinear factor analysis (McDonald, 1967, 1981, 1982) is a set of techniques directly related to the multidimensional item response theory (MIRT) procedures described in this chapter and chapter 6. Like linear factor analysis, it operates on the correlation matrix and is thus "partial information" factor analysis. As described earlier, the MIRT procedures described in this chapter are full-information analyses. Because nonlinear factor analysis is not as directly related to the commonly used models of unidemensional IRT that create the central theme of this volume, we leave its treatment to other accounts; foremost among those is that by McDonald (1999), which provides an integrated view of many of the test-theoretic concepts we discuss from a point of view that originates in the factor analytic tradition.

CONCLUSION

Using factor analysis to investigate the structure of a test's items is an empirical way of studying the construct validity of a test. When a test is designed to assess a specified number of factors, the items should group themselves according to the factors for which they were constructed to measure. If a group of items is constructed to test only one area (or construct), then each item should have a large loading on that one factor and very small or negligible loadings on any additional factors. The magnitude of the loadings describes the way items measuring the same construct are associated to indicate a factor. The consistency for this group of items is shown empirically by the amount of variability among the item scores explained by this factor.

In summary, every useful factor is more or less independent of the other factors in the analysis. Also, every useful factor accounts for a relatively large portion of the variance among the item scores. See Mislevy (1986) for more detailed discussion of item factor analysis, or McDonald (1985) or Gorsuch (1983) for a thorough review of factor analysis.

REFERENCES

Bock, R. D., & Aitkin, M. (1981). Marginal maximum likelihood estimation of item parameters: Application of an EM algorithm. *Psychometrika, 46*, 443–458.

Bock, R. D., Gibbons, R., & Muraki, E. (1988). Full-information factor analysis. *Applied Psychological Measurement, 12*, 261–280.

Bock, R. D., Gibbons, R., Schilling, S. G., Muraki, E., Wilson, D., & Wood, R. (2000). *TESTFACT 3.0: Test scoring, item statistics, and full-information item factor analysis.* Chicago: Scientific Software, Inc.

Bradlow, E. T., Wainer, H., & Wang, X. (1999). A Bayesian random effects model for testlets. *Psychometrika, 64*, 153–168.

Bridgeman, B., & Rock, D. A. (1993). Relationships among multiple-choice and open-ended analytical questions. *Journal of Educational Measurement, 30*, 313–329.

Browne, M. W. (1972). Orthogonal rotation to a partially specified target. *British Journal of Mathematical and Statistical Psychology, 25*, 115–120.

Browne, M. W., Cudeck, R., Tateneni, K., & Mels, G. (1998). *CEFA: Comprehensive exploratory factor analysis.* Columbus: Department of Psychology, Ohio State University.

Carroll, J. B. (1945). The effect of difficulty and chance success on correlations between items or between tests. *Psychometrika, 10*, 1–19.

Christoffersson, A. (1975). Factor analysis of dichotomous variables. *Psychometrika, 40*, 5–32.

Gibbons, R. D., & Hedeker, D. R. (1992). Full-information item bi-factor analysis. *Psychometrika, 57*, 423–436.

Gorsuch, R. L. (1983). *Factor analysis* (2nd ed.). Hillsdale, NJ: Lawrence Erlbaum Associates.

Hambleton, R. K., & Rovinelli, R. J. (1986). Assessing the dimensionality of a set of test items. *Applied Psychological Measurement, 10*, 287–302.

Harman, H. H. (1976). *Modern factor analysis* (3rd ed.). Chicago: University of Chicago Press.

Hattie, J., Krakowski, K., Rogers, H. J., & Swaminathan, H. (1996). An assessment of Stout's index of essential unidimensionality. *Applied Psychological Measurement, 20,* 1–14.

Jöreskog, K. G., & Sörbom, D. (1995). *LISREL 8 user's reference guide.* Chicago: Scientific Software, Inc.

Kaiser, H. F. (1958). The varimax criterion for analytic rotation in factor analysis. *Psychometrika, 23,* 187–200.

Kim, H. R. (1994). *New techniques for the dimensionality assessment of standardized test data.* Unpublished doctoral dissertation, University of Illinois at Urbana-Champaign.

McDonald, R. P. (1967). Nonlinear factor analysis. *Psychometric Monographs, 15.*

McDonald, R. P. (1981). The dimensionality of tests and items. *British Journal of Mathematical and Statistical Psychology, 34,* 100–117.

McDonald, R. P. (1982). 1981, 1982 Linear versus nonlinear models in item response theory. *Applied Psychological Measurement, 6,* 379–396.

McDonald, R. P. (1985). *Factor analysis and related methods.* Hillsdale, NJ: Lawrence Erlbaum Associates.

McDonald, R. P. (1999). *Test theory.* Hillsdale, NJ: Lawrence Erlbaum Associates.

McDonald, R. P., & Ahlawat, K. S. (1974). Difficulty factors in binary data. *British Journal of Mathematical and Statistical Psychology, 27,* 82–99.

Mislevy, R. J. (1986). Recent developments in the factor analysis of categorical variables. *Journal of Educational Statistics, 11,* 3–31.

Mislevy, R., & Bock, R. D. (1990). *PC Bilog 3: Item analysis and test scoring with binary logistic models* (2nd ed.). Chicago: Scientific Software, Inc.

Muthén, B. (1978). Contributions to factor analysis of dichotomous variables. *Psychometrika, 43,* 551–560.

Nandakumar, R. (1994). Assessing latent trait unidimensionality of a set of items—Comparison of different approaches. *Journal of Educational Measurement, 31,* 1–18.

Nandakumar, R., & Stout, W. F. (1993). Refinements of Stout's procedure for assessing latent trait multidimensionaltiy. *Journal of Educational Statistics, 18,* 41–68.

Reckase, M. D. (1985). The difficulty of test items that measure more than one ability. *Applied Psychological Measurement, 9,* 401–412.

Reckase, M. D. (1997). A linear logistic multidimensional model for dichotomous item response data. In W. J. van der Linden & Ronald K. Hambleton (Eds.), *Handbook of item response theory* (pp. 271–286). New York: Springer-Verlag.

Reckase, M. D., & McKinley, R. L. (1991). The discriminating power of items that measure more than one dimension. *Applied Psychological Measurement, 15,* 401–412.

Roussos, L. A., Stout, W. F., & Marden, J. I. (1998). Using new proximity measures with hierarchical cluster analysis to detect multidimensionality. *Journal of Educational Measurement, 35,* 1–30.

SAS Institute, Inc. (1989). *SAS/STAT user's guide, Version 6* (4th ed., Vol. 1). Cary, NC: Author.

Schmid, J., & Leiman, J. M. (1957). The development of hierarchical factor solutions. *Psychometrika, 22,* 53–61.

Stout, W. (1987). A nonparametric approach for assessing latent trait unidimensionality. *Psychometrika, 52,* 589–617.

Stout, W., Habing, B., Douglas, J., Kim, H. R., Roussos, L., & Zhang, J. (1996). Conditional covariance-based nonparametric multidimensionality assessment. *Applied Psychological Measurement, 20,* 331–354.

Thissen, D. (1991). *MULTILOG user's guide—Version 6* [Computer software]. Chicago: Scientific Software, Inc.

Thurstone, L. L. (1947). *Multiple factor analysis.* Chicago: University of Chicago Press.

Wilson, D., Wood, R., & Gibbons, R. D. (1991). *TESTFACT: Test scoring, item statistics, and item factor analysis.* Chicago: Scientific Software, Inc.

Yung, Y. F., Thissen, D., & McLeod, L. D. (1999). On the relationship between the higher-order factor model and the hierarchical factor model. *Psychometrika, 64,* 113–128.

Zhang, J., & Stout, W. F. (1999a). Conditional covariance structure of generalized compensatory multidimensional items. *Psychometrika, 64,* 129–152.

Zhang, J., & Stout, W. F. (1999b). The theoretical DETECT index of dimensionality and its application to approximate simple structure. *Psychometrika, 64,* 213–249.

Chapter 6

Factor Analysis for Items or Testlets Scored in More Than Two Categories

Kimberly A. Swygert
Law School Admission Council

Lori D. McLeod
Research Triangle Institute

David Thissen
University of North Carolina at Chapel Hill

Chapter 5 introduced the factor analytic model, and its development as an IRT model for items with dichotomous responses. We also laid the groundwork for the claim that it is dangerous to assume that all factor analytic techniques are appropriate for any data; there are necessary distinctions among continuous, dichotomous, and polytomous (categorical) data. Researchers sometimes assume that items with many categories are equivalent to items with continuous responses, but this is not always the case. It bears repeating here that the fewer categories the data have, the more likely it is that the distribution of the variables will be sufficiently nonnormal to disturb procedures designed for normally distributed continuous data. Two possible negative consequences are attenuation of the Pearson correlation coefficient, and the appearance of spurious factors composed of variables that have the same category splits and so correlate more highly with each other than with other variables, even if all variables measure the same construct.

In this chapter, we discuss factor analysis for items that may contain more than two categories, but not so many categories that the responses can be assumed to be continuous. Developers of psychometric techniques are currently active in this area; the result is that available procedures are in a state of flux, and less has been completely accomplished than is desired. Nevertheless, data analysis is required for many extant tests, and for tests under development; we describe currently available techniques and the extent to which those procedures accomplished desired goals for the analysis of those tests.

Many tests contain items that are scored in more than two categories. Often these polytomous items use an *open-ended* (or *short-answer* or *constructed-response*) format, and the item scores are categorical ratings provided by judges. Although these may comprise an entire test, open-ended items may also be administered along with conventional multiple-choice, dichotomously scored items. A second type of "item" that is scored in more than two categories is the item parcel (Cattell, 1956, 1974; Cattell & Burdsal, 1975; Cook, Dorans, Eignor, & Peterson, 1985; Dorans & Lawrence, 1987, 1991), which is created by summing scores on several multiple-choice items. Item parcels are created to provide appropriate data to use conventional factor analysis to examine the dimensional structure of tests with dichotomous items. Another polytomous item type is the testlet (Thissen & Steinberg, 1988; Wainer & Kiely, 1987), which bears a surface similarity to Cattell's parcel. Testlets are used when clusters of items may exhibit local dependence (see chap. 4).

STRUCTURAL EQUATION MODELS FOR POLYTOMOUS ITEMS

Traditional factor analytic procedures for polytomous data have evolved to become a subset of the techniques known collectively as *structural equation modeling*, or SEM. These techniques have become the standard for factor analysis of polytomous items that result from categorical items, item parcels, or testlets. The statistical theories for SEM were developed in the 1970s (Jöreskog, 1973; Wiley, 1973), and this procedure has grown in usefulness to the social sciences (for two comprehensive texts see Bollen, 1989, and Hoyle, 1995).

When using SEM, a researcher tests structural models to examine the relationship of sets of observed variables to one or two sets of latent variables. The observed variables are modeled as linear combinations of the latent variables. The fitted SEM model is divided into two sections: the measurement model and the structural model. The measurement portion of the model specifies how the observed variables are related to the latent variables, and the structural portion describes the relations among sets of latent variables. Models that incorporate both elements are referred to as full structural equation models, whereas a model that has only a measurement section (i.e., one set of observed variables relating to one latent variable set) is a factor analytic model.

The measurement portion of the structural equation model is relevant for our purposes here; that part, for a set of observed variables (the y

terms) and a set of latent variables (the f terms),[1] may be described by the following matrix equation:

$$y = \Lambda f + \varepsilon \tag{1}$$

Equation 1 (a matrix equivalent of Eq. 1 in chap. 5) describes the relationship of the observed variables y with the latent variables f; the Λ matrix contains the factor loadings (commonly referred to as the λ terms), with an added error component ε.

There are two approaches to factor analysis in the context of SEM: exploratory and confirmatory. When most researchers think of factor analysis, they imagine examining a set of variables to determine how many factors can usefully be extracted. This technique, in which a factor structure is not specified beforehand but is instead allowed to emerge from the data, is an exploratory one. Some factor analytic software allows the researcher to develop models only in this way. However, SEM also permits a hypothesized factor structure that can then be assessed in both an absolute way, using fit functions and fit indexes, and a relative way, by constructing alternate, nested models and comparing their goodness of fit to that of the original model. Confirmatory analysis has the advantage that the researcher can incorporate theory and prior knowledge into the data analyses. Three commonly used estimation procedures for structural equation factor analytic models are maximum Wishart likelihood (ML), unweighted least squares (ULS), and weighted least squares (WLS).

Estimation Procedures

Equation 1 implies that the covariance matrix among the observed variables is

$$\Sigma = \Lambda \Phi \Lambda' + \Delta \tag{2}$$

in which Λ contains the regression coefficients from Eq. 1, Δ is the covariance matrix among the ε terms, and Ψ is the covariance matrix among the f terms. Different estimation procedures can be used, depending on the nature of the sample covariance matrix S that is to be fitted by the modeled covariance matrix Σ.

---

[1]Presentations of structural equation models usually refer to the latent variables with the notation η, but here we use f to remain consistent with the traditional factor analytic literature.

Maximum Wishart Likelihood (ML). When **S** is the covariance matrix (the average squared deviations and their cross-products, for the observed variables), the ML method is most commonly used. The ML method minimizes the function

$$F = log||\mathbf{\Sigma}|| + \text{tr}(\mathbf{S\Sigma}^{-1}) - \log||\mathbf{S}|| - p \tag{3}$$

where p is the number of variables, $||\mathbf{S}||$ and $||\mathbf{\Sigma}||$ represent the determinants of the sample and estimated covariance matrices, and $\text{tr}(\mathbf{S\Sigma}^{-1})$ is the sum of the diagonal elements of the matrix product of **S** and the inverse of $\mathbf{\Sigma}$. While the derivation of Eq. 3 as the likelihood criterion depends on mathematical statistics beyond our scope here, intuitive explication is possible: For a model that fits well, $\mathbf{\Sigma}$ (the fitted covariance matrix) should be similar to **S**, so $\log||\mathbf{\Sigma}|| - \log||\mathbf{S}||$ should be small, and $\text{tr}(\mathbf{S\Sigma}^{-1}) - p$ should also be small; both are zero if $\mathbf{\Sigma} = \mathbf{S}$. The use of this estimation procedure assumes that the observed variables have a multinormal distribution, which implies that the covariance matrix **S** is sampled from a Wishart distribution with parameters $\mathbf{\Sigma}$ and n—hence the name (Jöreskog, 1967). The assumption of multinormality can rarely be safely made about polytomously scored item response data.

Unweighted Least Squares (ULS). If all of the variables are measured in the same units, the simpler ULS estimation procedure can be used. The criterion function that is minimized for ULS is

$$F = \frac{1}{2}\text{tr}[\mathbf{S} - \mathbf{\Sigma})^2] . \tag{4}$$

ULS is not optimally efficient, and the underlying statistical theory does not support as many diagnostic statistics as have been developed for use with ML or WLS, so ULS is rarely used.

Weighted Least Squares (WLS). The WLS estimation procedures minimizes, using Browne's (1984) notation:

$$F = (\mathbf{s} - \hat{\mathbf{\sigma}})' \mathbf{W}^{-1}(\mathbf{s} - \hat{\mathbf{\sigma}}) \tag{5}$$

where **W** is a weight matrix that depends on **S** and the sample size, **s** is the vector containing the elements in the lower half of the observed covariance matrix **S**, and $\hat{\mathbf{\sigma}}$ is a vector of the corresponding elements of the fitted covariance matrix $\mathbf{\Sigma}(\mathbf{\Lambda},\mathbf{\Psi},\mathbf{\Delta})$. Theoretically, any positive definite matrix **W** may be used to yield consistent estimates; because this procedure is a special case of the generalized least squares (GLS) algorithm, it is sometimes called the arbitrary generalized least squares estimator (AGLS).

Browne (1982, 1984) developed a specific weight function that always provides asymptotically correct goodness-of-fit and standard error estimates. Browne's weight matrix is used in the SEM computer package LISREL for the computation of WLS estimates (Jöreskog & Sörbom, 1995a). The WLS estimation procedure is equivalent to Browne's asymptotic-distribution-free procedure (Browne, 1984), and does not assume multivariate normality of the response data.

Although both the ML and ULS estimation procedures are said to be robust to nonnormality of data (Boomsma, 1983; Harlow, 1985), the WLS procedure produces asymptotically correct versions of the standard errors for the parameter estimates and the chi-square goodness-of-fit measures, whether the data are normal or not (Browne, 1982, 1984). Therefore, when tests include polytomous items, such as a test that is all open-ended items, or a mixture of binary and open-ended items, WLS may be the best choice for fitting a structural equation model.

Factor analytic tradition invites the (often) unwise analysis of Pearson correlation coefficients. Jöreskog and Sörbom (1995a) reiterated Gorsuch's (1983) claim that, for ordered categorical data that are not themselves normally distributed, but may be assumed to reflect underlying variables that are normally distributed, polychoric correlation coefficients are a better way to estimate the population correlation ρ. The polychoric coefficients may be assembled into a correlation matrix, and that matrix may be used as S in the estimation of the factor loadings (λ terms) using either Eq. 3, 4, or 5, with Eq. 5, the WLS model, being the preferred choice.

Polychoric correlations may differ noticeably from the Pearson coefficients for the same data. To illustrate this point, polychoric and Pearson correlation matrices were calculated for responses from a 33-item test of reading skills, where the first 30 items are dichotomous and the remaining 3 are short-answer, 0–3 scored items (these data are used later in this chapter as well). Both correlation matrices were calculated with PRELIS (Jöreskog & Sörbom, 1995b) and are presented in Table 6.1. The first five variables included in the correlations are testlets, where the scores are the summed scores of several dichotomous items measuring closely related reading skills. The results differ when the Pearson coefficients are calculated for these data in place of the more appropriate polychoric coefficients; the most striking differences involve the sixth variable (the first of the open-ended responses), for which the polychoric correlations are about 1.5 times the Pearson values. This is due to the fact that the responses for the first open-ended item are distributed very differently than the responses to the other open-ended items and the testlets.

TABLE 6.1
Polychoric and Pearson Correlation Matrices for the
Wisconsin Student Assessment System Eighth-Grade Reading Test
(Variables 1 Through 5 Represent the Grouping of the
Original 30 Multiple-Choice Items into Testlets)

				Polychoric Correlations				
Item	1	2	3	4	5	6	7	8
1	1.0							
2	.36	1.0						
3	.27	.47	1.0					
4	.31	.48	.41	1.0				
5	.30	.45	.39	.43	1.0			
6	.21	.37	.33	.33	.36	1.0		
7	.21	.35	.31	.31	.33	.33	1.0	
8	.24	.36	.29	.35	.34	.34	.43	1.0

				Pearson Correlations				
Item	1	2	3	4	5	6	7	8
1	1.0							
2	.34	1.0						
3	.25	.45	1.0					
4	.29	.45	.38	1.0				
5	.28	.43	.37	.40	1.0			
6	.14	.26	.23	.23	.24	1.0		
7	.19	.32	.27	.28	.30	.21	1.0	
8	.20	.33	.26	.31	.30	.22	.36	1.0

Assessment of Fit

To evaluate a confirmatory factor analytic model, there are several statistics that may be examined: The parameter estimates and their standard errors, and the correlations among the parameter estimates are essential results (Jöreskog & Sörbom, 1995a). Parameter estimates should be of a sensible magnitude and direction, and their standard errors should be small. A t-ratio is sometimes computed as the ratio of an estimate to its standard error; the resulting statistic can be interpreted using an ordinary t-distribution. A large t-ratio, resulting from a relatively small standard error, identifies a parameter that is well estimated, given the data. High correlations among the parameter estimates (i.e., redundancies) indicate areas of poor model identification.

Global fit indices are also considered in evaluating a factor analytic model; the most commonly used are the χ^2 index, the goodness-of-fit index (GFI; Tanaka & Huba, 1984), the adjusted-goodness-of-fit index

(AGFI), the root mean squared residual (RMR), and the root-mean-squared error of approximation (RMSEA). Expert advice is inconclusive about which of these indices (or several others) is best; see Hu and Bentler (1998, 1999) and MacCallum, Browne, and Sugawara (1996) for alternative strategies.

The χ^2 index, in the case of overall model fit, should not be seen as much as a test of significance as an indicator of how far the data deviate from the model. High values indicate large deviance, small values a small deviance.

For the GFI, the formula is:

$$\text{GFI} = 1 - \frac{(\mathbf{s} - \hat{\boldsymbol{\sigma}})' \mathbf{W}^{-1} (\mathbf{s} - \hat{\boldsymbol{\sigma}})}{\mathbf{s}' \mathbf{W}^{-1} \mathbf{s}} \tag{6}$$

where $\mathbf{s}$, $\hat{\boldsymbol{\sigma}}$, and $\mathbf{W}$ are as defined in Eq. 5. The AGFI is the GFI adjusted for the degrees of freedom in the model:

$$\text{AGFI} = 1 - \frac{p(p+1)}{2d}(1 - \text{GFI}) \tag{7}$$

where p is the number of observed variables in the model and d is the number of degrees of freedom for the model. Both of these indexes have a range of 0 to 1; the closer to 1 the value is, the better fitting is the model.

The RMR is

$$\text{RMR} = \left[2 \sum_{i=1}^{p} \sum_{j=1}^{i} (s_{ij} - \hat{\sigma}_{ij})^2 \Big/ p(p+1) \right]^{1/2} \tag{8}$$

where the s_{ij} and $\hat{\sigma}_{ij}$ values are the elements of the observed and fitted covariance matrices. This index is an average of the fitted residuals and should be interpreted in relation to the size of the observed variances and covariances. Ideally, the RMR value should be small; Hu and Bentler (1999) suggested that values <0.06 are acceptable (in conjunction with acceptable values of other fit statistics).

The root-mean-squared error of approximation, RMSEA, is

$$\text{RMSEA} = \sqrt{\hat{F}_0 / d} \quad \text{where } \hat{F}_0 = max[(\chi^2 - d) / (N - 1), 0]. \tag{9}$$

RMSEA is one of the few measures of goodness of fit with known distributional properties; as a result, it is sometimes recommended in contexts in which confidence intervals or tests of significance might be useful (Mac-

Callum et al., 1996). Hu and Bentler (1999) suggested that models that fit satisfactorily have values of RMSEA <0.05.

Many of the currently available SEM software packages, such as CALIS (SAS Institute, Inc., 1990), AMOS (Arbuckle, 1995), EQS (Bentler & Wu, 1995), MPLUS (Muthén & Muthén, 1998), and LISREL (Jöreskog & Sörbom, 1995a, 1995b), compute indexes of overall fit. In addition, the LISREL package provides modification indexes for the model parameters. These are approximately χ^2 values with 1 *df*; this value indicates that, if parameter estimation were to be modified (i.e., by freeing a fixed parameter), the total χ^2 goodness-of-fit value would decrease by approximately the amount of the modification index. A modification index may be used to suggest how to modify a model to fit the data. This is analogous to the practice, in analysis of variance (ANOVA), of doing post hoc tests after the planned comparisons have been examined (Hoyle, 1995).

Taken to an extreme, data-driven model fitting can result in an overfitted model that will not be useful for a different data set, and the probability of Type I errors is increased (MacCallum, Roznowski, & Necowitz, 1992). However, when there is no well-developed theory to guide the analyses, the modification indexes can provide clues as to why the model does not fit.

Modification indexes may be used as indexes of local dependence as well. The appearance of large modification indexes (or residuals) can be taken as indicators that, even if the data set appears to be unidimensional overall, there may be small groups of items that are otherwise correlated, perhaps due to context effects. Examination of the standardized residuals yields similar information, but the residuals are not as easily interpretable numerically.

A NEW APPROACH USING ITEM RESPONSE THEORY: FULL-INFORMATION FACTOR ANALYSIS FOR POLYTOMOUS ITEMS

As noted in chapter 5, there are problems with using factor analytic techniques that are based on the reduction of the data to interitem correlation matrices. Using tetrachoric or polychoric coefficients in place of Pearson coefficients (as described in chap. 5 and in the preceding section of this chapter) is one approach to solving the problem. However, for dichotomous data, the use of any correlation matrix as the information for factor analysis carries with it potential problems, such as spurious factors that may be introduced by differences in the marginal distributions of the variables. With polytomous data, this situation is not as likely to be problematic, because the data are not split into so few categories. Still, an ideal model would bypass the problems of the correlation matrices altogether; along these lines, a factor analytic technique based on IRT has recently been developed for polytomous data. This technique is largely parallel to the IRT-based technique for dichotomous data described in chapter 5. Unlike the technique for dichotomous data, this new approach is suggested here as a supplement to, not necessarily a replacement for, the conventional factor analytic techniques employed in SEM.

This approach, described by Muraki and Carlson (1995), is full-information factor analysis, eschewing the analysis of correlations to use all of the information contained in the response category pattern frequencies. A consequent advantage of this new technique is that matrix-sampled data are relatively easy to analyze.

As was discussed in chapter 5, the response process Y_i that underlies a set of observed responses is linearly related to the latent variable(s) θ_1, θ_2, ..., θ_M [all notation here is parallel to that of chap. 5; again, we use θ to represent the latent variables (factor scores) in this IRT-based section, in place of f in the more traditional factor analytic section]:

$$Y_i = \lambda_{i1}\theta_1 + \lambda_{i2}\theta_2 + \cdots + \lambda_{iM}\theta_M + \varepsilon_i$$

with θ_j representing the proficiency on dimension j. A polytomous equation (parallel to Eq. 6 of chap. 5) for the probability of any response k as a function of θ is

$$T(u_i = k|\theta) = \Phi[a_{i1}\theta_1 + a_{i2}\theta_2 + \cdots + a_{i1M}\theta_M + d_{ik}]$$
$$- \Phi[a_{i1}\theta_1 + a_{i2}\theta_2 + \cdots + a_{iM}\theta_M + d_{ik+1}] \qquad (10)$$

or

$$T(u_i = k|\theta) = \Phi[z_k] - \Phi[z_{k+1}] \qquad (11)$$

where

$$\Phi[z_0] = 0 \quad \text{and} \quad \Phi[z_{k+1}] = 1.$$

The translation of the a and d values into their equivalents in factor analytic notation is the same as listed in Table 5.1. The difference between the model as described in chapter 5 and Eq. 10 here is that the polytomous model is based on a graded response model (Samejima, 1969) that is described in chapter 4. Therefore, there is no parameter g for guessing, as guessing is not part of the multiple-category IRT model, and the probability is a difference. Maximum marginal likelihood (MML) may be used to estimate the a terms for each category within each item, and the d. This procedure has been implemented in the computer program POLYFACT (Muraki, 1993), which is currently available but has not been widely distributed. As with TESTFACT, good starting values are required for POLY-FACT. These values can be created by smoothing the interitem correlation matrix and then using a conventional factor analytic technique to obtain preliminary estimates of the factor loadings. These serve as the starting values for the iterative estimation procedure.

The IRT approach to item factor analysis yields multidimensional trace surfaces for each polytomous item. In chapter 5, one trace surface was created for each possible response, correct and incorrect; plots of those surfaces for correct responses were shown in Figs. 5.5 and 5.7. With the polytomous model, there is one trace surface for each response. Examples of these trace surfaces are presented in Figs. 6.1 through 6.4, for one testlet from a test of reading skills. Figure 6.1 shows the response surface for the lowest response (0), and Figs. 6.2–6.4 show the corresponding surfaces for responses 1, 2, and 3 (the highest response). These surfaces are graphical descriptions of the probability of each response as a function of two underlying latent variables, θ_1 and θ_2; they are four-category, two-dimensional analogs of the three-category, one-dimensional trace lines shown in the lower panel of Fig. 4.1.

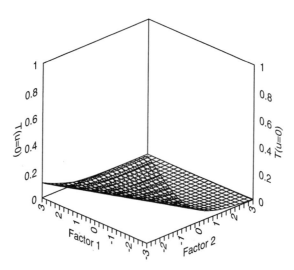

FIG. 6.1.   Trace surface for the lowest response (0) of a two-dimensional fit for a four-category item; the surface is graphical descriptions of the probability of response 0 as a function of two underlying latent variables, θ_1 (Factor 1) and θ_2 (Factor 2).

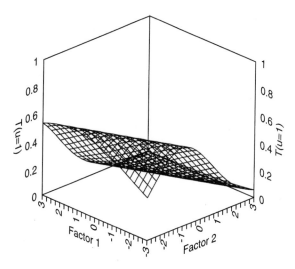

FIG. 6.2. Trace surface for response category 1 of a two-dimensional fit for a four-category item; the surface is graphical descriptions of the probability of response 1 as a function of two underlying latent variables, θ_1 (Factor 1) and θ_2 (Factor 2).

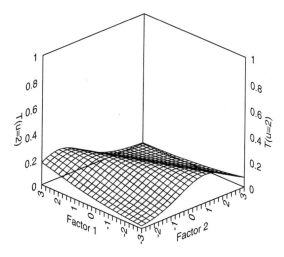

FIG. 6.3. Trace surface for response category 2 of a two-dimensional fit for a four-category item; the surface is graphical descriptions of the probability of response 2 as a function of two underlying latent variables, θ_1 (Factor 1) and θ_2 (Factor 2).

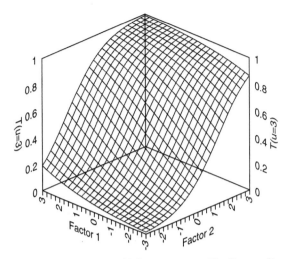

FIG. 6.4   Trace surface for the highest response (3) of a two-dimensional fit for a four-category item; the surface is graphical descriptions of the probability of response 3 as a function of two underlying latent variables, θ_1 (Factor 1) and θ_2 (Factor 2).

CHOOSING THE RIGHT ANALYSIS

One current problem, which may be resolved in the future, is that when tests are composed of both dichotomous and polytomous items, a choice must be made regarding which factor-analytic technique to use. There is no overall best solution at the time of this writing. The implementation of full-information item factor analysis for dichotomous items in TESTFACT (Bock, Gibbons, & Muraki, 1988) models multiple-choice item guessing, but not multiple-category items. The implementation of full-information item factor analysis for polytomous items in POLYFACT (Muraki & Carlson, 1995), or of WLS analysis of polychoric correlations, has useful models for multiple-category items, but has not been combined with a model for multiple-choice items with guessing. A combination of the two is theoretically possible but does not currently exist. In some of the examples to follow, we ignore guessing in the multiple-choice items; in other examples, we group sets of dichotomous and polytomous items into polytomous testlets, so that the techniques for polytomous items are more appropriate. Depending on the data and the theory underlying the data groupings (e.g., whether or not individual items accompany passages), there are several options open to the researcher.

A Relatively Unidimensional Test Combining Multiple-Choice and Open-Ended Items: The Wisconsin Student Assessment System Eighth-Grade Mathematics Test.   The data are the responses of 5,205 students who completed a Wisconsin Student Assessment System eighth-grade test of mathematics. This test is made up of 30 multiple-choice and 3 open-ended items. (The 30 multiple-choice items were also analyzed as the example in chap. 5.) The multiple-choice items test the student's knowledge of general arithmetic, algebra, fractions and percentages, table and graph interpretation, and some simple geometry. The multiple-choice items are graded as binary items (0, incorrect; 1, correct). The three open-ended items are word problems that assess knowledge of probability and algebra. These items, which require students to show their work and explain their reasoning, are scored from 0 to 3.

Here we examine the dimensionality of these data using confirmatory factor analysis and WLS estimation as implemented in LISREL (Jöreskog & Sörbom, 1995a). The process begins with the computation of the tetrachoric and polychoric correlations among the items, and the weight matrix $\mathbf{W}$, using PRELIS (Jöreskog & Sörbom, 1995b). Then a one-factor model is fitted using the WLS criterion; this model serves as the baseline model for comparison. The factor loadings of this model are shown in Table 6.2.

For these data, the values of GFI = 0.98 and AGFI = 0.98 are relatively large, so the models appears to fit well, and the values of RMR = 0.055 and RMSEA = 0.021 are also relatively small. However, the chi-square value is sufficiently large ($\chi^2 = 1662.36$ with 495 df, $p < .0001$) that it suggests that it might be possible to modify the model to fit better (again, the goal is to obtain a small χ^2 value, indicating that the data do not deviate significantly from the proposed model).

For the one-dimensional factor-analytic model, a few relatively large modification indexes appear in the error-covariance matrix of the items. Normally, errors among items are assumed to be uncorrelated, and large modification indices indicate that there is some covariance among the errors for item pairs that may be modeled. These large modification indices could be a suggestion of local dependence in the data, but here the large values do not appear to group together any sets of items that would make suitable testlets, and none of the item formats are sufficiently similar within the multiple-choice items to justify creating testlets on the basis of format. However, it is possible that the open-ended item group could explain some of the model misfit.

The next model fitted was a two-factor model, with the second factor having nonzero loadings for the open-ended items; the loadings are shown in Table 6.3. It is evident from the loadings that the three open-ended items do not constitute a valid second factor, as the last item is given an extreme loading—Factor 2 is effectively unique to the final open-ended item—and the first two open-ended item loadings are essentially zero. The fit statistics do not indicate a great deal of improvement in fit of

TABLE 6.2
WLS Factor Loading Estimates for the One-Factor Model for the
Wisconsin Student Assessment System Eighth-Grade Mathematics Test

Item	λ
1	.57
2	.40
3	.40
4	.68
5	.55
6	.46
7	.59
8	.46
9	.42
10	.77
11	.71
12	.62
13	.35
14	.52
15	.71
16	.58
17	.39
18	.65
19	.39
20	.44
21	.70
22	.57
23	.61
24	.52
25	.48
26	.52
27	.72
28	.70
29	.57
30	.62
31	.60
32	.37
33	.50

Note.   Items 1–30 are dichotomous, and items 31, 32, and 33 are open-ended.

the model to the data. The chi-square value barely drops (χ^2 with 492 $df =$ 1639.47, $p < .0001$), the GFI and AGFI indexes remain the same, and RMR = 0.054 and RMSEA = 0.021 barely decrease at all. (The factor loading estimates in Table 6.3 also represent a "Heywood case" [Lawley & Maxwell, 1971, p. 32]—that is the name given to the fairly common occurrence of improper solutions in factor analysis. The solution is improper because the sum of the squared loadings in the last row exceeds 1.)

For purposes of IRT scoring, then, it appears that the mathematics test can be considered unidimensional. There appear to be small pockets of

TABLE 6.3
WLS Factor Loading Estimates for the Two-Factor Model for the
Wisconsin Student Assessment System Eighth-Grade Mathematics Test

Item	λ_1	λ_2
1	.57	—
2	.40	—
3	.40	—
4	.68	—
5	.55	—
6	.46	—
7	.59	—
8	.46	—
9	.42	—
10	.78	—
11	.71	—
12	.62	—
13	.35	—
14	.52	—
15	.71	—
16	.58	—
17	.38	—
18	.65	—
19	.39	—
20	.44	—
21	.54	—
22	.70	—
23	.57	—
24	.61	—
25	.48	—
26	.52	—
27	.72	—
28	.70	—
29	.56	—
30	.62	—
31	.59	.03
32	.37	.02
33	.49	2.16

Note. Items 1–30 are dichotomous, and items 31, 32, and 33 are open-ended.

local dependence that may be due to pairs of items that are somewhat similar in format or that test almost the same concept, but the dependence in these data appears to be too small to be meaningfully modeled in this analysis. Most importantly, there is no evidence that the open-ended items measure any different construct than the multiple-choice items.

Testlets and Open-Ended Items: The Wisconsin Student Assessment System Eighth-Grade Reading Test. The data are 6,499 responses from a Wisconsin Student Assessment System eighth-grade reading test. The test is composed of 30 multiple-choice and 3 short-answer items. The multiple-choice items test the student's proficiency with reading short publications such as essays, stories, advertisements and menus, and are graded as binary items (0, incorrect; 1, correct). The short-answer items are 3 open-ended questions the student must answer after reading a short story. The student is asked to interpret the story, summarize the main idea of the story in a sentence, and write a short passage explaining why the story was titled as it was. These open-ended items are scored from 0 to 3.

In this example, we examine the dimensionality of these data using the WLS estimation procedure as implemented in LISREL, based on the tetrachoric and polychoric interitem correlations. A one-factor model is the first model to be fitted. The factor loadings of this model are shown in Table 6.4. The values of GFI = 0.99, AGFI = 0.99, RMR = 0.049, and RMSEA = 0.016 indicate that the model fits relatively well, but the chi-square value contradicts this interpretation (χ^2 = 1316.88 with 495 df, $p <$ .0001). The chi-square value is large enough to indicate a poor fit, indicating that the model could be modified to fit better.

For the one-dimensional factor analytic model, large modification indexes appeared in the error-covariance matrix of the items. These large modification indexes indicate that there is some covariance among the errors for item pairs that needs to be modeled. The largest modification index, with a value of 169.65, is for the last two, open-ended, items. The fitted residuals for the data, which show how well the observed covariance matrix is approximated by the fitted covariance matrix, show the largest residual value (.12) for this item pair as well.

There are other large residual values and modification indices for the one-factor model. These values appeared within small groups of items; for example, items 1, 2, 4, and 5 have higher modification indexes with each other than with the other items. The items are grouped by reading passage; first a section is provided for the student to read, and then several multiple-choice items are given that address the content of that section. This suggests that, rather than doing a factor analysis of all of the individual items, the items might be better grouped into testlets and a factor analysis then done on these testlets.

Therefore, we divide the items into testlets according to reading passage. Items 1 through 5 follow an advertisement passage, and those items are grouped into Testlet 1. Testlet 2 is composed of items 6 through 14, which all accompany a short story. Items 15 through 19 comprise Testlet 3, which tests for the student's understanding of a nonfiction essay. Items 20 through 25 make up Testlet 4, which asks students to synthesize information presented in a restaurant menu, and Testlet 5 is composed of items 26 through 30, all of which concern a history essay. The three open-

TABLE 6.4
WLS Factor Loading Estimates for the One-Factor Model for the
Wisconsin Student Assessment System Eighth-Grade Reading Test

Item	λ
1	.56
2	.57
3	.34
4	.16
5	.47
6	.58
7	.66
8	.61
9	.67
10	.35
11	.52
12	.64
13	.63
14	.65
15	.55
16	.58
17	.54
18	.44
19	.41
20	.48
21	.45
22	.42
23	.69
24	.64
25	.41
26	.42
27	.38
28	.65
29	.62
30	.47
31	.59
32	.55
33	.56

Note. Items 1–30 are dichotomous, and items 31, 32, and 33 are open-ended.

ended items are left separate. (The polychoric and Pearson correlations shown in Table 6.1 are for these data.)

A one-factor analysis of the testlet data shows that the fit improves tremendously. The values of RMR = 0.032 shows that the average difference between the observed and fitted correlations is substantially smaller for the testlet-level correlations; RMSEA = 0.032 is larger than it was for the item-level model, because RMSEA is sensitive to the number of variables

TABLE 6.5
WLS Factor Loading Estimates for the One-Factor
Model for Testlets for the Wisconsin Student
Assessment System Eighth-Grade Reading Test

Items/Testlets	λ
1	.46
2	.72
3	.62
4	.66
5	.64
6	.56
7	.55
8	.57

Note. Testlets 1–5 comprise dichotomous items, and items 6–8 are open-ended.

involved in the analysis. (The value of χ^2 for the testlet analysis, 220.15 with 20 *df*, $p < .001$, cannot be directly compared to the value obtained in the analysis of the individual items because a very different number of correlations, and hence degrees of freedom, is involved.). The values of GFI and AGFI did not change, but they were already close to the maximum with the ungrouped one-factor model. The factor loadings for this model are provided in Table 6.5. The chi-square value is still relatively large, however, indicating that some local dependence has not been addressed.

Recall that testlets 1 through 5 consist of grouped multiple-choice items, whereas items 6, 7, and 8 in the testlet analysis are the three open-ended items. Thissen, Wainer, and Wang (1994) presented several factor analytic studies in which they examined whether multiple-choice items and open-ended items appear to be measuring different constructs on a test, even if all the item types address the same general area of learning. In their study, they presented factor analyses of items from the advanced placement (AP) computer science and chemistry tests. In each case, the best-fitting models were ones in which the free-response item group was allowed to constitute a factor or factors orthogonal to the multiple-choice items. As we observed in chapter 5, Yung, McLeod, and Thissen (1999) have shown that this kind of hierarchical model is equivalent to a modified second-order factor model, and may be very useful for item factor analysis.

Therefore, the next model fitted to the testlet-scored data is a two-factor model, with the second factor having nonzero loadings only for the last three (open-ended) items; the estimated loadings are shown in Table 6.6. The results indicate a small improvement in fit of the model to the data: the *p* value drops, although not quite into the range of nonsignificance ($\chi^2 = 35.34$, $p = .0056$). The values of GFI = 1.0 and AGFI = 1.0 are as high as they can go, and RMR = 0.012 and RMSEA = 0.013 decrease a great deal.

TABLE 6.6
WLS Factor Loading Estimates for the Two-Factor Model
for Testlets for the Wisconsin Student Assessment
System Eighth-Grade Reading Test

Items/Testlets	λ_1	λ_2
1	.47	—
2	.73	—
3	.63	—
4	.66	—
5	.64	—
6	.53	.18
7	.49	.39
8	.51	.46

Note. Testlets 1–5 comprise dichotomous items, and items 6–8 are open-ended.

One more model is fitted, looking for continued improvement in fit: The five testlets that are made up of multiple-choice items are given non-zero loadings on a third factor, orthogonal to the first two. The three-factor model fits the data best of all, with the estimated factor loadings shown in Table 6.7. The p value of the chi-square statistic drops into the range of nonsignificance (χ^2 with 12 df = 18.45, p = .10). The GFI and AGFI values remain at their maximum (1.0), and the values of RMR = 0.008 and RMSEA = 0.009 fall yet again.

Another way to examine the relationship among the factor loadings for the eight testlets is to plot them on a two-dimensional set of axes. The plot of the loadings for the first two factors of the reading test is provided in Fig. 6.5. The loadings for testlets which load only on Factor 1 have all been placed at zero on Factor 2 (consistent with the constraints), and the other three testlets have their (λ_1, λ_2) loadings as the (x,y) values.

TABLE 6.7
WLS Factor Loading Estimates for the Three-Factor
Model for Testlets for the Wisconsin Student
Assessment System Eighth-Grade Reading Test

Items/Testlets	λ_1	λ_2	λ_3
1	.45	—	.13
2	.70	—	.32
3	.61	—	.13
4	.66	—	.06
5	.66	—	−.04
6	.53	.17	—
7	.50	.39	—
8	.51	.45	—

Note. Testlets 1–5 comprise dichotomous items, and items 6–8 are open-ended.

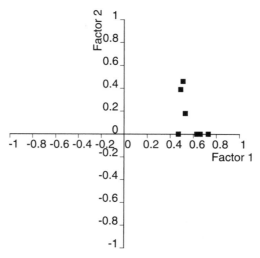

FIG. 6.5.   Plot of the WLS estimates of the loadings for the two-factor solution for the testlet analysis of the Wisconsin Student Assessment system
reading test.

For both the multiple-choice and open-ended testlets, the factor loadings are smaller on their separate orthogonal factors (Factor 2 for open-
ended, Factor 3 for multiple-choice) than on the first factor. In fact, some
of the factor loadings on the last two factors are very small (the highest one
for Factor 2 is Testlet 8, with a loading of .45; the highest for Factor 3 is
Testlet 2, with a loading of .32). These small loadings indicate that the
correlation of the observed open-ended scores with the underlying variable (proficiency at describing short-story information) being measured is
small, when that variable is considered separately from (or independent
of) the general factor underlying all responses. The same can be said for
the multiple-choice testlets, to an even greater extent; two of the testlets'
loadings on Factor 3 are very small, and two more are essentially zero. The
multiple-choice testlets thus correlate less with their individual factor than
with the first factor, which includes open-ended items.

This indicates that although a three-factor model provides the best fit
the data, in terms of giving the smallest chi-square and RMR and largest
GFI and AGFI, the two proficiencies on the test (the reading interpretation skills measured by the multiple-choice items and short-story description measured by the open-ended ones) are relatively indistinguishable.
One factor can be said to underlie the items, and the multiple-choice and
open-ended testlet scores may be combined to give one overall score on
the test.

To continue this example, the same data (testlet summed scores for the
multiple-choice items, and the open-ended scores) were also fitted with

the polytomous full-information factor analytic procedure using POLY-FACT (Muraki, 1993). The resulting factor loadings for the one-factor testlet data are provided in Table 6.8, and the varimax rotated loadings for the two-factor testlet data are provided in Table 6.9; a plot of the loadings is provided in Fig. 6.6.

The implementation of exploratory item factor analysis in POLYFACT requires the researcher to select some rotation; an oblique rotation is an option. Table 6.10 shows the oblique rotation of the two factors for the reading testlets, along with the correlation coefficient for the factors. The values of the factor loadings for the multiple-choice testlets are now much closer to zero for the open-ended factor 2. That and the estimated correlation between the two factors, which is 0.77, suggest that the correlated factors model may be more appropriate for the reading data than the uncorrelated simple-structure model.

TABLE 6.8
Full-Information Item Factor Analysis Loading Estimates
for the One-Factor Model for Testlets for the Wisconsin
Student Assessment System Eighth-Grade Reading Test

Items/Testlets	λ
1	.34
2	.45
3	.42
4	.43
5	.41
6	.37
7	.39
8	.41

Note. Testlets 1–5 comprise dichotomous items, and items 6–8 are open-ended.

TABLE 6.9
Varimax Rotation of the Full-Information Item Factor Analysis Loading
Estimates for the Two-Factor Model for Testlets for the Wisconsin
Student Assessment System Eighth-Grade Reading Test

Items/Testlets	λ_1	λ_2
1	.31	.14
2	.48	.19
3	.39	.18
4	.37	.21
5	.33	.22
6	.26	.28
7	.21	.48
8	.22	.49

Note. Testlets 1–5 comprise dichotomous items, and items 6–8 are open-ended.

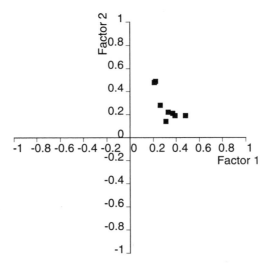

FIG. 6.6.   Plot of the full-information item factor analysis estimates of the loadings for the two-factor solution for the testlet analysis of the Wisconsin Student Assessment system reading test.

TABLE 6.10
Oblique Rotation of the Full-Information Item Factor Analysis
Loading Estimates for the Two-Factor Model for Testlets for the
Wisconsin Student Assessment System Eighth-Grade Reading Test

Items/Testlets	λ_1	λ_2
1	.36	−.02
2	.57	−.06
3	.43	−.00
4	.39	.04
5	.33	.08
6	.19	.22
7	−.02	.54
8	−.01	.55

Note.   Testlets 1–5 comprise dichotomous items, and items 6–8 are open-ended.

However, yet another rotation may be more interpretable still. Table 6.11 shows the loadings target-rotated to most nearly approximate the constrained solution in Table 6.6, using the Browne, Cudeck, Tateneni, and Mels (1998) CEFA software. This hierarchical structure shows a (relatively) strong general factor combined with a (relatively) weak second factor, which is essentially a doublet for the final two open-ended questions.

Multiple-category versions of the MIRT summary statistics described in chapter 5 (loadings that can be converted into angles with the reference

TABLE 6.11
Target Rotation of the Full-Information Item Factor Analysis Loading
Estimates for the Two-Factor Model for Testlets for the Wisconsin
Student Assessment System Eighth-Grade Reading Test

Items/Testlets	λ_1	λ_2
1	.34	−.01
2	.52	−.04
3	.43	−.01
4	.42	.02
5	.39	.05
6	.36	.14
7	.40	.34
8	.41	.34

Note. Testlets 1–5 comprise dichotomous items, and items 6–8 are open-ended.

axes, difficulty parameters that can be converted into points of highest discrimination, and MDISC) can be used to make vector graphics summarizing the performance of the testlets and items. Figure 6.7 shows an arrow
plot for the testlets and open-ended items of this reading test example, using the varimax-rotated full-information item factor analysis results. In
the multiple-category case, each item has one fewer arrows than there are
response categories; the location of the origin of each vector is at MDISC

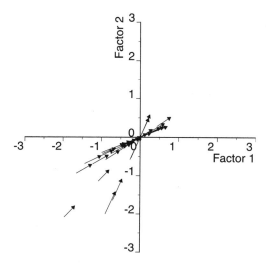

FIG. 6.7.   Arrow plot for the testlets and open-ended items of the Wisconsin reading test example, using the full-information item factor analysis results. Each item has three arrows; the location of the origin of each vector is
at the point of MDISC for the transition between category 0 and 1, and then
between category 1 and 2, and then between 2 and 3. The length of the vector reflects the item's maximum discrimination.

for the transition between category 0 and 1, and then between category 1 and 2, and so on. The length of the vector reflects the item's maximum discrimination. The fact that all of the arrows point in more or less the same direction in Fig. 6.7 indicates that the reading test is largely unidimensional; the variation from unidimensionality is shown in the cluster of three groups of arrows that are more vertical in orientation—those are the vectors associated with the open-ended items. (An arrow plot for the target-rotated loadings in Table 6.11 would rotate the axes in Fig. 6.7 around 30° counterclockwise, to place the axis for factor 1 coincident with the largest cluster of arrows.)

Thus, the conclusion with full-information item factor analysis is the same as the conclusion using WLS analysis of the polychoric correlations: Although the open-ended reading items do seem to form a factor separate from the grouped testlets, the factors are correlated highly enough that a single reading score would provide an adequate measure of a student's performance on this test.

This suggests a final model, which we return to the WLS analysis of polychoric correlations to fit: Along with the five testlets (one for each passage) for the multiple-choice items, we combine the responses to the three open-ended items to create a sixth summed-score testlet. Table 6.12 shows the factor loading estimates for the one-factor model fitted to the six passage summed scores. For this model, GFI = 1.00, AGFI = 1.00, RMR = 0.010, RMSEA = 0.028, and the value of the chi-square goodness-of-fit statistic is 34.14 with 9 df ($p < .0001$). The value of the chi-square statistic indicates lack of fit, but it is not particularly large for an analysis with a sample size in excess of 6,000. The other statistics suggest excellent fit. Based on this analysis, we used the six-testlet structure with unidimensional IRT models in examples in chapters 4, 7, and 8.

TABLE 6.12
WLS Factor Loading Estimates for the One-Factor
Model for Testlets for the Wisconsin Student
Assessment System Eighth-Grade Reading Test

Items/Testlets	λ
1	.47
2	.73
3	.63
4	.67
5	.64
6	.60

Note. Testlets 1–5 comprise dichotomous items, and item 6 is the summed score for the three open-ended questions.

Summary Comparison of WLS Analysis of Polychoric Correlations and Full-Information Item Factor Analysis. Two distinctions between the different model-fitting techniques implemented in LISREL and POLYFACT may be highlighted. One difference is that although the structural equations approach as implemented in LISREL provides several fit indices, the sole indicator of fit for the MIRT procedure implemented in POLYFACT (as with most IRT-based procedures) is the −2 times the loglikelihood. Although a full description of the −2loglikelihood is not suitable for this chapter, a useful fact is that the difference between a pair of −2loglikelihood values for nested models is distributed as a χ^2 variable. Therefore, although this index is not an indication of how each model fits, individually, the difference between the values for the one- and two-factor models tell us how much of an improvement the two-factor model is over the one-factor model. The index values for the one- and two-factor models for the eight-variable data are 123678 and 123491.1; the χ^2 difference between them is 186.9 with 7 *df*, $p < .001$, which shows that the two-factor model is a statistically significant improvement over the one-factor model.

A second difference between the structural equations model results and those obtained with the POLYFACT implementation of full-information item factor analysis is that there are nonzero factor loadings for all eight testlets for Factor 2 in Table 6.10, and small nonzero loadings in the target-rotated Table 6.11, where the loadings for the multiple-choice testlets were constrained to be zero in Table 6.6. The structural equations modeling system in LISREL requires that models be fitted as confirmatory models, so that fitting a model that has only testlets 6, 7, and 8 loading on Factor 2 requires that the other loadings be constrained to be zero. In a structural equations framework, the factor analytic model's indeterminacy of rotation does not arise; the model is identified by the placement of the so-called structural zeros in the matrix of loadings. Full-information item factor analysis is currently implemented only for the exploratory mode, so no such constraint is possible.

Testlets and Open-Ended Items That Do Not Measure the Same Thing: The Wisconsin Student Assessment System Eighth-Grade Language Test. These data include the responses of the 6,632 students who fully completed a Wisconsin Student Assessment System eighth-grade test of language skills. This test is composed of 30 multiple-choice and 2 open-ended items. The multiple-choice items focus on the student's knowledge of grammatical structure, expression of ideas, and sentence details such as punctuation and capitalization. These items are graded as binary items (0, incorrect; 1, correct). The open-ended items consist of a creative writing essay along with a letter-form essay that must display how well the student can present a point of view. Responses to these free-response writing prompts are scored by judges on a scale from 0 to 12.

First, we consider the results obtained with WLS analysis of polychoric correlations between the items. The initial computation of the tetrachoric and polychoric inter-item correlations is done using PRELIS, and the implementation of the WLS procedure in LISREL is used for the factor analysis. The one-factor model is the first to be fitted; the factor loadings for this model are shown in Table 6.13. For these data, the values of GFI = 0.98 and AGFI = 0.98 are sufficiently large to indicate that the model fits

TABLE 6.13
WLS Factor Loading Estimates for the One-Factor Model for the
Wisconsin Student Assessment System Eighth-Grade Language Test

Item	λ
1	.32
2	.35
3	.35
4	.62
5	.53
6	.51
7	.58
8	.42
9	.59
10	.28
11	.53
12	.49
13	.52
14	.45
15	.67
16	.70
17	.50
18	.65
19	.79
20	.52
21	.54
22	.65
23	.56
24	.52
25	.71
26	.49
27	.72
28	.68
29	.63
30	.57
31	.58
32	.59

Note. Items 1–30 are dichotomous, and items 31–32 are open-ended.

well, and RMR = 0.066 and RMSEA = 0.026 are also relatively small. However, the chi-square value is sufficiently large (χ^2 = 2503.18 with 464 df, $p <$ .0001) that the model could be modified to fit better. For the one-dimensional factor analytic model, large modification indexes appeared in the error-covariance matrix of the items, and these indicate that there is some covariance among the errors for item pairs that may be modeled. The largest modification index, with a value of 539.53, is for the last two, open-ended, items. The fitted residuals for the data, which show how well the observed covariance matrix is approximated by the fitted covariance matrix, showed the largest residual value (.14) for this item pair as well.

There are other large residual values and modification indices for the one-factor model. These values appear within small groups of items; for example, items 3, 4, 5, and 6 have higher modification indices with each other than with the other items. The items are grouped into different format types on the test form, each testing a different area of language knowledge. The groupings that appear in the modification indices corresponded somewhat with the item-type divisions. As was the case with the reading test, in which items were grouped by reading passage, these facts suggest that, rather than doing a factor analysis of all of the individual items, the items might be better grouped into testlets.

For the next analysis, the items are divided into testlets according to type. Items 1 through 10 consist of fill-in-the-blank sentence completions, and these are grouped into Testlet 1. Testlet 2 is composed of items 11 through 15, which measure capitalization and punctuation skills. Items 16 through 25 comprise Testlet 3, which measures understanding of sentence length and clarity, and items 26 through 30 make up Testlet 4, which asks students to synthesize information presented in separate sentences. The two open-ended items remain as separate items.

For the one-factor analysis of the grouped data, the fit is still not very good (χ^2 for grouped items = 497.57 with 9 df, $p <$ .0001). The value of GFI = 0.98 remains about the same and RMR = 0.061 decreases slightly (a sign of better fit), but the values of AGFI = 0.96 and RMSEA = 0.090 change in the direction of worse fit. The factor loadings for this model are shown in Table 6.14. Because the model fit is still not as good as it could be, it is possible that additional local dependence remains. Again, as with the reading test, it appears that a useful model is one in which a factor for the open-ended items is orthogonal to the general factor.

The next model fitted is a two-factor model for the testlet data, with the second factor having nonzero loadings only for the last two (open-ended) items. The results indicate a great improvement in fit of the model to the data. The p value has dropped into the range of nonsignificance (χ^2 = 7.86, p = .45), which indicates that the model fits the data satisfactorily. The GFI and AGFI are as high as they can go (1.0), RMSEA = 0.0, and the

TABLE 6.14
WLS Factor Loading Estimates for the One-Factor Model for the
Wisconsin Student Assessment System Eighth-Grade Language Test

Items/Testlets	λ
1	.69
2	.71
3	.72
4	.72
5	.59
6	.61

Note. Testlets 1–4 comprise dichotomous items, and items 5–6 are open-ended.

value of RMR = 0.005 has decreased a great deal. The loadings for the
two-factor model are shown in Table 6.15.

The data were next analyzed using full-information item factor analysis, with the items were divided into the same testlets (according to type) as
described earlier. The full-information item factor analysis loading estimates for the one-factor testlet data are provided in Table 6.16, with the

TABLE 6.15
WLS Factor Loading Estimates for the Two-Factor Model for the
Wisconsin Student Assessment System Eighth-Grade Language Test

Items/Testlets	λ_1	λ_2
1	.70	—
2	.71	—
3	.73	—
4	.73	—
5	.46	.51
6	.48	.51

Note. Testlets 1–4 comprise dichotomous items, and items 5–6 are open-ended.

TABLE 6.16
Full-Information Item Factor Analysis Loading Estimates
for the One-Factor Model for the Wisconsin Student
Assessment System Eighth-Grade Language Test

Items/Testlets	λ
1	.43
2	.53
3	.46
4	.53
5	.16
6	.15

Note. Testlets 1–4 comprise dichotomous items, and items 5–6 are open-ended.

TABLE 6.17
Varimax Rotation of the Full-Information Item Factor Analysis
Loading Estimates for the Two-Factor Model for the Wisconsin
Student Assessment System Eighth-Grade Language Test

Items/Testlets	λ_1	λ_2
1	.41	.12
2	.52	.13
3	.46	.10
4	.52	.14
5	.12	.38
6	.10	.51

Note. Testlets 1–4 comprise dichotomous items, and items 5–6 are open-ended.

two-factor testlet loadings provided in Table 6.17; an arrow plot for the two-dimensional solution is shown in Fig. 6.8.

As with the reading example, the main indicator of fit for the full-information item factor analysis model is the −2 loglikelihood. The WLS analysis of the polychoric correlations indicated that the one-factor model fit the language data much more poorly than the reading data, so we would expect the one-factor versus two-factor χ^2 value for the language data to be larger than for the reading data. That is what we find—the index values for the one- and two-factor models are 126101.2 and 125137.8;

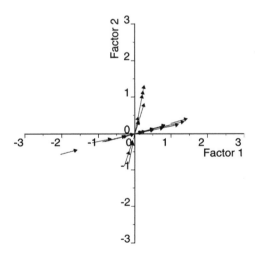

FIG. 6.8.   Arrow plot for the testlets and open-ended items of the Wisconsin language test example, using the full-information item factor analysis results. Each item has three arrows; the location of the origin of each vector is at the point of MDISC for the transition between category 0 and 1, and then between category 1 and 2, and then between 2 and 3. The length of the vector reflects the item's maximum discrimination.

the χ^2 difference between them is 963.4 with 5 df, $p < .001$. There are factor loadings for all six testlets for both factors in the full-information analysis; the loadings for the last two testlets on Factor 1 and the first four testlets on Factor 2 are relatively small, indicating that two open-ended items form a different construct than do the assembled testlets.

It is possible that the language constructs may be correlated, so an oblique rotation was performed. The results are shown in Table 6.18: The factor loadings are now much more distinct for the various testlets, and the intercorrelation is .46. The factors for this pair of constructs appear much more separate and distinct than for the reading constructs, yet the factors are still somewhat related. Table 6.19 shows the results of target rotation (again using the Browne et al. [1998] CEFA software) to the orthogonal hierarchical structure of the confirmatory analysis shown in Table 6.15. In both Table 6.15 and Table 6.19, there is clearly a factor general to the multiple-choice testlets, on which the open-ended items load weakly, and the open-ended writing items also identify their own factor more strongly.

TABLE 6.18
Oblique Rotation of the Full-Information Item Factor Analysis
Loading Estimates for the Two-Factor Model for the Wisconsin
Student Assessment System Eighth-Grade Language Test

Items/Testlets	λ_1	λ_2
1	.42	.01
2	.54	−.05
3	.48	−.02
4	.53	.01
5	.03	.38
6	.02	.53

Note. Testlets 1–4 comprise dichotomous items, and items 5–6 are open-ended.

TABLE 6.19
Target Rotation of the Full-Information Item Factor Analysis Loading
Estimates for the Two-Factor Model for the Wisconsin Student
Assessment System Eighth-Grade Language Test

Items/Testlets	λ_1	λ_2
1	.43	.02
2	.54	−.00
3	.47	−.02
4	.54	.01
5	.21	.34
6	.22	.47

Note. Testlets 1–4 comprise dichotomous items, and items 5–6 are open-ended.

With respect to scoring, the results of both two-factor analyses leave us impaled on the horns of a dilemma: Although the essay scores (testlets 5 and 6 in the analysis) are correlated with the general factor of language skills dominated by the multiple-choice testlets, those correlations are substantially lower than the loadings for the multiple choice testlets. In addition, the loadings for the essay scores are higher on Factor 2. This suggests that it would be better to give separate scores for the multiple-choice and essay components of the test. However (to refer specifically to the WLS results in Table 6.15), the loadings of the essays on Factor 2 are only .51 (equal, to identify the model); that is an estimate of the correlation of the observed essay scores with the underlying essay-writing skill variable being measured, when that variable is considered separately from, or independent of, what the multiple-choice items measure. This implies that the reliability of a score computed from the two essay scores alone would be

$$\frac{2(0.51 \times 0.51)}{1 + (0.51 \times 0.51)} = 0.41,$$

when computed using the Spearman–Brown formula to correct the fitted correlation between the two essays to the value of the reliability of a two-essay test. This level of reliability is usually not considered suitable for individual score reporting. Repeating the calculation using the factor loading estimates from the full-information analysis (in Table 6.19) yields an equally unsuitable reliability of 0.28. The ultimate question is: Does one report a single score that reflects a relatively unbalanced mixture of two distinguishable proficiencies (the editing skills measured by the multiple-choice items and essay-writing skill), or does one report two separate scores, with the essay score an extremely unreliable one?

CONCLUSIONS

An examination of the various theories, factor-analytic models, and results from real data in chapters 5 and 6 leads to several less-than-satisfying conclusions (at least for the time being). Item factor analysis is sometimes possible, but is currently very difficult to implement. The theory underlying the full-information models is complex, and may require more knowledge of item response theory than most educational researchers are interested in acquiring. The software itself is difficult to use, as it still lacks many user-friendly features that have come to be expected. POLYFACT is an infant in developmental terms (whereas LISREL has been around for 25 or so years). At the very least, applying one of the full-information programs to a set of item-level data is very time-consuming.

There are other limitations to be considered. No currently available implementation of full-information item factor analysis for polytomous items permits confirmatory analysis, or correlated error structures (which are two of the great advantages of SEM systems), and full-information item factor analysis is computationally intensive. On the other hand, any software that works with polychoric correlations and the WLS model is limited to a relatively small number of items for most realistic sample sizes.

Very recent alternative developments include POLY-DIMTEST (Li & Stout, 1995), which is an extension of the nonparametric DIMTEST procedure (mentioned in chap. 5) for polytomous item data. A simulation study of its performance has been reported by Nandakumar, Yu, Li, and Stout (1998).

Future developments in this area may reasonably be expected. At some time, implementation of structural equation model-like constraints in software that performs full-information item factor analysis may be expected; when that is available, the complications involved in arbitrary rotation can be set aside for item factor analysis, as they often are in traditional factor analysis. The nonparametric approaches to the investigation of dimensionality for polytomous response data has only just begun to be developed, so we can reasonably expect a good deal of future advancement in that area.

REFERENCES

Arbuckle, J. L. (1995). *AMOS for Windows: Analysis of moment structures (Version 3.5)*. Chicago: SmallWaters.

Bentler, P. M., & Wu, E. J. C. (1995). *EQS 5.4 for Windows*. Encino, CA: Multivariate Software.

Bock, R. D., Gibbons, R., & Muraki, E. (1988). Full-information factor analysis. *Applied Psychological Measurement, 12*, 261–280.

Bollen, K. A. (1989). *Structural equations with latent variables*. New York: Wiley.

Boomsma, A. (1983). On the robustness of LISREL against small sample sizes in factor analysis models. In K. G. Jöreskog & H. Wold (Eds.), *Systems under direct observation: Causality, structure, prediction (Part 1)* (pp. 149–173). Amsterdam: North-Holland.

Browne, M. W. (1982). Covariance structures. In D. M. Hawkins (Ed.), *Topics in applied multivariate analysis* (pp. 72–141). Cambridge: Cambridge University Press.

Browne, M. W. (1984). Asymptotically distribution-free methods for the analysis of covariance structures. *British Journal of Mathematical and Statistical Psychology, 37*, 62–83.

Browne, M. W., Cudeck, R., Tateneni, K., & Mels, G. (1998). *CEFA: Comprehensive exploratory factor analysis*. Columbus: Department of Psychology, Ohio State University.

Cattell, R. B. (1956). Validation and intensification of the Sixteen Personality Factor Questionnaire. *Journal of Clinical Psychology, 12*, 205–214.

Cattell, R. B. (1974). Radial parcel factoring versus item factoring in defining personality structure in questionnaires: Theory and experimental checks. *Australian Journal of Psychology, 26*, 103–119.

Cattell, R. B., & Burdsal, C. A., Jr. (1975). The radial parcel double factoring design: A solution to the item-vs.-parcel controversy. *Multivariate Behavioral Research, 10*, 165–179.

Cook, L. L., Dorans, N. J., Eignor, D. R., & Peterson, N. S. (1985). *An assessment of the relationship between the assumption of unidimensionality and the quality of IRT true-score equating* (RR-85-30). Princeton, NJ: Educational Testing Service.

Dorans, N. J., & Lawrence, I. M. (1987). *The internal construct validity of the SAT* (RR-87-35). Princeton, NJ: Educational Testing Service.

Dorans, N., & Lawrence, I. M. (1991, November). *The role of the unit of analysis in dimensionality assessment*. Paper presented at the International Symposium on Modern Theories in Measurement: Problems and Issues, Montebello, Quebec, Canada.

Gorsuch, R. L. (1983). *Factor analysis* (2nd ed.). Hillsdale, NJ: Lawrence Erlbaum Associates.

Harlow, L. L. (1985). *Behavior of some elliptical theory estimators with nonnormal data in a covariance structures framework: A Monte Carlo study*. Unpublished doctoral thesis, University of California, Los Angeles.

Hoyle, R. H. (1995). The structural equation modeling approach: Basic concepts and fundamental issues. In R. H. Hoyle (Ed.), *Structural equation modeling: Concepts, issues, and applications* (pp. 1–13). Thousand Oaks, CA: Sage.

Hu, L., & Bentler, P. M. (1998). Fit indices in covariance structure modeling: Sensitivity to underparameterized model misspecification. *Psychological Methods*, *3*, 424–453.

Hu, L., & Bentler, P. M. (1999). Cutoff criteria for fit indexes in covariance structure analysis: Conventional criteria versus new alternatives. *Structural Equation Modeling*, *6*, 1–55.

Jöreskog, K. G. (1967). Some contributions to maximum likelihood factor analysis. *Psychometrika*, *32*, 443–482.

Jöreskog, K. G. (1973). A general method for estimating a linear structural equation system. In A. S. Goldberger & O. D. Duncan (Eds.), *Structural equation models in the social sciences* (pp. 85–112). New York: Academic.

Jöreskog, K. G., & Sörbom, D. (1995a). *LISREL 8 user's reference guide*. Chicago: Scientific Software, Inc.

Jöreskog, K. G., & Sörbom, D. (1995b). *PRELIS: A program for multivariate data screening and data summarization*. Chicago: Scientific Software, Inc.

Lawley, D. N., & Maxwell, A. E. (1971). *Factor analysis as a statistical method*. New York: American Elsevier.

Li, H.-H., & Stout, W. F. (1995, April). *Assessment of dimensionality for mixed polytomous and dichotomous item data: Refinements of POLY-DIMTEST*. Paper presented at the Annual Meeting of the National Council on Measurement in Education, San Francisco.

MacCallum, R. C., Browne, M. W., & Sugawara, H. M. (1996). Power analysis and determination of sample size for covariance structure modeling. *Psychological Methods*, *1*, 130–149.

MacCallum, R. C., Roznowski, M., & Necowitz, L. B. (1992). Model modifications in covariance structure analysis: The problem of capitalization on chance. *Psychological Bulletin*, *111*, 490–504.

Muraki, E. (1993). POLYFACT [Computer software]. Princeton, NJ: Educational Testing Service.

Muraki, E., & Carlson, J. E. (1995). Full-information factor analysis for polytomous item responses. *Applied Psychological Measurement*, *19*, 73–90.

Muthén, L. K., & Muthén, B. O. (1998). *MPLUS: The comprehensive modeling program for applied researchers, user's guide*. Los Angeles, CA: Muthén & Muthén.

Nandakumar, R., Yu, F., Li, H.-H., & Stout, W. F. (1998). Assessing unidimensionality of polytomous data. *Applied Psychological Measurement*, *22*, 99–115.

Samejima, F. (1969). Estimation of latent ability using a response pattern of graded scores. *Psychometric Monograph*, No. 17, *34*, Part 2.

SAS Institute, Inc. (1990). *SAS/STAT user's guide, version 6* (4th ed., Vols. 1 and 2). Cary, NC: Author.

Tanaka, J. S., & Huba, G. J. (1984). Confirmatory hierarchical factor analyses of psychological distress measures. *Journal of Personality and Social Psychology*, *46*, 621–635.

Thissen, D., & Steinberg, L. (1988). Data analysis using item response theory. *Psychological Bulletin, 104,* 385–395.

Thissen, D., Wainer, H., & Wang, X. (1994). Are tests comprising both multiple-choice and free-response items necessarily less unidimensional than multiple-choice tests? An analysis of two tests. *Journal of Educational Measurement, 31,* 113–123.

Wainer, H., & Kiely, G. L. (1987). Item clusters and computerized adaptive testing: A case for testlets. *Journal of Educational Measurement, 24,* 185–201.

Wiley, D. E. (1973). The identification problem for structural equation models with unmeasured variables. In A. S. Goldberger & O. D. Duncan (Eds.), *Structural equation models in the social sciences* (pp. 85–112). New York: Academic Press.

Yung, Y. F., McLeod, L. D., & Thissen, D. (1999). On the relationship between the higher-order factor model and the hierarchical factor model. *Psychometrika, 64,* 113–128.

Part III

SPECIAL PROBLEMS, SPECIAL SOLUTIONS (A SECTION OF APPLICATIONS)

Chapter 7

Item Response Theory Applied to Combinations of Multiple-Choice and Constructed-Response Items—Scale Scores for Patterns of Summed Scores

Kathleen Rosa
University of North Carolina at Chapel Hill

Kimberly A. Swygert
Law School Admission Council

Lauren Nelson
David Thissen
University of North Carolina at Chapel Hill

Many contemporary tests include both multiple-choice items and extended constructed-response items, for which the item scores are ordered categorical ratings provided by judges. Examples include the National Assessment of Educational Progress (NAEP) (Calderone, King, & Horkay, 1997), many of the Advanced Placement (AP) examinations (College Entrance Examination Board, 1988), state assessments that have been administered at times in North Carolina, Wisconsin, and in many other states, and other less visible testing programs. If the collection of items is sufficiently well represented by a unidimensional IRT model, scale scores may be a viable plan for scoring such a test.

Some tests that combine multiple-choice and constructed-response items are nearly unidimensional with respect to the variation in proficiency that they measure; in chapter 6, we saw that the Wisconsin mathematics and reading tests are two examples. After obtaining similar results to those shown for the mathematics and reading examples in chapter 6, Thissen, Wainer, and Wang (1994) similarly concluded that the AP computer science and chemistry examinations they considered could be well approximated with a unidimensional model. On the other hand, there are

253

also certainly other tests in which different item types measure different dimensions of proficiency; the Wisconsin language test analyzed in chapter 6 is a striking example. When that is the case, combining the scores from the separate parts of the test may have negative utility—the combined score may be the same for examinees who are not particularly similar. However, for the large class of tests that combine item types to measure the same aspects of proficiency in different ways, combined scores are efficient and sensible.

Score combination is often motivated in the context of assessment that uses performance tasks, or portfolios, because the reliability of such performance tasks or portfolio scoring may be low. (For an example of an analysis of a portfolio-based assessment that yielded low reliability, see Klein, McCaffrey, Stecher, and Koretz [1995]. However, note that if a standardized performance assessment is sufficiently long, it may produce scores that reach the usual reliability expected of most large-scale assessments [Yen & Ferrara, 1997].) One solution to the dilemma produced by the perceived desirability of performance assessment and a need for high reliability for individual-level scores is to combine performance assessments with multiple-choice sections in scoring.

In cases for which combined scoring is desirable, either the EAP or MAP estimates of proficiency (θ) based on response patterns, as described in chapter 4, are traditional (IRT) solutions. However, in many contexts response-pattern scoring carries nonpsychometric penalties, and some alternative solution is required. Weighted combinations of the summed scores are widely used, but, as noted in chapter 2, there is no clearly superior solution to the problem of selecting the weights. When committees select the weights, there is a real (empirical) risk that the combination may be less reliable than one of its components; Lukhele, Thissen, and Wainer (1994) presented data summarized in Table 7.1 that illustrate realizations of this possibility. Table 7.1 shows 5-year medians for the period 1982–1986 of the reliabilities of the multiple-choice and constructed-response sections of seven AP tests, as well as the correlation between the two sections and the reliability of the composite. For the AP tests, the composite is a weighted sum of the multiple-choice and constructed-response scores, where the weights are chosen by subject-matter experts. For five of the seven tests listed in Table 7.1, the composite reliability is lower than the reliability of the multiple-choice section alone.

It is by no means a universal result that arbitrary linear composites exhibit lower reliability than one of their components, either for the AP tests (Bridgeman, Morgan, & Wang, 1996, listed many AP examinations for which the composite reliability was at least as great as that for the multiple-choice section), or for other tests that are scored as weighted combinations. However, the fact that ill-chosen weights can and do result in low-

TABLE 7.1
Five-Year Medians (1982–1986) of Reliability Coefficients
for Some Selected Advanced Placement Examinations

| Test | Reliability | | | Reliability of Composite Score |
	Multiple-Choice (MC)	Constructed-Response (CR)	Correlation MC and CR	
European History	0.90	0.46	.50	0.80
Biology	0.93	0.68	.73	0.89
Chemistry	0.91	0.77	.84	0.90
French Language	0.93	0.75	.78	0.92
Music: Listening & Lit.	0.85	0.29	.47	0.84
Computer Science	0.88	0.79	.80	0.90
Mathematics: Calculus AB	0.89	0.80	.83	0.92

Note. Data are from the College Entrance Examination Board (1988).

ered reliability of composite scores led to the development of the techniques presented in this chapter[1]: Here we develop a technique for combining scores based on IRT that is simpler than response-pattern scoring, both to implement and to explain to consumers, but that uses the data to determine what are, in effect, the relative weights of the components. In the process, we will find (in chap. 8) that IRT suggests, for many tests, that the "weights" vary as a function of the actual performance of the examinee.

RECAPITULATION: THE BACKGROUND IN IRT FOR SCALE SCORES BASED ON PATTERNS OF SUMMED SCORES

Expected A Posteriori (EAP) Estimates Based on Response Patterns. As described in chapters 3 and 4, for any IRT model for items indexed by i with item scores u, the likelihood for each response pattern is

$$L_{\mathbf{u}}(\theta) = L(_{\mathbf{u}}|\theta) = \prod_i T_{u_i}(\theta) , \qquad (1)$$

where $T_{u_i}(\theta)$ is the trace line for response u to item i. The probability of each response pattern $\mathbf{u}$ in a population with population distribution $\phi(\theta)$ for θ is

---

[1]There have been other proposals to solve this problem as well. For example, Longford (1997) described a non-IRT-based system to produce linear combination weights to combine multiple-choice and constructed-response section scores; that system is closely related to the procedure we describe to compute augmented (sub)scores in chapter 9.

$$P_{\mathbf{u}} = \int L_{\mathbf{u}}(\theta)\phi(\theta)\,d\theta \,. \qquad (2)$$

The average of the joint likelihood for the item responses and the population distribution is widely used as a point estimate of proficiency; that is,

$$\mathrm{EAP}[\theta|\mathbf{u}] = \frac{\int \theta L_{\mathbf{u}}(\theta)\phi(\theta)\,d\theta}{P_{\mathbf{u}}}\,, \qquad (3)$$

and the corresponding conditional variance,

$$\mathrm{var}[\theta|\mathbf{u}] = \frac{\int (\theta - \mathrm{EAP}[\theta|\mathbf{u}])^2 L_{\mathbf{u}}(\theta)\phi(\theta)\,d\theta}{P_{\mathbf{u}}}\,, \qquad (4)$$

is often used to compute a reportable standard error for each score as $\sqrt{\mathrm{var}[\theta|\mathbf{u}]}$.

Summed Scores From the Perspective of IRT. The likelihood for any summed score $x = \Sigma u_i$ is

$$L_x(\theta) = \sum_{(u_i)=x} L(\mathbf{u}|\theta)\,, \qquad (5)$$

where the summation is over the all response patterns that contain x correct responses. That is, for all values of θ the likelihood of a summed score is obtained as the sum of the likelihoods of all of the response patterns that have that summed score. The probability of each score x is

$$P_x = \int L_x(\theta)\phi(\theta)\,d\theta\,, \qquad (6)$$

where $\phi(\theta)$ is the population density.

An algorithm to compute $L_x(\theta)$ was described in chapters 3 and 4. Using that algorithm to compute a representation of $L_x(\theta)$ as a list of ordinates at specified values of θ, it is straightforward to compute the average value of θ associated with each score,

$$\mathrm{EAP}[\theta|x] = \frac{\int \theta L_x(\theta)\phi(\theta)\,d\theta}{P_x}\,, \qquad (7)$$

and the corresponding conditional variance,

$$\text{var}[\theta|x] = \frac{\int (\theta - \text{EAP}[\theta|x])^2 L_x(\theta)\phi(\theta)\,d\theta}{P_x}, \tag{8}$$

or the standard deviation $\sqrt{\text{var}[\theta|x]}$.

SCALE SCORES BASED ON PATTERNS
OF SUMMED SCORES

A solution based on IRT to the problem of combining binary-scored multiple-choice (MC) sections with open-ended (OE) items scored in multiple categories involves a hybridization of summed-score and response-pattern computation of scaled scores. That hybridization is to compute scale scores for patterns of testlet summed scores.

To do that, one first jointly calibrates all of the items (i.e., one estimates the item parameters), using suitable IRT models for each item. Then one computes $L_x^{MC}(\theta)$, the likelihood for summed score x for the multiple-choice section, and $L_{x'}^{OE}(\theta)$, the likelihood for summed score x' for the open-ended section, in both cases as described in chapters 3 and 4, and summarized briefly in the preceding section (see Eq. 5). Then, for each combination of a given summed score x on the multiple-choice section with any summed score x' on the open-ended section, compute the product

$$L_{xx'}(\theta) = L_x^{MC}(\theta)L_{x'}^{OE}(\theta). \tag{9}$$

The product in Eq. 9 is the likelihood for the response pattern defined as {score x on the multiple-choice section, score x' on the open ended section}. Then, following the same procedures that were used to compute scale scores associated with summed scores in chapters 3 and 4, we can compute the modeled probability of the response pattern of summed scores $\{x,x'\}$,

$$P_{xx'} = \int L_{xx'}(\theta)\phi(\theta)\,d\theta. \tag{10}$$

We may also compute the expected value of θ, given the response pattern of summed scores $\{x,x'\}$,

$$\text{EAP}[\theta|x, x'] = \frac{\int \theta L_{xx'}(\theta)\phi(\theta)\,d\theta}{P_{xx'}}, \tag{11}$$

and the corresponding standard deviation,

$$SD[\theta|x, x'] = \left(\frac{\int \left\{ \theta - EAP[\theta|x, x'] \right\}^2 L_{xx'}(\theta)\phi(\theta)\,d\theta}{P_{xx'}} \right)^{1/2}. \qquad (12)$$

Equations 11 and 12 define two-way score translation tables that provide scaled scores and their standard errors for each such response pattern, where the "pattern" refers to the ordered pair {score x on the multiple-choice section, score x' on the open-ended section}. This procedure offers many of the practical advantages of summed-scores, while preserving the differences in scale scores that may be associated with very different values of "points" on the multiple-choice and open-ended sections.

Using IRT Scale Scores for Patterns of Summed Scores to Score Tests Combining Multiple-Choice and Constructed-Response Sections: Wisconsin Third-Grade Reading Field Test.

To illustrate the construction of scale scoring tables using Eqs. 11 and 12, we revisit the Wisconsin third-grade reading test previously discussed in chapters 3 and 4. In chapter 4, we fitted the 16-item multiple-choice section and 4 open-ended items, each rated 0–3, with the 3PL and GR models (Birnbaum, 1968; Samejima, 1969), respectively, using the computer program MULTILOG (Thissen, 1991). The item parameter estimates are in Table 4.8; those were used to compute scale scores for the response patterns to these 20 items. Here, we use the same item response models and item parameter estimates to compute the values of $EAP[\theta|x,x']$ and $SD[\theta|x,x']$, using Eqs. 11 and 12.

The values of $EAP[\theta|x,x']$ for the 221 combinations of x, the summed score on the MC section, and x', the summed score on the OE section, are shown in Table 7.2. Tabulations such as that shown in Table 7.2 can be used in score-translation systems; one enters the table with the summed scores on the two parts of the test, and locates the scale score for that combination in the body of the table. A similar array of the values of $SD[\theta|x,x']$ is shown in Table 7.3; those may be reported as the standard errors of the scores.

Table 7.2 shows some interesting features of IRT-based score combination, as opposed to the more commonly used simple weighted combinations of summed scores. Reading across each row, or down each column, of Table 7.2, note that the effect of an additional "point" on either the open-ended section or the multiple-choice section depends on its context. In a simple weighted combination of the scores, obtaining 12 points instead of 11 on the open-ended portion would have the same effect on the score as obtaining 1 point instead of 0. That is not true for the IRT system; to anthropomorphize, the likelihood-based system "considers" the two scores and, in addition, their consistency as pieces of evidence. Where the two pieces of evidence essentially agree (roughly, near the main diagonal of the table), the summed score on each part has a larger effect on the

TABLE 7.2
Values of EAP[θ|x,x'] for Combinations of Multiple-Choice (MC)
and Open-Ended (OE) Summed Scores on a Wisconsin
Reading Tryout Form (θ Is Standardized)

MC Sum	Open–Ended (Summed) Rated Score												
	0	1	2	3	4	5	6	7	8	9	10	11	12
0	-3.2	-3.0	-2.8	-2.7	-2.5	-2.4	-2.2	-2.1	-2.0	-1.9	-1.8	-1.8	-1.7
1	-3.2	-3.0	-2.8	-2.6	-2.4	-2.3	-2.1	-2.0	-1.9	-1.8	-1.7	-1.7	-1.6
2	-3.1	-2.9	-2.7	-2.5	-2.3	-2.2	-2.0	-1.9	-1.8	-1.7	-1.6	-1.6	-1.5
3	-3.1	-2.8	-2.6	-2.4	-2.2	-2.1	-1.9	-1.8	-1.7	-1.6	-1.5	-1.4	-1.4
4	-3.0	-2.7	-2.5	-2.3	-2.1	-1.9	-1.8	-1.7	-1.6	-1.5	-1.4	-1.3	-1.3
5	-2.9	-2.6	-2.3	-2.1	-1.9	-1.8	-1.6	-1.5	-1.4	-1.3	-1.3	-1.2	-1.1
6	-2.7	-2.4	-2.2	-1.9	-1.8	-1.6	-1.5	-1.4	-1.3	-1.2	-1.1	-1.0	-1.0
7	-2.5	-2.2	-2.0	-1.7	-1.6	-1.4	-1.3	-1.2	-1.1	-1.0	-1.0	-0.9	-0.9
8	-2.3	-1.9	-1.7	-1.5	-1.4	-1.3	-1.2	-1.1	-1.0	-0.9	-0.8	-0.8	-0.7
9	-1.9	-1.6	-1.4	-1.3	-1.2	-1.1	-1.0	-0.9	-0.8	-0.8	-0.7	-0.6	-0.6
10	-1.5	-1.3	-1.2	-1.1	-1.0	-0.9	-0.8	-0.7	-0.7	-0.6	-0.5	-0.5	-0.4
11	-1.2	-1.0	-0.9	-0.9	-0.8	-0.7	-0.6	-0.6	-0.5	-0.4	-0.4	-0.3	-0.2
12	-0.8	-0.8	-0.7	-0.6	-0.6	-0.5	-0.5	-0.4	-0.3	-0.3	-0.2	-0.1	0.0
13	-0.6	-0.5	-0.5	-0.4	-0.4	-0.3	-0.3	-0.2	-0.1	0.0	0.1	0.2	0.3
14	-0.3	-0.3	-0.3	-0.2	-0.2	-0.1	-0.1	0.0	0.1	0.2	0.3	0.5	0.6
15	-0.1	-0.1	0.0	0.0	0.1	0.1	0.2	0.3	0.4	0.5	0.7	0.9	1.1
16	0.2	0.2	0.2	0.3	0.3	0.4	0.5	0.6	0.7	0.9	1.1	1.4	1.7

Note. The unshaded area in the table represents the central 99% HDR for the response patterns.

scaled score than it may when the scores disagree. In the latter case, when the scores are inconsistent, the open-ended score is (effectively) given less weight, because the open-ended section is less reliable (or discriminating).

Figure 7.1 illustrates the scoring system graphically, for the entry in Table 7.2 for $x_{MC} = 15$ and $x'_{OE} = 9$; shown in the three panels of Figure 7.1 are the population distribution [$\phi(\theta)$], the likelihoods for OE score 9

TABLE 7.3
Values of $SD[\theta|x,x']$ for Combinations of Multiple-Choice (MC)
and Open-Ended (OE) Summed Scores on a
Wisconsin Reading Tryout Form (θ Is Standardized)

MC	Open–Ended (Summed) Rated Score												
Sum	0	1	2	3	4	5	6	7	8	9	10	11	12
0	0.6	0.6	0.5	0.5	0.5	0.4	0.4	0.4	0.4	0.4	0.4	0.4	0.3
1	0.6	0.6	0.5	0.5	0.5	0.5	0.4	0.4	0.4	0.4	0.4	0.4	0.3
2	0.6	0.6	0.6	0.5	0.5	0.5	0.4	0.4	0.4	0.4	0.4	0.4	0.3
3	0.6	0.6	0.6	0.5	0.5	0.5	0.4	0.4	0.4	0.4	0.4	0.3	0.3
4	0.7	0.6	0.6	0.6	0.5	0.5	0.4	0.4	0.4	0.4	0.4	0.3	0.3
5	0.7	0.7	0.6	0.6	0.5	0.5	0.4	0.4	0.4	0.4	0.3	0.3	0.3
6	0.8	0.7	0.6	0.6	0.5	0.5	0.4	0.4	0.4	0.3	0.3	0.3	0.3
7	0.8	0.7	0.6	0.6	0.5	0.4	0.4	0.4	0.3	0.3	0.3	0.3	0.3
8	0.8	0.7	0.6	0.5	0.5	0.4	0.4	0.4	0.3	0.3	0.3	0.3	0.3
9	0.8	0.7	0.6	0.5	0.4	0.4	0.4	0.3	0.3	0.3	0.3	0.3	0.3
10	0.8	0.6	0.5	0.4	0.4	0.4	0.3	0.3	0.3	0.3	0.3	0.3	0.3
11	0.6	0.5	0.4	0.4	0.4	0.3	0.3	0.3	0.3	0.3	0.3	0.3	0.3
12	0.5	0.4	0.4	0.4	0.3	0.3	0.3	0.3	0.3	0.3	0.3	0.3	0.4
13	0.4	0.4	0.4	0.3	0.3	0.3	0.3	0.3	0.3	0.4	0.4	0.4	0.4
14	0.4	0.4	0.4	0.3	0.3	0.3	0.4	0.4	0.4	0.4	0.4	0.5	0.5
15	0.4	0.4	0.4	0.4	0.4	0.4	0.4	0.4	0.4	0.5	0.5	0.5	0.6
16	0.4	0.4	0.4	0.4	0.4	0.4	0.5	0.5	0.5	0.5	0.6	0.6	0.7

Note. The unshaded area in the table represents the central 99% HDR for the response patterns.

$[L_9^{OE}(\theta)]$ and for MC score 15 $[L_{15}^{MC}(\theta)]$, and the product of those three densities, the likelihood for θ given OE score 9 and MC score 15 $[L_{15\&9}(\theta)]$. Referring to Table 7.2, we find that the value of $EAP[\theta|x,x']$ for the score combination shown in Fig. 7.1 is 0.5, whereas the MC $EAP[\theta|x]$ is also 0.5, and the OE $EAP[\theta|x']$ is 0.1. Thus, although the likelihood in Fig. 7.1 for

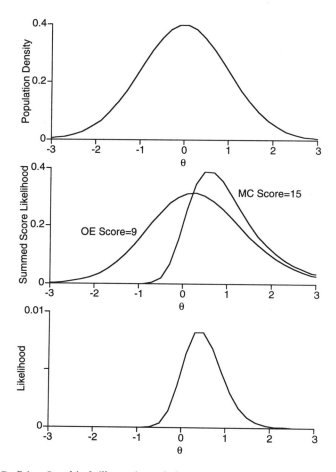

FIG. 7.1. Graphical illustration of the IRT pattern-of-summed-scores combination system, using data from the Wisconsin third-grade reading test. Top panel: Population distribution [$\phi(\theta)$]. Center panel: Likelihood for OE score 9 [$L_9^{OE}(\theta)$] and the likelihood for MC score 15 [$L_{15}^{MC}(\theta)$]. Lower panel: Product of the three densities in the upper two panels, which is the likelihood for θ given OE score 9 and MC score 15 [$L_{15\&9}(\theta)$].

the combination appears to be between those for the MC score and the OE score, the "average" computed using the combination likelihood is approximately in the same location as the MC EAP scale score. Table 7.2 gives the value of $SD[\theta\,|\,x,x'] = 0.5$ for this combination, and the likelihood plotted in Fig. 7.1 shows that to be a rather accurate description: The inflection points are a little above 0 and a little below 1.

Figure 7.2 shows a similarly constructed graphic for the combination with MC score 16 and OE score 12—the maximum summed score for each

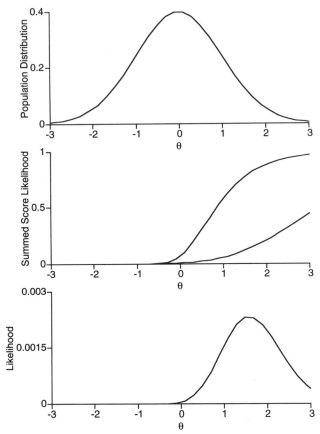

FIG. 7.2. Graphical illustration of the IRT pattern-of-summed-scores combination system, using data from the Wisconsin third-grade reading test. Top panel: Population distribution [$\phi(\theta)$]. Center panel: Likelihood for OE score 12 [$L_{12}^{OE}(\theta)$] and the likelihood for MC score 16 [$L_{16}^{MC}(\theta)$]. Lower panel: Product of the three densities in the upper two panels, which is the likelihood for θ given OE score 12 and MC score 16 [$L_{16\&12}(\theta)$].

component. In this case, the combination likelihood (the product of both component likelihoods and the population distribution) has EAP[$\theta \mid x,x'$] = 1.7 (from Table 7.2), while the EAPs for the two components are 1.1 (for the MC section) and 1.4 (for the OE section). Again, this kind of likelihood-based score-combination system is better taken as a system for combining evidence (about θ) than as an averaging system, with or without weights; for example, here, where the examinee obtains the maximum score on both of the two components, the evidence is compounded that the examinee's proficiency is very high—far from the mean of the population distribution.

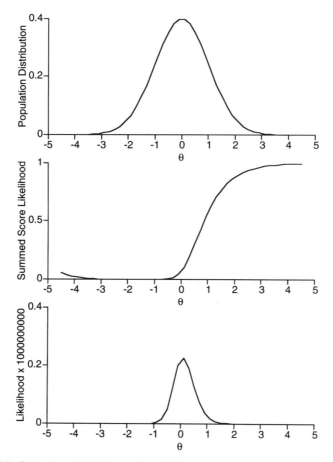

FIG. 7.3. Graphical illustration of the IRT pattern-of-summed-scores combination system, using data from the Wisconsin third-grade reading test. Top panel: Population distribution [$\phi(\theta)$]. Center panel: Likelihood for OE score 0 [$L_0^{OE}(\theta)$] and the likelihood for MC score 16 [$L_{16}^{MC}(\theta)$]. Lower panel: Product of the three densities in the upper two panels, which is the likelihood for θ given OE score 0 and MC score 16 [$L_{16\&0}(\theta)$]; this curve has been multiplied by 10^9 to give it visible height.

Figure 7.3 shows the likelihoods for an extremely unlikely combination: all items correct on the MC section (a summed score of 16), and no points on the OE section (summed score 0). This is a difficult situation for any score combination system: The value of EAP[$\theta|x$] for the MC section alone is 1.1, indicating relatively high proficiency, while that for EAP[$\theta|x'$] for the OE section alone is -2.8, indicating very low proficiency. The value of EAP[$\theta|x,x'$] for the combination likelihood is 0.2, which is a kind of compromise, but it is a compromise with a warning.

The Probabilities of Score Combinations. The IRT model also gives the probability for each combination of scores x and x' (Eq. 10). For the score-combinations in Table 7.2, the values of $P_{xx'}$ range from about 0.07 to less than 0.000005; a truncated representation of those values of $P_{xx'}$ is shown in Table 7.4. Considered individually, the values of $P_{xx'}$ are not readily interpretable as reflecting likely or unlikely events in any absolute

TABLE 7.4
Values of $P_{xx'}$ for Combinations of Multiple-Choice (MC)
and Open-Ended (OE) Summed Scores on a
Wisconsin Reading Tryout Form

MC	Open–Ended (Summed) Rated Score												
Sum	0	1	2	3	4	5	6	7	8	9	10	11	12
0	000	000	000	000	000	000	000	000	000	000	000	000	000
1	000	000	000	001	002	003	003	002	001	000	000	000	000
2	000	000	001	003	006	009	009	007	004	001	000	000	000
3	000	000	001	005	011	019	022	018	010	004	001	000	000
4	000	000	002	007	017	030	038	034	022	009	002	000	000
5	000	000	002	007	020	039	055	055	039	018	005	001	000
6	000	000	002	006	020	043	067	075	059	030	009	001	000
7	000	000	001	005	017	043	074	092	081	046	015	002	000
8	000	000	001	004	014	039	075	105	102	065	023	004	000
9	000	000	000	002	011	033	072	112	122	087	034	007	001
10	000	000	000	002	008	027	067	116	142	112	050	011	001
11	000	000	000	001	006	022	060	117	161	145	072	018	002
12	000	000	000	001	004	018	054	118	184	189	108	031	003
13	000	000	000	001	003	015	049	119	213	254	171	058	008
14	000	000	000	000	002	011	043	119	246	348	284	120	021
15	000	000	000	000	001	008	034	109	267	464	483	271	065
16	000	000	000	000	001	004	019	073	218	482	676	542	196

Note. Entries in the table are $10,000P_{xx'}$, truncated, with a leading 0.0 suppressed (that is, 001 is 0.0001). The unshaded area in the table represents the central 99% HDR for the response patterns.

sense, because the magnitude of the individual $P_{xx'}$ terms depends on the number of row and column score points. However, the values of $P_{xx'}$ may be used to construct a $(1 - \alpha)100\%$ "highest density region" (HDR; see Novick & Jackson, 1974, pp. 119–120) for the response combinations.

To construct the HDR, first sort the cells in order of $P_{xx'}$, from largest to smallest, and construct the cumulative distribution of $P_{xx'}$ using that sorted list. Then, to locate, say, the 99% HDR, include in the region all of those cells contributing to the first 99% of the cumulative total of $P_{xx'}$. This region has the properties that it includes 99% of the modeled response probability (by construction), and that the probability of any response combination within the region is higher than the probability of any response combination excluded from the region. According to the model, 99% of the examinees should obtain score combinations in that list of cells.

To illustrate, the 99% HDR was located for the Wisconsin reading data, as well as the 99.9% HDR; they are shown with shading in Table 7.4 (the same cells are shaded in Tables 7.2 and 7.3). In Table 7.4 (along with Tables 7.2 and 7.3), the 99% HDR is shown with no shading, and the region excluded from the 99.9% HDR is shown shaded darkly. The light gray shading and the unshaded area together represent the 99.9% HDR. Any response combination in the darkly shaded area in Tables 7.2–7.4 is unusual, in the sense that, according to the model, fewer than 1 in 1000 examinees should produce responses in that region.

Returning our attention to the unlikely score combination illustrated in Fig. 7.4, we now note that the likelihood for the combination has been multiplied by 10^9 to make it visible on the graphic. And the shadings in Tables 7.2–7.4 indicate that, according the IRT model, that score combination is one that the model says should occur only rarely. Rather than accept any score for this combination (Which one should we accept? The high MC score? The low OE score? An average that represents neither?), this information could be used in some testing systems to indicate that either the test or the model is somehow inappropriate for examinees with this response pattern—and that some further testing might be useful.

Response-Pattern Scores and Section Score-Pattern Scores. Figure 7.4 shows the values of the EAPs associated with each pattern of MC and OE summed scores, plotted against the EAPs (computed using the methods of chap. 4) associated with the corresponding item response patterns, for the 522 examinees who responded to the Wisconsin third-grade reading test. The correlation is .994; that value, and the scatter plot, indicate that there is very little difference between the scores (EAPs) obtained using only the information contained in the two section summed scores and the scores (EAPs) obtained using the complete response-pattern data. There is some difference for some response patterns, due to the fact that the items are

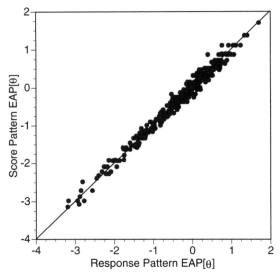

FIG. 7.4. Values of the EAPs associated with each pattern of MC and OE summed scores, plotted against the EAPs associated with the corresponding item response patterns, using data from the Wisconsin third-grade reading test.

differentially discriminating; if a Rasch-family (Masters & Wright, 1984) model was used, the response-pattern EAPs and the summed score EAPs would be identical, and the scatter plot would be a straight line and the correlation would be 1.0. However, for the relatively ordinary or expected amount of differential discrimination that appears in these data (recall the item parameters in Table 4.8), the result shown in Fig. 7.4 is obtained.

Figure 7.5 shows the values of the standard errors ($SD[\theta]$) associated with each pattern of MC and OE summed scores, superimposed on those associated with the corresponding item response patterns, both plotted against the values of the corresponding EAPs, using data from the Wisconsin third-grade reading test. The score-pattern standard errors are slightly larger than the minimum response-pattern standard errors obtained at each level of θ; that is to be expected, because there is some loss of information involved when all response patterns with the same section score are collapsed to obtain the same score. However, the loss of precision is small; generally, it is of the order of 10%.

The Relation of Likelihood-Based Score Combination With Rasch Model Scores. As we observed in chapter 4, analysis of data like these with a Rasch-family (Masters & Wright, 1984) model produces scale scores that are the same for any score combination that yields the same total summed score. In the case of Rasch-family models, the two-way array of values of

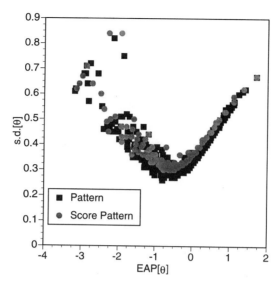

FIG. 7.5. Values of the standard errors ($SD[\theta]$) associated with each pattern of MC and OE summed scores, and those associated with the corresponding item response patterns, both plotted against the values of the corresponding EAPs, using data from the Wisconsin third-grade reading test.

$EAP[\theta|x,x']$, such as is shown in Table 7.2, is superfluous; any combination of x and x' that have the same total score have the same scale score. When applied to data that the 3PL/GR model combination fits with different discrimination values for the MC items (as a set) and the OE items (as a set), Rasch-family model scale scores and the 3PL/GR model combination scale scores differ somewhat.

Figure 7.6 shows the 3PL/GR score-combination values of $EAP[\theta|x,x']$ plotted against the Rasch-family $MAP[\theta|x,x']$ estimates, as computed with the computer program BIGSTEPS (Wright & Linacre, 1992) (because the Rasch-family estimates are originally computed on a different scale [see chap. 3], their values in Fig. 7.6 have been standardized to have the same mean and variance as the values of $EAP[\theta|x,x']$). (Only the points for the same central 95% HDR of the score-combinations are plotted in Fig. 7.6; the computation of the HDR is based on the 3PL/GR model.) We see in Fig. 7.6 that there are some score combinations for which the Rasch-family values of $MAP[\theta|x,x']$ and the 3PL/GR values of $EAP[\theta|x,x']$ differ fairly substantially. Because the 3PL/GR scale scores are computed accounting for guessing on the multiple-choice items, which almost certainly exists, as well as different relative values of the "points" for the number-correct MC score as opposed to the rated OE score, which also almost certainly contains some truth, we are inclined to believe that where the two scores differ, the 3PL/GR scores may well be more valid.

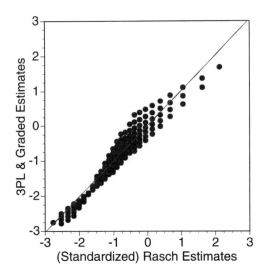

FIG. 7.6.   Values of EAP[θ|*x,x'*], computed using the 3PL/GR model combination, plotted against the values of MAP[θ|*x,x'*], computed using the Rasch model, using data from the Wisconsin third-grade reading test. (Only the points for the central 95% HDR of the score combinations are plotted.)

IRT Scale Scores for Patterns of Summed Scores Combining Multiple-Choice and Constructed-Response Sections: The 1993 North Carolina Open-Ended End-of-Grade Tests—Eighth-Grade Mathematics.   To provide another brief example of the relation between response-pattern scores (EAPs) and the EAPs for pattern-of-summed-scores, here we consider data from the 1993 administration of one form (A) of the North Carolina Open-Ended End-of-Grade Test of Mathematics, combined with the 80-item North Carolina Multiple-Choice End-of-Grade Test of Mathematics. Form A included three open-ended items, two rated 0–3 and the third rated 0–2, so the sum score range was 0–8 for the OE items. We jointly calibrated the multiple-choice items (using the 3PL model) and the open-ended items (using Samejima's 1969 graded model), and then computed response-pattern scores (EAPs) and the EAPs for pattern-of-summed-scores. Figure 7.7 shows a scatterplot of the EAPs for pattern-of-summed-scores against the response-pattern scores (EAPs) for a random sample of 870 of the examinees. The correlation is .984; that value is slightly lower than we obtained with the Wisconsin third-grade reading data, because in this example the discrimination parameters are more variable among the multiple-choice items, and between the multiple-choice items and the open-ended items. Nevertheless, there is only slight loss of precision due to using only the information in the section summed scores, as opposed to the complete response patterns.

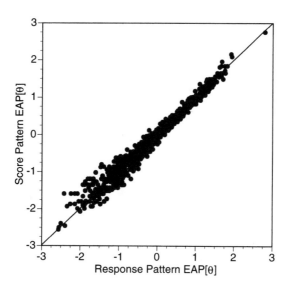

FIG. 7.7.   Values of the EAPs associated with each pattern of MC and OE summed scores, plotted against the EAPs associated with the corresponding item response patterns, using data from the North Carolina eighth-grade mathematics test.

An Anomaly That Can Arise With IRT Scale Scores for Patterns of Summed Scores Combining Multiple-Choice and Constructed-Response Sections: An Example from the North Carolina End-of-Course Geometry Test.   Table 7.5 shows the values of EAP[θ|x,x'] for combinations of multiple-choice (MC) and open-ended (OE) summed scores on Form E of the North Carolina End-of-Course Geometry test; θ is standardized. This table gives an idea of the size of the scoring tables for longer tests; in this case, there are 60 MC items, and the OE section yields a total of 12 score points.

Table 7.5 also illustrates an anomaly that can arise using this IRT-based method to combine scores for MC and OE sections: Close examination of the values in the first row of the table (for a score of 0 on the MC section) reveals that the combined scores (EAPs) increase, as we would expect, for OE scores of 0, 1, 2, and 3, but then they decrease to a lower value for an OE score of 4! The standardized scores then remain lower for OE scores of 5, 6, 7, and 8. Figure 7.8 shows some of the likelihood curves involved: the likelihoods for OE score 3, 4, 5, and 6, the likelihood for MC score 0, and the products of the MC curve and the four OE curves.

This kind of anomalous result is more of an esthetic annoyance than a real problem; nevertheless it is an annoyance that is best understood. The curves in Fig. 7.8 illustrate the source of the problem: Given the score of zero on the MC section (and the associated likelihood, decreasing from

TABLE 7.5
Values of EAP[θ|x,x'] for Combinations of Multiple-Choice (MC)
and Open-Ended (OE) Summed Scores on Form E of the
North Carolina End-of-Course Geometry Test (θ Is Standardized)

MC	Open-Ended (Summed) Rated Score												
Sum	0	1	2	3	4	5	6	7	8	9	10	11	12
0	-3.5	-3.2	-3.1	-2.9	**-3.0**	**-3.0**	**-3.1**	**-3.0**	**-3.1**	-2.8	-2.7	-2.7	-2.7
1	-3.5	-3.1	-3.1	-2.9	**-3.0**	**-2.9**	**-3.0**	**-3.0**	**-3.0**	-2.7	-2.7	-2.7	-2.7
2	-3.4	-3.1	-3.0	-2.8	**-2.9**	**-2.8**	**-2.9**	**-2.9**	**-2.9**	-2.7	-2.6	-2.6	-2.6
3	-3.4	-3.0	-2.9	-2.7	**-2.8**	**-2.8**	**-2.9**	**-2.8**	**-2.9**	-2.6	-2.5	-2.5	-2.5
4	-3.3	-3.0	-2.9	-2.7	**-2.8**	**-2.7**	**-2.8**	**-2.8**	**-2.8**	-2.5	-2.5	-2.5	-2.5
5	-3.2	-2.9	-2.8	-2.6	**-2.7**	**-2.6**	**-2.7**	**-2.7**	**-2.7**	-2.5	-2.4	-2.4	-2.4
6	-3.2	-2.9	-2.7	-2.5	**-2.6**	**-2.5**	**-2.6**	**-2.6**	**-2.7**	-2.4	-2.3	-2.3	-2.3
7	-3.1	-2.8	-2.7	-2.5	-2.5	-2.5	**-2.6**	**-2.5**	**-2.6**	-2.3	-2.3	-2.3	-2.3
8	-3.1	-2.7	-2.6	-2.4	**-2.5**	**-2.4**	**-2.5**	**-2.4**	**-2.5**	-2.2	-2.2	-2.2	-2.2
9	-3.0	-2.7	-2.5	-2.3	**-2.4**	**-2.3**	**-2.4**	**-2.4**	**-2.4**	-2.2	-2.1	-2.1	-2.1
10	-2.9	-2.6	-2.5	-2.2	**-2.3**	**-2.2**	**-2.3**	**-2.3**	**-2.3**	-2.1	-2.0	-2.0	-2.0
11	-2.9	-2.5	-2.4	-2.2	-2.2	-2.2	-2.2	-2.2	**-2.3**	-2.0	-2.0	-2.0	-2.0
12	-2.8	-2.5	-2.3	-2.1	-2.1	-2.1	-2.2	-2.1	**-2.2**	-2.0	-1.9	-1.9	-1.9
13	-2.7	-2.4	-2.2	-2.0	-2.1	-2.0	-2.1	-2.0	**-2.1**	-1.9	-1.8	-1.8	-1.8
14	-2.6	-2.3	-2.2	-2.0	-2.0	-1.9	**-2.0**	**-1.9**	**-2.0**	-1.8	-1.7	-1.7	-1.7
15	-2.5	-2.3	-2.1	-1.9	-1.9	-1.8	**-1.9**	**-1.9**	**-1.9**	-1.7	-1.7	-1.7	-1.7
16	-2.5	-2.2	-2.0	-1.8	-1.8	-1.8	-1.8	-1.8	-1.8	-1.7	-1.6	-1.6	-1.6
17	-2.4	-2.1	-2.0	-1.8	-1.7	-1.7	-1.7	-1.7	-1.7	-1.6	-1.5	-1.5	-1.5
18	-2.3	-2.0	-1.9	-1.7	-1.7	-1.6	-1.6	-1.6	**-1.7**	-1.5	-1.4	-1.4	-1.4
19	-2.2	-1.9	-1.8	-1.6	-1.6	-1.5	**-1.6**	**-1.5**	**-1.6**	-1.5	-1.4	-1.4	-1.3
20	-2.1	-1.9	-1.7	-1.5	-1.5	-1.4	**-1.5**	**-1.4**	**-1.5**	-1.4	-1.3	-1.3	-1.3
21	-2.0	-1.8	-1.7	-1.5	-1.4	-1.4	-1.4	-1.4	-1.4	-1.3	-1.2	-1.2	-1.2
22	-1.9	-1.7	-1.6	-1.4	-1.3	-1.3	-1.3	-1.3	-1.3	-1.2	-1.1	-1.1	-1.1
23	-1.8	-1.6	-1.5	-1.3	-1.3	-1.2	-1.2	-1.2	-1.2	-1.2	-1.0	-1.0	-1.0
24	-1.7	-1.5	-1.4	-1.3	-1.2	-1.1	-1.1	-1.1	-1.1	-1.1	-1.0	-1.0	-1.0
25	-1.6	-1.4	-1.3	-1.2	-1.1	-1.1	-1.1	-1.0	-1.1	-1.0	-0.9	-0.9	-0.9
26	-1.5	-1.4	-1.3	-1.1	-1.0	-1.0	-1.0	-1.0	-1.0	-0.9	-0.8	-0.8	-0.8
27	-1.4	-1.3	-1.2	-1.0	-0.9	-0.9	-0.9	-0.9	-0.9	-0.9	-0.8	-0.7	-0.7
28	-1.3	-1.2	-1.1	-1.0	-0.9	-0.8	-0.8	-0.8	-0.8	-0.8	-0.7	-0.7	-0.7
29	-1.2	-1.1	-1.0	-0.9	-0.8	-0.8	-0.7	-0.7	-0.7	-0.7	-0.6	-0.6	-0.6
30	-1.1	-1.0	-0.9	-0.8	-0.7	-0.7	-0.7	-0.7	-0.6	-0.6	-0.5	-0.5	-0.5
31	-1.0	-0.9	-0.8	-0.7	-0.7	-0.6	-0.6	-0.6	-0.6	-0.6	-0.5	-0.5	-0.4
32	-0.9	-0.8	-0.8	-0.7	-0.6	-0.5	-0.5	-0.5	-0.5	-0.5	-0.4	-0.4	-0.4
33	-0.8	-0.7	-0.7	-0.6	-0.5	-0.5	-0.4	-0.4	-0.4	-0.4	-0.3	-0.3	-0.3
34	-0.7	-0.6	-0.6	-0.5	-0.4	-0.4	-0.4	-0.4	-0.3	-0.3	-0.3	-0.2	-0.2
35	-0.7	-0.6	-0.5	-0.4	-0.4	-0.3	-0.3	-0.3	-0.3	-0.3	-0.2	-0.2	-0.2
36	-0.6	-0.5	-0.4	-0.4	-0.3	-0.3	-0.2	-0.2	-0.2	-0.2	-0.1	-0.1	-0.1
37	-0.5	-0.4	-0.4	-0.3	-0.2	-0.2	-0.2	-0.1	-0.1	-0.1	-0.1	0.0	0.0
38	-0.4	-0.3	-0.3	-0.2	-0.2	-0.1	-0.1	-0.1	-0.1	0.0	0.0	0.0	0.1
39	-0.3	-0.2	-0.2	-0.2	-0.1	-0.1	0.0	0.0	0.0	0.0	0.1	0.1	0.1
40	-0.2	-0.2	-0.1	-0.1	0.0	0.0	0.0	0.1	0.1	0.1	0.2	0.2	0.2
41	-0.1	-0.1	-0.1	0.0	0.0	0.1	0.1	0.1	0.2	0.2	0.2	0.3	0.3
42	-0.1	0.0	0.0	0.1	0.1	0.1	0.2	0.2	0.2	0.2	0.3	0.3	0.4
43	0.0	0.1	0.1	0.1	0.2	0.2	0.3	0.3	0.3	0.3	0.4	0.4	0.4

(Continued)

TABLE 7.5
(Continued)

MC	Open-Ended (Summed) Rated Score												
Sum	0	1	2	3	4	5	6	7	8	9	10	11	12
44	0.1	0.2	0.2	0.2	0.3	0.3	0.3	0.3	0.4	0.4	0.4	0.5	0.5
45	0.2	0.2	0.2	0.3	0.3	0.4	0.4	0.4	0.5	0.5	0.5	0.6	0.6
46	0.3	0.3	0.3	0.4	0.4	0.4	0.5	0.5	0.5	0.5	0.6	0.6	0.7
47	0.4	0.4	0.4	0.4	0.5	0.5	0.6	0.6	0.6	0.6	0.7	0.7	0.8
48	0.4	0.5	0.5	0.5	0.6	0.6	0.6	0.7	0.7	0.7	0.8	0.8	0.8
49	0.5	0.6	0.6	0.6	0.6	0.7	0.7	0.7	0.8	0.8	0.8	0.9	0.9
50	0.6	0.7	0.7	0.7	0.7	0.8	0.8	0.8	0.8	0.9	0.9	1.0	1.0
51	0.7	0.7	0.8	0.8	0.8	0.8	0.9	0.9	0.9	1.0	1.0	1.1	1.1
52	0.8	0.8	0.9	0.9	0.9	0.9	1.0	1.0	1.0	1.1	1.1	1.2	1.2
53	0.9	0.9	1.0	1.0	1.0	1.0	1.1	1.1	1.1	1.2	1.2	1.3	1.3
54	1.0	1.0	1.1	1.1	1.1	1.1	1.2	1.2	1.2	1.3	1.3	1.4	1.5
55	1.1	1.1	1.2	1.2	1.2	1.2	1.3	1.3	1.3	1.4	1.4	1.5	1.6
56	1.2	**1.3**	**1.3**	**1.3**	**1.3**	1.4	1.4	1.4	1.5	1.5	1.6	1.6	1.8
57	1.4	1.4	1.4	1.4	1.5	1.5	1.6	1.6	1.6	1.6	1.7	1.8	1.9
58	1.5	1.5	1.6	1.6	1.6	1.6	1.7	1.7	1.8	1.8	1.9	1.9	2.1
59	1.7	1.7	1.7	1.7	1.8	1.8	1.9	1.9	2.0	2.0	2.1	2.1	2.4
60	1.9	1.9	1.9	1.9	2.0	2.0	2.1	2.1	2.2	2.2	2.3	2.3	2.7

Note. Anomalous values are boldface; see text for discussion.

the left in the center panel of Fig. 7.8), the likelihoods for increasing OE scores become increasingly distant—the product is of the (extreme) tails of the MC and OE likelihoods. The shapes of the tails of the 3PL and graded-model likelihoods are such that for some score combinations the average of the product-likelihood moves left when we would expect it to move right.

These combinations are exceedingly rare. First of all, obtaining an MC score of 0 on a 60-item four-alternative multiple-choice test is a rare event; the chance score is 15. The IRT model (and good sense) suggests that obtaining a score of zero on the MC section, *and* a relatively high score on the OE section, is an very rare event. These score combinations should not actually arise in data, except through such unmodeled behaviors as malingering or data-entry errors.

The IRT model does not handle such unlikely score combinations exactly as one would expect. However, such score combinations are so rare that this potential anomaly may not appear in operational use.

IRT Scale Scores for Patterns of Summed Scores Combining Multiple-Choice and Constructed-Response Section, Using the Graded Model for Items Combined Into Summed-Scored Testlets, Combined With Open-Ended Ratings: The Wisconsin Eighth-Grade Reading Test. As an example of score combination that uses multiple-cateogry IRT models throughout, we

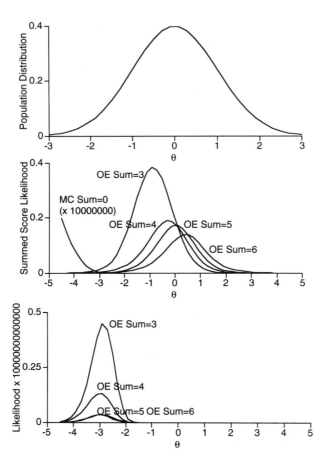

FIG. 7.8.   Graphical illustration of an anomaly that can arise using the IRT pattern-of-summed-scores combination system, using data from the North Carolina geometry test. Top panel: Population distribution [$\phi(\theta)$]. Center panel: Likelihoods for OE score 3, 4, 5, and 6, and the likelihood for MC score 0. Lower panel: Products of the MC curve and the four OE curves in the upper two panels.

return our attention to the data from the Wisconsin Student Assessment System eighth-grade reading comprehension test in 1995, which we previously considered in examples in chapters 4 and 6. The test included six reading passages; the first five passages were each followed by five to nine four-alternative multiple-choice questions, whereas the sixth passage formed the basis for three relatively short constructed-response questions that were each subsequently rated 0–3. In chapter 6, we described the results of factor analysis of these data; after the test is redefined as six testlet scores, (one summed score for each passage) it may be considered unidimensional.

In chapter 4 we illustrated the computation of MAP[θ], using the graded IRT model for the six testlet scores (the trace lines, one set for each passage, are shown in Figs. 4.17 and 4.18, and the item parameter estimates are in Table 4.9). To continue this extended example, here we present the values of EAP[θ|x,x'] for summed scores x on the multiple-choice section and x' on the constructed response section in Table 7.6, again using the graded model trace line for the number-correct after each passage construed as testlets. For the 6,499 examinees, the correlation be-

TABLE 7.6
Values of EAP[θ|x,x'] for Combinations of Multiple-Choice (MC)
and Open-Ended (OE) Summed Scores on the
Wisconsin Eighth-Grade Reading Test (θ Is Standardized)

MC	Open-Ended (Summed) Rated Score									
Sum	0	1	2	3	4	5	6	7	8	9
0	−4.2	−4.1	−4.1	−4.0	−3.8	−3.7	−3.7	−3.7	−3.6	−3.6
1	−4.1	−4.1	−4.0	−3.9	−3.7	−3.6	−3.6	−3.5	−3.5	−3.5
2	−4.0	−4.0	−3.9	−3.8	−3.6	−3.5	−3.4	−3.4	−3.3	−3.3
3	−3.8	−3.8	−3.7	−3.6	−3.4	−3.3	−3.2	−3.2	−3.1	−3.1
4	−3.7	−3.7	−3.6	−3.4	−3.3	−3.1	−3.0	−3.0	−3.0	−2.9
5	−3.5	−3.5	−3.4	−3.3	−3.1	−3.0	−2.9	−2.8	−2.8	−2.7
6	−3.3	−3.3	−3.2	−3.1	−2.9	−2.8	−2.7	−2.6	−2.6	−2.6
7	−3.1	−3.1	−3.0	−2.9	−2.8	−2.6	−2.5	−2.5	−2.4	−2.4
8	−2.9	−2.9	−2.9	−2.8	−2.6	−2.5	−2.4	−2.3	−2.2	−2.2
9	−2.7	−2.7	−2.7	−2.6	−2.5	−2.3	−2.2	−2.1	−2.1	−2.0
10	−2.6	−2.6	−2.5	−2.4	−2.3	−2.2	−2.1	−2.0	−1.9	−1.9
11	−2.4	−2.4	−2.4	−2.3	−2.2	−2.1	−1.9	−1.8	−1.8	−1.7
12	−2.2	−2.2	−2.2	−2.2	−2.1	−1.9	−1.8	−1.7	−1.6	−1.6
13	−2.1	−2.1	−2.1	−2.0	−1.9	−1.8	−1.7	−1.6	−1.5	−1.4
14	−1.9	−1.9	−1.9	−1.9	−1.8	−1.7	−1.5	−1.4	−1.3	−1.3
15	−1.8	−1.8	−1.8	−1.7	−1.6	−1.5	−1.4	−1.3	−1.2	−1.1
16	−1.6	−1.6	−1.6	−1.6	−1.5	−1.4	−1.3	−1.2	−1.0	−1.0
17	−1.5	−1.5	−1.4	−1.4	−1.4	−1.3	−1.2	−1.0	−0.9	−0.8
18	−1.3	−1.3	−1.3	−1.3	−1.2	−1.1	−1.0	−0.9	−0.8	−0.7
19	−1.1	−1.1	−1.1	−1.1	−1.1	−1.0	−0.9	−0.8	−0.6	−0.5
20	−1.0	−1.0	−1.0	−1.0	−0.9	−0.8	−0.7	−0.6	−0.5	−0.4
21	−0.8	−0.8	−0.8	−0.8	−0.8	−0.7	−0.6	−0.5	−0.3	−0.2
22	−0.6	−0.6	−0.6	−0.6	−0.6	−0.5	−0.4	−0.3	−0.2	0.0
23	−0.5	−0.5	−0.5	−0.4	−0.4	−0.4	−0.3	−0.2	0.0	0.1
24	−0.3	−0.3	−0.3	−0.3	−0.2	−0.2	−0.1	0.0	0.1	0.3
25	−0.1	−0.1	−0.1	−0.1	0.0	0.0	0.1	0.2	0.3	0.5
26	0.1	0.1	0.2	0.2	0.2	0.2	0.3	0.4	0.5	0.7
27	0.4	0.4	0.4	0.4	0.4	0.4	0.5	0.6	0.7	0.9
28	0.6	0.6	0.6	0.6	0.7	0.7	0.7	0.8	0.9	1.2
29	0.9	0.9	0.9	0.9	1.0	1.0	1.0	1.1	1.2	1.5
30	1.3	1.3	1.3	1.3	1.3	1.3	1.3	1.4	1.5	1.9

tween the pattern of summed-score-pattern EAPs and complete response-pattern EAPs (computed using the methods presented in chap. 4) is .994.

For this test, with the passage structure used to recombine the items into testlet summed scores, there is obviously very little loss in precision involved in using the relatively simpler score-combination method proposed in this chapter instead of full response-pattern scoring. This example also illustrates the fact that this score combination method is equally applicable to tests in which all of the items use multiple-category IRT models; it is not restricted to the combination of the 3PL model with a multiple-category section.

Using IRT Scale Scores for Patterns of Summed Scores to Score Tests Combining Multiple-Choice and Constructed-Response Sections: The North Carolina Test of Computer Skills.

In this extended example, we describe a sequence of analyses that culminate in combined scoring for the North Carolina Test of Computer skills. In chapters 2, 3, and 4, we used parts of this test to illustrate concepts in traditional test theory and IRT. Here, we describe preliminary analyses of item tryout forms for this test, and the decision-making process that led to combined scores.[2]

The item tryout for the North Carolina Computer Skills Test included four forms (labeled 1–4) for the multiple-choice portion and 12 forms (labeled 13–24) of the performance (constructed-response) test. In all of the data analyses reported here, a sample of 3,099 students who responded to both the multiple-choice and performance forms in the field test was used. The performance, or open-ended, forms of the Computer Skills Test comprise four parts: keyboarding techniques (KB), word processing/editing (ED), database use (DB), and spreadsheet use (SS). The KB portion included three ratings scored 0–3, while the ED, DB, and SS sections included 6–10 items that were each scored either 0–1 or 0–1–2.

Traditional Analysis of the Performance Forms.

We examined the reliability (coefficient α) for the 12 open-ended forms, computing the statistics with the test as items, as well as with the KB, ED, DB, and SS sections taken to be four testlets. The computation of α as items assumes that the items of the test equally measure some overall level of computer skill. For the treatment of the performance forms as testlets, the items within each of the four sections (KB, ED, DB, and SS) are summed, and then the test is taken to be made up of four large items (or testlets). In either event, coeffi-

---

[2]As a matter of fact, the combined scores for the North Carolina Test of Computer Skills have never been used; a decision was made to consider the multiple-choice and constructed-response sections' scores separately in the actual implementation of the test. Nevertheless, it is an interesting early example of this method of score combination.

TABLE 7.7
Reliability Coefficients for the Performance Forms
of the North Carolina Test of Computer Skills

OE	Coefficient α	
Form	Items	Testlets
1 (13)	.85	.67
2 (14)	.85	.64
3 (15)	.85	.67
4 (16)	.84	.67
5 (17)	.83	.66
6 (18)	.84	.68
7 (19)	.77	.56
8 (20)	.83	.70
9 (21)	.82	.62
10 (22)	.82	.65
11 (23)	.80	.62
12 (24)	.82	.64
Average	.83	.65

cient α is an estimate of the reliability of the same (summed) test score. If all of the items on the test reflect computer skill equally—that is, if there is no local dependence among the items within KB or ED or DB or SS—then coefficient α will be the same regardless of whether it is computed for the items or the testlets. If coefficient α is substantially smaller for the testlet computation than for the item computation, that means that there is local dependence among the items within the four parts. If there is local dependence, then coefficient α computed at the item level does not provide an appropriate estimate of alternate-form reliability—that is, the correlation that would be obtained if two different performance forms were used—due to the fact that item-level coefficient α includes increased correlations among items in a particular performance section that would not be present across items on alternate forms.

We found that testlet-level coefficient α is substantially smaller than item-level α for the performance forms; average item α is .83, while average testlet α is .65 (see Table 7.7). Under these circumstances, testlet α reflects more closely true alternate-form reliability, and gives a better estimate of the precision of the test as a measure of overall computer skill (defined as a composite of KB, ED, DB, and SS). Therefore, in subsequent analyses we treated the performance forms as comprising four testlets.

Exploration of the Dimensionality of the Test. To explore the dimensionality of the multiple-choice forms, we divided the items into parcels based on the objectives being measured by the test, and factor ana-

TABLE 7.8
Factor Loadings for the Combined Multiple-Choice Parcel
and Performance Testlet Analysis for Multiple-Choice Form 1
of the North Carolina Test of Computer Skills

MC	Factor Loadings		
Objective	General	OE	MC
1	0.6		0.1
2	0.6		0.1
3	0.6		0.2
4	0.5		0.1
5	0.6		-.2
6	0.8		0.2
7	0.8		0.3
8	0.7		0.4
9	0.7		0.3
OE Testlet			
KB	0.5	0.3	
ED	0.5	0.3	
DB	0.6	0.3	
SS	0.5	0.3	

lyzed the correlations among the parcel summed scores, as described in chapter 6. This analysis showed no clear evidence of multidimensionality. To further explore the dimensionality of the multiple-choice objective parcels in combination with the performance testlets, we factor analyzed the parcels and summed testlet scores jointly. To provide adequate sample sizes for the factor analysis while correcting for the differences in difficulty between the performance forms, we standardized the summed scores within testlets for each of the performance forms, and did four factor analyses, one for each multiple choice form. Standardized testlet scores from all of the performance forms were aggregated to become the performance testlet scores in each analysis.[3]

The joint factor analyses indicated that a unidimensional model did not fit the combined data well. For all four forms, a three-factor structured (confirmatory) model, with loadings arranged as shown in Table 7.8, provided an adequate fit (only the results for multiple-choice form 1 are tabulated here). The results of the factor analysis suggest that a strong general factor pervades the test, regardless of objectives or testlet sections of the performance forms. In addition, there is a factor reflecting individual differences on the performance testlets, with loadings approximately equal

[3]Because the design of the multiform item tryout yielded regrettably small sample sizes for any given form combination, we actually used Pearson correlations and ML estimation in the factor analysis instead of the superior procedures recommended in chapter 6.

to 0.3 for all four testlets. In principle, that means that the performance portion measures a somewhat different aspect of computer skill than does the multiple-choice section. However, that additional performance skill would not be measured reliably by a separate performance score that removed the general level of computer skill: The correlation of each of the four testlets with the performance-specific factor is only .3. That means that the correlation among the performance testlets due to the specific performance factor is $.3^2 = .09$, and Spearman–Brown extrapolation of an intertestlet correlation of .09 yields a 4-testlet reliability of 0.28. Of course, the performance scores have substantially higher reliability than 0.28, but most of that higher reliability is due to the general computer skills factor. If we were to use these data to create a test that measured only the distinct aspect of performance skill, as opposed to general computer skill measured by both the multiple-choice and performance tests, such a separate performance score would be extremely unreliable. There was even less evidence of a factor specific to the multiple-choice format.

Therefore, we proceeded with the plan to combine the scores for the multiple-choice and performance sections for students who respond to both. Simply summing the multiple-choice and performance scores, with both taken at their numerical value, proved unwise. Table 7.9 shows the values of coefficient α that are obtained for the multiple-choice forms alone, and after the raw summed scores for each of the performance sections are added to those scores.

Note in all cases that the reliability of simple sums of the multiple-choice scores and the summed performance scores is less than (or, rarely, equal to) the reliability of the multiple-choice scores alone. That is due to the fact that "points" on the performance section are not equal to "points" on the multiple-choice section—simply summing the two numbers-of-points has the effect of overweighting the performance scores, in a way that reduces reliability. Thus, scaled scores are needed to combine the multiple-choice and performance scores.

TABLE 7.9
Reliability Coefficients for the Multiple-Choice Forms
of the North Carolina Test of Computer Skills Alone,
and After the Raw Summed Scores for Each
of the Performance Sections Are Added to Those Scores

MC		With OE Form Number (as Testlets)											
Form	α	1	2	3	4	5	6	7	8	9	10	11	12
1	.93	.89	.89	.92	.89	.91	.91	.91	.90	.91	.91	.91	.91
2	.91	.89	.89	.88	.87	.90	.89	.89	.86	.88	.90	.87	.91
3	.93	.91	.89	.89	.91	.89	.89	.88	.92	.89	.91	.91	.90
4	.92	.84	.89	.91	.89	.87	.90	.88	.91	.90	.92	.89	.92

Scale Scores.   To compute scale scores, we first need item parameter estimates for IRT models appropriate for the multiple-choice items and the performance testlets. For the multiple choice items, we used the three-parameter logistic model. For the performance testlets, we used the graded item response model.

In preliminary analyses of the performance testlets, we noted that for many of the testlets, several of the low-score categories and a few of the high-score categories had few or no respondents in the field test data. With little data, it is not possible to accurately estimate item response functions for those responses. We collapsed these empty (or near empty) score categories; then we fitted the graded model to the collapsed categories. Scoring is on the basis of the sums of the testlet score categories as collapsed.

After recoding the testlet score categories, the 48 testlets (12 forms times 4 testlets each) were jointly calibrated with the 280 multiple-choice items (4 forms of 70 items each) in a single joint estimation of the item parameters using the computer program MULTILOG (Thissen, 1991). The three-parameter logistic model was used for the multiple choice items and the graded model was used for the performance testlets.

Subsequently, the expected a posteriori (EAP) scale scores were computed for each summed score on the multiple-choice forms, for each sum of the (recoded, collapsed) testlet scores for each performance form, and for each combination of summed multiple choice and summed (recoded) testlet scores. As examples, the scoring table for the multiple choice form 1 is in Table 7.10, and that for performance form 13 is in Table 7.11. In this realistic example, the scaled scores (in Tables 7.10, 7.11, and 7.12) are presented on a scale with an average of 50 and a standard deviation of approximately 10, and they are tabulated as integers for more attractive score reporting.

One of the 48 scoring tables for the IRT-scaled EAPs for combinations of summed multiple-choice and summed testlet scores (for MC form 1 and OE form 13) is shown in Table 7.12 (scores) and Table 7.13 (for the standard errors). These tables give the optimal IRT scaled scores for each combined score.

Although the four multiple-choice forms were essentially summed-score equivalent, the performance forms differed substantially in average difficulty (and consequently in average summed score). The IRT scaling (combined with the assumption of equivalent groups for the spiraled form administration) produced scores that are nearly the same, on average, for all forms. Tables 7.14 and 7.15 show the average scaled scores for the multiple-choice section, the performance section, and the combination for each of the performance forms and multiple-choice forms, respectively. In addition, Tables 7.14 and 7.15 include the correlation between the multi-

TABLE 7.10
Scoring Tables for Multiple Choice Form 1
of the North Carolina Test of Computer Skills

MC Form 1 Sum	Scaled Score	Standard Error
0	21	4
1	21	4
2	21	4
3	22	5
4	22	5
5	22	5
6	23	5
7	23	5
8	24	5
9	24	5
10	25	5
11	26	5
12	26	5
13	27	5
14	28	5
15	29	5
16	29	5
17	30	5
18	31	5
19	32	5
20	33	5
21	34	4
22	35	4
23	36	4
24	37	4
25	38	4
26	38	4
27	39	4
28	40	3
29	41	3
30	42	3
31	42	3
32	43	3
33	44	3
34	45	3
35	45	3
36	46	3
37	47	3
38	47	3
39	48	3
40	49	2
41	49	2
42	50	2
43	51	2
44	51	2

(Continued)

TABLE 7.10
(Continued)

MC Form 1 Sum	Scaled Score	Standard Error
45	52	2
46	53	2
47	53	2
48	54	2
49	55	2
50	55	2
51	56	2
52	57	2
53	57	2
54	58	2
55	59	2
56	60	3
57	61	3
58	62	3
59	62	3
60	63	3
61	64	3
62	66	3
63	67	3
64	68	3
65	69	3
66	71	3
67	73	4
68	75	4
69	77	4
70	79	5

ple-choice and performance scaled scores—the average value of .63 is somewhat less than would be expected if the multiple-choice and perform-ance tests measured exactly the same thing, but it is about the value we ex-pect given the factor analytic results described earlier.

THE GENERALIZATION OF SCALE SCORES BASED ON PATTERNS OF SUMMED SCORES TO CASES WITH MORE THAN TWO SUMMED SCORES

Thus far, we have developed the implications of IRT for combinations of summed scores on a pair of test sections, concentrating on tests combining multiple-choice and constructed-response items. However, it is possible to conceive of tests that combine more than two sections. One example might be a test with a multiple-choice section, a short-answer constructed-

TABLE 7.11
Scoring Tables for Performance Form 13
of the North Carolina Test of Computer Skills

OE Form 13 Sum	Scaled Score	Standard Error
0	26	8
1	28	8
2	29	8
3	31	7
4	33	7
5	35	7
6	37	7
7	39	7
8	40	7
9	42	7
10	43	7
11	45	7
12	46	7
13	47	7
14	49	7
15	50	7
16	51	7
17	53	7
18	54	7
19	56	7
20	58	7
21	59	7
22	61	7
23	63	7
24	64	7
25	67	7
26	70	8

response section, and one or more larger rated performance exercises, scored as three sections. Another class of examples may be derived from the idea of a multistage adaptive test, in which examinees respond to items on a routing test and, depending on their score, are adaptively administered one or more additional short tests in stages. The idea of the testlet computerized adaptive test (CAT) (Wainer & Kiely, 1987; Wainer & Lewis, 1990) is a variation of a multistage adaptive test with explicit consideration of questions of local dependence and independence within the test. Armstrong, Jones, Berliner, and Pashley (1998) described in detail the possible construction of one such CAT.

One IRT solution for scoring such multiple-section tests was introduced in chapter 4, where we described using multiple-category IRT models to score tests made up of testlets. In a multisection test, each section could be

TABLE 7.12
NC Computer Skills MC Form 1, OE Form 13

		26	25	24	23	22	21	20	19	18	17	16	15	14	13	12	11	10	9	8	7	6	5	4	3	2	1	0
		70	67	64	63	61	59	58	56	54	53	51	50	49	47	46	45	43	42	40	39	37	35	33	31	29	28	26
0	21	26	26	26	26	26	26	25	25	25	25	25	24	24	24	23	23	23	22	22	22	21	21	20	20	19	18	17
1	21	26	26	26	26	26	26	26	26	25	25	25	24	24	24	24	23	23	23	22	22	21	21	20	20	19	18	17
2	21	27	27	27	27	27	26	26	26	26	26	25	25	25	24	24	24	23	23	23	22	22	21	20	20	19	18	17
3	22	27	27	27	27	27	27	27	26	26	26	26	25	25	25	25	24	24	23	23	23	22	22	21	21	20	18	17
4	22	28	28	28	27	27	27	27	27	27	26	26	26	26	25	25	25	24	24	24	23	23	22	22	21	20	19	18
5	22	28	28	28	28	28	28	27	27	27	27	27	26	26	26	25	25	25	24	24	24	23	23	22	22	20	19	18
6	23	29	29	29	28	28	28	28	28	28	27	27	27	26	26	26	26	25	25	25	24	24	23	22	22	21	19	18
7	23	29	29	29	29	29	29	28	28	28	28	27	27	27	27	26	26	26	25	25	25	24	24	23	23	21	20	18
8	24	29	29	29	29	29	29	29	29	29	28	28	28	27	27	27	26	26	26	25	25	25	24	23	23	22	20	19
9	24	30	30	30	30	29	29	29	29	29	29	28	28	28	27	27	27	26	26	26	25	25	24	24	23	22	20	19
10	25	31	30	30	30	30	30	30	30	29	29	29	29	28	28	28	27	27	26	26	26	25	25	24	23	23	20	19
11	26	31	31	31	31	31	31	30	30	30	30	30	29	29	29	28	28	28	27	27	26	26	25	25	24	22	21	20
12	26	32	32	32	31	31	31	31	31	31	31	30	30	30	29	29	28	28	28	27	27	26	26	25	24	23	21	20
13	27	32	32	32	32	32	32	31	31	31	31	31	30	30	30	29	29	29	28	28	27	27	26	25	25	24	22	20
14	28	34	33	33	33	33	33	32	32	32	32	32	31	31	31	30	30	30	29	29	28	28	27	26	26	25	23	21
15	29	34	34	34	34	34	34	33	33	33	33	32	32	32	31	31	31	30	30	29	29	28	28	27	26	26	24	22
16	29	35	35	35	35	34	34	34	34	34	34	33	33	33	32	32	31	31	31	30	30	29	29	28	27	26	24	22
17	30	36	36	36	35	35	35	35	35	35	34	34	34	33	33	33	32	32	31	31	31	30	30	29	28	27	25	22
18	31	36	36	36	36	36	36	36	36	35	35	35	34	34	34	33	33	32	32	32	31	31	30	29	28	27	26	23
19	32	37	37	37	37	37	36	36	36	36	36	36	35	35	35	34	34	33	33	32	32	32	31	30	29	28	27	24
20	33	38	38	38	37	37	37	37	37	37	37	37	36	36	36	35	35	34	34	33	33	32	32	31	30	29	28	25
21	34	38	38	38	38	38	38	38	38	38	37	37	37	36	36	36	36	35	35	34	34	33	33	32	31	30	29	26
22	35	39	39	39	39	39	39	39	39	38	38	38	38	37	37	37	36	36	36	35	35	34	34	33	33	31	30	28
23	36	40	40	40	39	39	39	39	39	39	38	38	38	38	37	37	37	36	36	36	35	35	34	34	33	32	30	29
24	37	40	40	40	40	40	40	40	40	39	39	39	39	38	38	38	37	37	37	36	36	36	35	34	34	33	31	30
25	38	41	41	41	41	41	41	40	40	40	40	40	39	39	39	38	38	38	37	37	37	36	36	35	34	34	32	31

26	38	32	33	34	35	35	36	37	37	38	38	38	39	39	39	39	40	40	40	40	41	41	41	41	41	42	42	42
27	39	34	34	35	36	37	37	38	38	38	39	39	40	40	40	41	41	41	42	42	42	42	42	42	42	42	42	42
28	40	35	35	36	37	38	38	39	39	40	40	40	41	41	41	42	42	42	42	43	43	43	43	43	43	43	43	43
29	41	36	36	37	38	39	39	40	40	41	41	41	42	42	42	43	43	43	43	43	43	43	44	44	43	43	44	44
30	42	37	37	38	39	40	40	41	41	41	42	42	43	43	43	43	44	44	44	44	44	44	44	45	44	44	44	44
31	42	38	38	39	40	40	41	42	42	42	42	43	44	44	44	44	45	45	45	45	45	45	45	45	45	45	45	45
32	43	39	39	40	41	41	42	43	42	42	43	43	44	44	44	45	45	46	46	46	46	46	46	46	46	45	46	46
33	44	40	40	41	41	42	43	43	43	43	44	44	45	44	45	45	46	46	46	46	47	47	47	47	46	46	46	46
34	45	41	41	42	42	43	43	44	44	44	44	45	46	45	46	46	47	47	47	47	47	47	48	48	47	47	47	47
35	45	42	42	43	43	44	44	45	44	45	45	46	46	46	47	47	47	48	48	48	48	48	48	48	48	48	48	48
36	46	43	43	44	44	45	45	45	45	46	46	46	47	47	47	48	48	48	48	48	49	49	48	48	49	49	49	49
37	47	44	43	44	45	45	46	46	46	46	47	47	47	48	48	48	49	49	49	49	49	49	49	49	49	49	49	49
38	47	45	44	45	46	46	46	47	47	47	47	48	48	48	49	49	49	49	49	50	50	50	50	50	50	50	50	50
39	48	46	45	46	46	47	47	47	48	47	48	48	48	49	49	49	50	50	50	50	50	50	51	51	50	50	50	50
40	49	46	46	47	47	48	48	48	48	48	49	49	49	49	50	50	50	51	51	51	51	51	51	51	51	51	51	51
41	49	47	46	47	48	48	48	49	49	49	49	50	50	50	50	51	51	51	51	52	52	52	52	52	51	51	52	52
42	50	48	47	48	48	49	49	49	49	50	50	50	50	51	51	51	52	52	52	52	52	52	52	53	52	52	53	53
43	51	48	48	49	49	50	49	50	50	50	51	51	51	51	52	52	52	53	53	53	53	53	53	53	53	53	53	53
44	51	49	48	49	49	50	50	51	50	51	51	51	52	52	52	53	53	53	53	53	54	54	54	54	53	54	54	54
45	52	50	49	50	50	51	50	51	51	51	52	52	52	52	53	53	53	54	54	54	54	54	54	54	54	54	54	54
46	53	50	50	51	51	52	51	52	52	52	52	53	53	53	53	53	54	54	54	55	55	55	55	55	54	55	55	55
47	53	51	51	51	52	52	52	52	53	52	53	53	53	54	54	54	55	55	55	55	55	55	56	56	55	55	55	55
48	54	52	51	52	52	53	52	53	53	53	53	54	54	54	54	55	55	55	55	56	56	56	56	56	56	56	56	56
49	55	53	52	53	53	53	53	54	54	54	54	54	55	54	55	55	56	56	56	56	56	56	57	57	56	56	57	57
50	55	53	53	53	54	54	54	54	55	54	55	55	55	55	56	56	56	57	57	57	57	57	57	57	57	57	57	57
51	56	54	53	54	54	55	55	55	55	55	56	56	56	56	56	56	57	58	57	58	58	58	58	58	58	58	58	58
52	57	55	54	55	55	56	55	56	56	56	56	57	57	57	57	57	58	58	58	58	58	58	58	59	58	59	59	59
53	57	55	55	56	56	56	56	57	57	57	57	57	58	57	58	58	59	59	59	59	59	59	60	60	59	59	59	59
54	58	56	55	56	57	57	57	57	58	57	58	58	58	59	59	59	60	60	60	60	60	60	60	60	60	60	60	60
55	59	57	56	57	57	58	58	58	58	58	59	59	59	59	59	59	60	61	60	61	61	61	61	61	61	61	60	61

(Continued)

TABLE 7.12
(Continued)

		0	1	2	3	4	5	6	7	8	9	10	11	12	13	14	15	16	17	18	19	20	21	22	23	24	25	26
		26	*28*	*29*	*31*	*33*	*35*	*37*	*39*	*40*	*42*	*43*	*45*	*46*	*47*	*49*	*50*	*51*	*53*	*54*	*56*	*58*	*59*	*61*	*63*	*64*	*67*	*70*
56	*60*	58	58	58	58	58	58	58	58	58	58	58	59	59	59	59	59	59	60	60	60	60	60	61	61	61	61	61
57	*61*	58	58	58	59	59	59	59	59	59	59	59	59	60	60	60	60	60	60	61	61	61	61	61	61	62	62	62
58	*62*	59	59	59	59	59	59	60	60	60	60	60	60	60	61	61	61	61	61	61	62	62	62	62	62	63	63	63
59	*62*	60	60	60	60	60	60	60	61	61	61	61	61	61	61	62	62	62	62	62	62	63	63	63	63	64	64	64
60	*63*	61	61	61	61	61	61	61	61	62	62	62	62	62	62	62	63	63	63	63	63	64	64	64	64	65	65	65
61	*64*	62	62	62	62	62	62	62	62	63	63	63	63	63	63	63	63	64	64	64	64	64	65	65	65	65	66	66
62	*66*	63	63	63	63	63	63	63	63	64	64	64	64	64	64	64	64	65	65	65	65	65	66	66	66	66	67	67
63	*67*	64	64	64	64	64	64	64	64	64	65	65	65	65	65	65	65	66	66	66	66	67	67	67	67	68	68	69
64	*68*	65	65	65	65	65	65	65	65	65	65	66	66	66	66	66	66	66	67	67	67	68	68	68	69	69	69	70
65	*69*	66	66	66	66	66	66	66	66	67	67	67	67	67	67	68	68	68	68	69	69	69	69	70	70	70	71	71
66	*71*	67	67	67	67	67	67	67	68	68	68	68	68	68	69	69	69	69	69	70	70	70	71	71	71	72	72	73
67	*73*	68	68	68	69	69	69	69	70	69	69	69	70	71	70	69	70	71	71	71	71	72	72	73	73	73	74	75
68	*75*	70	70	70	70	71	70	70	70	71	71	71	71	71	73	72	72	72	72	73	73	73	74	74	75	75	76	77
69	*77*	71	71	71	71	71	72	72	72	72	72	72	73	73	73	73	74	74	74	75	75	75	76	76	77	77	78	80
70	*79*	73	73	73	73	73	73	73	74	74	74	74	75	75	75	75	76	76	76	77	77	78	78	79	79	80	81	82

Note. Rows are MC **summed**, *scaled* scores; columns are OE **summed**, *scaled* scores.

TABLE 7.13
SEs for NC Computer Skills MC Form 1, OE Form 13

	0	1	2	3	4	5	6	7	8	9	10	11	12	13	14	15	16	17	18	19	20	21	22	23	24	25	26
0	8	8	8	7	7	7	7	7	7	7	7	7	7	7	7	7	7	7	7	7	7	7	7	7	7	7	8
1	4	4	4	4	4	4	4	4	4	4	4	4	4	4	4	4	4	4	4	4	4	3	3	3	3	3	3
2	4	4	4	4	4	4	4	4	4	4	4	4	4	4	4	4	4	4	4	4	4	3	3	3	3	3	3
3	4	4	4	4	4	4	4	4	4	4	4	4	4	4	4	4	4	4	4	4	4	4	3	3	3	3	3
4	5	4	4	4	4	4	4	4	4	4	4	4	4	4	4	4	4	4	4	4	4	4	4	4	4	4	4
5	5	5	4	4	4	4	4	4	4	4	4	4	4	4	4	4	4	4	4	4	4	4	4	4	4	4	4
6	5	5	5	4	4	4	5	4	4	4	4	4	4	4	4	4	4	4	4	4	4	4	4	4	4	4	4
7	5	5	5	5	4	4	4	4	4	4	4	4	4	4	4	4	4	4	4	4	4	4	4	4	4	4	4
8	5	5	5	5	5	4	4	4	4	4	4	4	4	4	4	4	4	4	4	4	4	4	4	4	4	4	4
9	5	5	5	5	5	4	5	4	4	4	4	4	4	4	4	4	4	4	4	4	4	4	4	4	4	4	4
10	5	5	5	5	5	5	4	4	4	4	4	4	4	4	4	4	4	4	4	4	4	4	4	4	4	4	4
11	5	5	5	5	5	5	4	4	4	4	4	4	4	4	4	4	4	4	4	4	4	4	4	4	4	4	4
12	5	5	5	5	5	5	4	4	4	4	4	4	4	4	4	4	4	4	4	4	4	4	4	4	4	4	4
13	5	5	5	5	5	5	5	4	4	4	4	4	4	4	4	4	4	4	4	4	4	4	4	4	4	4	4
14	5	5	5	5	5	5	5	4	4	4	4	4	4	4	4	4	4	4	4	4	4	4	4	3	3	3	3
15	5	5	5	5	5	5	5	4	4	4	4	4	4	4	4	4	4	4	4	4	4	3	3	3	3	3	3
16	6	5	5	5	5	5	5	4	4	4	4	4	4	4	4	3	3	3	3	3	3	3	3	3	3	3	3
17	6	5	5	5	5	5	5	4	4	4	4	4	4	4	3	3	3	3	3	3	3	3	3	3	3	3	3
18	6	6	5	5	5	5	4	4	4	4	4	4	4	3	3	3	3	3	3	3	3	3	3	3	3	3	3
19	6	6	6	5	5	5	4	4	4	4	4	4	4	3	3	3	3	3	3	3	3	3	3	3	3	3	3
20	6	6	6	5	5	4	4	4	4	4	4	4	4	3	3	3	3	3	3	3	3	3	3	3	3	3	3
21	6	6	6	5	4	4	4	4	4	4	4	4	3	3	3	3	3	3	3	3	3	3	3	3	3	3	3
22	6	6	5	5	4	4	4	4	4	4	4	4	3	3	3	3	3	3	3	3	3	3	3	3	3	3	3
23	6	6	5	5	4	4	4	4	4	4	4	4	3	3	3	3	3	3	3	3	3	3	3	3	3	3	3

(Continued)

TABLE 7.13
(Continued)

	0	1	2	3	4	5	6	7	8	9	10	11	12	13	14	15	16	17	18	19	20	21	22	23	24	25	26
	8	8	8	7	7	7	7	7	7	7	7	7	7	7	7	7	7	7	7	7	7	7	7	7	7	7	8
24	6	5	5	5	5	4	4	4	4	4	4	4	3	3	3	3	3	3	3	3	3	3	3	3	3	3	3
25	6	5	5	5	4	4	4	4	4	4	4	3	3	3	3	3	3	3	3	3	3	3	3	3	3	3	3
26	6	5	5	5	4	4	4	4	4	4	3	3	3	3	3	3	3	3	3	3	3	3	3	3	3	3	3
27	5	5	5	4	4	4	4	4	4	3	3	3	3	3	3	3	3	3	3	3	3	3	3	3	3	3	3
28	5	5	5	4	4	4	4	4	3	3	3	3	3	3	3	3	3	3	3	3	3	3	3	3	3	3	3
29	5	4	4	4	4	4	4	3	3	3	3	3	3	3	3	3	3	3	3	3	3	3	3	3	3	3	3
30	5	4	4	4	4	4	3	3	3	3	3	3	3	3	3	3	3	3	3	3	3	3	3	3	3	3	3
31	5	4	4	4	4	3	3	3	3	3	3	3	3	3	3	3	3	3	3	3	3	3	3	3	3	3	3
32	4	4	4	4	4	3	3	3	3	3	3	3	3	3	3	3	3	3	3	3	3	3	3	3	3	3	3
33	4	4	4	4	3	3	3	3	3	3	3	3	3	3	3	3	3	3	3	3	3	3	3	3	3	3	3
34	4	3	3	3	3	3	3	3	3	3	3	3	3	3	3	3	3	3	3	2	2	2	2	2	2	2	2
35	4	3	3	3	3	3	3	3	3	3	3	3	3	3	3	3	3	2	2	2	2	2	2	2	2	2	2
36	4	3	3	3	3	3	3	3	3	3	3	3	3	3	3	2	2	2	2	2	2	2	2	2	2	2	2
37	3	3	3	3	3	3	3	3	3	3	3	3	2	2	2	2	2	2	2	2	2	2	2	2	2	2	2
38	3	3	3	3	3	3	3	3	3	3	2	2	2	2	2	2	2	2	2	2	2	2	2	2	2	2	2
39	3	3	3	3	3	3	3	3	3	2	2	2	2	2	2	2	2	2	2	2	2	2	2	2	2	2	2
40	3	3	3	3	3	3	3	3	2	2	2	2	2	2	2	2	2	2	2	2	2	2	2	2	2	2	2
41	3	3	3	3	3	3	3	2	2	2	2	2	2	2	2	2	2	2	2	2	2	2	2	2	2	2	2
42	3	3	3	3	3	3	2	2	2	2	2	2	2	2	2	2	2	2	2	2	2	2	2	2	2	2	2
43	3	3	3	3	2	2	2	2	2	2	2	2	2	2	2	2	2	2	2	2	2	2	2	2	2	2	2
44	3	3	3	3	2	2	2	2	2	2	2	2	2	2	2	2	2	2	2	2	2	2	2	2	2	2	2
45	3	3	2	2	2	2	2	2	2	2	2	2	2	2	2	2	2	2	2	2	2	2	2	2	2	2	2

MC																												
46	2	2	2	2	2	2	2	2	2	2	2	2	2	2	2	2	2	2	2	2	2	2	2	2	2	2	2	2
47	2	2	2	2	2	2	2	2	2	2	2	2	2	2	2	2	2	2	2	2	2	2	2	2	2	2	2	2
48	2	2	2	2	2	2	2	2	2	2	2	2	2	2	2	2	2	2	2	2	2	2	2	2	2	2	2	2
49	2	2	2	2	2	2	2	2	2	2	2	2	2	2	2	2	2	2	2	2	2	2	2	2	2	2	2	2
50	2	2	2	2	2	2	2	2	2	2	2	2	2	2	2	2	2	2	2	2	2	2	2	2	2	2	2	2
51	2	2	2	2	2	2	2	2	2	2	2	2	2	2	2	2	2	2	2	2	2	2	2	2	2	2	2	2
52	2	2	2	2	2	2	2	2	2	2	2	2	2	2	2	2	2	2	2	2	2	2	2	2	2	2	2	2
53	2	2	2	2	2	2	2	2	2	2	2	2	2	2	2	2	2	2	2	2	2	2	2	2	2	2	2	2
54	2	2	2	2	2	2	2	2	2	2	2	2	2	2	2	2	2	2	2	2	3	3	3	3	3	3	3	3
55	2	2	2	2	2	2	2	2	2	2	3	3	3	3	3	3	3	3	3	3	3	3	3	3	3	3	3	3
56	3	3	3	3	3	3	3	3	3	3	3	3	3	3	3	3	3	3	3	3	3	3	3	3	3	3	3	3
57	3	3	3	3	3	3	3	3	3	3	3	3	3	3	3	3	3	3	3	3	3	3	3	3	3	3	3	3
58	3	3	3	3	3	3	3	3	3	3	3	3	3	3	3	3	3	3	3	3	3	3	3	3	3	3	3	3
59	3	3	3	3	3	3	3	3	3	3	3	3	3	3	3	3	3	3	3	3	3	3	3	3	3	3	3	3
60	3	3	3	3	3	3	3	3	3	3	3	3	3	3	3	3	3	3	3	3	3	3	3	3	3	3	3	3
61	3	3	3	3	3	3	3	3	3	3	3	3	3	3	3	3	3	3	3	3	3	3	3	3	3	3	3	3
62	3	3	3	3	3	3	3	3	3	3	3	3	3	3	3	3	3	3	3	3	3	3	3	3	3	3	3	3
63	3	3	3	3	3	3	3	3	3	3	3	3	3	3	3	3	3	3	3	3	3	3	3	3	3	3	3	3
64	3	3	3	3	3	3	3	3	3	3	3	3	3	3	3	3	3	3	3	3	3	3	3	3	3	3	3	3
65	3	3	3	3	3	3	3	3	3	3	3	3	3	3	3	3	3	3	3	3	3	3	3	3	3	3	3	3
66	3	3	3	3	3	3	3	3	3	3	3	3	3	3	3	3	3	3	3	3	3	3	3	3	3	3	3	3
67	3	3	3	3	3	3	3	3	3	3	3	3	3	3	3	3	3	3	3	3	3	3	3	3	3	3	3	3
68	3	3	3	3	3	3	3	3	3	3	3	3	3	3	4	4	4	4	4	4	4	4	4	4	4	4	4	4
69	4	4	4	4	4	4	4	4	4	4	4	4	4	4	4	4	4	4	4	4	4	4	4	4	4	4	4	4
70	4	4	4	4	4	4	4	4	4	4	4	4	4	4	4	4	4	4	4	4	4	4	4	4	4	5	5	5

Note. Rows are MC **summed**, *scaled* scores; columns are OE **summed**, *scaled* scores.

TABLE 7.14
Average Scaled Scores for the Groups Responding to the
12 Performance Forms of the North Carolina Test
of Computer Skills, and the Correlation Between
Multiple-Choice and Performance Scaled Scores

OE	Average			
Form	MC	OE	Both	$r_{MC\text{-}OE}$
1 (13)	50.31	50.22	50.28	.573
2 (14)	49.65	49.78	49.62	.620
3 (15)	50.76	50.46	50.77	.694
4 (16)	50.19	50.23	50.10	.591
5 (17)	50.44	50.12	50.35	.649
6 (18)	49.71	49.88	49.68	.644
7 (19)	50.51	50.22	50.48	.579
8 (20)	50.17	50.30	50.17	.678
9 (21)	49.56	49.75	49.52	.629
10 (22)	49.62	49.83	49.60	.657
11 (23)	49.41	49.57	49.38	.652
12 (24)	49.68	49.83	49.63	.617
Average	50.00	50.02	49.96	.632

TABLE 7.15
Average Scaled Scores for the Groups Responding to the Four
Multiple-Choice Forms of the North Carolina Test
of Computer Skills, and the Correlation Between
Multiple-Choice and Performance Scaled Scores

MC	Average			
Form	MC	OE	Both	$r_{MC\text{-}OE}$
1	49.96	50.03	49.87	.654
2	50.31	50.27	50.23	.637
3	49.72	49.75	49.73	.621
4	50.03	50.03	50.03	.617
Average	50.00	50.02	49.96	.632

regarded as a testlet, and multiple-category models could be used to produce trace lines for each testlet score. Alternatively, if local independence can be assumed for the items both within and between testlets (here, for ease of language use, we refer to any of "sections" or "stages" in a test as testlets), the methods of this chapter may be generalized to use IRT to score combinations of testlet summed scores.

In general, for T testlet summed scores indexed by t in a vector $\mathbf{x}$, we can compute

$$L_x(\theta) = L(x|\theta) = \prod_t L_x^t(\theta) , \tag{13}$$

where $L_x^t(\theta)$ is the likelihood for summed score x on testlet t. Then, just as before, probability of each response pattern of summed scores $\mathbf{x}$ in a population with population distribution $\phi(\theta)$ for θ is

$$P_\mathbf{x} = \int L_\mathbf{x}(\theta)\phi(\theta)\, d\theta . \tag{14}$$

The average of the joint likelihood for the pattern of summed scores and the population distribution may used as a point estimate of proficiency; that is,

$$\text{EAP}[\theta|\mathbf{x}] = \frac{\int \theta L_\mathbf{x}(\theta)\phi(\theta)\, d\theta}{P_\mathbf{x}} ; \tag{15}$$

It differs from the response-pattern EAP only in that it uses less information. The corresponding conditional variance

$$\text{var}[\theta|\mathbf{x}] = \frac{\int (\theta - \text{EAP}[\theta|\mathbf{x})^2 L_\mathbf{x}(\theta)\phi(\theta)\, d\theta}{P_\mathbf{x}} , \tag{16}$$

may be used to compute a reportable standard error for each score as $\sqrt{\text{var}[\theta|\mathbf{x}]}$.

The Problem of the Size of the Scoring Tables. A major drawback of the use of this IRT likelihood-based system to score tests that combine several sections is the size of the scoring tables. Equations 15 and 16 yield tables that have as many dimensions as there are testlets (or sections); three- or four- or five-way tables quickly become large and unwieldy. For some computerized scoring applications, such tables may be invisible (except to the system's programmers); in such cases, this system may be practical. However, for many uses such large and complex scoring tables would be a problem. In chapter 8, we introduce a system to approximate this IRT based scoring with linear combinations of scaled testlet scores—that approximation replaces the excessively large tables with simple computations.

An Aside: Use of $P_{xx'}$ as the Basis of an "Appropriateness Index." For any test that is constructed of testlets (blocks of items, like MC and OE items; or stages in a testlet CAT), and for any number of testlets, tables of the same general form as Table 7.4 may also be constructed using Eq. 14:

$$P_{\mathbf{x}} = \int L_{\mathbf{x}}(\theta)\phi(\theta)\,d\theta.$$

These values may be used to construct a $(1 - \alpha)100\%$ HDR for scores for any combination of any number of blocks, generalizing the procedure that was used to make Table 7.4. These represent the model's predictions of score combinations that are likely and unlikely. Any score combination that lies outside the $(1 - \alpha)100\%$ HDR could be flagged, in much the same way that it has been proposed that appropriateness indices such as l_z (Drasgow, Levine, & Williams, 1985) be used to flag response patterns that are relatively unlikely, according to an IRT model. However, unlike l_z, which relies on a Gaussian approximation for the distribution of the loglikelihood for its (questionable) p values (Reise & Flannery, 1996), the probability statements associated with use of a $(1 - \alpha)100\%$ HDR for two- (or three- or four-) way classifications of the item responses blockwise may be computed directly from the IRT model.

What should be done with examinees whose responses are flagged as unlikely, according to the model? This question raises difficult policy questions, and its answer certainly depends on the purpose of the test. The mismatch between the examinee's performance on one block and another may mean the examinee cheated on one block (in which case the better measure may be the person's lower performance), or it may be that something else went wrong (distraction? computer difficulties?) with the examinee's performance on the block on which he or she scored lower, in which case the higher of the two scores is more valid. The context of high-stakes testing, which is expensive in time and money for the examinee, may add further considerations. Davis and Lewis (1996) and McLeod and Lewis (1999) suggested several possible courses of action that could be followed if the test was computerized: One set of possible actions include on-line extension of the test, either switching from a CAT system to a long linear form, or using a special block of "silver bullet items" to more accurately estimate the proficiency of the examinee. Other possible actions include score cancellation, and retesting.

CONCLUSION

Item response theory is a very flexible system for scoring tests. Suitably extended, as it has been in this chapter, it can be used to provide scores on the same scale for any of a variety of combinations of scores, either for individual items or for blocks of items (sections on a test, or testlets). The technology developed in this chapter yields scoring tables that appear to test users much like familiar score-translation tables commonly used in large-scale testing to convert summed scores to scale scores. Given that the IRT model is appropriate for the data, these score-translation tables provide optimal proficiency estimates if we are limited to the use of combinations of summed scores.

The only obvious disadvantage of the scoring system introduced in this chapter is the potentially unwieldy size of the scoring tables. In chapter 8, we introduce approximate methods that replace the scoring tables with weighted linear combinations of the component scores.

REFERENCES

Armstrong, R. D., Jones, D. H., Berliner, N., & Pashley, P. (1998, June). *Computerized adaptive tests with multiple forms structures*. Paper presented at the annual meeting of the Psychometric Society, Champaign-Urbana, IL.

Birnbaum, A. (1968). Some latent trait models and their use in inferring an examinee's ability. In F. M. Lord & M. R. Novick, *Statistical theories of mental test scores* (pp. 395–479). Reading, MA: Addison-Wesley.

Bridgeman, B., Morgan, R., & Wang, M. M. (1996). *Reliability of Advanced Placement examinations* (RR 96-3). Princeton, NJ: Educational Testing Service.

Calderone, J., King, L. M., & Horkay, N. (Eds.). (1997). *The NAEP guide*. Washington, DC: U.S. Department of Education, National Center for Education Statistics.

College Entrance Examination Board. (1988). *Technical manual for the Advanced Placement Program 1982–1986*. New York: Author.

Davis, L. A., & Lewis, C. (1996, April). *Person-fit indices and their role in the CAT environment*. Paper presented at the annual meeting of the National Council on Measurement in Education, New York.

Drasgow, F., Levine, M. V., & Williams, E. A. (1985). Appropriateness measurement with polytomous item response models and standardized indices. *British Journal of Mathematical and Statistical Psychology, 38*, 67–86.

Klein, S. P., McCaffrey, D., Stecher, B., & Koretz, D. (1995). The reliability of mathematics portfolio scores: Lessons from the Vermont experience. *Applied Measurement in Education, 8*, 243–260.

Longford, N. T. (1997). Shrinkage estimation of linear combinations of true scores. *Psychometrika, 62*, 237–244.

Lukhele, R., Thissen, D., & Wainer, H. (1994). On the relative value of multiple-choice, constructed-response, and examinee-selected items on two achievement tests. *Journal of Educational Measurement, 31*, 234–250.

Masters, G. N., & Wright, B. D. (1984). The essential process in a family of measurement models. *Psychometrika, 49*, 529–544.

McLeod, L. D., & Lewis, C. (1999). Detecting item memorization in the CAT environment. *Applied Psychological Measurement, 23*, 147–160.

Novick, M. R., & Jackson, P. H. (1974). *Statistical methods for educational and psychological research*. New York: McGraw-Hill.

Reise, S. P., & Flannery, W. P. (1996). Assessing person-fit on measures of typical performance. *Applied Psychological Measurement, 9*, 9–26.

Samejima, F. (1969). Estimation of latent ability using a response pattern of graded scores. *Psychometric Monograph, 17*.

Thissen, D. (1991). Multilog user's guide—Version 6 [Computer software]. Chicago: Scientific Software, Inc.

Thissen, D., Wainer, H., & Wang, X. B. (1994). Are tests comprising both multiple-choice and free-response items necessarily less unidimensional than multiple-choice tests? An analysis of two tests. *Journal of Educational Measurement, 31,* 113–123.

Wainer, H., & Kiely, G. L. (1987). Item clusters and computerized adaptive testing: A case for testlets. *Journal of Educational Measurement, 24,* 185–201.

Wainer, H., & Lewis, C. (1990). Toward a psychometrics for testlets. *Journal of Educational Measurement, 27,* 1–14.

Wright, B. D., & Linacre, J. M. (1992). Bigsteps Rasch analysis [Computer software] Chicago: MESA Press.

Yen, W. M., & Ferrara, S. (1997). The Maryland school performance assessment program: Performance assessment with psychometric quality suitable for high stakes usage. *Educational and Psychological Measurement, 57,* 60–84.

Chapter 8

Item Response Theory Applied to Combinations of Multiple-Choice and Constructed-Response Items— Approximation Methods for Scale Scores

David Thissen
Lauren Nelson
University of North Carolina at Chapel Hill

Kimberly A. Swygert
Law School Admission Council

In chapter 7, we introduced a novel IRT-based score combination method to produce scale scores for tests that combine multiple-choice and constructed-response items; to use unidimensional IRT, we assumed that the tests, although they mix item types, are essentially unidimensional with respect to the variation in proficiency that they measure. The only obvious disadvantage of the scoring system introduced in chapter 7 is the potentially unwieldy size of the scoring tables. In this chapter, we develop approximate methods that replace the scoring tables with weighted linear combinations of the component scores.

After decades of high-visibility tests with scoring systems that are "sums of points," many test users expect test scores to be exactly that; the fact that IRT does not naturally yield scores in that format has been an impediment to the adoption of IRT scale scores in some contexts. However, Green (1997) and others observed that IRT scale scores may be approximated as linear combinations of values that reflect the relative difficulty of items and weights that reflect different degrees of discrimination; in this chapter we develop and illustrate the use of a system to approximate the IRT scores for patterns of summed scores using linear combinations: "points" and "weights" (Thissen, 1998a, 1998b). By computing the scale scores as weighted linear combinations, we are able to replace the large (and potentially unwieldy) score-translation tables of chapter 7 with straightforward computations, which are easier to do, and which may be easier to explain to test users.

A LINEAR APPROXIMATION FOR THE EXTENSION TO COMBINATIONS OF SCORES

As developed in chapter 7, using an IRT model for a combination of a multiple-choice (MC) section with open-ended (OE) items scored in multiple categories, the likelihood for score combination x,x' is

$$L_{xx'}(\theta) = L_x^{MC}(\theta)L_{x'}^{OE}(\theta) . \tag{1}$$

The modeled probability of the response pattern of summed scores $\{x,x'\}$ is

$$P_{xx'} = \int L_{xx'}(\theta)\phi(\theta)\, d\theta ;$$

The expected value of θ, given the response pattern of summed scores $\{x,x'\}$ is

$$\text{EAP}[\theta\,|\,x,x'] = \frac{\int \theta L_{xx'}(\theta)\phi(\theta)\, d\theta}{P_{xx'}} , \tag{2}$$

and the corresponding conditional variance is

$$\text{var}[\theta\,|\,x,x'] = \frac{\int (\theta - \text{EAP}[\theta\,|\,x,x'])^2\, L_{xx'}(\theta)\phi(\theta)\, d\theta}{P_{xx'}} . \tag{3}$$

It may be useful for many purposes to approximate $\text{EAP}[\theta\,|\,x,x']$ and $\text{var}[\theta\,|\,x,x']$ as linear combinations of values associated with score x on the MC section and score x' on the OE section. If we assume that the joint likelihood for each summed score, and the population distribution, are Gaussian, we obtain (see the appendix to this chapter) estimates of the form

$$\text{EAP}^*[\theta\,|\,x,x'] = \frac{w_x \text{EAP}[\theta|x] + w_{x'} \text{EAP}[\theta|x']}{w_x + w_{x'} - 1} , \tag{4}$$

with $w_x = 1/\text{var}[\theta|x]$, and

$$\text{var*}[\theta \,|\, x, x'] = \frac{1}{w_x + w_{x'} - 1},\tag{5}$$

in which the asterisks indicate that EAP* and var* are approximations for EAP and var. The value of $\sqrt{\text{var*}[\theta \,|\, x, x']}$ is an approximation that may be used as the reported standard error of the scale score.

Equations 4 and 5 form the basis of the linear approximation to the IRT-based score combination system: We compute the value of the EAP associated with each summed score x on the MC section of the test (i.e., EAP$[\theta \,|\, x]$), and the EAP associated with summed score x' on the OE section of the test (i.e., EAP$[\theta \,|\, x']$), using the methods described in chapters 3 and 4, and recapitulated briefly in chapter 7. At the same time, we compute the variance associated with each of those EAPs; those are var$[\theta \,|\, x]$ and var$[\theta \,|\, x']$. Then using Eq. 4, we compute the approximation for the scale score as (what appears to be nearly) a weighted average of the two EAPs, using weights computed as the inverses of the variances.

The algebraic development of this result in the appendix to this chapter reveals that Eqs. 4 and 5 are slightly more complicated than weighted averages of the EAPs; the relatively mysterious appearance of -1 in the denominators arises from several adjustments having to do with the population distribution in Eqs. 2 and 3. Actually, the approximate values of the EAP for the combination is

$$\text{EAP*}[\theta \,|\, x, x'] = \frac{\dfrac{1}{v_x^*}\,\theta_x^* + \dfrac{1}{v_{x'}^*}\,\theta_{x'}^* + \dfrac{1}{1}\,0}{\dfrac{1}{v_x^*} + \dfrac{1}{v_{x'}^*} + \dfrac{1}{1}}.\tag{6}$$

in which the values of θ_x^* and v_x^* may be interpreted as the mean and variance of a Gaussian approximation to the likelihood for score x, L_x^{MC}, and the values of $\theta_{x'}^*$ and $v_{x'}^*$ may be interpreted as the mean and variance of a Gaussian approximation to the likelihood for score x', $L_{x'}^{\text{OE}}$. The values of θ_x^* and v_x^* are computed from our standard summed-score IRT analysis as

$$\theta_x^* = \frac{\text{EAP}_x[\theta]}{1 - \text{var}_x[\theta]}\tag{7}$$

and

$$v_x^* = \frac{1}{\dfrac{1}{\text{var}_x[\theta]}} - 1 \;\; = \frac{\text{var}_x[\theta]}{1 - \text{var}_x[\theta]}.\tag{8}$$

These are curious values, because in some cases (e.g., for scores equal to the maximum obtainable on the test), the likelihood cannot be normed, and its mean and variance are undefined (the mode is not finite). Although Eq. 6 is not convenient for computation, it is useful to clarify the fact that the approximation is a weighted linear combination of three components—an approximation to the average of the likelihood for score x on the MC section, an approximation to the average of the likelihood for score x' on the OE section, and the zero that is the average of the population distribution—all weighted by the inverse of their respective variances. Equation 6 simplifies to Eq. 4 when we intend to use the readily available EAPs and the variances associated with summed scores on the components.

Using Approximated IRT Scale Scores for Patterns of Summed Scores to Score Tests Combining Multiple-Choice and Constructed-Response Sections: Wisconsin Third-Grade Reading Field Test.

To illustrate the computation of scale scores using Eqs. 4 and 5, we revisit the Wisconsin third-grade reading test previously discussed in chapters 3, 4, and 7. In chapter 7, we tabulated the scale scores for the combination of the 16-item multiple-choice section and the 4 open-ended items, each rated 0–3, using the 3PL and GR models (Birnbaum, 1968; Samejima, 1969) respectively. Here, we use the same item response models and item parameter estimates to compute the values of $EAP^*[\theta|x,x']$ and $SD^*[\theta|x,x']$.

Figure 8.1 illustrates the computations for the score combination $x_{MC} = 15$ and $x_{OE} = 9$ that was used as an example in Fig. 7.1. Figure 8.1 shows the population distribution in the top panel, the likelihoods for scores 15 and 9 as dashed curves in the center panel, and the joint likelihood (which is the product of the population distribution and the two likelihoods) as a dashed curve in the lower panel. The two solid curves in the center panel of Fig. 8.1 are Gaussian distributions with averages of θ_x^* and $\theta_{x'}^*$ and variances equal to v_x^* and $v_{x'}^*$. The solid curve in the lower panel of Fig. 8.1 is the Gaussian approximation for the joint likelihood, which may be computed either by multiplying the three solid curves in the upper two panels or, more simply, as the Gaussian distribution with mean and variance given by Eq. 4 (or Eq. 6) and Eq. 5. In Fig. 8.1, $EAP[\theta|15,9] = 0.51$, and $SD[\theta|15,9]$ is 0.45; $EAP^*[\theta|15,9] = 0.53$, and $SD^*[\theta|15,9]$ is 0.47. Because score reporting is rarely done to more than one decimal place in standard units, the differences of 0.02 between the approximations and the direct likelihood computations would have no apparent consequences.

Turning to the scores for the entire test, Tables 8.1 and 8.2 show the components for the MC and OE sections, respectively, that are used to compute the values of $EAP^*[\theta|x,x']$ and $SD^*[\theta|x,x']$ that are shown in Tables 8.3 and 8.4. Equation 4 is used to compute the values of $EAP^*[\theta|x,x']$ shown in Table 8.3. For each combination of a score x on the MC section and x' on the OE section, we use the values of $EAP[\theta]$, weighted by the val-

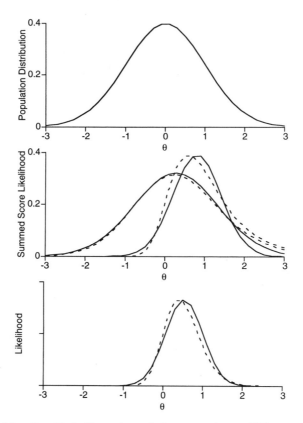

FIG. 8.1. Graphical illustration of the approximate IRT pattern-of-summed-scores combination system, using data from the Wisconsin third-grade reading test. Top panel: The population distribution $[\phi(\theta)]$. Center panel: Dashed curves are the likelihood for OE score 9 $[L_9^{OE}(\theta)]$ and the likelihood for MC score 15 $[L_{15}^{MC}(\theta)]$; solid curves are Gaussian distributions with averages of θ_{15}^* and θ_9^* and variances equal to v_{15}^* and v_9^*. Lower panel: The dashed curve is the likelihood for θ given OE score 9 and MC score 15 $[L_{15\&9}(\theta)]$; the solid curve is the Gaussian approximation.

ues of w that correspond with the scores x and x'. For example, for the combination illustrated in Fig. 8.1,

$$EAP^*[\theta|15,9] = \frac{3.71 \times 0.59 + 1.87 \times 0.13}{3.71 + 1.87 - 1} = 0.53 \ ,$$

and

$$SD^*[\theta|15,9] = \sqrt{\frac{1}{3.71 + 1.87 - 1}} = 0.47 \ .$$

TABLE 8.1
EAP[θ], SD[θ], w, and the Probability for Each Score
for the Multiple-Choice Section of the Wisconsin Third-Grade
Reading Field Test, as Computed With the 3PL Model

Sum	EAP[θ]	SD[θ]	w	Probability
0	−2.33	0.49	4.10	.00016
1	−2.22	0.50	4.02	.00114
2	−2.09	0.50	3.97	.00395
3	−1.95	0.50	3.99	.00916
4	−1.79	0.49	4.10	.01625
5	−1.61	0.48	4.37	.02400
6	−1.43	0.45	4.87	.03131
7	−1.24	0.42	5.62	.03769
8	−1.05	0.39	6.61	.04320
9	−0.87	0.36	7.68	.04825
10	−0.69	0.34	8.55	.05361
11	−0.51	0.34	8.90	.06056
12	−0.30	0.34	8.48	.07119
13	−0.07	0.37	7.25	.08891
14	0.21	0.43	5.48	.11943
15	0.59	0.52	3.71	.17005
16	1.12	0.64	2.41	.22113

Note. The values of EAP[θ] differ slightly from those shown in Table 3.14, because the item parameters used here are from a joint calibration of the 16 MC items with 4 OE items, and differ slightly from those for the 16 MC items alone used to compute the values in Table 3.14. The item parameters used here are in Table 4.8.

TABLE 8.2
EAP[θ], SD[θ], w, and the Probability for Each Score
for the Open-Ended Section of the Wisconsin Third-Grade
Reading Field Test, as Computed with the Graded Model

Sum	EAP[θ]	SD[θ]	w	Probability
0	−2.88	0.76	1.74	.00001
1	−2.55	0.76	1.71	.00017
2	−2.22	0.76	1.75	.00106
3	−1.90	0.75	1.80	.00448
4	−1.59	0.74	1.85	.01434
5	−1.27	0.73	1.89	.03631
6	−0.95	0.72	1.92	.07416
7	−0.61	0.72	1.92	.12716
8	−0.25	0.73	1.89	.18702
9	0.13	0.73	1.87	.22546
10	0.53	0.75	1.80	.19341
11	0.96	0.76	1.71	.10676
12	1.41	0.79	1.62	.02966

Note that these computations are based solely on the values of $EAP[\theta|x,x']$ and $SD[\theta|x,x']$ for each summed score that are computed exactly as described in chapters 3 and 4. (Remember that the values of the weights, w, are the inverse of $var[\theta|x]$.) Thus, all of the values in Tables 8.3 and 8.4 are easily computed from the values in Tables 8.1 and 8.2; the rectangular scoring tables are superfluous in operational use, and are shown here solely for didactic purposes.

TABLE 8.3
Values of the Linear Approximation $EAP^*[\theta|x,x']$ for Combinations
of Multiple-Choice (MC) and Open-Ended (OE) Summed Scores
on a Wisconsin Reading Tryout Form (θ Is Standardized)

MC	Open–Ended (Summed) Rated Score												
Sum	0	1	2	3	4	5	6	7	8	9	10	11	12
0	-3.0	-2.9	-2.8	-2.6	-2.5	-2.4	-2.3	-2.1	-2.0	-1.9	-1.8	-1.6	-1.5
1	-2.9	-2.8	-2.7	-2.6	-2.4	-2.3	-2.2	-2.0	-1.9	-1.8	-1.7	-1.5	-1.4
2	-2.8	-2.7	-2.6	-2.5	-2.3	-2.2	-2.1	-1.9	-1.8	-1.7	-1.5	-1.4	-1.3
3	-2.7	-2.6	-2.5	-2.3	-2.2	-2.1	-2.0	-1.8	-1.7	-1.6	-1.4	-1.3	-1.2
4	-2.6	-2.4	-2.3	-2.2	-2.1	-2.0	-1.8	-1.7	-1.6	-1.4	-1.3	-1.2	-1.1
5	-2.4	-2.2	-2.1	-2.0	-1.9	-1.8	-1.7	-1.6	-1.4	-1.3	-1.2	-1.1	-1.0
6	-2.1	-2.0	-1.9	-1.8	-1.7	-1.6	-1.5	-1.4	-1.3	-1.2	-1.1	-1.0	-0.9
7	-1.9	-1.8	-1.7	-1.6	-1.5	-1.4	-1.3	-1.2	-1.1	-1.0	-0.9	-0.8	-0.8
8	-1.6	-1.5	-1.5	-1.4	-1.3	-1.3	-1.2	-1.1	-1.0	-0.9	-0.8	-0.7	-0.6
9	-1.4	-1.3	-1.3	-1.2	-1.1	-1.1	-1.0	-0.9	-0.8	-0.8	-0.7	-0.6	-0.5
10	-1.2	-1.1	-1.1	-1.0	-0.9	-0.9	-0.8	-0.7	-0.7	-0.6	-0.5	-0.5	-0.4
11	-1.0	-0.9	-0.9	-0.8	-0.8	-0.7	-0.6	-0.6	-0.5	-0.4	-0.4	-0.3	-0.2
12	-0.8	-0.8	-0.7	-0.6	-0.6	-0.5	-0.5	-0.4	-0.3	-0.3	-0.2	-0.1	0.0
13	-0.7	-0.6	-0.6	-0.5	-0.4	-0.4	-0.3	-0.2	-0.1	0.0	0.1	0.1	0.2
14	-0.6	-0.5	-0.4	-0.4	-0.3	-0.2	-0.1	0.0	0.1	0.2	0.3	0.5	0.6
15	-0.6	-0.5	-0.4	-0.3	-0.2	0.0	0.1	0.2	0.4	0.5	0.7	0.9	1.0
16	-0.7	-0.5	-0.4	-0.2	-0.1	0.1	0.3	0.5	0.7	0.9	1.1	1.4	1.6

Note. The unshaded area in the table represents the central 99% HDR for the response patterns.

TABLE 8.4
Values of the Linear Approximation $SD^*[\theta|x,x']$ for Combinations
of Multiple-Choice (MC) and Open-Ended (OE) Summed Scores
on a Wisconsin Reading Tryout Form (θ Is Standardized)

MC	Open–Ended (Summed) Rated Score												
Sum	0	1	2	3	4	5	6	7	8	9	10	11	12
0	0.5	0.5	0.5	0.5	0.4	0.4	0.4	0.4	0.4	0.4	0.5	0.5	0.5
1	0.5	0.5	0.5	0.5	0.5	0.5	0.4	0.5	0.5	0.5	0.5	0.5	0.5
2	0.5	0.5	0.5	0.5	0.5	0.5	0.5	0.5	0.5	0.5	0.5	0.5	0.5
3	0.5	0.5	0.5	0.5	0.5	0.5	0.5	0.5	0.5	0.5	0.5	0.5	0.5
4	0.5	0.5	0.5	0.5	0.4	0.4	0.4	0.4	0.4	0.4	0.5	0.5	0.5
5	0.4	0.4	0.4	0.4	0.4	0.4	0.4	0.4	0.4	0.4	0.4	0.4	0.4
6	0.4	0.4	0.4	0.4	0.4	0.4	0.4	0.4	0.4	0.4	0.4	0.4	0.4
7	0.4	0.4	0.4	0.4	0.4	0.4	0.4	0.4	0.4	0.4	0.4	0.4	0.4
8	0.4	0.4	0.4	0.4	0.4	0.4	0.4	0.4	0.4	0.4	0.4	0.4	0.4
9	0.3	0.3	0.3	0.3	0.3	0.3	0.3	0.3	0.3	0.3	0.3	0.3	0.3
10	0.3	0.3	0.3	0.3	0.3	0.3	0.3	0.3	0.3	0.3	0.3	0.3	0.3
11	0.3	0.3	0.3	0.3	0.3	0.3	0.3	0.3	0.3	0.3	0.3	0.3	0.3
12	0.3	0.3	0.3	0.3	0.3	0.3	0.3	0.3	0.3	0.3	0.3	0.3	0.3
13	0.4	0.4	0.4	0.4	0.4	0.4	0.3	0.4	0.4	0.4	0.4	0.4	0.4
14	0.4	0.4	0.4	0.4	0.4	0.4	0.4	0.4	0.4	0.4	0.4	0.4	0.4
15	0.5	0.5	0.5	0.5	0.5	0.5	0.5	0.5	0.5	0.5	0.5	0.5	0.5
16	0.6	0.6	0.6	0.6	0.6	0.5	0.5	0.5	0.5	0.6	0.6	0.6	0.6

Note.   The unshaded area in the table represents the central 99% HDR for the response patterns.

It is tedious to compare the values of EAP$^*[\theta|x,x']$ in Table 8.3 with the values of EAP$[\theta|x,x']$ in Table 7.2 to see that, for the most part, the approximation yields scores that are very similar to the exact IRT computation. Table 8.5 shows the differences between corresponding values of the approximation EAP$^*[\theta|x,x']$ and EAP$[\theta|x,x']$; almost all of the values in

TABLE 8.5

Values of the Difference Between the Linear Approximation
for EAP*[θ|x,x'] (Table 8.3) and EAP[θ|x,x'] (Table 7.2) for
Combinations of Multiple-Choice (MC) and Open-Ended (OE) Summed
Scores on a Wisconsin Reading Tryout Form (θ Is Standardized)

MC	Open–Ended (Summed) Rated Score												
Sum	0	1	2	3	4	5	6	7	8	9	10	11	12
0	-0.2	-0.1	-0.1	0.0	0.0	0.0	0.0	0.0	0.0	0.0	-0.1	-0.1	-0.2
1	-0.3	-0.2	-0.1	0.0	0.0	0.0	0.0	0.0	0.0	0.0	-0.1	-0.1	-0.2
2	-0.3	-0.2	-0.1	0.0	0.0	0.0	0.0	0.0	0.0	0.0	-0.1	-0.1	-0.2
3	-0.4	-0.2	-0.1	-0.1	0.0	0.0	0.0	0.0	0.0	0.0	-0.1	-0.1	-0.2
4	-0.4	-0.3	-0.2	-0.1	0.0	0.0	0.0	0.0	0.0	0.0	-0.1	-0.1	-0.2
5	-0.5	-0.3	-0.2	-0.1	0.0	0.0	0.0	0.0	0.0	0.0	-0.1	-0.1	-0.2
6	-0.6	-0.4	-0.2	-0.1	0.0	0.0	0.0	0.0	0.0	0.0	-0.1	-0.1	-0.1
7	-0.7	-0.4	-0.2	-0.1	-0.1	0.0	0.0	0.0	0.0	0.0	0.0	-0.1	-0.1
8	-0.6	-0.4	-0.2	-0.1	-0.1	0.0	0.0	0.0	0.0	0.0	0.0	0.0	-0.1
9	-0.5	-0.3	-0.2	-0.1	-0.1	0.0	0.0	0.0	0.0	0.0	0.0	0.0	0.0
10	-0.4	-0.2	-0.1	-0.1	0.0	0.0	0.0	0.0	0.0	0.0	0.0	0.0	0.0
11	-0.2	-0.1	-0.1	0.0	0.0	0.0	0.0	0.0	0.0	0.0	0.0	0.0	0.0
12	0.0	0.0	0.0	0.0	0.0	0.0	0.0	0.0	0.0	0.0	0.0	0.0	0.0
13	0.1	0.1	0.1	0.1	0.0	0.0	0.0	0.0	0.0	0.0	0.0	0.0	0.0
14	0.3	0.2	0.2	0.1	0.1	0.1	0.0	0.0	0.0	0.0	0.0	0.0	0.1
15	0.5	0.4	0.3	0.3	0.2	0.2	0.1	0.0	0.0	0.0	0.0	0.0	0.1
16	0.9	0.7	0.6	0.5	0.4	0.3	0.2	0.1	0.1	0.0	0.0	0.0	0.1

Note. The unshaded area in the table represents the central 99% HDR for the response patterns.

the unshaded (high-probability) region of Table 8.5[1] are 0.0, meaning that with the common score-reporting convention that standardized test scores are reported in units no more precise than tenths of a standard unit, there is no difference. To aid comparison of the approximate $SD^*[\theta|x,x']$ values in Table 8.4 with the exact values of $SD[\theta|x,x']$ in Table 7.3, Table 8.6 shows the ratios of the former to the latter. The ratios are generally between 0.9 and 1.1, indicating that, for the most part, in the high-likelihood portion of the scoring tables, the approximate values of the standard deviation (which would be reported as the standard error of the standardized score) are within 10% of the exact value.

Surprisingly, the error of approximation can be small even for extreme scores, and for some unlikely score combinations. Figure 8.2 shows the likelihoods and the Gaussian approximations for the score combination that represents the maximum score for both sections of the test; both score likelihoods increase monotonically. In Fig. 8.2, $EAP[\theta|16,12] = 1.69$, and $SD[\theta|16,12]$ is 0.67; $EAP^*[\theta|16,12] = 1.64$, and $SD^*[\theta|16,12]$ is 0.57. The posterior standard deviation is more poorly approximated in this extreme combination, but not to the extent that score reporting would likely be compromised. It is especially curious that the Gaussian approximation works so well for this particular score combination, because, as shown in Fig. 8.2, the Gaussian distributions that underlie the linear combination system are approximating strictly monotonic likelihoods that are not at all bell shaped. Nevertheless, the approximated joint likelihood in the lower panel of Fig. 8.2 is very similar to the joint likelihood computed as the product of the population distribution with the monotonically increasing likelihoods.

The residual values in Table 8.5 show that the approximation fails rather seriously for some score combinations in the unlikely (shaded) parts of the table. The largest residual is associated with the most unlikely event: a perfect score of 16 on the MC section and a score of zero on the OE section. Figure 8.3 shows the population distribution, likelihoods, and the Gaussian approximations for the 16,0 combination. Note that the joint likelihood is the product of sections well into the tails of the two likelihoods (also note that the posterior has been magnified by nine orders of magnitude to appear on the plot at all). Because the Gaussian approximations and the likelihoods have different shapes in the tails, the product computed in the tails is very different: In Fig. 8.3, $EAP[\theta|16,0] = 0.15$, whereas $EAP^*[\theta|16,0] = -0.73$. If it is wise to report any score for such an unlikely combination of evidence, it is clear that the approximate computation does not give the same estimate of θ as the likelihood computation.

---

[1]Tables 8.3–8.7 are shaded as was described in detail with respect to Tables 7.2–7.4; the unshaded area represents 99% of the modeled probability, the darkly shaded area represents 0.1%, and the unshaded and lightly shaded areas combined represent 99.9%.

TABLE 8.6
Values of the Ratio Between the Linear Approximation for $SD^*[\theta|x,x']$
(Table 8.5) and $SD[\theta|x,x']$ (Table 7.3) for Combinations of
Multiple-Choice (MC) and Open-Ended (OE) Summed Scores
on a Wisconsin Reading Tryout Form (θ Is Standardized)

MC	Open–Ended (Summed) Rated Score												
Sum	0	1	2	3	4	5	6	7	8	9	10	11	12
0	0.8	0.8	0.8	0.9	1.0	1.0	1.1	1.1	1.2	1.2	1.2	1.3	1.3
1	0.8	0.8	0.8	0.9	0.9	1.0	1.1	1.1	1.2	1.2	1.3	1.3	1.3
2	0.7	0.8	0.8	0.9	0.9	1.0	1.1	1.1	1.2	1.2	1.3	1.3	1.4
3	0.7	0.7	0.8	0.8	0.9	1.0	1.0	1.1	1.2	1.2	1.3	1.3	1.4
4	0.7	0.7	0.8	0.8	0.9	1.0	1.0	1.1	1.2	1.2	1.3	1.3	1.4
5	0.6	0.7	0.7	0.8	0.9	0.9	1.0	1.1	1.2	1.2	1.3	1.3	1.4
6	0.6	0.6	0.7	0.7	0.8	0.9	1.0	1.1	1.1	1.2	1.3	1.3	1.4
7	0.5	0.5	0.6	0.7	0.8	0.9	1.0	1.0	1.1	1.2	1.2	1.3	1.3
8	0.4	0.5	0.6	0.7	0.8	0.9	1.0	1.0	1.1	1.1	1.2	1.2	1.2
9	0.4	0.5	0.6	0.7	0.8	0.9	0.9	1.0	1.1	1.1	1.1	1.1	1.2
10	0.4	0.5	0.6	0.7	0.8	0.9	0.9	1.0	1.0	1.1	1.1	1.1	1.1
11	0.5	0.6	0.7	0.8	0.9	0.9	1.0	1.0	1.0	1.0	1.0	1.0	1.0
12	0.7	0.8	0.8	0.9	0.9	1.0	1.0	1.0	1.0	1.0	1.0	1.0	0.9
13	0.9	0.9	1.0	1.0	1.0	1.0	1.0	1.0	1.0	1.0	1.0	0.9	0.9
14	1.1	1.1	1.1	1.1	1.1	1.1	1.1	1.1	1.1	1.0	1.0	0.9	0.8
15	1.3	1.3	1.3	1.3	1.2	1.2	1.2	1.1	1.1	1.0	1.0	0.9	0.8
16	1.4	1.4	1.4	1.4	1.3	1.3	1.2	1.2	1.1	1.0	1.0	0.9	0.9

Note. The unshaded area in the table represents the central 99% HDR for the response patterns.

However, it is also clear from Fig. 8.3 that neither computation is particularly meaningful: Evidence from the MC section of the test implies very high θ, whereas evidence from the OE section implies very low θ.

The Relation of IRT and Weights. Details of the derivation of Eq. 4 (in the appendix to this chapter) show that the weights are actually equal to

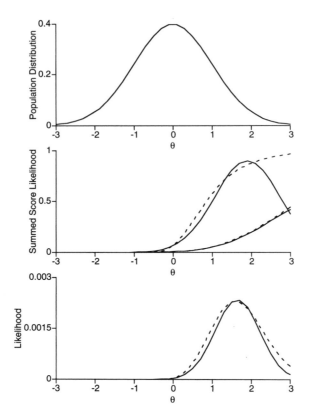

FIG. 8.2. Graphical illustration of the approximate IRT pattern-of-summed-scores combination system, using data from the Wisconsin third-grade reading test. Top panel: The population distribution [$\phi(\theta)$]. Center panel: Dashed curves are the likelihood for OE score 12 [$L_{12}^{OE}(\theta)$] and the likelihood for MC score 16 [$L_{16}^{MC}(\theta)$]; solid curves are Gaussian distributions with averages of θ_{16}^* and θ_{12}^* and variances equal to v_{16}^* and v_{12}^*. Lower panel: The dashed curve is the likelihood for θ given OE score 12 and MC score 16 [$L_{16\&12}(\theta)$]; the solid curve is the Gaussian approximation.

$$\frac{1}{\text{var}[\theta|x]} - 1 ;$$

If one follows traditional true-score theory in assuming that $\rho = 1 - \text{var}[\theta|x]$, that is equivalent to

$$\frac{\rho}{1-\rho} ,$$

the weights proposed by Kelley (1927, pp. 211–213; see also Kelley, 1947, pp. 423–425, and Gulliksen, 1950/1987, pp. 331–334) for combining

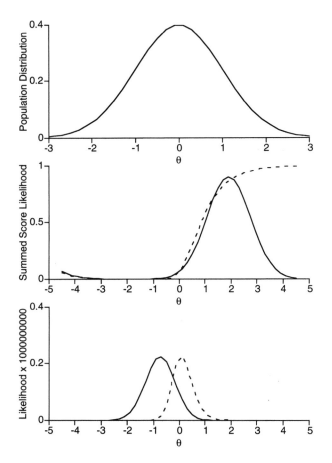

FIG. 8.3. Graphical illustration of the approximate IRT pattern-of-summed-scores combination system, using data from the Wisconsin third-grade reading test. Top panel: The population distribution [$\phi(\theta)$]. Center panel: Dashed curves are the likelihood for OE score 0 [$L_0^{OE}(\theta)$] and the likelihood for MC score 16 [$L_{16}^{MC}(\theta)$]; solid curves are Gaussian distributions with averages of θ_{16}^* and θ_0^* and variances equal to v_{16}^* and v_0^*. Lower panel: The dashed curve is the likelihood for θ given OE score 0 and MC score 16 [$L_{16\&0}(\theta)$]; the solid curve is the Gaussian approximation (both curves are multiplied by 10^9 to make them visible).

scores weighted by their reliability. The difference between the true score development due to Kelley and the IRT-based system described here is that in the IRT system the values of var[$\theta|x$], and hence the weights, vary as a function of the score, whereas in true score theory ρ is a constant.

The relative weights underlying the IRT system, computed as the ratio of the weight for the MC section to the weight for the OE section in the Gaussian approximation, are shown in Table 8.7. To the extent that the

TABLE 8.7
Relative Weights, MC/OE, Implicit in the Estimation of Expected
A Posteriori (EAP*) Estimates for Combinations of Multiple-Choice (MC)
and Open-Ended (OE) Summed Scores on a
Wisconsin Reading Tryout Form (θ Is Standardized)

MC	Open–Ended (Summed) Rated Score												
Sum	0	1	2	3	4	5	6	7	8	9	10	11	12
0	2.1	2.3	2.3	2.3	2.3	2.2	2.2	2.2	2.2	2.2	2.3	2.4	2.6
1	2.0	2.2	2.3	2.2	2.1	2.1	2.1	2.1	2.3	2.3	2.3	2.4	2.5
2	2.0	2.2	2.2	2.2	2.2	2.1	2.1	2.1	2.1	2.2	2.2	2.3	2.4
3	2.0	2.2	2.2	2.2	2.1	2.1	2.1	2.1	2.1	2.2	2.2	2.4	2.5
4	2.0	2.2	2.3	2.3	2.2	2.2	2.2	2.2	2.2	2.2	2.3	2.4	2.5
5	2.3	2.4	2.4	2.4	2.4	2.3	2.3	2.3	2.3	2.4	2.4	2.6	2.7
6	2.4	2.6	2.7	2.7	2.6	2.6	2.5	2.6	2.6	2.6	2.7	2.8	3.0
7	2.8	3.0	3.1	3.1	3.0	3.0	2.9	2.9	3.0	3.0	3.1	3.3	3.5
8	3.3	3.6	3.7	3.6	3.6	3.5	3.4	3.4	3.5	3.5	3.7	3.9	4.1
9	3.8	4.2	4.3	4.2	4.1	4.1	4.0	4.0	4.1	4.1	4.3	4.5	4.7
10	4.2	4.6	4.7	4.7	4.6	4.5	4.5	4.5	4.5	4.6	4.8	5.0	5.3
11	4.4	4.8	4.9	4.9	4.8	4.7	4.6	4.6	4.7	4.8	4.9	5.2	5.5
12	4.2	4.6	4.7	4.7	4.6	4.5	4.4	4.4	4.5	4.6	4.7	5.0	5.2
13	3.6	3.9	4.0	4.0	3.9	3.8	3.8	3.8	3.8	3.9	4.0	4.2	4.4
14	2.7	3.0	3.0	3.0	3.0	2.9	2.9	2.9	2.9	2.9	3.0	3.2	3.4
15	1.8	2.0	2.1	2.0	2.0	2.0	1.8	1.9	2.0	2.0	2.1	2.2	2.3
16	1.2	1.3	1.3	1.3	1.3	1.3	1.3	1.3	1.3	1.3	1.3	1.4	1.5

Note. The unshaded area in the table represents the central 99% HDR for the response patterns.

Gaussian system approximates the IRT likelihood-based system, these are the effective IRT weights for the two parts of the test. The weights range from just over unity to about five. They are highest for scores 9–12 on the MC section, in the region where the MC section is most precise, and lower at the extremes. To the extent that IRT is an accurate model for the two part scores and their combination, this shows that no constant-weighting (linear combination) model is likely to yield optimal results.

The Overall Quality of the Approximation. Table 8.8 shows the means and standard deviations of the residuals in Table 8.5, as well as the means and standard deviations for the residuals for the values of SD^*, using the normal approximation. In addition, Table 8.8 shows all of these statistics for two other tests, the North Carolina Computer Skills test, Forms Z1 and Z2. Table 8.8 shows that there is no bias in any of the approximations; all of the residual means are zero. The normal approximation system performed very well for all three tests, for both the EAP and the SD, which would be reported as the standard error of the test score.

Figure 8.4 shows a bubble plot of the values of the Gaussian-approximated EAP* terms associated with each pattern of MC and OE summed scores (from Table 8.3), plotted against the pattern of summed-score-pattern EAPs (from Table 7.2); the area of the bubbles is proportional to the probability of each score combination (from Table 7.4). The relation is strikingly linear, and for likely response patterns, shown as the larger bubbles in Fig. 8.4, the points fall nearly on the identity (45°) line; the points that exhibit the largest disagreement between the exact EAP terms and the approximate EAP* terms are associated with very unlikely response patterns.

Figure 8.5 shows a scatter plot of the values of the Gaussian-approximated EAP* terms associated with each pattern of MC and OE summed scores, plotted against the (theoretically optimal) EAP terms associated with the corresponding item response patterns, for the 522 observations in the data. The correlation is .991; the slight deviations from linearity that appear at the lower end of the point cloud are there because a handful of the observations *are* the very unlikely score combinations represented by very small bubbles at the lower end of the plot in Fig. 8.4. Even there, the disagreement between the two scoring systems is not large. Fig-

TABLE 8.8
Weighted Means and Standard Deviations of Residuals
(IRT Combination Values, Estimates) Resulting From the Estimation
of Scores for Combinations of Multiple-Choice (MC)
and Open-Ended (OE) Summed Scores on Three Tests

Test	For EAP − EAP*		For SD − SD*	
	Mean	*SD*	*Mean*	*SD*
WI Rdg	.00	.03	.00	.04
NC Z1	.00	.01	.00	.02
NC Z2	.00	.01	.00	.02

Note. θ Is standardized; the weights are IRT score-combination probabilities.

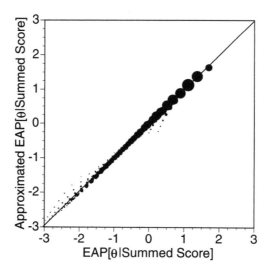

FIG. 8.4. Bubble plot of the values of the Gaussian-approximated EAP*s associated with each pattern of MC and OE summed scores, plotted against the corresponding pattern of summed-score-pattern EAPs, using data from the Wisconsin third-grade reading test; the area of the bubbles is proportional to the probability of each score combination.

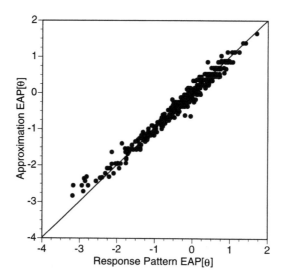

FIG. 8.5. Scatter plot of the values of the Gaussian-approximated EAP*s associated with each pattern of MC and OE summed scores, plotted against the EAPs associated with the corresponding item response patterns, for the 522 observations from the Wisconsin third-grade reading test.

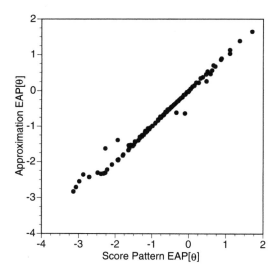

FIG. 8.6. Scatter plot of the values of the Gaussian-approximated EAP*s associated with each pattern of MC and OE summed scores, plotted against the EAPs associated with the corresponding summed-score pattern, for the 522 observations from the Wisconsin third-grade reading test.

ure 8.6 shows a scatter plot of the values of the Gaussian-approximated EAP* terms associated with each pattern of MC and OE summed scores, plotted against the EAP terms associated with the corresponding summed-score pattern, again for the 522 observations in the data. The correlation is .997, with only 4 or 5 of the 522 observations deviating from essentially perfect linearity.

The values of the standard errors ($SD[\theta]$) associated with each item response pattern, with each pattern of MC and OE summed scores, and the approximate computation (from Eq. 5), all plotted against the values of the corresponding EAPs, are shown in Fig. 8.7. For the most part, all of these alternative estimates of the error variation in the IRT test scores tell the same story: Their values are around 0.3 for examinees just below average ($\theta = 0$), and increase to around 0.5 at the extremes of the score range, with a few higher values. Although it is true that the response-pattern scoring yields the smallest standard errors, that effect is very small—usually less than 0.1.

IRT Approximated Scale Scores for Patterns of Summed Scores Combining Multiple-Choice and Constructed-Response Sections: The 1993 North Carolina Open-Ended End-of-Grade Tests—Eighth-Grade Mathematics. To provide another brief example of the relation between response-pattern scores (EAPs) and the approximate EAP*s for patterns-of-summed-scores, we reconsider the same data from the 1993 of the North

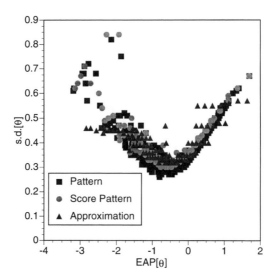

FIG. 8.7.   Values of the standard errors ($SD[\theta]$) associated with each pattern of MC and OE summed scores, the approximate computation, and those associated with the corresponding item response patterns, all plotted against the values of the corresonding EAPs, using data from the Wisconsin third-grade reading test.

Carolina Open-Ended End-of-Grade Test of Mathematics that provided one of the illustrations in chapter 7. This test combines an 80-item multiple-choice test with 3 open-ended items. Figure 8.8 shows a scatter plot of the EAP*s for the patterns-of-summed-scores plotted against the response-pattern scores (EAPs) for a random sample of 870 of the examinees. The correlation is .983; that is ever so slightly lower than the value (.984) we obtained with these data when we compared the EAPs for patterns-of-summed scores with response-pattern EAPs (in Fig. 7.7). The values of the EAP*s associated with each pattern of MC and OE summed scores are plotted against the EAPs associated with the corresponding summed-score patterns in Fig. 8.9; the correlation coefficient is .998. There is clearly only a slight loss of precision due to using the linear approximation.

The Approximation Changes the Anomalous Scores That Can Arise With IRT Scale Scores for Patterns of Summed Scores: The Example From the North Carolina End-of-Course Geometry Test, Revisited.   Tables 8.9–8.11 show the components and results obtained using the approximation in Eq. 4 to compute values of EAP*[$\theta|x,x'$] for combinations of multiple-choice (MC) and open-ended (OE) summed scores on Form E of the North Carolina End-of-Course Geometry test, for which we described anomalous results in chapter 7. These tables illustrate the size and content of the scoring tables for longer tests; in this case, there are 60 MC items,

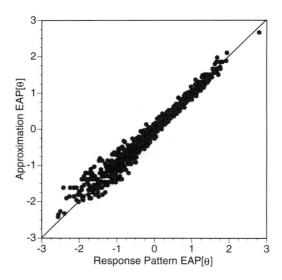

FIG. 8.8. Values of the EAP*s associated with each pattern of MC and OE summed scores, plotted against the EAPs associated with the corresponding item response patterns, using data from the North Carolina eighth-grade mathematics test.

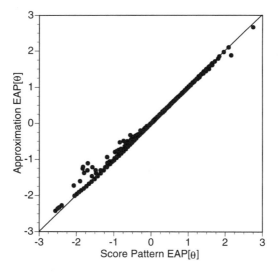

FIG. 8.9. Values of the EAP*s associated with each pattern of MC and OE summed scores, plotted against the EAPs associated with the corresponding summed-score patterns, using data from the North Carolina eighth-grade mathematics test.

and the OE section yields a total of 12 score-points. As a result, Table 8.9 contains 61 lines for the summed scores from 0 to 60 on the multiple-choice section, and Table 8.10 has 13 lines for the summed scores from 0 to 12 on the open-ended part. For the sake of illustration, Table 8.11 contains the 61 by 13 table of values of EAP*[θ|x,x']. Note, however, that all of the 793 values in Table 8.11 are computed very simply from the entries in the EAP[θ] and w columns in Tables 8.9 and 8.10, using Eq. 4, so Table 8.11 is redundant for operational computation of the EAP*s as test scores.

When the approximation proposed in this chapter is used, the values in Table 8.11 replace the similar values of EAP[θ|x,x'] that are shown in Table 7.5. As we observed in chapter 7, the values in the first row of Table 7.5 illustrate an anomaly that can arise using the IRT-based method to combine scores for MC and OE sections: In Table 7.5, the combined scores (EAPs) increase for OE scores of 0, 1, 2 and 3; but then they decrease to a lower value for an OE score of 4, and remain lower for OE scores of 5, 6, 7, and 8. When the linear combination system of this chapter is used to compute approximate values (EAP*s), inspection of Table 8.11 shows that the anomaly has moved: The values of EAP* in the first row of Table 8.11 increase monotonically (as those in Table 7.5 do not) for OE scores from 0 to 11. However, a different anomaly appears in other (even more unlikely) score combinations: The values of EAP* for very low MC scores (from 0 to 17—roughly, those below chance) combined with the maximum score (12) on the OE section are lower than the value of EAP* for the same MC score and a score of 11 on the OE section.

TABLE 8.9
EAP[θ], SD[θ], w, and the Probability for Each Score for the
Multiple-Choice Section of the of Form E of the North Carolina
End-of-Course Geometry Test, as Computed With the 3PL Model

Sum	EAP[θ]	SD[θ]	w	Probability
0	−3.44	0.48	4.36	.00000
1	−3.38	0.49	4.23	.00000
2	−3.32	0.49	4.11	.00000
3	−3.26	0.50	4.00	.00000
4	−3.19	0.51	3.91	.00000
5	−3.12	0.51	3.83	.00000
6	−3.05	0.52	3.77	.00000
7	−2.97	0.52	3.72	.00000
8	−2.89	0.52	3.69	.00001
9	−2.81	0.52	3.67	.00003
10	−2.73	0.52	3.67	.00008
11	−2.64	0.52	3.69	.00017
12	−2.55	0.52	3.72	.00034

(Continued)

TABLE 8.9
(Continued)

Sum	EAP[θ]	SD[θ]	w	Probability
13	−2.46	0.51	3.78	.00062
14	−2.36	0.51	3.86	.00108
15	−2.27	0.50	3.96	.00176
16	−2.17	0.49	4.08	.00269
17	−2.07	0.49	4.24	.00389
18	−1.97	0.48	4.42	.00537
19	−1.87	0.46	4.64	.00707
20	−1.77	0.45	4.89	.00896
21	−1.67	0.44	5.18	.01096
22	−1.57	0.43	5.52	.01300
23	−1.46	0.41	5.90	.01501
24	−1.37	0.40	6.33	.01694
25	−1.27	0.38	6.81	.01875
26	−1.17	0.37	7.34	.02042
27	−1.08	0.36	7.91	.02195
28	−0.98	0.34	8.52	.02335
29	−0.89	0.33	9.15	.02461
30	−0.80	0.32	9.80	.02576
31	−0.72	0.31	10.45	.02680
32	−0.63	0.30	11.08	.02774
33	−0.55	0.29	11.69	.02858
34	−0.47	0.29	12.27	.02933
35	−0.39	0.28	12.81	.02998
36	−0.31	0.27	13.30	.03052
37	−0.23	0.27	13.75	.03096
38	−0.15	0.27	14.15	.03129
39	−0.07	0.26	14.51	.03150
40	0.01	0.26	14.81	.03160
41	0.08	0.26	15.07	.03159
42	0.16	0.26	15.27	.03147
43	0.24	0.25	15.40	.03124
44	0.32	0.25	15.48	.03092
45	0.40	0.25	15.48	.03050
46	0.49	0.25	15.40	.03000
47	0.57	0.26	15.24	.02941
48	0.66	0.26	14.98	.02875
49	0.75	0.26	14.61	.02800
50	0.85	0.27	14.13	.02716
51	0.95	0.27	13.53	.02622
52	1.06	0.28	12.81	.02515
53	1.17	0.29	11.95	.02394
54	1.30	0.30	10.96	.02252
55	1.43	0.32	9.86	.02085
56	1.59	0.34	8.66	.01881
57	1.76	0.37	7.40	.01626
58	1.97	0.40	6.14	.01301
59	2.22	0.45	4.93	.00892
60	2.52	0.51	3.91	.00413

TABLE 8.10
EAP[θ], *SD*[θ], *w*, and the Probability for Each Score for the
Open-Ended Section of Form E of the North Carolina End-of-Course
Geometry Test, as Computed With the Graded Model

Sum	EAP[θ]	SD[θ]	w	Probability
0	−1.84	0.70	2.04	.02119
1	−1.29	0.69	2.08	.04134
2	−1.01	0.66	2.33	.09357
3	−0.55	0.61	2.65	.18329
4	−0.18	0.62	2.57	.11309
5	0.01	0.62	2.62	.10378
6	0.24	0.64	2.41	.08155
7	0.33	0.64	2.42	.07307
8	0.51	0.66	2.33	.07016
9	0.62	0.66	2.31	.07151
10	0.95	0.61	2.65	.06123
11	1.21	0.61	2.69	.03828
12	1.64	0.69	2.13	.04794

TABLE 8.11
Values of EAP*[θ|x,x'] for Combinations of Multiple-Choice (MC)
and Open-Ended (OE) Summed Scores on Form E of the
North Carolina End-of-Course Geometry Test (θ Is Standardized)

MC Sum	Open-Ended (Summed) Rated Score												
	0	1	2	3	4	5	6	7	8	9	10	11	12
0	−3.5	−3.2	−3.0	−2.7	−2.6	−2.5	−2.5	−2.5	−2.4	−2.4	−2.1	−1.9	−2.1
1	−3.4	−3.2	−3.0	−2.7	−2.5	−2.4	−2.4	−2.4	−2.4	−2.3	−2.0	−1.9	−2.0
2	−3.4	−3.1	−2.9	−2.6	−2.5	−2.4	−2.4	−2.3	−2.3	−2.3	−1.9	−1.8	−1.9
3	−3.3	−3.1	−2.9	−2.6	−2.4	−2.3	−2.3	−2.3	−2.2	−2.2	−1.9	−1.7	−1.9
4	−3.3	−3.0	−2.8	−2.5	−2.4	−2.2	−2.2	−2.2	−2.2	−2.1	−1.8	−1.6	−1.8
5	−3.2	−3.0	−2.8	−2.4	−2.3	−2.2	−2.2	−2.1	−2.1	−2.0	−1.7	−1.6	−1.7
6	−3.2	−2.9	−2.7	−2.4	−2.2	−2.1	−2.1	−2.1	−2.0	−2.0	−1.7	−1.5	−1.6
7	−3.1	−2.9	−2.7	−2.3	−2.2	−2.1	−2.0	−2.0	−2.0	−1.9	−1.6	−1.4	−1.6
8	−3.1	−2.8	−2.6	−2.3	−2.1	−2.0	−2.0	−1.9	−1.9	−1.8	−1.5	−1.4	−1.5
9	−3.0	−2.7	−2.5	−2.2	−2.1	−1.9	−1.9	−1.9	−1.8	−1.8	−1.5	−1.3	−1.4
10	−2.9	−2.7	−2.5	−2.2	−2.0	−1.9	−1.9	−1.8	−1.8	−1.7	−1.4	−1.3	−1.4
11	−2.9	−2.6	−2.4	−2.1	−1.9	−1.8	−1.8	−1.8	−1.7	−1.7	−1.4	−1.2	−1.3
12	−2.8	−2.5	−2.3	−2.0	−1.9	−1.8	−1.7	−1.7	−1.6	−1.6	−1.3	−1.2	−1.2
13	−2.7	−2.5	−2.3	−2.0	−1.8	−1.7	−1.7	−1.6	−1.6	−1.5	−1.2	−1.1	−1.2
14	−2.6	−2.4	−2.2	−1.9	−1.8	−1.7	−1.6	−1.6	−1.5	−1.5	−1.2	−1.1	−1.1
15	−2.5	−2.3	−2.1	−1.9	−1.7	−1.6	−1.6	−1.5	−1.5	−1.4	−1.2	−1.0	−1.1
16	−2.5	−2.2	−2.1	−1.8	−1.7	−1.5	−1.5	−1.5	−1.4	−1.4	−1.1	−1.0	−1.0

(Continued)

TABLE 8.11
(Continued)

MC	Open–Ended (Summed) Rated Score												
Sum	0	1	2	3	4	5	6	7	8	9	10	11	12
17	−2.4	−2.2	−2.0	−1.7	−1.6	−1.5	−1.5	−1.4	−1.4	−1.3	−1.1	−0.9	−1.0
18	−2.3	−2.1	−1.9	−1.7	−1.5	−1.4	−1.4	−1.4	−1.3	−1.3	−1.0	−0.9	−0.9
19	−2.2	−2.0	−1.8	−1.6	−1.5	−1.4	−1.3	−1.3	−1.3	−1.2	−1.0	−0.9	−0.9
20	−2.1	−1.9	−1.8	−1.5	−1.4	−1.3	−1.3	−1.2	−1.2	−1.2	−0.9	−0.8	−0.9
21	−2.0	−1.8	−1.7	−1.5	−1.3	−1.3	−1.2	−1.2	−1.1	−1.1	−0.9	−0.8	−0.8
22	−1.9	−1.7	−1.6	−1.4	−1.3	−1.2	−1.2	−1.1	−1.1	−1.1	−0.9	−0.7	−0.8
23	−1.8	−1.6	−1.5	−1.3	−1.2	−1.1	−1.1	−1.1	−1.0	−1.0	−0.8	−0.7	−0.7
24	−1.7	−1.5	−1.4	−1.3	−1.2	−1.1	−1.0	−1.0	−1.0	−0.9	−0.8	−0.7	−0.7
25	−1.6	−1.4	−1.3	−1.2	−1.1	−1.0	−1.0	−1.0	−0.9	−0.9	−0.7	−0.6	−0.6
26	−1.5	−1.3	−1.3	−1.1	−1.0	−1.0	−0.9	−0.9	−0.9	−0.8	−0.7	−0.6	−0.6
27	−1.4	−1.2	−1.2	−1.0	−0.9	−0.9	−0.9	−0.8	−0.8	−0.8	−0.6	−0.5	−0.6
28	−1.3	−1.2	−1.1	−1.0	−0.9	−0.8	−0.8	−0.8	−0.7	−0.7	−0.6	−0.5	−0.5
29	−1.2	−1.1	−1.0	−0.9	−0.8	−0.8	−0.7	−0.7	−0.7	−0.6	−0.5	−0.5	−0.5
30	−1.1	−1.0	−0.9	−0.8	−0.7	−0.7	−0.7	−0.6	−0.6	−0.6	−0.5	−0.4	−0.4
31	−1.0	−0.9	−0.8	−0.7	−0.7	−0.6	−0.6	−0.6	−0.5	−0.5	−0.4	−0.3	−0.3
32	−0.9	−0.8	−0.8	−0.7	−0.6	−0.6	−0.5	−0.5	−0.5	−0.5	−0.4	−0.3	−0.3
33	−0.8	−0.7	−0.7	−0.6	−0.5	−0.5	−0.4	−0.4	−0.4	−0.4	−0.3	−0.2	−0.2
34	−0.7	−0.6	−0.6	−0.5	−0.4	−0.4	−0.4	−0.4	−0.3	−0.3	−0.2	−0.2	−0.2
35	−0.6	−0.6	−0.5	−0.4	−0.4	−0.3	−0.3	−0.3	−0.3	−0.3	−0.2	−0.1	−0.1
36	−0.5	−0.5	−0.4	−0.4	−0.3	−0.3	−0.2	−0.2	−0.2	−0.2	−0.1	−0.1	0.0
37	−0.5	−0.4	−0.4	−0.3	−0.2	−0.2	−0.2	−0.2	−0.1	−0.1	0.0	0.0	0.0
38	−0.4	−0.3	−0.3	−0.2	−0.2	−0.1	−0.1	−0.1	−0.1	0.0	0.0	0.1	0.1
39	−0.3	−0.2	−0.2	−0.2	−0.1	−0.1	0.0	0.0	0.0	0.0	0.1	0.1	0.2
40	−0.2	−0.2	−0.1	−0.1	0.0	0.0	0.0	0.1	0.1	0.1	0.2	0.2	0.2
41	−0.2	−0.1	−0.1	0.0	0.0	0.1	0.1	0.1	0.1	0.2	0.2	0.3	0.3
42	−0.1	0.0	0.0	0.1	0.1	0.1	0.2	0.2	0.2	0.2	0.3	0.3	0.4
43	0.0	0.1	0.1	0.1	0.2	0.2	0.3	0.3	0.3	0.3	0.4	0.4	0.4
44	0.1	0.1	0.2	0.2	0.3	0.3	0.3	0.3	0.4	0.4	0.4	0.5	0.5
45	0.2	0.2	0.2	0.3	0.3	0.4	0.4	0.4	0.4	0.5	0.5	0.6	0.6
46	0.2	0.3	0.3	0.4	0.4	0.4	0.5	0.5	0.5	0.6	0.6	0.7
47	0.3	0.4	0.4	0.4	0.5	0.5	0.6	0.6	0.6	0.6	0.7	0.7	0.7
48	0.4	0.5	0.5	0.5	0.6	0.6	0.6	0.7	0.7	0.7	0.7	0.8	0.8
49	0.5	0.5	0.5	0.6	0.7	0.7	0.7	0.7	0.8	0.8	0.8	0.9	0.9
50	0.5	0.6	0.6	0.7	0.7	0.8	0.8	0.8	0.9	0.9	0.9	1.0	1.0
51	0.6	0.7	0.7	0.8	0.8	0.8	0.9	0.9	0.9	1.0	1.0	1.1	1.1
52	0.7	0.8	0.8	0.8	0.9	0.9	1.0	1.0	1.0	1.1	1.1	1.2	1.2
53	0.8	0.9	0.9	0.9	1.0	1.0	1.1	1.1	1.1	1.2	1.2	1.3	1.3
54	0.9	1.0	1.0	1.0	1.1	1.1	1.2	1.2	1.3	1.3	1.3	1.4	1.5
55	1.0	1.0	1.1	1.1	1.2	1.2	1.3	1.3	1.4	1.4	1.4	1.5	1.6
56	1.0	1.1	1.1	1.2	1.3	1.3	1.4	1.4	1.5	1.5	1.6	1.6	1.8
57	1.1	1.2	1.2	1.3	1.4	1.4	1.5	1.6	1.6	1.7	1.7	1.8	1.9
58	1.2	1.3	1.3	1.4	1.5	1.6	1.7	1.7	1.8	1.8	1.9	2.0	2.1
59	1.2	1.4	1.4	1.4	1.6	1.7	1.8	1.8	1.9	2.0	2.0	2.1	2.4
60	1.2	1.4	1.4	1.5	1.7	1.8	2.0	2.0	2.1	2.2	2.2	2.3	2.6

To reiterate observations made previously: In chapter 7, we noted that these anomalous score-combination results involve pairs of summed scores that are unlikely to co-occur, and they involve combining likelihoods that do not overlap very much. The shapes of the tails of the 3PL and graded-model likelihoods are such that for some score combinations the average of the product-likelihood moves left when we would expect it to move right. When those likelihoods are replaced by Gaussian distributions, as they are when we use the linear approximation, different surprising results may arise. However, these combinations remain exceedingly rare. Although it is true that the IRT model does not handle such unlikely score combinations exactly as one would expect, such score combinations are so unusual that this potential anomaly may not appear in operational use.

IRT Approximated Scale Scores for Patterns of Summed Scores Combining Multiple-Choice and Constructed-Response Sections: Using the Graded Model for Items Combined Into Summed-Scored Testlets, Combined With Open-Ended Ratings: The Wisconsin Eighth-Grade Reading Test. Here we revisit the data from the Wisconsin Student Assessment System eighth-grade reading comprehension test in 1995, which we considered in examples in chapters 4, 6, and 7. The test included six reading passages; the first five passages were each followed by five to nine four-alternative multiple-choice questions, and the sixth passage formed the basis for three relatively short constructed-response questions that were each subsequently rated 0–3. In chapter 6, we described the results of factor analysis of these data; after the test is redefined as six testlet scores (one summed score for each passage), it may be considered unidimensional. In chapter 4 we illustrated the computation of MAP[θ], using the graded IRT model for the six testlet scores (the trace lines, one set for each passage, are shown in Figs. 4.17 and 4.18), and in chapter 7 we computed the scale scores associated with each combination of a summed score on the multiple-choice part with a summed score on the constructed-response section, again using the graded model trace line for the number correct after each passage construed as testlets.

To complete this extended example, here we present the values of EAP*[$\theta | x, x'$] for summed scores x on the multiple-choice section and x' on the constructed response section, in Table 8.12. Comparing the linear-approximation values in Table 8.12 with the exact IRT values in Table 7.6, we find that 80% of the EAP* values round to the same values as the corresponding EAPs when presented with the usual precision of tenths of a standard unit. Only 7% of the scores differ by as much as ±0.2, and those differences are associated with extremely unlikely combinations of low scores on the multiple-choice section and high scores on the constructed-response section, or vice versa.

TABLE 8.12
Values of EAP*[θ|x,x'] for Combinations of Multiple-Choice (MC)
and Open-Ended (OE) Summed Scores on the Wisconsin
Eighth-Grade Reading Test (θ Is Standardized)

MC	Open-Ended (Summed) Rated Score									
Sum	0	1	2	3	4	5	6	7	8	9
0	−4.2	−4.2	−4.2	−4.1	−4.0	−3.8	−3.7	−3.6	−3.5	−3.5
1	−4.1	−4.1	−4.1	−4.0	−3.9	−3.7	−3.6	−3.4	−3.3	−3.4
2	−4.0	−4.0	−4.0	−3.9	−3.8	−3.6	−3.4	−3.3	−3.1	−3.2
3	−3.9	−3.9	−3.8	−3.7	−3.6	−3.4	−3.2	−3.1	−2.9	−3.0
4	−3.7	−3.7	−3.7	−3.6	−3.4	−3.2	−3.1	−2.9	−2.8	−2.8
5	−3.5	−3.5	−3.5	−3.4	−3.2	−3.1	−2.9	−2.7	−2.6	−2.6
6	−3.3	−3.3	−3.3	−3.2	−3.0	−2.9	−2.7	−2.6	−2.4	−2.4
7	−3.1	−3.1	−3.1	−3.0	−2.9	−2.7	−2.6	−2.4	−2.3	−2.3
8	−2.9	−2.9	−2.9	−2.8	−2.7	−2.6	−2.4	−2.3	−2.1	−2.1
9	−2.7	−2.7	−2.7	−2.6	−2.5	−2.4	−2.3	−2.1	−2.0	−2.0
10	−2.6	−2.6	−2.5	−2.5	−2.4	−2.3	−2.1	−2.0	−1.8	−1.8
11	−2.4	−2.4	−2.4	−2.3	−2.2	−2.1	−2.0	−1.8	−1.7	−1.7
12	−2.2	−2.2	−2.2	−2.2	−2.1	−2.0	−1.8	−1.7	−1.6	−1.5
13	−2.1	−2.1	−2.1	−2.0	−1.9	−1.8	−1.7	−1.6	−1.4	−1.4
14	−1.9	−1.9	−1.9	−1.9	−1.8	−1.7	−1.6	−1.4	−1.3	−1.2
15	−1.8	−1.8	−1.8	−1.7	−1.6	−1.5	−1.4	−1.3	−1.2	−1.1
16	−1.6	−1.6	−1.6	−1.6	−1.5	−1.4	−1.3	−1.2	−1.0	−1.0
17	−1.5	−1.5	−1.5	−1.4	−1.4	−1.3	−1.2	−1.0	−0.9	−0.8
18	−1.3	−1.3	−1.3	−1.3	−1.2	−1.1	−1.0	−0.9	−0.8	−0.7
19	−1.1	−1.1	−1.1	−1.1	−1.1	−1.0	−0.9	−0.8	−0.6	−0.5
20	−1.0	−1.0	−1.0	−1.0	−0.9	−0.8	−0.7	−0.6	−0.5	−0.4
21	−0.8	−0.8	−0.8	−0.8	−0.8	−0.7	−0.6	−0.5	−0.3	−0.2
22	−0.6	−0.6	−0.6	−0.6	−0.6	−0.5	−0.4	−0.3	−0.2	0.0
23	−0.5	−0.5	−0.5	−0.4	−0.4	−0.4	−0.3	−0.2	0.0	0.1
24	−0.3	−0.3	−0.3	−0.3	−0.2	−0.2	−0.1	0.0	0.1	0.3
25	−0.1	−0.1	−0.1	−0.1	−0.1	0.0	0.1	0.2	0.3	0.5
26	0.1	0.1	0.1	0.1	0.1	0.2	0.2	0.4	0.5	0.7
27	0.4	0.4	0.4	0.3	0.4	0.4	0.5	0.6	0.7	0.9
28	0.6	0.6	0.6	0.6	0.6	0.6	0.7	0.8	1.0	1.2
29	0.9	0.9	0.9	0.9	0.9	0.9	0.9	1.0	1.2	1.5
30	1.3	1.3	1.2	1.2	1.2	1.2	1.2	1.3	1.6	1.9

Figure 8.10 shows a bubble plot of the values of the Gaussian-approximated EAP*s associated with each pattern of multiple-choice and constructed-response summed scores, plotted against the pattern of summed-score-pattern EAPs; the area of the bubbles is proportional to the IRT-modeled probability of each score combination. All of the points fall on, or very near, the identity line. For the 6,499 examinees, the correlation between the EAP*s and the pattern of summed-score-pattern EAPs (from chap. 7) is .999; the correlation between the EAP*s and response pattern EAPs (computed using the methods presented in chap. 4) is .994.

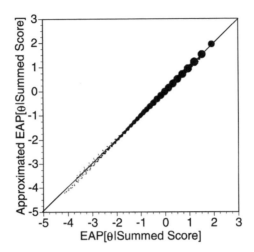

FIG. 8.10.   Bubble plot of the values of the Gaussian-approximated EAP*s associated with each pattern of MC and OE summed scores, plotted against the pattern of summed-score-pattern EAPs associated, using data from the Wisconsin eighth-grade reading test; the area of the bubbles is proportional to the probability of each score combination.

Holding in mind that the standard scale scores in Table 8.12 were computed from the EAPs and weights associated with each summed score (from 0 to 30) on the multiple-choice section, and a second collection of EAPs and weights associated with each summed score (0–9) on the constructed-response section, it is clear that this represents a quick and easy way to provide scores on the IRT scale for this test.

THE GENERALIZATION OF TWO OR MORE SCORES

If there are scores on $T \geq 2$ testlets, indexed by t, we have $\text{EAP}_x^t[\theta]$, representing a list of the values of $\text{EAP}[\theta|x]$ for testlet t, and w_x^t, representing a list of the values of $1/\text{var}[\theta|x]$ for testlet t. Then the generalization for the scale score given the vector $\mathbf{x} = [x_1, x_2, \ldots, x_T]$ is

$$\text{EAP}^*[\theta|\mathbf{x}] = \frac{\displaystyle\sum_{t=1}^{T} w_x^t \text{EAP}_x^t[\theta]}{\displaystyle\sum_{t=1}^{T} w_x^t - (T-1)} . \tag{9}$$

The conditional variance is

$$\text{var*}[\theta|\mathbf{x}] = \frac{1}{\sum_{t=1}^{T} w_x^t - (T - 1)} . \tag{10}$$

This generalization has potential use in multistage tests, especially some kinds of computerized adaptive tests.

POTENTIAL APPLICATIONS OF LINEAR APPROXIMATIONS TO IRT IN COMPUTERIZED ADAPTIVE TESTS

Most descriptions of computerized adaptive tests (CATs) suggest that the testing system selects each item adaptively, based on an item-by-item updating of some estimate of the examinee's proficiency (see, e.g., Wainer et al., 1990). There are other ways to construct a CAT, however, that bear more resemblance to multistage tests. Consider a CAT that comprises blocks of items, or testlets, that are administered as fixed sets—after an examinee responds to all of the items in the first set, the CAT chooses the next set of items adaptively. The data derived from administration of those blocks of items look very much like the data that are obtained in a paper-and-pencil test with different sections: Each section (or block of items) has a score, and the problem is to combine those scores optimally, and probably onto a specified scale that may be derived from an IRT model. Of course, response-pattern IRT scoring could be used with such a CAT—but we assume here that there are good reasons to avoid that strategy, so we consider scoring systems for the blocked CAT based on block summed scores. For simplicity, assume that the CAT item pool is unidimensional, or sufficiently close to that so that local independence holds both within and between testlets (although it is not clear that we want to call them *testlets* in such a fully unidimensional case, because that word may imply local dependence within blocks).

After the first block is administered, scaled scores for the summed scores on that block (from 0 to I, the maximum score) could be obtained from a tabulation of the EAPs associated with each summed score. Then, for any second block that could be administered, a two-way table of EAPs could be constructed using the methods described in chapter 7, in which the entries would be the EAPs for the ordered pair {score on block 1, score on block 2}.

So EAPs for each combination of summed scores on any of the possible first two blocks could be obtained by a table lookup procedure. There would have to be as many tables as there are first–second block combinations in the CAT algorithm; this may or may not be practical, depending on the details of the implementation—specifically, the number of blocks that could be administered as the first block, and the number that could follow each. Even if practical, it is not a very attractive idea.

The Gaussian approximation described in this chapter provides a simpler scheme: For each block, lists of $\text{EAP}[\theta|x]$ and w_x are maintained; then the approximate score for any combined scores on set of blocks could be computed using Eq. 4. The only difference between the appearance of this system and a system that uses standard linearly weighted scores is that the weight for each block's summed score reflects the relative discrimination of that block *at a given score level*.

Two blocks may or may not make a CAT. If the CAT had two blocks, it would be a two-stage test—and there have been suggestions that two-stage tests include sufficient adaptation. If the CAT consisted of three blocks, then the generalization of the approximation in Eq. 9 would be used, producing linear equations that approximate the EAPs for any set of summed scores.

This proposal is not intended to be computationally simpler than conventional IRT approaches to scoring—it is probably not. Its interesting feature is that, if it can be implemented, for some public-relations purposes, it replaces the arcane computations involved in IRT scoring with a system that may be presented as a linear combination of (score-table transformed) summed scores obtained on sections of the test. The scores, computed as linear combinations of (transformed) summed scores, have the scale properties of IRT scaled scores, to the extent that the linear system reproduced the EAPs from which it was derived, as well as the properties of weighted summed scores, which may facilitate some algebraic analyses of their properties.

An Alternative (Testlet) Formulation for the CAT System.

In the preceding section, we assumed local independence both within and between blocks in the CAT. Local independence between blocks is probably likely in a CAT designed to produce a single score: If the blocks are not locally independent, adaptation between blocks, based on the results of preceding blocks, is unlikely to be efficient. So we continue to assume between-block local independence.

Local independence within blocks of the CAT is necessary to justify the computation of the joint likelihoods and the EAPs for the summed scores for each block by multiplying the trace lines for the binary items that comprise the block. If there is some degree of local dependence within blocks, that procedure would not produce accurate joint likelihoods, or EAPs, for the summed scores, with respect to θ measured by the CAT as a whole. In this case, the blocks would be best treated as testlets.

However, all that is really necessary to construct the tables of EAPs on which the scoring is based is that we have the likelihood, as a function of θ, for each summed score for each testlet. Those could be obtained by calibrating the summed scores for each testlet, using either Samejima's (1969, 1997) graded model or some version of Bock's (1972, 1997) nominal model, as is appropriate for the data. Using these models, as described in chapter 4, the trace lines themselves would be the likelihoods for each summed score for the testlet. Using those trace lines as the likelihoods, the entire scoring procedure would be otherwise the same as described earlier.

An Illustration of Testlet CAT Scoring. Here we consider computing scale scores for a multistage adaptive test made up of testlets—specifically, for testlets in a multiform structure (MFS; Armstrong, Jones, Berliner, & Pashley, 1998). We examine in some detail one particular MFS, in which each examinee responds to two fixed 5-item testlets (that is, effectively, a 10-item routing test), followed by three 5-item testlets that are selected adaptively, based on the summed score obtained on the preceding testlets. Testlets in the adaptively administered stages are arranged in five layers, for very low (VL), low (L), medium (M), high (H), and very high (VH) levels of proficiency. After the 10-item routing testlet, examinees who score 0–2 are administered one of the VL testlets, those who score 3–4 receive an L testlet, those who score 5–8 receive an M testlet, and those with scores of 9 and 10 are routed to H and VH testlets, respectively. After the first and second adaptive stages, examinees who score 0–1 on a 5-item testlet receive an easier testlet in the next stage, whereas those who score 5 receive a more difficult testlet; otherwise the difficulty level is unchanged. The MFS administration protocol is designed to accrue the advantages of testlet CAT construction cited by Wainer and Kiely (1987), with additional useful features provided by the satisfaction of a number of constraints that must be met in large-scale test construction (Armstrong et al., 1998).

The testlet scoring system associates a distinct scale score, and a distinct weight, with each summed score for each testlet; these numbers are shown in Table 8.13 for a particular assembly of testlets. In Table 8.13, the IRT scale score associated with each summed score on each testlet is labeled "EAP," and the weights are labeled "Wt." There is one routing test comprising two 5-item testlets—which is effectively a 10-item routing test. Then in the columns representing stages 2, 3, and 4, there are five testlets, ranging in difficulty (encoded at the right of Table 8.13) from very low (VL) to very high (VH). Predetermined cutpoints determine which testlets an examinee sees, based on his or her score on the preceding testlet(s).

Table 8.14 illustrates an example of the IRT-based scoring system, using the Gaussian linear approximation. The examinee scored 8 of 10 on the routing test, was passed on to a testlet of medium difficulty, and ob-

TABLE 8.13
IRT Scale Score (Labeled "EAP") and Weights (Labeled "Wt")
Associated With Each Summed Score on Each Testlet
in a Multiform Structure

Stage 1 — Routing (pair of) testlets:

Sum	EAP	Wt
0	-1.6	2.2
1	-1.4	2.2
2	-1.2	2.2
3	-0.8	2.2
4	-0.5	2.2
5	-0.2	2.3
6	0.1	2.4
7	0.5	2.5
8	0.9	2.5
9	1.3	2.5
10	1.8	2.3

	Stage 2			Stage 3			Stage 4			
	Sum	EAP	Wt	Sum	EAP	Wt	Sum	EAP	Wt	Diff.
	0	-1.8	2.1	0	-1.9	2.7	0	-1.8	1.8	VL
	1	-1.3	2.0	1	-1.5	2.8	1	-1.4	1.7	
	2	-0.8	2.0	2	-1.1	2.8	2	-1.0	1.6	
	3	-0.3	1.9	3	-0.6	2.8	3	-0.5	1.6	
	4	0.3	1.7	4	-0.1	2.4	4	0.1	1.5	
	5	0.9	1.5	5	0.7	1.7	5	0.6	1.4	
	0	-1.5	1.8	0	-1.7	2.2	0	-1.8	2.4	L
	1	-1.1	1.8	1	-1.3	2.2	1	-1.4	2.4	
	2	-0.7	1.7	2	-0.9	2.2	2	-1.0	2.4	
	3	-0.2	1.6	3	-0.4	2.2	3	-0.5	2.3	
	4	0.3	1.6	4	0.2	2.0	4	0.1	2.0	
	5	0.9	1.5	5	0.9	1.7	5	0.8	1.6	
	0	-1.2	2.0	0	-1.4	2.1	0	-1.5	1.9	M
	1	-0.8	1.9	1	-1.0	2.0	1	-1.1	1.8	
	2	-0.4	1.8	2	-0.5	2.0	2	-0.7	1.8	
	3	0.1	1.8	3	0.0	2.0	3	-0.2	1.7	
	4	0.7	1.8	4	0.5	2.1	4	0.3	1.6	
	5	1.3	1.8	5	1.1	1.8	5	0.9	1.5	
	0	-0.8	1.8	0	-0.6	1.5	0	-0.8	1.5	H
	1	-0.6	1.7	1	-0.3	1.4	1	-0.4	1.5	
	2	-0.3	1.5	2	0.0	1.3	2	0.0	1.4	
	3	0.2	1.4	3	0.5	1.2	3	0.4	1.3	
	4	0.7	1.4	4	1.0	1.2	4	1.0	1.2	
	5	1.4	1.6	5	1.6	1.3	5	1.8	1.6	
	0	-0.3	1.4	0	-0.8	1.4	0	-0.6	1.6	VH
	1	-0.2	1.2	1	-0.4	1.4	1	-0.4	1.5	
	2	0.0	1.1	2	0.0	1.3	2	0.0	1.3	
	3	0.4	0.9	3	0.5	1.2	3	0.4	1.2	
	4	1.0	0.9	4	1.0	1.2	4	1.0	1.3	
	5	1.9	0.9	5	1.6	1.2	5	1.7	1.6	

Note. At the left of the table, there is a representation of a routing test comprising two five-item testlets. Then in the columns representing stages 2, 3, and 4, there are five testlets, ranging in difficulty (encoded at the right) from very low (VL) to very high (VH). Predetermined cutpoints determine which testlets an examinee sees, based on his or her score on the preceding testlet(s).

TABLE 8.14
A Person Responds to Items on the Testlet CAT Illustrated in
Table 8.13: The Examinee Obtains a Score of 8 on a 10-Item Routing
Testlet (Pair), a Score of 5 on a Medium-Difficulty 5-Item Testlet,
and Then Scores of 3 and 4 on Two High-Difficulty Testlets

Scale Score Computation:
$$\frac{0.9 \times 2.5 + 1.3 \times 1.8 + 0.5 \times 1.2 + 1.0 \times 1.2}{2.5 + 1.8 + 1.2 + 1.2 - (4-1)} = 1.7$$

Sum	EAP	Wt
0	−1.6	2.2
1	−1.4	2.2
2	−1.2	2.2
3	−0.8	2.2
4	−0.5	2.2
5	−0.2	2.3
6	0.1	2.4
7	0.5	2.5
8	**0.9**	**2.5**
9	1.3	2.5
10	1.8	2.3

Sum	EAP	Wt
0	−1.2	2.0
1	−0.8	1.9
2	−0.4	1.8
3	0.1	1.8
4	0.7	1.8
5	**1.3**	**1.8**

Sum	EAP	Wt	Sum	EAP	Wt
0	−0.6	1.5	0	−0.8	1.5
1	−0.3	1.4	1	−0.4	1.5
2	0.0	1.3	2	0.0	1.4
3	**0.5**	**1.2**	3	0.4	1.3
4	1.0	1.2	**4**	**1.0**	**1.2**
5	1.6	1.3	5	1.8	1.6

tained a score of 5 (of 5). After that, this examinee was moved to a testlet of
high difficulty for stage 3, and obtained a score of 3 (of 5), and then 4 of 5
on another testlet of high difficulty. The computation of this examinee's
scale score (in standard units) is shown inset in Table 8.14. Other examinees might be administered other combinations of testlets, but would
be scored on the same scale.

How does this compare to other alternative methods for CAT scoring?
The first illustration in Table 8.15 shows the estimates of proficiency (in
standard units) computed at the end of each stage of testing, for an
examinee that responds correctly to all items; in this case (as well as the
example with all items incorrect, at the bottom of the table), the response-
pattern and summed-score-pattern estimates are identical. The approximation is "off" by 0.4 standard units at the end of the test; however, the estimates exceed 3 standard deviations above the mean, and would probably
be truncated to identical values on the usual score-reporting scale.

TABLE 8.15

Illustrative Response Patterns for the Testlet CAT Illustrated in Table 8.13, With Standard Scores Computed Using Three Alternative Systems

Stage 1 (Routing)		Stage 2		Stage 3		Stage 4	
Item Responses	Sum	Responses	Sum	Responses	Sum	Responses	Sum
1111111111	10	11111	5	11111	5	11111	5
Response Pattern EAP(SD)	1.80(.7)		2.60(.6)		2.92(.5)		3.07(.5)
Summed Score Pattern EAP(SD)	1.80(.7)		2.60(.6)		2.92(.5)		3.07(.5)
Linear Approximation EAP(SD)			2.63(.7)		3.17(.6)		3.43(.6)
1111111100	8	11111	5	11100	3	11110	4
Response Pattern EAP(SD)	0.78(.6)		1.17(.5)		1.19(.4)		1.43(.4)
Summed Score Pattern EAP(SD)	0.87(.6)		1.32(.5)		1.37(.5)		1.58(.4)
Linear Approximation EAP(SD)			1.34(.6)		1.43(.5)		1.67(.5)
1111111000	7	11100	3	11100	3	11100	3
Response Pattern EAP(SD)	0.57(.5)		0.55(.5)		0.38(.4)		0.29(.4)
Summed Score Pattern EAP(SD)	0.48(.6)		0.46(.5)		0.34(.5)		0.22(.4)
Linear Approximation EAP(SD)			0.44(.6)		0.31(.5)		0.18(.4)
0000000000	0	00000	0	00000	0	00000	0
Response Pattern EAP(SD)	-1.65(.7)		-2.24(.6)		-2.56(.6)		-2.89(.5)
Summed Score Pattern EAP(SD)	-1.65(.7)		-2.24(.6)		-2.56(.6)		-2.89(.5)
Linear Approximation EAP(SD)			-2.21(.5)		-2.47(.4)		-2.70(.4)

Note. The "Response Pattern EAP" is the conventional method of computing the expected a posteriori estimate of proficiency, based on the pattern of item responses (Wainer et al., 1990); the "Summed Score Pattern EAP" is the expected a posteriori estimate of proficiency, based on the pattern of summed scores (Thissen et al., 1995); and the "Linear Approximation EAP" is our currently-proposed approximation to the summed score pattern EAP, computed as a linear combination of scaled summed scores. For all estimates, the posterior standard deviation is shown in parentheses.

The second block of values in Table 8.15 illustrates one set of response patterns that are associated with the summed-score pattern 8–5–3–4 shown in Table 8.14. The third block of values in Table 8.15 shows a lower-scoring set of response patterns, with summed scores 7–3–3–3 on the four testlets, whereas the final block of the table shows the estimates for examinees who respond to all items incorrectly. In most cases, the result of the linear approximation is within approximately one-half standard error of the summed-score-pattern estimate and/or the response-pattern estimate.

EVALUATION OF THE PATTERN-OF-SUMMED-SCORES, AND GAUSSIAN APPROXIMATION, ESTIMATES OF PROFICIENCY

In chapter 7, we proposed that in some cases, the usual IRT response-pattern estimate of proficiency could usefully be replaced with an estimate based on summed scores for sections of a test; in this chapter, we have proposed a linear approximation, based on Gaussian assumptions, for the estimate based on section summed scores. In this section, we examine the relative accuracy of three scoring methods—response-pattern EAP[$\theta | \mathbf{u}$], pattern-of-summed-scores EAP[$\theta | \mathbf{x}$], and the linear approximation EAP*[$\theta | \mathbf{x}$]. For convenience in this section, we use the notation $\hat{\theta}$ to refer generically to any of {EAP[$\theta | \mathbf{u}$], EAP[$\theta | \mathbf{x}$], and EAP*[$\theta | \mathbf{x}$]}; that risks some confusion, because in the 1960s and 1970s, much of the IRT literature used the notation $\hat{\theta}$ to refer to the mode of the response-pattern likelihood, and here that estimator is not even considered. However, $\hat{\theta}$ is a natural notation for "any estimator for θ," and it is used in that sense here.

Some Statistics Useful in the Evaluation of IRT Estimates of Proficiency—Conditional Descriptions of Accuracy. Summaries of the precision of IRT estimates of θ are usually conditional on θ. Perhaps the most stringent measure of precision is mean squared error (MSE):

$$\text{MSE}(\theta) = \varepsilon[(\hat{\theta} - \theta)^2] . \tag{11}$$

In model-based simulations, MSE is often estimated by simulating the responses of many examinees, given a value of θ and the model, and then computing $\hat{\theta}$ and the value of Eq. 11. However, given sufficient computational time, the theoretical value of MSE can be computed, as

$$\text{MSE}(\theta) = \sum_{\text{all } \mathbf{u}} (\hat{\theta} - \theta)^2 L(\mathbf{u} | \theta) . \tag{12}$$

Summing over all response patterns **u** sums over all possible observations, and weighting by the joint likelihood, $L(\mathbf{u}|\theta)$, reflects the relative likelihood of that response pattern, given θ.

We use as the basis of the evaluation the testlet CAT design described in the preceding section, with two 5-item testlets assembled into a 10-item routing test, followed by three 5-item testlets; there are a total of $2^{10} \times 2^5 \times 2^5 \times 2^5 = 1024 \times 32 \times 32 \times 32 = 33,554,432$ response patterns. That is rather a large number, but not insurmountable with current computational equipment, so here we compute the theoretical value of MSE(θ) using Eq. 12—this is a simulation, but there is no "Monte Carlo" or sampling. We compute the value of MSE (and other statistics, to follow) at 46 equally spaced values of θ, between -4.5 and 4.5.

MSE(θ) comprises two obviously separable parts—bias and random variance. We expect that all EAP estimates of θ are biased (toward zero when computed in standard units; this is often called "shrinkage"). The component of MSE(θ) that is bias may or may not be a problem: If the estimates are rescaled or equated to some other scale after they are computed, shrinkage bias may be scaled away. However, if estimates, say from different tests or MFSs, are to be compared to each other without intervening rescaling, then differential bias (between tests or MFSs) is part of the error.

In any event, we compute and report bias separately, as

$$\text{Bias}(\theta) = \sum_{\text{all } \mathbf{u}} (\hat{\theta} - \theta)L(\mathbf{u}|\theta) ; \qquad (13)$$

again summing over all response patterns and weighting by the joint likelihood given θ. Then we compute the variance of $\hat{\theta}$ given θ, as

$$\text{var}(\theta) = \text{MSE}(\theta) - [\text{Bias}(\theta)]^2 . \qquad (14)$$

Each estimator $\hat{\theta}$ has associated with it a model-based estimate of error, for which we use the notation σ_e^2 in this section. The term σ_e^2 represents an estimate of the variance of θ given the observed response pattern **u**, or the pattern of summed scores **x**. The square roots of these values are often reported as the standard errors of $\hat{\theta}$s computed with IRT. In the most traditional IRT, the information function (the inverse of the expected value of σ_e^2 for the modal estimate of θ) is often used as a measure of the precision of the test. For estimates other than the mode of the joint likelihood, we can compute the expected value of the modeled error variance as

$$E(\sigma_e^2) = \sum_{\text{all } \mathbf{u}} \sigma_e^2 L(\mathbf{u}|\theta) ; \qquad (15)$$

It is instructive to compare these values (the variance of θ given $\mathbf{u}$, which is effectively given $\hat{\theta}$) to the value of var(θ), which is the variance $\hat{\theta}$ given θ (Eq. 14).

Reliabilities. Green, Bock, Humphreys, Linn, and Reckase (1984) suggested that an IRT analog to the traditional reliability coefficient, which they called *marginal reliability*, could be computed as

$$\bar{\rho} = \frac{\sigma_{\theta}^2 - \bar{\sigma}_e^2}{\sigma_{\theta}^2}, \tag{16}$$

in which[2]

$$\bar{\sigma}_e^2 = \int E(\sigma_e^2)\phi(\theta)\,d\theta. \tag{17}$$

If the variance of θ in the population is fixed at a value of 1.0, as it usually is for purposes of parameter estimation, Eq. 16 simplifies to become

$$\bar{\rho} = 1 - \bar{\sigma}_e^2. \tag{18}$$

For a specified value of θ, the expected value of σ_e^2 is

$$E(\sigma_e^2) = \sum_{\text{all } \mathbf{u}} \sigma_e^2 L(\mathbf{u}|\theta), \tag{19}$$

where σ_e^2 is calculated as var[$\theta|\mathbf{u}$] or var[$\theta|\mathbf{x}$] or var*[$\theta|\mathbf{x}$], and the weighted average over all response patterns is computed to yield $E(\sigma_e^2)$.

Marginal reliability was derived from the basic traditional definition of reliability—that reliability is the ratio of true score variance to observed score variance. However, a brief algebraic exercise in the traditional test theory shows that reliability, defined as the ratio of true score variance to observed score variance, is also the squared correlation between the observed scores and the (unobservable) true scores (Gulliksen, 1950/1987, pp. 22–23). That suggests an alternative IRT analog to the traditional reliability coefficient: the squared correlation of $\hat{\theta}$ with θ. The correlation of an estimate $\hat{\theta}$ with θ can be computed as

---

[2]Equation 17 is not exactly what Green et al. (1984, p. 353) said, but it is no doubt what they meant. Green et al. did not include the expectation operator around σ_e^2; however, that is probably because they considered using the inverse of the Fisher information function for that value, as is usually used for modal estimates, and the inverse of Fisher information is $E(\sigma_e^2)$. Green et al. (1984, p. 352) mentioned the use of the "posterior variance of θ" (with "Bayesian," or EAP estimates), but they do not pursue that idea into the notation for the computation of the average error variance.

$$\sqrt{\rho} = \frac{\sum\limits_{\text{all } \mathbf{u}} \int [\hat{\theta}\theta L(\mathbf{u}|\theta)\phi(\theta)]\, d\theta}{\sigma_{\hat{\theta}}}. \tag{20}$$

(The fact that the expected value of θ is 0 and its variance is 1 simplifies Eq. 20 to become the weighted sum of the cross-products of θ and the estimates, divided by the standard deviation of the estimates.)

Results—Conditional Descriptions of Accuracy.   Figure 8.11 shows the values of Bias(θ) over the range $\theta = -3$ to $+3$ in standard units for the three estimators: $\hat{\theta}_1$ ("Pattern"), $\hat{\theta}_2$ ("Sum Score Pattern"), and $\hat{\theta}_3$ ("Linear Approx."). For the most part, all three estimators show the expected form of shrinkage bias—bias toward the mean, zero. There is one unusual feature shown in Fig. 8.11: $\hat{\theta}_3$, the Gaussian linear approximation, exhibits unusually low bias for values of θ between $+1$ and $+3$. This appears to be due to the fact that the values of $\hat{\theta}_3$ associated with all-correct, and nearly all-correct, response patterns are higher than the corresponding values for the other two estimators. For example, in Table 8.15 we see that the value of $\hat{\theta}_3$ for the response pattern that is all correct is 3.43, as opposed to the values for $\hat{\theta}_1$ and $\hat{\theta}_2$, which are (identically) 3.07. As θ increases, the probability of all-correct (and nearly all-correct) response patterns increase, and the higher estimates from $\hat{\theta}_3$ limit the bias for that estimator.

If the problem is considered a little more deeply, it becomes apparent that the linear approximation's underlying Gaussian approximation to the likelihoods produces this result. The actual likelihoods for the all-

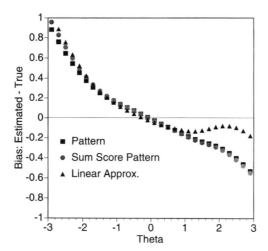

FIG. 8.11.   Values of Bias(θ) over the range $\theta = -3$ to $+3$ in standard units for three estimators: $\hat{\theta}_1$ ("Pattern"), $\hat{\theta}_2$ ("Sum Score Pattern"), and $\hat{\theta}_3$ ("Linear Approx.").

correct (and nearly all-correct) response patterns are negatively skewed; that negative skew pulls their averages lower (toward zero) and contributes to the shrinkage bias. The Gaussian approximation eliminates the negative skew, and reduces shrinkage bias for high values of θ.

Although this result is theoretically curious, it is best not to make a mountain out of this particular molehill: Because the reduced bias of $\hat\theta_3$ is due largely to values of the estimator that exceed +3 standard units, and most large-scale testing programs truncate reported scores at +3 standard units (or less), this reduced bias would probably never be observed in operational scoring. The phenomenon also does not appear for low values of θ, presumably because the response-pattern likelihoods there are less skewed (for the three-parameter logistic model). Nevertheless, the bias results are important for the understanding of the results with respect to mean squared error.

Figure 8.12 shows the values of MSE(θ) over the range θ = −3 to +3 in standard units for the three estimators: $\hat\theta_1$ ("Pattern"), $\hat\theta_2$ ("Sum Score Pattern"), and $\hat\theta_3$ ("Linear Approx."). MSE for all three estimators is at or below 0.2 for most values between θ = −1.5 and +1.5; outside that range, MSE rises fairly sharply as the Bias² component increases (see Fig. 8.11). An exception, expected after the results shown in Fig. 8.11, is the low MSE for $\hat\theta_3$ for θ > +2; that is due to the relative lack of bias in that range for $\hat\theta_3$, discussed above.

It is fairly difficult to disentangle the three curves plotted in Fig. 8.12; Fig. 8.13 shows the ratio MSE(θ for $\hat\theta_1$)/MSE(θ for $\hat\theta_s$), for s = 2 and 3 for two estimators: $\hat\theta_2$ ("Sum Score Pattern") and $\hat\theta_3$ ("Linear Approx."). For unbi-

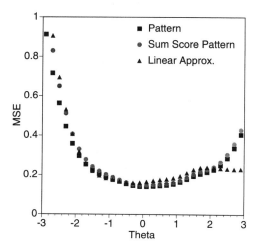

FIG. 8.12.   Values of MSE(θ) over the range θ = −3 to +3 in standard units for three estimators: $\hat\theta_1$ ("Pattern"), $\hat\theta_2$ ("Sum Score Pattern"), and $\hat\theta_3$ ("Linear Approx.").

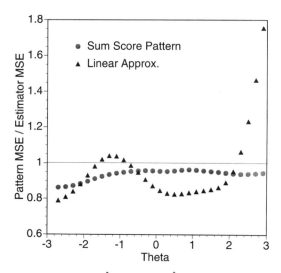

FIG. 8.13. Ratio MSE(θ for $\hat{\theta}_1$)/MSE(θ for $\hat{\theta}_s$), for $s = 2$ and 3 for two estimators: $\hat{\theta}_2$ ("Sum Score Pattern"), and $\hat{\theta}_3$ ("Linear Approx.").

ased estimators, this ratio would be relative efficiency; because all of the estimators considered here are biased, the ratio is a kind of pseudo relative efficiency, but in this context it may be interpreted for many purposes as relative efficiency. The value for $\hat{\theta}_2$, the summed score pattern estimator, is usually greater than 0.9 and always greater than 0.85—this shows that the loss of information involved in using patterns of summed scores in place of item response pattern data is relatively small. For high values of θ, $\hat{\theta}_3$ is superefficient; this is a reflection of the (relatively) lower bias of this estimator in that region.

Reliabilities. Table 8.16 shows, for all three estimators, the squared correlation of $\hat{\theta}$ with $\theta(\rho)$, the marginal reliability $(\bar{\rho})$, the average conditional variance (σ_e^2), and the population variance of the estimator $(\sigma_{\hat{\theta}}^2)$. The squared correlation of $\hat{\theta}$ with $\theta(\rho)$ is .8235 for the optimal response

TABLE 8.16
Squared Correlation of $\hat{\theta}$ with $\theta(\rho)$, Marginal Reliability $(\bar{\rho})$, Average Conditional Variance (σ_e^2), and Population Variance of the Estimator $(\sigma_{\hat{\theta}}^2)$ for Three Estimators of Proficiency (θ)

Estimator	Squared Correlation of $\hat{\theta}$ with $\theta(\rho)$	Marginal Reliability $(\hat{\rho})$	Average Conditional Variance (σ_e^2)	Population Variance of the Estimator $(\sigma_{\hat{\theta}}^2)$
$\hat{\theta}_1$	.8235	0.8235	0.1765	0.8235
$\hat{\theta}_2$	.8129	0.8130	0.1870	0.8129
$\hat{\theta}_3$	.8078	0.7860	0.2140	0.9106

TABLE 8.17
Overall Bias $(\hat{\theta} - \theta)$, Root Average Conditional Variance (σ_e),
Root Average Conditional MSE, and Average Conditional
MSE for Three Estimators of Proficiency (θ)

Estimator	Overall Bias $(\hat{\theta} - \theta)$	Root Average Conditional Variance (σ_e)	Root Average Conditional MSE	Average Conditional MSE
$\hat{\theta}_1$	0.0	0.420	0.420	0.1765
$\hat{\theta}_2$	0.0	0.432	0.432	0.1870
$\hat{\theta}_3$	0.014	0.462	0.442	0.1953

pattern EAP $(\hat{\theta}_1)$, and decreases only to .8078 for the most approximate estimator $(\hat{\theta}_3)$; converted with the Spearman–Brown formula, that decrease in reliability is equivalent to a decrease in test length from 25 to 23 items.

Marginal reliability (Eq. 16) is numerically equal to the squared correlation of $\hat{\theta}$ with θ (ρ; Eq. 20) for the two truly IRT EAP estimators, $\hat{\theta}_1$ and $\hat{\theta}_2$. In addition, for those two estimators, the sum of the average conditional variance (σ_e^2) and the population variance of the estimator $(\sigma_{\hat{\theta}}^2)$ is equal to the population variance, 1.0. Those nice relations do not apply to the linear approximation $(\hat{\theta}_3)$; for the linear approximation, marginal reliability consistently underestimates the correlation of $\hat{\theta}$ with θ (ρ), and that phenomenon increases with the degree of approximation. This appears to be due to both the facts that the conditional variance (σ_e^2) appears to be overestimated, on the average, for these estimators by Eq. 10, and the population variance of the estimators themselves is somewhat larger than one would expect from the results obtained with $\hat{\theta}_1$ and $\hat{\theta}_2$, which the linear approximations are supposed to approximate.

Table 8.17 shows the overall bias $(\hat{\theta} - \theta)$, the root average conditional variance (σ_e), the root average conditional MSE, and the average conditional MSE for all three estimators of proficiency (θ). These average values are computed using the density of the (normal) population distribution to weight the conditional values. The overall bias of the two truly IRT EAP estimators, $\hat{\theta}_1$ and $\hat{\theta}_2$, is zero. The linear approximation exhibits a small amount of overall bias, about 0.01. For the two truly IRT EAP estimators, $\hat{\theta}_1$ and $\hat{\theta}_2$, the root average conditional variance (σ_e) is equal to the root average conditional MSE; the results for those estimators differ very little. For the linear approximation, on average the modeled error variance (σ_e) exceeds the actual MSE slightly.

CONCLUSION

In this chapter we have developed an IRT-based system to combine scores from parts of a test using weighted linear scoring rules: "points" and "weights." In some contexts, this system may be more acceptable to the varied consumers of tests and test scores: Persons unschooled in the mysteries of IRT may consider response-pattern scoring, as described in chapters 3 and 4, or even summed-score-pattern scoring, as described in chapter 7, to be arcane or mystical. However, there is a very long and very public tradition associated with educational and psychological tests that provides an apparent basis for assigning some number of "points" to each summed-score outcome, and also the use of weights to combine the points into a total score. The advantage of the scores provided by the system proposed here is that the total scores are on the IRT scale, so they can be used in the context of IRT-linked multiple forms, or developmental scales, in the same way as more conventional IRT scores have been (as illustrated in chaps. 3 and 4).

This analysis of IRT score combination also provides IRT's answer to the vexing problem of weight selection, first raised in chapter 2. Table 8.7, for example, shows the relative weights (the weight for the multiple choice score of that combined test relative to a weight of one for the open-ended score) that are, in some sense, implicit in the IRT analysis of those particular reading test data. Those relative weights vary, depending on the values of the scores being combined. That means that the IRT analysis does not agree with *any* arbitrarily chosen weights that simply take one value for the multiple-choice score and another for the open-ended score—so IRT cannot agree with any of the traditional weighting schemes discussed or mentioned in chapter 2.

This IRT-based scoring system based on linear combinations was first developed for scoring two-part tests, like those that combine multiple-choice and open-ended sections. However, further development has led to the conclusion that it can also form a basis for scoring testlet-based CATs. Response-pattern scoring is currently used, at the time of this writing, in most operational CAT systems; that is difficult to explain, or even justify, to many consumers of large-scale test results. An apparently simpler method of scoring that equally yields results on the IRT scale could have many applications.

There is a price for simplicity; in this case, the price is a loss of precision in the test scores themselves. If the IRT model fits the data, response-pattern scores (such as described in chaps. 3 and 4) are optimal. Scores based on patterns of section summed scores (as described in chap. 7) lose some information relative to complete response-pattern scoring, so they must be less precise. And the *approximation* to scores based on patterns of section summed scores proposed in this chapter must be less precise yet. However, results summarized in this chapter indicate that the loss of information may be sufficiently small that the advantages of a simpler explanation of the results may justify that loss. The judgment of the relative values of precision and simplicity has to be made in each individual context, holding in mind, as always, the purposes of the testing program and the test scores.

REFERENCES

Armstrong, R. D., Jones, D. H., Berliner, N., & Pashley, P. (1998, June). *Computerized adaptive tests with multiple forms structures*. Paper presented at the annual meeting of the Psychometric Society, Champaign-Urbana, IL.

Birnbaum, A. (1968). Some latent trait models and their use in inferring an examinee's ability. In F. M. Lord & M. R. Novick (Eds.), *Statistical theories of mental test scores* (pp. 395–479). Reading, MA: Addison-Wesley.

Bock, R. D. (1972). Estimating item parameters and latent ability when responses are scored in two or more nominal categories. *Psychometrika, 37*, 29–51.

Bock, R. D. (1997). The nominal categories model. In W. van der Linden & R. K. Hambleton (Eds.), *Handbook of modern item response theory* (pp. 33–50). New York: Springer.

Green, B. F. (1997, March). *Alternate methods of scoring computer-based adaptive tests*. Paper presented at the annual meeting of the American Educational Research Association, Chicago.

Green, B. F., Bock, R. D., Humphreys, L. G., Linn, R. L., & Reckase, M. D. (1984). Technical guidelines for assessing computerized adaptive tests. *Journal of Educational Measurement, 21*, 347–360.

Gulliksen, H. O. (1987). *Theory of mental tests*. Hillsdale, NJ: Lawrence Erlbaum Associates. (Original work published 1950)

Kelley, T. L. (1927). *The interpretation of educational measurements*. New York: World Book.

Kelley, T. L. (1947). *Fundamentals of statistics*. Cambridge, MA: Harvard University Press.

Masters, G. N., & Wright, B. D. (1984). The essential process in a family of measurement models. *Psychometrika, 49*, 529–544.

Samejima, F. (1969). Estimation of latent ability using a response pattern of graded scores. *Psychometric Monograph, 17*.

Samejima, F. (1997). Graded response model. In W. van der Linden & R. K. Hambleton (Eds.), *Handbook of modern item response theory* (pp. 85–100). New York: Springer.

Thissen, D. (1998a, April). *Scaled scores for CATs based on linear combinations of testlet scores*. Paper presented at the annual meeting of the National Council on Measurement in Education, San Diego, CA.

Thissen, D. (1998b, June). *Some item response theory to provide scale scores based on linear combinations of testlet scores, for computerized adaptive tests*. Paper presented at the annual meeting of the Psychometric Society, Champaign-Urbana, IL.

Thissen, D., Pommerich, M., Billeaud, K., & Williams, V. S. L. (1995). Item response theory for scores on tests including polytomous items with ordered responses. *Applied Psychological Measurement, 19*, 39–49.

Wainer, H., Dorans, N., Flaugher, R., Green, B., Mislevy, R. M., Steinberg, L., & Thissen, D. (1990). *Computerized adaptive testing: A primer*. Hillsdale, NJ: Lawrence Erlbaum Associates.

Wainer, H., & Kiely, G. L. (1987). Item clusters and computerized adaptive testing: A case for testlets. *Journal of Educational Measurement, 24*, 185–201.

TECHNICAL APPENDIX:
IRT FOR PATTERNS OF SUMMED SCORES,
AND A GAUSSIAN APPROXIMATION

Summed Scores From the Perspective of IRT.   For any IRT model for items indexed by i with item scores u, the likelihood for any summed score $x = \sum u_i$ is

$$L_x(\theta) = \sum_{(u_i) = x} L(\mathbf{u}|\theta) , \qquad (21)$$

where the summation is over the all response patterns that contain x correct responses. That is, for all values of θ the likelihood of a summed score is obtained as the sum of the likelihoods of all of the response patterns that have that summed score. The likelihood for each response pattern is

$$L(\mathbf{u}|\theta) = \prod_i T_{u_i}(\theta) , \qquad (22)$$

where $T_{u_i}(\theta)$ is the trace line for response u to item i. The probability of each score x is

$$P_x = \int L_x(\theta)\phi(\theta) \, d\theta , \qquad (23)$$

where $\phi(\theta)$ is the population density.

An algorithm to compute $L_x(\theta)$ was described in chapters 3 and 4. Using that algorithm to compute a representation of $L_x(\theta)$ as a list of ordinates at specified values of θ, it is straightforward to compute the average value of θ associated with each score,

$$\mathrm{EAP}[\theta|x] = \mathrm{EAP}[\theta|x = \sum u_i] = \frac{\int \theta L_x(\theta)\phi(\theta) \, d\theta}{P_x} , \qquad (24)$$

and the corresponding conditional variance,

$$\mathrm{var}[\theta|x] = \mathrm{var}[\theta|x = \sum u_i] = \frac{\int (\theta - \mathrm{EAP}[\theta|x])^2 L_x(\theta)\phi(\theta) \, d\theta}{P_x} , \qquad (25)$$

or the standard deviation $\sqrt{\mathrm{var}[\theta|x]}$.

Scale Scores Based on Patterns of Summed Scores.   Historically, IRT scale scores have usually been computed for response patterns; for all IRT models with the exception of "Rasch-family" (Masters & Wright, 1984) models, the scale scores may differ for response patterns that have the same summed score. If the IRT model being used is an accurate representation of the data, the response-pattern scale scores are more precise than are those based on summed scores, because more information about θ is available from the response pattern. However, the loss of information involved in using summed scores instead of response patterns may be small, and there are many practical reasons to prefer scale score-translation tables based on summed scores (Thissen, Pommerich, Billeaud, & Williams, 1995).

When a test comprises testlets, or other units containing more than one item but fewer than all of the items on the test, IRT provides a strategy for computing scale scores that is intermediate between response-pattern scale scores and summed-score scale scores. That intermediate strategy is to compute scale scores for patterns of testlet summed scores.

As this approach applies to combining testlet scores, say for testlets t and t', one computes $L_x^t(\theta)$, the likelihood for summed score x for testlet t, and $L_{x'}^{t'}(\theta)$, the likelihood for summed score x' for testlet t', in both cases as described above. Then, for each combination of a given summed score x on testlet t with any summed score x' on testlet t', compute the product

$$L_{xx'}(\theta) = L_x^t(\theta)L_{x'}^{t'}(\theta) . \tag{26}$$

The product in Eq. 26 is the likelihood for the response pattern defined as {score x on testlet t, score x' on testlet t'}. Then, following standard IRT procedures, we can compute the modeled probability of the response pattern of summed scores $\{x,x'\}$,

$$P_{xx'} = \int L_{xx'}(\theta)\phi(\theta) \, d\theta . \tag{27}$$

We may also compute the expected value of θ, given the response pattern of summed scores $\{x,x'\}$,

$$\text{EAP}[\theta \,|\, x,x'] = \frac{\int \theta L_{xx'}(\theta)\phi(\theta) \, d\theta}{P_{xx'}} , \tag{28}$$

and the corresponding conditional variance,

$$\text{var}[\theta|x,x'] = \frac{\int (\theta - \text{EAP}[\theta \,|\, x,x'])^2 L_{xx'}(\theta)\phi(\theta) \, d\theta}{P_{xx'}} , \tag{29}$$

which can be used to compute the conditional standard deviation as $\sqrt{\text{var}[\theta \,|\, x,x']}$; that may be reported as the standard error of the scale score.

A Linear Approximation for the Extension to Combinations of Scores.   According to the IRT model, as described in the preceding section, the likelihood for testlet score combination x,x' is

$$L_{xx'}(\theta) = L_x^t(\theta)L_{x'}^{t'}(\theta) \ .$$

It may be useful for many purposes to approximate the mean and standard deviation of the density $L_{xx'}(\theta)$ as a linear combination of values associated with score x on testlet t and score x' on testlet t'. To construct such an approximation, we begin by constructing an approximation for the likelihood for score x on each testlet:

$$L_x(\theta)\phi(\theta) = L_x(\theta)N(0,1) \ . \tag{30}$$

[Here, the Gaussian density with mean μ and variance σ^2 is denoted $N(\mu,\sigma^2)$.] We assume that we have available the values of the expected a posteriori estimate of θ for score x, $\text{EAP}_x[\theta]$, and the posterior variance of θ for score x, $\text{var}_x[\theta]$; those are estimates of the mean and variance of $L_x(\theta)\phi(\theta)$.

Then we approximate $L_x(\theta)\phi(\theta)$ in Eq. 30 with a Gaussian distribution with the same mean and variance; because we have already assumed that the population distribution $\phi(\theta)$ is $N(0,1)$, that implies that there is a corresponding approximation for $L_x(\theta)$ that is also Gaussian. That is, Eq. 30 may be rewritten as a relation among three (approximately) Gaussian densities:

$$N(\text{EAP}_x[\theta], \text{var}_x[\theta]) = N(\theta_x^*, v_x^*)N(0,1) \ . \tag{31}$$

The values of θ_x^* and v_x^* may be determined by noting that Eq. 31 is the likelihood representation of a combination of normal data, for which the mean is the average of the component means, weighted by the inverses of the variances,

$$\text{EAP}_x[\theta] = \frac{\dfrac{1}{v_x^*}\theta_x^* + \dfrac{1}{1}0}{\dfrac{1}{v_{x'}^*} + \dfrac{1}{1}} \ ,$$

and the variance is the inverse of the sum of the inverse variances,

$$\text{var}_x[\theta] = \cfrac{1}{\cfrac{1}{v_x^*} + \cfrac{1}{1}} \, .$$

Solving for θ_x^* and v_x^*, we obtain

$$\theta_x^* = \frac{\text{EAP}_x[\theta]}{1 - \text{var}_x[\theta]} \tag{32}$$

and

$$v_x^* = \cfrac{1}{\cfrac{1}{\text{var}_x[\theta]} - 1} = \frac{\text{var}_x[\theta]}{1 - \text{var}_x[\theta]} \, . \tag{33}$$

The values of θ_x^* and v_x^* may be interpreted as the mean and variance of (an approximation to) the likelihood for score x.

Having obtained θ_x^* and v_x^*, we approximate the score-combination likelihood, for example, for testlet t score x and testlet t' score x',

$$L_{xx'}(\theta) = L_x^t(\theta) \, L_{x'}^{t'}(\theta)$$

as

$$N(\theta_{xx'}^*, v_{xx'}^*) = N(\theta_x^*, v_x^*) N(\theta_{x'}^*, v_{x'}^*)$$

in which

$$\theta_{xx'}^* = \cfrac{\cfrac{1}{v_x^*}\theta_x^* + \cfrac{1}{v_{x'}^*}\theta_{x'}^*}{\cfrac{1}{v_x^*} + \cfrac{1}{v_{x'}^*}} \, , \tag{34}$$

and

$$v_{xx'}^* = \cfrac{1}{\cfrac{1}{v_x^*} + \cfrac{1}{v_{x'}^*}} \, . \tag{35}$$

Approximation of the mean and variance of the posterior density for score combination x, x' also must include shrinkage due to the inclusion of the population distribution in the complete joint likelihood

$$L_{xx'}^t(\theta)\phi(\theta) = L_x^t(\theta)L_{x'}^{t'}(\theta)\phi(\theta) .$$

Continuing with the Gaussian approximation strategy, that is

$$N(\text{EAP*}[\theta|x, x'], \text{var*}[\theta|x, x']) = N(\theta_x^*, v_x^*)N(\theta_{x'}^*, v_{x'}^*)N(0, 1) .$$

So the Gaussian-approximated estimate of $\text{EAP}[\theta|x, x']$ is

$$\text{EAP*}[\theta|x, x'] = \frac{\dfrac{1}{v_x^*}\theta_x^* + \dfrac{1}{v_{x'}^*}\theta_{x'}^* + \dfrac{1}{1}0}{\dfrac{1}{v_x^*} + \dfrac{1}{v_{x'}^*} + \dfrac{1}{1}} . \tag{36}$$

This may be simplified by remembering that

$$\theta_x^* = \frac{\text{EAP}_x[\theta]}{1 - \text{var}_x[\theta]}$$

(Eq. 32), and

$$v_x^* = \frac{\text{var}_x[\theta]}{1 - \text{var}_x[\theta]}$$

(Eq. 33). So Eq. 36 may be rewritten as

$$\text{EAP*}[\theta|x, x'] = \frac{\dfrac{1 - \text{var}_x[\theta]}{\text{var}_x[\theta]}\dfrac{\text{EAP}_x[\theta]}{1 - \text{var}_x[\theta]} + \dfrac{1 - \text{var}_{x'}[\theta]}{\text{var}_{x'}[\theta]}\dfrac{\text{EAP}_{x'}[\theta]}{1 - \text{var}_{x'}[\theta]}}{\dfrac{1 - \text{var}_x[\theta]}{\text{var}_x[\theta]} + \dfrac{1 - \text{var}_{x'}[\theta]}{\text{var}_{x'}[\theta]} + 1}$$

$$= \frac{\dfrac{1}{\text{var}_x[\theta]}\text{EAP}_x[\theta] + \dfrac{1}{\text{var}_{x'}[\theta]}\text{EAP}_{x'}[\theta]}{\dfrac{1}{\text{var}_x[\theta]} - 1 + \dfrac{1}{\text{var}_{x'}[\theta]} - 1 + 1}$$

$$= \frac{\dfrac{1}{\mathrm{var}_x[\theta]}\,\mathrm{EAP}_x[\theta] + \dfrac{1}{\mathrm{var}_{x'}[\theta]}\,\mathrm{EAP}_{x'}[\theta]}{\dfrac{1}{\mathrm{var}_x[\theta]} + \dfrac{1}{\mathrm{var}_{x'}[\theta]} - 1}$$

$$= \frac{w_x\,\mathrm{EAP}[\theta|x] + w_{x'}\,\mathrm{EAP}[\theta|x']}{w_x + w_{x'} - 1}, \tag{37}$$

which is Eq. 4, with $w_x = 1/\mathrm{var}[\theta|x]$. Although Eq. 37 appears to be (almost) a weighted average of the original summed-score EAPs, it is useful to remember that they actually represent weighted averages of the values of θ_x^*.

The formula for the (approximated) variance similarly simplifies:

$$\mathrm{var}^*[\theta|x, x'] = \frac{1}{\dfrac{1}{v_x^*} + \dfrac{1}{v_{x'}^*} + \dfrac{1}{1}}$$

$$= \frac{1}{\dfrac{1 - \mathrm{var}_x[\theta]}{\mathrm{var}_x[\theta]} + \dfrac{1 - \mathrm{var}_{x'}[\theta]}{\mathrm{var}_{x'}[\theta]} + 1}$$

$$= \frac{1}{\dfrac{1}{\mathrm{var}_x[\theta]} - 1 + \dfrac{1}{\mathrm{var}_{x'}[\theta]} - 1 + 1}$$

$$= \frac{1}{\dfrac{1}{\mathrm{var}_x[\theta]} + \dfrac{1}{\mathrm{var}_{x'}[\theta]} - 1}$$

$$= \frac{1}{w_x + w_{x'} - 1}. \tag{38}$$

The Generalization for More Than Two Testlets. For $T \geq 2$ testlets, indexed by t, we have $\mathrm{EAP}_x^t[\theta]$, a list of the values of $\mathrm{EAP}[\theta|x]$ for testlet t, and w_x^t, a list of the values of $1/\mathrm{var}[\theta|x]$ for testlet t. Then the generalization of Eq. 37 for the scale score given the vector $\mathbf{x} = [x_1, x_2, \ldots, x_T]$ is

$$
\text{EAP}^*[\theta \mid \mathbf{x}] = \frac{\displaystyle\sum_{t=1}^{T} \frac{1}{v_x^{*t}} \theta_x^{*t} + \frac{1}{1} 0}{\displaystyle\sum_{t=1}^{T} \frac{1}{v_x^{*t}} + \frac{1}{1}}
$$

$$
= \frac{\displaystyle\sum_{t=1}^{T} \frac{1 - \text{var}_x^t[\theta]}{\text{var}_x^t[\theta]} \frac{\text{EAP}_x^t[\theta]}{1 - \text{var}_x^t[\theta]}}{\displaystyle\sum_{t=1}^{T} \frac{1 - \text{var}_x^t[\theta]}{\text{var}_x^t[\theta]} + 1}
$$

$$
= \frac{\displaystyle\sum_{t=1}^{T} \frac{1}{\text{var}_x^t[\theta]} \text{EAP}_x^t[\theta]}{\displaystyle\sum_{t=1}^{T} \left(\frac{1}{\text{var}_x^t}[\theta] - 1 \right) + 1}
$$

$$
= \frac{\displaystyle\sum_{t=1}^{T} \frac{1}{\text{var}_x^t[\theta]} \text{EAP}_x^t[\theta]}{\displaystyle\sum_{t=1}^{T} \frac{1}{\text{var}_x^t[\theta]} - T + 1}
$$

$$
= \frac{\displaystyle\sum_{t=1}^{T} w_x^t \, \text{EAP}_x^t[\theta]}{\displaystyle\sum_{t=1}^{T} w_x^t - (T - 1)} \; .
$$

The conditional variance is

$$
\text{var}^*[\theta \mid \mathbf{x}] = \frac{1}{\displaystyle\sum_{t=1}^{T} \frac{1}{v_x^{*t}} + \frac{1}{1}}
$$

$$
= \frac{1}{\displaystyle\sum_{t=1}^{T} \frac{1 - \text{var}_x^t[\theta]}{\text{var}_x^t[\theta]} + 1}
$$

$$
= \frac{1}{\displaystyle\sum_{t=1}^{T} \left(\frac{1}{\text{var}_x^t[\theta]} - 1 \right) + 1}
$$

$$= \cfrac{1}{\displaystyle\sum_{t=1}^{T} \cfrac{1}{\mathrm{var}_x^t[\theta]} - T + 1}$$

$$= \cfrac{1}{\displaystyle\sum_{t=1}^{T} w_x^t - (T - 1)}.$$

The overall consequence of this proposal is that it replaces the arcane computations involved in IRT scoring with a system that may be presented as a linear combination of (score-table transformed) summed scores obtained on sections of the test. The overall scores, computed as linear combinations of (transformed) summed testlet scores, have the scale properties of IRT scaled scores, to the extent that the linear system reproduced the EAPs from which it was derived, as well as the properties of weighted summed scores, which may facilitate some algebraic analyses.

Augmented Scores—"Borrowing Strength" to Compute Scores Based on Small Numbers of Items

Howard Wainer
Educational Testing Service

Jack L. Vevea
University of North Carolina at Chapel Hill

Fabian Camacho
Wake Forest School of Medicine

Bryce B. Reeve III
Kathleen Rosa
Lauren Nelson
University of North Carolina at Chapel Hill

Kimberly A. Swygert
Law School Admission Council

David Thissen
University of North Carolina at Chapel Hill

A test is rarely given with a single purpose in mind. For example, aside from their intended use, scores on college admissions tests like the SAT and the ACT are also used in related tasks like awarding scholarships, as well as for completely unrelated tasks like the evaluation of states' educational policies. Sometimes multiple uses of the scores are complementary, and the same test construction procedures that build a test that is good for one purpose also yield a test that works well for the others. Sometimes, however, the goals are antithetical: A test that is built to precisely rank examinees is likely to be rather poor at providing specific diagnostic information for remediation. An ability test that is built to measure an examinee's potential for learning may generalize far more broadly than a performance assessment that is built to measure how well an examinee can perform a specific task. Conversely, if we want to know if someone can change a tire, it is best to ask that they do exactly that, rather than use the indirect and inefficient approach of administering a general test of mechanical aptitude.

The world is complex, and with limited resources tests must usually serve many purposes. In this chapter we describe a statistical procedure that is helpful in permitting a test to better serve two commonly co-occurring and yet fundamentally antithetical purposes: ranking individuals and providing diagnostic feedback.

A test that is to rank individuals must yield scores that establish the ordering of those individuals as reliably as possible, while covering a broad range of material. The latter requirement emerges from considerations of fairness and validity: To be fair to all examinees the test cannot focus narrowly on any subset of the material being considered; validity usually requires broad content coverage.

A test that is to serve diagnostic purposes must also yield scores that are as reliable as possible, both for the overall score and for subscores associated with specific areas of the content domain. To be of diagnostic value, scores are needed that focus as narrowly as possible on the areas of the domain in which the examinee may be having difficulty.

Mixing the simultaneous requirements of breadth and narrowness with practical limitations on examinee testing time yields what appears at first to be a problem of insurmountable difficulty. How can we obtain highly reliable scores on whatever small region of the domain spanned by the test that might be required for a particular examinee, without taking an inordinate amount of time for all other examinees?

There are two answers. One strategy is to administer the test in an adaptive mode, and expand some portions of the test as needed to achieve adequately accurate estimates of diagnostic subscores. Such a solution is expensive and is practical only with computerized administration, which carries with it a different set of problems.

The second approach is to stabilize the diagnostic subscores by augmenting data from any particular subscale with information obtained from other portions of the test. It is this latter approach that this chapter espouses.[1] Yen (1987) developed a procedure to combine information from the responses to subsets of items representing some specific educational objective with the score on the test as a whole, to produce estimates of the true score for the subset of items. That procedure forms the basis of the *objective performance index* (OPI) reported for some tests published by

---

[1]Of course, these two approaches are not mutually exclusive. One can easily stabilize the subscores obtained in an adaptive test and doubly gain. We would strongly advocate such an approach for a test that is already being administered by computer.

CTB/McGraw-Hill. The methods we describe in this chapter are closely related to Yen's proposal; they differ only in computational detail. Yen's procedure is based on assumed binomial distributions for the (proportion-correct) scores, whereas the methods we describe use the same normal distribution theory that formed the basis of Kelley's (1927, 1947) true score estimates, as described in chapter 2.

In addition, Yen's (1987) procedure treats the rest of the test as a unit in subscore estimation, whereas the methods we describe in this chapter distinguish among the other subscale scores in the estimation of any one of them. A consequence of the latter approach is that the methods of this chapter are well suited to the estimation of subscale scores even when the test is truly multidimensional. In this respect, the methods described here are closely related to a system proposed by Longford (1997) to estimate linear combinations of scores on multidimensional tests. Indeed, if the linear combination in question is made degenerate—by weighting a single subscale 1 and the others 0—the procedures are the same. However, here we expand the concept to emphasize subscore augmentation, and we treat variants that work with IRT scale scores.

There have been other approaches that use both IRT and collateral information to estimate subscores; Gessaroli (1997) and Folske, Gessaroli, and Swanson (1999) described a system that combines IRT and *forced classification* (Nishisato, 1984) to yield augmented subscores. However, that system is not as closely integrated with the methods of the traditional test theory, or IRT as it is explained here, as the procedure that follows. Indeed, the procedure described in this chapter is most closely related to the way collateral information is used in the computation of subscores in the National Assessment of Educational Progress (NAEP; see Mislevy, Johnson, & Muraki, 1992). The difference between the two systems is less conceptual than computational: the NAEP procedures calibrate the items and make use of collateral information to estimate all subscores in one large iterative estimation system, whereas the system we describe here proceeds in steps, using conventional summed scores or scale scores and adding augmentation.

REGRESSED ESTIMATES: STATISTICAL AUGMENTATION OF MEAGER INFORMATION

Predicting a baseball player's season-long batting average from his first few weeks' performance is a problem that is closely related to predicting an examinee's true score on a subscale from a small sample of items. In both cases an efficient estimate is influenced by how everyone else is doing, by the player's (examinee's) past performance, and by the size of the sample of behavior we have observed. There are at least three different ways to approach prediction problems of this sort, although all use the notions of empirical Bayes estimation. In the testing context, we can use:

1. A fully observed score approach, using elements of the traditional theory.
2. A hybrid approach, using elements of both the traditional theory and item response theory.
3. Or an approach completely based on item response theory.

In this discussion we describe and use the first two methods and show sufficient improvement in the efficiency of estimation of subscores to warrant reporting them to examinees. The third (all-IRT) procedure is used in scoring the National Assessment of Educational Progress (NAEP); a full account of that method is beyond our scope here, but see Mislevy et al. (1992).

A General Description of Empirical Bayes Theory

The basic notion of what has come to be called *empirical Bayes* estimation is to use ancillary information to increase the precision of estimates. In general, the precision of an estimate can be improved if we shrink, or *regress*, the estimate toward some aggregate value. The amount of shrinkage depends on the size of the relationship between the statistic of interest and the ancillary information, as well as the amount of information we have about the specific statistic of interest. We use the term *ancillary information* in a general way, subsuming under it aggregate statistics like group means. Empirical Bayes methods have a long history in psychometrics, considerably predating the invention of the nomenclature, and much of the theory: Kelley's (1927, 1947) equation (see chap. 2),

$$\hat{\tau} = \rho x + (1 - \rho)\mu ,$$

in which an improved estimate of true score (τ) is obtained by shrinking the observed score (x) toward the group mean (μ) by an amount equal to the complement of the reliability of the measurement (ρ), is one well-known example. When the observed score is very reliable, its contribution dominates the estimate; a very unreliable observed score is largely ignored and the estimate shrinks from either extreme toward the group mean.

Let us consider a simple example, taken from Casella (1985).[2] Suppose, when the baseball season begins, a particular player gets a hit at his first

---

[2]For those familiar with the concepts of Bayesian estimation, this introduction is already overlong, and we suggest those experienced readers jump ahead to the more technical next section.

time at bat; his batting average is 1.000. What would we predict his season-long average will turn out to be? Obviously lower. Suppose another made an out initially and thus is batting 0.000. Our prediction about the end of the season would surely be higher. If we knew nothing more about these two players, we might sensibly predict that they would both end the season with a batting average equal to the observed mean, for all major league players, of .286; we would shrink the player who started with a hit *down* toward .286, and the player who made an out initially *up* toward .286. If their initial batting averages were based on 20 or 30 at-bat opportunities, we would still shrink the estimates, but not as much, because the initial data contain more information.

Placed into the context of Kelley's equation, the initial data (*x*) when there is only a single at-bat is very unreliable, so we shrink the estimate a great deal toward the group mean. As the estimate of *x* becomes increasingly reliable, we shrink it less. Of course, if we knew what these players' batting averages were in previous years we would shrink their estimates in that direction. Casella (1985) reported the batting averages of seven major league players after 45 at-bats, and then compared those averages with their final batting averages at the end of the season. He found that there was a remarkable 67% reduction in mean square error if regressed estimates were used as the predictor of final batting average instead. In Fig. 9.1 is a graphic depiction of these data and the empirical Bayes estimation process.

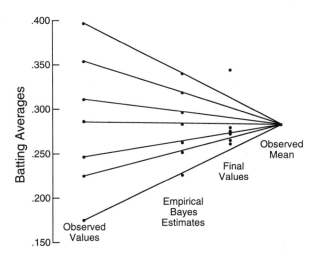

FIG. 9.1.   Graphical depiction of the effect of empirical Bayes shrinkage on the estimation of season-long batting averages of seven baseball players after only 45 at-bats (inspired by Casella, 1985).

One can think of the line joining each observed data point with the observed mean in Fig. 9.1 as a depiction of all of the (linear) empirical Bayes possibilities. If the initial data were very reliable, the empirical Bayes estimates would be very close to the observed data (toward the left of the picture). If the data were very unreliable, the estimate would shift further to the right, toward the group mean. Again, thinking in terms of Kelley's equation, the size of ρ tells us how far to the right to move; large ρ moves only a little, and small ρ moves more. In this instance we can see that the empirical Bayes estimates are a great deal better than the observed data, but that a bit more shrinkage would have been better still.

When we observe the performance of an examinee on a subscale of a test, our information is typically more meager than what we know about that examinee from the entire test. The trick is to use the information from the rest of the test, insofar as it is relevant, to increase the precision of our estimate of that examinee's score on that subscale. In the next section we formalize this idea.

AN OBSERVED SCORE APPROACH TO AUGMENTED SCORES

Using the usual true score model for an observed test score, let us define

$$x_{jv} = \tau_{jv} + \varepsilon_{jv}, \tag{1}$$

where x_{jv} is the observed score of person j on subscale v, τ_{jv} is the true score for person j on subscale v, and ε_{jv} is the error of measurement. The observed score x_{jv} is calculated in the obvious way, as the number of correct responses observed for subscale v. If desired, we may use the summed scores x_{jv} in the computations that follow, to obtain improved estimates on the summed score scale. However, in most large-scale testing contexts, there are multiple forms and score reporting is done on some arbitrary scale; in such contexts, it may be more convenient to use the standardized scores,

$$z_{jv} = \frac{x_{jv} - \bar{x}_{jv}}{s_{x_{jv}}};$$

That is what we do in most of the examples to follow. One may also use the scaled scores themselves, as we do in the first illustration (with SAT scores).

Kelley's equation for the estimated true score,

$$\hat{\tau} = \rho x + (1 - \rho)\mu,$$

may be rewritten as

$$\hat{\tau} = x_. + r(x - x_.)$$

by substituting a sample estimate of reliability, r, for ρ and the sample estimate x. for μ, and rearranging terms. In vector notation, for the multivariate situation involving several test scores collected in the vector **x**, this becomes

$$\hat{\tau} = \mathbf{x}_. + \mathbf{B}(\mathbf{x} - \mathbf{x}_.),$$

where **B** is a matrix that is the multivariate analog for the estimated reliability. The matrix **B** contains weights that combines the scores in x into estimates of the true scores in τ. If $\mathbf{B} = \mathbf{I}$, the scores are perfectly reliable and the observed scores **x** are the estimated true scores; if $\mathbf{B} = \mathbf{0}$ all observed scores are regressed to the mean, **x.**. Useful results are obtained between those two extremes.

All we need to be able to calculate regressed estimates of the true scores is to derive an estimate of **B** that we can obtain using the data. To do this, we first calculate the observed covariance matrix of the subscores, denoted $\mathbf{S}^{\text{obs}}$. The diagonal elements of $\mathbf{S}^{\text{obs}}$ contain the observed variances of the subscores. To do empirical Bayes estimation we will also need the covariance matrix of the true scores, $\mathbf{S}^{\text{true}}$. How can we estimate $\mathbf{S}^{\text{true}}$? The off-diagonal elements are the covariances between pairs of true scores, but because errors are uncorrelated with true scores, it is easy to see that $\sigma_{\tau_{jv}\tau_{jv'}} = \sigma_{x_{jv}x_{jv'}}$. Therefore the off-diagonal elements of $\mathbf{S}^{\text{obs}}$, providing, as they do, estimates of $\sigma_{x_{jv}x_{jv'}}$, may be used as the off-diagonal elements of our estimate of $\mathbf{S}^{\text{true}}$ as well.

It is in the diagonal elements of the two matrices that the difference arises. In the diagonal of $\mathbf{S}^{\text{true}}$ are the true score variances σ_τ^2, whereas in the diagonal of $\mathbf{S}^{\text{obs}}$ are the observed score variances σ_x^2. However, if we multiply the diagonal elements of $\mathbf{S}^{\text{obs}}$ by the fraction σ_τ^2/σ_x^2, the result will be what we need. But σ_τ^2/σ_x^2 is merely the reliability of the subscale in question (see chap. 2). This gives us the tool we need to estimate $\mathbf{S}^{\text{true}}$: We can compute $\mathbf{S}^{\text{true}}$, the estimated covariance matrix of the true scores, element-wise using:

$$s_{vv'}^{\text{true}} = s_{vv'}^{\text{obs}} \quad \text{for } v \neq v',$$

and

$$s_{vv'}^{\text{true}} = \rho_v s_{vv}^{\text{obs}} \quad \text{for } v = v'.$$

[It is customary to estimate reliability (ρ) with Cronbach's coefficient α (Eq. 13 from chap. 2).]

Alternatively, if the computations are to be done in matrix format, it is useful to construct the diagonal matrix $\mathbf{D}$ (Eq. 2), the diagonal elements of which are estimates of error variance. Error variance for each subscale is estimated as the product of the observed score variance for that subscale with 1 minus the reliability of that subscale.

$$\mathbf{D} = \begin{bmatrix} (1-\rho_1)s_{11}^{\text{obs}} & 0 & \cdots & 0 \\ 0 & (1-\rho_2)s_{22}^{\text{obs}} & \cdots & 0 \\ \cdots & \cdots & \cdots & \cdots \\ 0 & 0 & \cdots & (1-\rho_V)s_{VV}^{\text{obs}} \end{bmatrix} \tag{2}$$

We can then estimate $\mathbf{S}^{\text{true}}$ directly from the difference between $\mathbf{S}^{\text{obs}}$ and $\mathbf{D}$:

$$\mathbf{S}^{\text{true}} = \mathbf{S}^{\text{obs}} - \mathbf{D}. \tag{3}$$

The raw score and true score variance–covariance matrices are the components needed to obtain empirical Bayes estimates of the true subscale scores τ_{jv}. These estimates are $E(\tau_{jv}|x_{jv})$, the expected value of the true score on each subscale, given the scores on all of the subscales.

Assuming that the subscores are normally distributed, such an estimate is straightforward to calculate: To establish notation, suppose we have two variables, $\mathbf{y}_1$ and $\mathbf{y}_2$, whose distribution is multivariate normal (to be completely general, we note that $\mathbf{y}_1$ and $\mathbf{y}_2$ may each be either scalar or vector valued). Notationally:

$$\begin{bmatrix} \mathbf{y}_1 \\ \mathbf{y}_2 \end{bmatrix} \sim N\left(\begin{bmatrix} \mu_1 \\ \mu_2 \end{bmatrix}, \begin{bmatrix} \Sigma_{11} & \Sigma_{12} \\ \Sigma_{21} & \Sigma_{22} \end{bmatrix} \right).$$

For any such multivariate normal distribution, given any value of $\mathbf{y}_2$, the variable $\mathbf{y}_1$ is also distributed normally:

$$(\mathbf{y}_1|\mathbf{y}_2) \sim N(\mu_1 + \Sigma_{12}\Sigma_{22}^{-1}(\mathbf{y}_2 - \mu_2), \Sigma_{11} - \Sigma_{12}\Sigma_{22}^{-1}\Sigma_{21})$$

Put another way, the expected value of $\mathbf{y}_1$, given any value of $\mathbf{y}_2$, is

$$E(\mathbf{y}_1 | \mathbf{y}_2) = \mu_1 + \Sigma_{12} \Sigma_{22}^{-1} (\mathbf{y}_2 - \mu_2) \tag{4}$$

and the conditional covariance matrix of $\mathbf{y}_1$, given any value of $\mathbf{y}_2$, is

$$\Sigma_{(\mathbf{y}_1 | \mathbf{y}_2)} = \Sigma_{11} - \Sigma_{12} \Sigma_{22}^{-1} \Sigma_{21}. \tag{5}$$

Equation 4 is the definition of the statistical technique commonly known as *regression*; that fact is the reason that empirical Bayes estimates are also often called regressed estimates.

Using these standard results for the problem of subscore estimation, we assume that the true score τ and the observed score x follow a multivariate normal distribution, with common mean μ:

$$\begin{bmatrix} \tau \\ \mathbf{x} \end{bmatrix} \sim N \left(\begin{bmatrix} \mu \\ \mu \end{bmatrix}, \begin{bmatrix} \Sigma^{\text{true}} & \Sigma^{\text{true}} \\ \Sigma^{\text{true}} & \Sigma^{\text{obs}} \end{bmatrix} \right).$$

Then the empirical Bayes estimate of the vector of true subscale scores for examinee j, τ_j, conditioned on the observed scores, is

$$E(\tau_j | \mathbf{x}_j) = \mu + \Sigma^{\text{true}} (\Sigma^{\text{obs}})^{-1} (\mathbf{x}_j - \mu)$$

which we estimate using

$$\hat{\tau} = \mathbf{x}. + \mathbf{S}^{\text{true}} (\mathbf{S}^{\text{obs}})^{-1} (\mathbf{x}_j - \mathbf{x}.) = \mathbf{x}. + \mathbf{B} (\mathbf{x}_j - \mathbf{x}.) \tag{6}$$

by substituting the observed estimates $\mathbf{x}.$ (the vector mean of the subscale scores) and $\mathbf{S}^{\text{true}}$ and $\mathbf{S}^{\text{obs}}$ (the sample estimates of the true and observed covariance matrices) for the population quantities μ, Σ^{true} and Σ^{obs}.

$$\mathbf{B} = \mathbf{S}^{\text{true}} (\mathbf{S}^{\text{obs}})^{-1} \tag{7}$$

is conventional notation for the matrix of regression coefficients; these are the *weights* for the linear combination of the deviation scores that produce the best estimates of the subscale scores $\hat{\tau}$.

Note that in the absence of any error, the true and the raw covariance matrices coincide, the test is perfectly reliable, and the right side of Eq. 6 reduces to $\mathbf{x}_j$; in this case, the estimate of the true subscale scores is equal to the observed subscale scores. As error increases, the second term in Eq. 6 shrinks toward zero, so the best estimate of true score becomes $\mathbf{x}.$, the mean over all examinees. This effect, of shrinking the observed score toward the mean as a function of the error of measurement, or the unreliability of the subscores, operationalizes mathematically what was shown graphically in Fig. 9.1. Actually, Eq. 6 is simply the multivariate generalization of Kelley's equation.

We can also obtain an estimate of the conditional covariance matrix of the estimated true score by substituting appropriate sample quantities into Eq. 5. Specifically,

$$\mathbf{S}_{\hat{\tau}|x_i} = \mathbf{S}^{true} - \mathbf{S}^{true}(\mathbf{S}^{obs})^{-1}\mathbf{S}^{true}. \tag{8}$$

and the diagonal elements of $\mathbf{S}_{\hat{\tau}|x_j}$ are the conditional variances of the regression estimates of the true scores.

Equations 6 and 8 define the empirical Bayes estimate of subscores. These regressed subscore estimates are more accurate, or more reliable, in the sense that they have smaller mean squared error, than estimates based solely on an examinee's performance on the items within each subscale, if the rest of the test bears any relation at all to what is being measured by the items on that subscale. Vevea, Billeaud, and Nelson (1998) described a simulation that confirmed the increased precision of the regressed, or *augmented*, subscores under realistic conditions.

We can derive an estimate of subscale reliability by calculating the ratio of the unconditional true score variance to unconditional estimated true score variance. The numerator of this fraction is the unconditional true score variance of the vth subscale, which is the vth diagonal element of the matrix,

$$\mathbf{A} = \mathbf{S}^{true}(\mathbf{S}^{obs})^{-1}\mathbf{S}^{true}(\mathbf{S}^{obs})^{-1}\mathbf{S}^{true}. \tag{9}$$

The denominator, the unconditional score variance of the estimates for the vth subscale, is the vth diagonal element of the matrix

$$\mathbf{C} = \mathbf{S}^{true}(\mathbf{S}^{obs})^{-1}\mathbf{S}^{true}. \tag{10}$$

Or, summarizing, the reliability r_v^2 of subscale v is

$$r_v^2 = a_{vv}/c_{vv}. \tag{11}$$

Before going on to some examples, it will be valuable to discuss an important diagnostic statistic. $\mathbf{S}^{obs}$ must be a positive definite matrix; all of its eigenvalues must be positive. Σ^{true} must also be positive definite, although its estimate, $\mathbf{S}^{true}$, may not be. There are schemes for estimating $\mathbf{S}^{true}$ that assure that it is positive definite (see, e.g., ten Berge, Snijders, & Zegers, 1981), but they are not necessary for these computations. It profits us, however, to examine the eigenstructure of $\mathbf{S}^{\text{true}}$: If it is dominated by a single eigenvalue, it tells us that despite being made up of V separate subscales, the test is largely unidimensional, and all subscales are estimates of the same underlying proficiency. This is good news and bad news. It is good news, in that we can report subscores of very high reliability, because the other items carry a great deal of information about the scales on which they are not included. It is bad news, in that what we thought of as separate pieces of information (the different subscales) are not separate. If $\mathbf{S}^{\text{true}}$ is of full rank, with V substantial eigenvalues, it means that the subscales are indeed carrying independent information, and that the empirical Bayes estimates of the subscale scores may not yield massive improvements in precision.

Before examining examples of the use of this technology, it may be helpful to look at a simple special case. We believe that by going through this small, but very interesting, plausible application, the reader will develop both intuition about the technology and a deeper appreciation of the benefits that it can yield.

More Accurate Mathematics Scores
on a Test Like the SAT

Let us consider the simplest possible subscore problem: Suppose we have a test made up of two parts, say a mathematics section and a verbal section. Further, suppose we wish to report scores on each section separately. The solution currently employed by major testing organizations is to be sure that each section is sufficiently long that the reported scores are reliable enough on their own for their prospective use. But can we do better using the empirical Bayes technology just described?

An Example of Augmented Scores Specialized for Two Scores.   Following the notation introduced in chapter 2, let us define the observed scores for each section as

$$x_{\text{M}} = \tau_{\text{M}} + e_{\text{M}}$$

for the scores on the mathematics (M) section and

$$x_{\text{V}} = \tau_{\text{V}} + e_{\text{V}}$$

for the scores on the verbal (V) section.

Considering the score on the mathematics section first, we want to estimate the expected value of the true mathematics score, given the observed mathematics and verbal scores,

$$E(\tau_M | x_M, x_V),$$

as a linear regression from the two observed scores. Or

$$\hat{\tau}_M = \beta_0 + \beta_M x_M + \beta_V x_V. \tag{12}$$

Let us assume, plausibly for any large operational program, that we have good estimates of all of the summary statistics for the test, specifically the variances of the observed scores (s_M^2 and s_V^2), the covariance between the verbal and mathematical scores (s_{VM}), the means of the two sections ($\bar{x}_V$ and $\bar{x}_M$), and the reliability of the two sections (r_M and r_V).

We can then estimate the parameters for Eq. 12 by solving the matrix equation $\mathbf{B} = \mathbf{S}^{true}(\mathbf{S}^{obs})^{-1}$, from Eq. 7. But in this case, where there are only two sections, and because we are only interested in the results for the math test, this specializes to[3]

$$\begin{bmatrix} \beta_M \\ \beta_V \end{bmatrix} = \begin{bmatrix} s_M^2 & s_{VM} \\ s_{VM} & s_V^2 \end{bmatrix}^{-1} \begin{bmatrix} r_M s_M^2 \\ s_{VM} \end{bmatrix}, \tag{13}$$

and

$$\beta_0 = \bar{x}_M - \beta_M \bar{x}_M - \beta_V \bar{x}_V.$$

Solving Eq. 13 yields:

$$\beta_V = \frac{s_M^2 s_{VM}(1 - r_M)}{s_M^2 s_V^2 - s_{VM}}, \tag{14}$$

and

$$\beta_M = 1 - \frac{s_V^2}{s_{VM}} \beta_V. \tag{15}$$

How does the implementation of this affect SAT scores? Using approximate, but rather plausible, estimates, lets us calculate the consequences by assuming that each section of the SAT has a mean of 500, a standard deviation of 100, and a reliability of .90. Moreover, let us assume that the scores on the two sections correlate at .7 with each other.

---

[3]We note that Eq. 13 is directly analogous with the standard matrix formulation for the computation of regression coefficients,

$$\beta = (\mathbf{X}'\mathbf{X})^{-1}(\mathbf{X}'\mathbf{y}).$$

Substituting these values into Eqs. 14 and 15, and those results into Eq. 12, we obtain the estimation equation

$$\hat{\tau}_M = 30 + 0.80x_M + 0.14x_V.$$

Using this equation we generated some expected true scores for a range of observed scores; these results are shown in Table 9.1. We have reproduced the value of the Kelley regressed true scores [$E(\tau_M|x_M)$, the expected value of the true mathematics score given only the value of the observed mathematics score] as the last column of Table 9.1 for comparison. Consider the (extremely hypothetical) situation of an examinee who obtained an observed score of 800 on the math section but only a 200 on the verbal. The regressed estimate of that person's mathematics true score is 698, whereas if the verbal score had also been 800 we estimate a mathematics true score of 782.

It is illuminating to examine the more plausible circumstances associated with the set of cells highlighted along the diagonal and compare them with the associated Kelley estimate in the last column. For example, if someone has an observed score of 200 on the SAT-M the Kelley estimate regresses it upward 30 points toward the mean of 500. But if that same person also scored 200 on the SAT-V this is viewed as additional evidence of this person's lack of mathematics proficiency, so the estimate that also uses the SAT-V score regresses the true score estimate upward only 18 points. Note that the size of the shrinkage is proportional to the distance that the observed score is from the mean; a score of 500 is not moved at all. Of course, because the shrinkage is symmetric around the mean, the higher scores shrink downward by exactly the same amount as their low-end counterparts are moved upward.

TABLE 9.1
Empirical Bayes Estimates of the True Score for SAT Mathematics
for Various Values of Observed Mathematics and Verbal Scores

| | *SAT-V* | | | | | | | *Kelley* |
SAT-M	*200*	*300*	*400*	*500*	*600*	*700*	*800*	*True Score*
200	**218**	232	246	260	274	288	302	230
300	298	**312**	326	340	354	368	382	320
400	378	392	**406**	420	434	448	462	410
500	458	472	486	**500**	514	528	542	500
600	538	552	566	580	**594**	608	622	590
700	618	632	646	660	674	**688**	702	680
800	698	712	726	740	754	768	**782**	770

Note. The Kelley estimate, which does not use the verbal observed score, is included for comparison.

One way to think about this is that the regressed estimate is a prediction of what score this person would obtain if they took the test again. It uses the information contained in the verbal score to affect this estimate. The Kelley estimates, not having the benefit of the information in the verbal scores, suggest a different value.

The observed scores have the statistical property of being unbiased; their expected value is equal to their true score. Regressed true score estimates are not unbiased, but they are more accurate estimates than the observed score in that they have a smaller mean square error.

How much more accurate are these estimates than the observed scores? We can use Eq. 11 to compute the reliability of these scores. When this is done we discover that these scores have a reliability of .92. This is somewhat larger than the original reliability of .90, and corresponds, using the Spearman–Brown "prophesy" formula (Eq. 12 in chap. 2), to increasing the length of the mathematics section by about 26%. Thus we conclude that using the information in the verbal section of the SAT allows us to improve the precision of the scores of the mathematics section equivalent to increasing that section's length by 26%. Through a symmetric argument, the precision of the verbal score can be improved by an identical amount if the information in the mathematics section is used in its computation.

What Score Should Be Reported?   Should we report estimated true scores or observed scores? And if we report the former, what does that do to the original scale of the test? This is not a particularly complex question, but the answer requires precision. If the observed scores are placed on a scale from 200 to 800 we have seen that the estimates of true score will shrink inward. The Kelley estimates shrink most, yielding a score range of 230 to 770. The estimates that use the information available in the verbal score shrink to a scale from 218 to 782. These results leave us with a number of questions.

For example one might ask, based on these results, "Is there no one whose true score is 800?" Or, "Why does a person's true score change depending on what information is used to estimate it?" These questions are part of the more general question of "What is the right scale?" The answer to the last question is, "all of them"; it depends on what one wants to know.

If we want to know what math score someone achieved on this form of the SAT, then the answer is the observed (scaled) score (x_M), which runs from 200 to 800. If we want to know what score they are likely to get if they take the test again, then we want to estimate the true score. Note that what we estimate $[E(\tau_M | x_M)]$ is the mean of the conditional distribution. These estimates have a narrower range then the observed scores. But this does not mean that no one has a true score of 800 (or 200). Consider the Kelley estimates: An observed score of 800 yields an estimate of 770, but that 770 is merely the mean of a distribution (as was shown in the bottom panel of Fig. 2.4). Some of the examinees who scored 800 the first time will score 800 the second time as well; an approximately equal number will score 740 or lower. The average of all of these people who originally scored 800 on the second testing will be 770. This distribution will have some variance, computable from Eq. 8.

If we estimate SAT-M true scores with more information than is used in Kelley's equation, say by using the SAT-V score as well, two things happen: The variance of the means of the posterior distributions increases (hence, the posterior means spread out to a range of 218 to 782), and the conditional posterior variance decreases, so that the variation on SAT-M retest scores of all those who scored 800 on both the SAT-V and the SAT-M will be more tightly clustered around 782.

Regressed Observed Subscores for a 1994 American Production and Inventory Control Society (APICS) Certification Examination

The American Production and Inventory Control Society (APICS) certifies expertise in a variety of areas. Their 1994 Just-in-Time Examination is part of certification in production and inventory management. It consists of 100 multiple-choice items that comprise six subscales. These subscales and the number of items that make up each subscale are shown in Table 9.2. The test administration that provided the data analyzed here involved 2,410 examinees.

The reliability of each subscale (Cronbach's coefficient α) is shown in the third column of Table 9.2. Although the overall test score is very reliable, only the longest of the subscales (3, 4, and 6) have reliabilities that even approach levels that permit responsible reporting to examinees. In the fourth column of Table 9.2, labeled "expected reliability," is the reliability we would expect, based on the overall test reliability, the subscale's length, and the Spearman–Brown formula. When expected reliability is about equal to the actual reliability for each subscale, as in Table 9.2, it is evidence that the test is relatively homogeneous—that is, that all of the sections are basically measuring the same thing. For such an essentially unidimensional test, empirical Bayes estimated subscores are much more reliable than the observed subscores.

The rightmost column of Table 9.2, listing the empirical Bayes estimates of reliability, shows just how much more stable subscale estimates can be made. The fact that all subscores are almost as reliable as the test as a whole (they are all less reliable than the total, but only in the third decimal place) provides very strong evidence that the test is essentially unidimensional. We show later in greater detail how the regressed subscore

TABLE 9.2
Comparison of Subscale Reliabilities for the APICS Subscales Computed
in the Traditional Way and With Empirical Bayes Estimates

	Number of Items	Coefficient α	Expected Reliability	Empirical Bayes
Overall	100	.88		
1. Concepts	12	.43	.47	.88
2. Human Resources	12	.47	.47	.88
3. Total QC	17	.62	.56	.87
4. Techniques	23	.67	.63	.88
5. Integration	14	.53	.51	.88
6. Implementation	22	.65	.62	.88
Average	17	.56	.54	.88

TABLE 9.3
Eigenvalues of $\mathbf{S}^{true}$ for the Standardized Subscale Scores for APICS

Number	Eigenvalue	Percent of Total
1	3.23	96
2	0.08	2
3	0.04	1
4	0.03	<1
5	0.02	<1
6	−0.02	—

estimates are computed for this test, and how the improved reliability is obtained.

As discussed in the previous section, the dimensionality of the test can also be examined by computing the eigenvalues of $\mathbf{S}^{true}$, shown for the standardized subscale scores[4] for the APICS data in Table 9.3. It is clear from the eigenstructure that this test is extremely unidimensional. The four smallest roots appear to be random fluctuations from zero. The implications for the computation of subscale scores are obvious: For any subscale one can choose items from the test essentially at random and obtain a good estimate; for greater precision, choose more items. The empirical Bayes estimates reflect a formal way of using what is essentially the score on the entire test, for each subscore.

To obtain the regressed estimates of the subscale scores, we begin with the sample estimates of $\mathbf{S}^{obs}$ and $\mathbf{S}^{true}$ shown in Table 9.4. Because we are

---

[4]In this chapter we use standardized summed scores (z-scores) to illustrate the summed-scores computations. The subscore augmentation procedure works equally well for the number-correct scores; however, because those are all on different number-correct scales from subscale to subscale, the results are difficult to interpret for an unfamiliar test.

working with standardized subscale scores, $\mathbf{S}^{obs} = \mathbf{R}$, the correlation matrix among the subscale scores. The diagonal elements of $\mathbf{S}^{true}$ are the values of coefficient α for each subscale. Using $\mathbf{S}^{obs}$ and $\mathbf{S}^{true}$, we compute $\mathbf{B}$, the matrix of weights that are used to combine the observed subscale scores into the regressed estimates, as shown in Eq. 7. For the standardized subscale scores from the APICS data, the resulting weights are shown in Table 9.5.

TABLE 9.4
$\mathbf{S}^{obs}$ and $\mathbf{S}^{true}$ for the APICS Subscales

| | \multicolumn{6}{c}{$\mathbf{S}^{obs}$} |
	1	2	3	4	5	6
1	1.0					
2	0.443	1.0				
3	0.504	0.512	1.0			
4	0.525	0.535	0.578	1.0		
5	0.489	0.465	0.514	0.576	1.0	
6	0.511	0.522	0.576	0.630	0.569	1.0
	\multicolumn{6}{c}{$\mathbf{S}^{true}$}
	1	2	3	4	5	6
1	0.429					
2	0.443	0.474				
3	0.504	0.512	0.620			
4	0.525	0.535	0.578	0.674		
5	0.489	0.465	0.514	0.576	0.534	
6	0.511	0.522	0.576	0.630	0.569	0.650

TABLE 9.5
$\mathbf{B}$, the Matrix of Weights That Are Used to Combine the Observed
Subscale Scores Into the Regressed Estimates, for the APICS Subscales

| | \multicolumn{6}{c}{$\mathbf{B}$} |
	1	2	3	4	5	6
1	0.073	0.094	0.165	**0.167**	0.149	0.139
2	0.087	0.139	0.164	**0.175**	0.087	0.150
3	0.110	0.118	**0.289**	0.144	0.088	0.151
4	0.096	0.108	0.123	**0.298**	0.137	0.188
5	0.121	0.077	0.108	**0.196**	0.163	0.188
6	0.085	0.100	0.139	**0.202**	0.141	0.266

Note. Each row gives the weights that multiply each of the six observed subscale scores to provide the regressed subscore estimate for that subscale. The largest weight in each row is emphasized in boldface.

We note that the scoring weights in Table 9.5 are characterized by striking uniformity, which is a result of the undimensional nature of this test. Because the subscales do not appear to measure different dimensions of individual differences, the empirical Bayes system assigns the larger weights to the more reliable subscores: For example, the largest weight in the computation of the regressed estimate for subscale 1 is assigned to subscale 4, because subscale 4 is more reliable than subscale 1. Were we to anthropomorphize the empirical Bayes regression system, we would write that "it says that subscale 4 provides a better estimate of the score on subscale 1 than does the observed score on subscale 1, because all of the subscales appear to measure the same thing, and subscale 4 does so more reliably."

Because the empirical Bayes subscores are regressed estimates, they vary less than the observed subscale scores. Shown in Fig. 9.2 is a plot of the distributions of the standardized subscale scores with the empirical Bayes estimates. As is evident, the distributions of the empirical Bayes (regressed) estimates are considerably less variable, although they are generally centered on about the same value.

Our intuitions about how the scores are modified may be strengthened by examining the scores for a few examinees. Shown in Table 9.6 are the

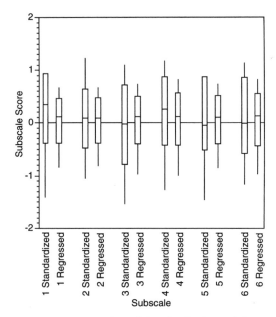

FIG. 9.2.   Box-and-whisker plots of the distributions of the standardized and regressed (empirical Bayes) estimates of subscores for each of the six subscales in the APICS test. For each distribution, the top, center, and bottom lines of the box represent the 75th, 50th, and 25th percentiles respectively; the whiskers extend to the 90th and 10th percentiles.

TABLE 9.6
Standardized Subscores, and Their Regressed (Empirical Bayes)
Values, for 12 Representative APICS Examinees

	APICS Subscale					
Examinee	1	2	3	4	5	6
	Standardized Subscores					
1	0.94	1.22	1.47	1.17	1.35	1.72
2	0.94	1.22	1.10	0.87	−0.05	1.14
3	0.94	0.09	0.72	0.56	0.88	1.14
4	0.35	1.22	0.72	0.56	−0.52	0.86
5	0.35	−0.48	0.72	0.87	0.88	−0.01
6	−1.41	0.65	0.72	0.56	−0.52	0.86
7	−0.24	0.65	0.35	0.26	−0.52	0.28
8	0.94	−1.61	0.35	−1.26	−0.05	1.14
9	−0.24	0.09	−0.03	−0.35	−0.99	−0.01
10	0.35	−1.61	−1.91	0.56	−0.05	−0.29
11	0.94	−0.48	−0.78	−0.66	−0.99	−1.73
12	−0.83	0.09	−1.91	−1.87	−1.46	−0.87
	Regressed Standardized Subscores					
1	1.06	1.07	1.22	1.26	1.14	1.29
2	0.66	0.75	0.86	0.82	0.70	0.83
3	0.58	0.56	0.65	0.69	0.67	0.73
4	0.40	0.50	0.55	0.51	0.40	0.52
5	0.37	0.31	0.39	0.45	0.40	0.38
6	0.21	0.27	0.29	0.28	0.14	0.31
7	0.11	0.17	0.18	0.15	0.08	0.15
8	−0.09	−0.14	0.00	−0.21	−0.02	0.01
9	−0.22	−0.16	−0.16	−0.26	−0.26	−0.23
10	−0.40	−0.46	−0.67	−0.27	−0.24	−0.37
11	−0.60	−0.57	−0.62	−0.72	−0.62	−0.81
12	−1.02	−0.96	−1.16	−1.23	−1.07	−1.14

observed standardized subscores and the regressed estimates for 12 examinees. These 12 examinees are equally spaced across the range of total score on the APICS examination. We can examine these scores in conjunction with Fig. 9.3, which shows the observed and augmented standardized scores for three of these examinees plotted as profiles.

The extraordinarily salient difference between the profiles for the standardized and regressed subscores in Fig. 9.3 is that the regressed subscores are all very nearly the same within each person, whereas the standardized subscores are highly variable within persons—especially for the examinees whose scores are shown in the upper two panels. Returning our attention to Table 9.6, note that the score values show that the regressed estimates are near the observed estimates when the observed estimates are

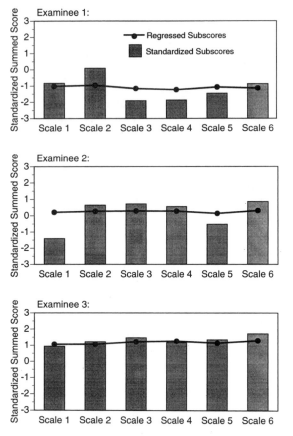

FIG. 9.3. Standardized subscores (shaded bars) and regressed (empirical Bayes) standardized subscores (points) on the six subscales for three representative APICS examinees.

near average for any particular examinee, and that the regressed estimates are corrected back toward that score level when the observed subscores deviate. The regularity of the empirical Bayes estimates is a direct result of the unidimensionality of the covariance matrix of true scores.

Regressed Observed Subscores for the Performance Assessment Part of the North Carolina Test of Computer Skills

The North Carolina Test of Computer Skills was developed as part of a system to ensure basic computer proficiency for graduates of the North Carolina Public Schools. The test is intended for eighth-grade students.

TABLE 9.7
Comparison of Subscale Reliabilities for North Carolina
Test of Computer Skills Subscales Computed
in the Traditional Way and With Empirical Bayes Estimates

	Number of Items	Coefficient α	Expected Reliability	Empirical Bayes
Overall	26	.86		
Keyboarding (KB)	3	.52	.33	.74
Editing (ED)	10	.85	.62	.86
Database (DB)	7	.60	.53	.74
Spreadsheet (SS)	6	.77	.49	.81
Average	6	.68	.49	.79

The performance assessment included in the North Carolina Test of Computer Skills consists of four parts: Keyboarding Techniques (KB), Word Processing/Editing (ED), Database Use (DB), and Spreadsheet Use (SS). We examined the KB and ED sections using data from the item try-out administration and traditional test theory in chapter 2, and we considered IRT scale scores for the ED section in chapter 3 and for the KB section in chapter 4. Here we examine the use of data from all four parts of the performance assessment to compute augmented estimates of the true subscores for the KB, ED, DB, and SS sections. In this illustration, we use data from the 267 examinees who responded to Form 1 of the item tryout.

The reliability estimate for the summed score of the entire test for this sample is .86; however, subscores for three of the four sections are insufficiently reliable to allow individual student reporting (see the values in Table 9.7).[5] This test is not as unidimensional as APICS; multidimensionality is suggested both by the difference between the observed values of coefficient α for the sections and the values of "expected reliability" in Table 9.7, and the eigenvalues of $\mathbf{S}^{true}$ shown in Table 9.8.

The values of $\mathbf{S}^{obs}$ and $\mathbf{S}^{true}$ shown in Table 9.9 show that this test is an extremely promising candidate for improvement of the precision of the subscale scores using the empirical Bayes approach. The subscales are all correlated with each other, indicating that to some extent each subscale measures some aspects of proficiency in common with the others, so the possibility of borrowing strength exists. On the other hand, in this example, unlike the APICS example, the correlations among the four subscales are substantially lower than their reliabilities (which are the diagonal val-

---

[5]The reliability estimates in Table 9.7 for the KB and ED sections differ slightly from those reported for those sections in chapter 2, because the estimates reported in chapter 2 were computed using all 3,104 students in the item tryout sample, all of whom completed the same KB and ED sections. Because the DB and SS sections varied for subsamples of the item tryout, only 267 examinees responded to all four of the particular sections considered here.

TABLE 9.8
Eigenvalues of S^{true} for the Standardized Subscale Scores
for the North Carolina Test of Computer Skills,
Performance Assessment Tryout Form 1

Number	Eigenvalue	Percent of Total
1	1.748	64
2	0.501	18
3	0.260	9
4	0.234	9

TABLE 9.9
S^{obs} and S^{true} for the North Carolina Test of Computer Skills,
Performance Assessment Tryout Form 1

	S^{obs}			
	KB	ED	DB	SS
KB	1.00			
ED	0.371	1.00		
DB	0.301	0.314	1.00	
SS	0.346	0.345	0.417	1.00

	S^{true}			
	KB	ED	DB	SS
KB	0.518			
ED	0.371	0.853		
DB	0.301	0.314	0.604	
SS	0.346	0.345	0.417	0.768

ues of S^{true} in Table 9.9). That indicates that each subscale measures a distinguishable aspect of proficiency.

When the values in Table 9.9 are used in Eq. 7, the result is the weight matrix (**B**) shown in Table 9.10. In **B**, each row gives the weights that multiply each of the four observed subscale scores to provide the regressed subscore estimate for that subscale. As we would expect (but as was not the case with the APICS data), each subscale has the largest weight in the row that defines the regressed estimate for its own subscore. In this case, the empirical Bayes system is actually using data from the other three subscales only to help out estimation of each subscale's score; it is not entirely replacing some of the subscales with the total score on the test, as it did for APICS.

Nevertheless, the reliability estimates in the rightmost column of Table 9.7 show that the empirical Bayes estimates of the subscale scores are sub-

TABLE 9.10
B, the Matrix of Weights That Are Used to Combine the Observed
Subscale Scores Into the Regressed Estimates, for the North Carolina
Test of Computer Skills, Performance Assessment Tryout Form 1

| | *B* | | | |
	KB	ED	DB	SS
KB	**0.393**	0.158	0.083	0.121
ED	0.048	**0.814**	0.029	0.035
DB	0.068	0.079	**0.492**	0.161
SS	0.058	0.056	0.095	**0.689**

Note. Each row gives the weights that multiply each of the four observed subscale scores to provide the regressed subscore estimate for that subscale. The largest weight in each row is emphasized in boldface.

stantially more reliable than the observed subscale scores for KB, DB, and SS (ED was already as reliable as the test as a whole, so it could not become substantially more reliable).

A more detailed impression of the effect of the score stabilization can be gained by examining some individual score profiles. As we did with APICS, we selected three examinees (spaced equally across the total score distribution) and plotted their observed subscores, as well as their empirical Bayes subscores, in Fig. 9.4. These three examinees clearly exhibit different patterns of performance across the four parts of the test, and those patterns of performance are preserved in the regressed estimates. However, wild fluctuations in performance, like a pattern with one poor subscore and three much higher ones, are attenuated in the empirical Bayes estimates.

AN APPROACH TO AUGMENTED SCORES
THAT USES LINEAR COMBINATIONS
OF IRT SCALE SCORES

There are many reasons that a large-scale testing program may use IRT scale scores instead of observed summed scores—an important one of these reasons is that IRT procedures yield scores that are comparable across forms. As we observed in chapter 4, this property of IRT scale scores is especially useful for performance assessments, in which alternate forms may each include relatively few large items, and those items may vary widely in difficulty and/or discrimination. Subscale scores, which, in a performance assessment, may well correspond to scores on individual items(!), might have the greatest need for the useful properties of IRT.

Therefore, it is useful to generalize the empirical Bayes technology described thus far so that it can be applied to IRT scale scores, like MAP[θ]

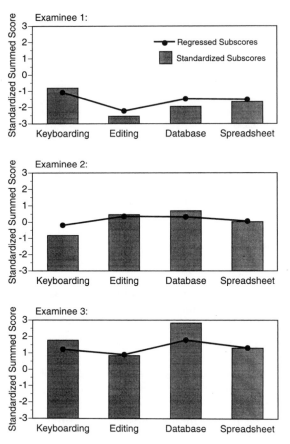

FIG. 9.4. Standardized subscores (shaded bars) and regressed (empirical Bayes) standardized subscores (points) on the four subscales for three representative North Carolina Test of Computer Skills examinees.

or EAP[θ], when those scale scores are computed for each subscale on a test. The generalization is straightforward, but modest adjustments are required because we begin with scores that have slightly different properties.

Empirical Bayes (Regressed) Estimates Based on IRT Scale Scores for Response Patterns

In this description, we assume that values of MAP[θ] or EAP[θ] have been computed for each examinee for each subscale, using the methods described in chapters 3 and 4. Those IRT scale scores may be treated almost, but not quite, as if they were observed scores. The important difference between MAP[θ] or EAP[θ] and the observed scores is that, as we observed in chapter 3, MAP[θ] and EAP[θ] are already analogous to Kelley's regressed estimates, in that they shrink toward the mean for the population. The analogy with Kelley's regressed estimates is not correct in detail: Kelley regressed estimates of the true score shrink linearly, or proportionally, toward the mean, whereas the amount that MAP[θ] or EAP[θ] shrink toward the mean is proportional to their variance—values of MAP[θ] or EAP[θ] shrink more toward the mean when they are associated with response patterns that provide relatively less information, and they shrink less when the response pattern provides more information.

Nevertheless, if the ultimate goal of the subscore estimation procedure is to compute the estimates as linear combinations of the subscale MAP[θ]s or EAP[θ]s, we know that we will ultimately ignore the variability in the precision of those estimates. In addition, that variability is usually relatively small for any well-constructed test. Therefore, to facilitate treating values of MAP[θ] or EAP[θ] in the same way we treat observed scores, we:

1. Ignore the variable standard errors associated with different values of MAP[θ] or EAP[θ], and treat them as though the error of measurement is constant—that is, we treat the error of measurement for the IRT scale scores just as we assume the error of measurement to be for the summed scores in the traditional theory.

2. Make a correction, based in part on IRT and in part on the traditional theory, to the values of MAP[θ] or EAP[θ], to remove their regression toward the mean. Then the methods described in the previous section may be applied to IRT scale scores without alteration.

In what follows, we use MAP[θ_v] to refer to the IRT response-pattern scale score for subscale v,[6] computed as described in chapters 3 and 4, and we assume that the mean subscore for each subscale is zero for notational convenience. If we ignore the fact that the estimate of measurement error (and consequently, the amount of shrinkage) associated with each value of MAP[θ_v] is different, then, by analogy with Kelley's equation,

$$\text{MAP}[\theta_v] \approx \rho_v \, \text{MAP}*[\theta_v], \qquad (16)$$

where ρ_v is an estimate of the reliability of subscale v, and MAP*[θ_v] is a (somewhat hypothetical) IRT scale estimate of θ_v that is *not* regressed toward the mean. That is, the values of MAP*[θ_v] are like the observed summed scores in the previous section. Then, we can solve Eq. 16 for MAP*[θ_v]:

---

[6]EAP[θ] could be substituted for MAP[θ_v] in any of these equations, and probably produce slightly superior results.

$$\text{MAP}*[\theta_v] \approx \frac{\text{MAP}[\theta_v]}{\rho_v} . \tag{17}$$

[Note: In chap. 8 we used a more elaborate system to "unshrink" IRT scale scores; that more elaborate system is less motivated here, because in what follows we are not able to maintain the different error variances for each value of MAP[θ_v], as we did in the score-combination algorithm in chap. 8.]

To compute MAP*[θ_v] for each subscale, we require some estimate of the reliability (ρ_v) of the IRT scale scores for that subscale. One plausible way to do that is to compute

$$\rho_v = \frac{\text{Variance}[\text{MAP}[\theta_v]]}{\text{Variance}[\text{MAP}[\theta_v]] + \text{Average}[SE^2[\theta_v]]}, \tag{18}$$

in which Variance[MAP[θ_v]] is the variance of the IRT scale scores for subscale v, and Average[$SE^2[\theta_v]$] is the average value of the variances of the error of measurement associated with those scores; for response-pattern data, the average and variance may be computed as the usual summary statistics, making use of the observations at hand.

After computing an estimate of ρ_v for each subscale using Eq. 18, we may compute MAP*[θ_v] for each examinee for each subscale using Eq. 17, and then compute $\mathbf{S}^{\text{obs}}$ as the covariance matrix among the scale scores MAP*[θ_v]. Alternatively (and equivalently), we can compute $\mathbf{S}^{\text{MAP}}$, the covariance matrix among the original IRT scale scores, and then correct that matrix using

$$\mathbf{S}_{vv'}^{\text{obs}} = \mathbf{S}_{vv'}^{\text{MAP}}/\rho_v\rho_{v'} \quad \text{for } v \neq v', \text{ and}$$

$$\mathbf{S}_{vv}^{\text{obs}} = \mathbf{S}_{vv'}^{\text{MAP}}/\rho_v^2 \quad \text{for } v = v', \tag{19}$$

to compute the elements $\mathbf{S}_{vv'}^{\text{obs}}$ of $\mathbf{S}^{\text{obs}}$.

Once we have estimates of $\mathbf{S}^{\text{obs}}$ and ρ_v, we may use Eq. 3 to compute $\mathbf{S}^{\text{true}}$, and then compute the empirical Bayes estimates of the IRT scale scores as

$$\underline{\widehat{\text{MAP}}}[\theta] = \underline{\text{MAP}}[\theta]. + \mathbf{S}^{\text{true}}(\mathbf{S}^{\text{obs}})^{-1}(\underline{\text{MAP}}*[\theta]_j - \underline{\text{MAP}}[\theta].)$$

$$= \underline{\text{MAP}}[\theta]. + \mathbf{B}*(\underline{\text{MAP}}*[\theta]_i - \underline{\text{MAP}}[\theta].), \tag{20}$$

where $\underline{\text{MAP}}*[\theta]_j$ is the vector of IRT scale scores for the subscales for examinee j, $\underline{\text{MAP}}[\theta]$. is the average vector of IRT subscale scores, $\underline{\widehat{\text{MAP}}}[\theta]$ is the vector of empirical Bayes estimates of the IRT scale scores, and

$$\mathbf{B}* = \mathbf{S}^{\text{true}}(\mathbf{S}^{\text{obs}})^{-1} . \tag{21}$$

The weights in the matrix $\mathbf{B}^*$ may not be the most convenient, because those are the coefficients for the values of $\underline{\mathbf{MAP}}^*[\theta]$ for each examinee; for a large sample, it may be undesirable to compute $\underline{\mathbf{MAP}}^*[\theta]$ as an intermediate for all examinees, and it is not necessary. Because $\underline{\mathbf{MAP}}^*[\theta]$ is computed from $\underline{\mathbf{MAP}}[\theta]$ by the simple expedient of dividing each subscore $MAP[\theta_v]$ by the corresponding reliability estimate (see Eq. 17), we can, instead, divide the weights $b_{vv'}$ for subscale v regressed on subscale v' in $\mathbf{B}^*$ by the reliability estimates to obtain

$$b_{vv'} = \frac{b_{vv'}^*}{\rho_{v'}}. \tag{22}$$

Then we use the weights $\mathbf{B}$ to compute the augmented estimates from the original values of $\underline{\mathbf{MAP}}[\theta]$:

$$\overset{\wedge}{\underline{\mathbf{MAP}}}[\theta] = \underline{\mathbf{MAP}}[\theta]. + \mathbf{B}(\underline{\mathbf{MAP}}[\theta]_i - \underline{\mathbf{MAP}}[\theta].). \tag{23}$$

To compute the conditional covariance matrix among the empirical Bayes estimates of the IRT scale scores, Eq. 8 may be used.

Regressed IRT Scale Scores Based on Subscale Response Patterns for the Performance Assessment Part of the North Carolina Test of Computer Skills. We now revisit the North Carolina Test of Computer Skills, to compute augmented estimates of the true subscores for the KB, ED, DB, and SS sections, based on the values of $MAP[\theta]$ for the response patterns for each of those sections. For this illustration, we computed the values of $MAP[\theta]$ for each of the 267 examinees who responded to Form 1 of the item tryout, using the 2PL model for the dichotomous items and the graded model for the items scored in more than two categories. The values of $MAP[\theta]$ for each response pattern for the ED and KB sections are very similar to the values of $EAP[\theta]$ shown for some of those response patterns in chapters 3 and 4. The item parameters used to compute the response-pattern values of $MAP[\theta]$ were estimated using larger numbers of examinees who responded to each of the items in a matrix-sampled item tryout design.

The fourth column of Table 9.11 shows the estimates of ρ_v computed using the average values of $SE^2[\theta]$ and the variance of $MAP[\theta]$ for each subscale in Eq. 18, compared to the values of coefficient α for the summed scores in the third column of the table. We note that the reliability estimates derived from the IRT scale scores are somewhat different than those for the summed scores. This difference is due to the fact that the

TABLE 9.11
Comparison of Subscale Reliabilities for North Carolina
Test of Computer Skills Subscales Computed
in the Traditional Way and With IRT

	Number of Items	Coefficient α	IRT ρ	For IRT (Regressed)
Keyboarding (KB)	3	.52	.67	.73
Editing (ED)	10	.85	.70	.76
Database (DB)	7	.60	.67	.75
Spreadsheet (SS)	6	.77	.74	.79

IRT scale scores effectively use item weights: The different values of the slope parameters associated with the items have the consequence that some of the items count more or less in the estimated scale score. Thus, the IRT scale scores for each subscale are really estimates of something slightly different from the summed scores—the IRT scale scores are the best estimate of the underlying variable that explains the covariance of the item response data, whereas the summed scores are just that, the total number of arbitrary "points" for this particular set of items. The values of IRT ρ_v and coefficient α differ because they estimate the reliability of different scores.

Because of the central place that the subscale reliabilities play in the empirical Bayes approach, the differences between the IRT and summed score reliabilities (shown in Table 9.11) have the consequence that the empirical Bayes estimates for the IRT scale scores are somewhat different from those computed in the previous section for the standardized summed scores.

The values of $\mathbf{S}^{obs}$ and $\mathbf{S}^{true}$ for the MAP[θ] response pattern scale scores for the four subscales are shown in Table 9.12. These values were computed using Eq. 19 to correct the observed covariance matrix among the MAP[θ]s, and then Eq. 3 to compute $\mathbf{S}^{true}$. Because the scale scores are not standardized, $\mathbf{S}^{obs}$ is not a correlation matrix.

The weights that are used to linearly combine the subscale values of MAP*[θ] to form the regressed estimates are computed using Eq. 21; those values are shown in Table 9.13, along with the values of $\mathbf{B}$ (computed using Eq. 22) that are used to form the linear combinations of the MAP[θ]s.

Figure 9.5 shows the profiles of the MAP[θ] subscores, and the profiles using the empirical Bayes (regressed) estimates computed using MAP[θ], for the same three examinees whose summed scores were plotted in Fig. 9.4. Notice that the overall variability of the empirical Bayes estimates in Fig. 9.5 is *greater* than that of the MAP[θ]s—for the low-scoring examinee in the top panel, the augmented estimates (represented by the points) are

TABLE 9.12

S^{obs} and S^{true} for the IRT Response-Pattern Scale Scores MAP[θ]
for the North Carolina Test of Computer Skills,
Performance Assessment Tryout Form 1

	S^{obs}			
	KB	*ED*	*DB*	*SS*
KB	1.311			
ED	0.419	1.227		
DB	0.339	0.433	1.468	
SS	0.360	0.385	0.506	1.059
	S^{true}			
	KB	*ED*	*DB*	*SS*
KB	0.880			
ED	0.419	0.863		
DB	0.339	0.433	0.986	
SS	0.360	0.385	0.506	0.786

TABLE 9.13

B*, the Matrix of Weights That Are Used to Combine the Subscale
Scores MAP*[θ], and **B**, the Matrix of Weights That Are Used to
Combine the Subscale Scores MAP[θ], Into the Regressed Estimates, for
the IRT Response-Pattern Scale Scores for the North Carolina Test
of Computer Skills, Performance Assessment Tryout Form 1

	$B*$			
	KB	*ED*	*DB*	*SS*
KB	**0.609**	0.096	0.034	0.081
ED	0.081	**0.630**	0.064	0.077
DB	0.038	0.085	**0.585**	0.155
SS	0.052	0.058	0.088	**0.661**
	B			
	KB	*ED*	*DB*	*SS*
KB	**0.909**	0.137	0.051	0.109
ED	0.121	**0.900**	0.096	0.104
DB	0.057	0.121	**0.873**	0.209
SS	0.078	0.080	0.131	**0.893**

Note. Each row gives the weights that multiply each of the four subscale scores to provide the regressed subscore estimate for that subscale. The largest weight in each row is emphasized in boldface.

371

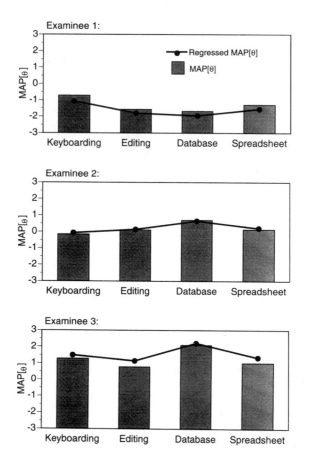

FIG. 9.5 Values of MAP[θ] (shaded bars) and regressed (empirical Bayes) values of MAP[θ] (points) on the four subscales for three representative North Carolina Test of Computer Skills examinees.

lower than the corresponding values of MAP[θ], and for the high-scoring examinee in the lower panel, the augmented estimates (represented by the points) are higher. Recall that MAP[θ] scale scores are analogous to Kelly regressed estimates of the true score in the traditional theory, so they are already regressed toward their mean. The multivariate empirical Bayes estimates plotted in Fig. 9.5 are *less* regressed toward the overall mean, just as the bivariate empirical Bayes estimates in the SAT example were less regressed toward the mean than the Kelley estimates in Table 9.1. When we apply the empirical Bayes technology to IRT scale scores, the effect is to regress each individual's subscore estimates toward a different value, depending on that individual's scores on the other subscales; that *reduces* the regression of each score toward the overall average.

The individual profiles for the augmented subscore estimates in Fig. 9.5 are somewhat "flattened" when compared to their corresponding patterns for the MAP[θ] subscores. This is the primary effect of the empirical Bayes combination of all of the subscale estimates into each subscore estimate—in this respect, the results in Fig. 9.5 are similar to those for the regressed standardized subscore estimates in Fig. 9.4. The reliability of the empirical Bayes estimates is shown in the rightmost column of Table 9.11; the values are about 10% higher than IRT ρ.

Regressed IRT Scale Scores Based on Subscale Response Patterns for a 1994 American Production and Inventory Control Society (APICS) Certification Examination. We computed the values of MAP[θ] for the response patterns on the six subscales of the APICS examination using item parameter estimates for the 3PL model; all 2,410 examinees in the sample were used for item parameter estimation. The profiles of response-pattern MAP[θ] are shown in Fig. 9.6 for the same three examinees whose summed scores were plotted in Fig. 9.3. Relative to the standardized summed scores in Fig. 9.3, the values of MAP[θ] in Fig. 9.6 are regressed toward the mean—sometimes extremely so, as for subscales 1 and 2. For those short subscales, with their low reliability (in Table 9.2), the values of MAP[θ] shrink a great deal.

Following procedures that parallel those that we used in the preceding section for the Computer Skills subscores, we computed empirical Bayes estimates for the subscores on the APICS examination, using the values of MAP[θ] for the response pattern to each subscale. The resulting profiles of empirical Bayes subscores are also shown in Fig. 9.6. As was the case when we computed empirical Bayes subscores for APICS using (standardized) summed scores, the empirical Bayes profiles in Fig. 9.6 are flattened to the extent that (almost) the only variation that remains is captured by rank order on the total score. The empirical Bayes estimates in Fig. 9.6 are much less regressed toward the mean, because each (entire profile) is basically a replicate of the highly reliable total score on the examination.

Empirical Bayes (Regressed) Estimates Based on IRT Scale Scores for Summed Scores

As we observed in chapters 3 and 4, there are many reasons why a large-scale testing program may choose to use IRT scale scores, and at the same time perform the computations using only the summed score on a test or subscale, as opposed to the item response patterns. These two goals are simultaneously accomplished by using EAP[θ|summed score] as a test or subscale score, and SD[θ|summed score] as the corresponding estimate of

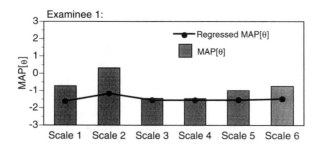

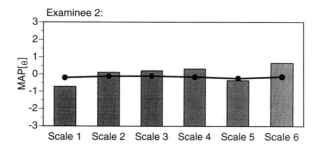

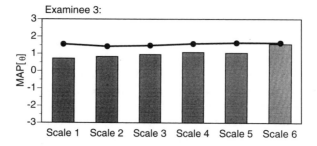

FIG. 9.6. Values of MAP[θ] (shaded bars) and regressed (empirical Bayes) values of MAP[θ] (points) on the six subscales for three representative APICS examinees.

the error of measurement—both as computed using the methods described in chapters 3 and 4.

To obtain the advantages of empirical Bayes estimation for subscale scores based on EAP[θ | summed score], the procedures similar to those we described in the preceding section for response-pattern MAP[θ] may be applied. By analogy to Eq. 17, one may compute

$$\text{EAP} *[\theta_v | \text{summed score}] \approx \frac{\text{EAP}[\theta_v | \text{summed score}]}{\rho_v}, \qquad (24)$$

using as an estimate of ρ_v marginal reliability, as proposed by Green, Bock, Humphreys, Linn, and Reckase (1984), and as used previously in chapter 8. For standardized θ,

$$\rho_v = 1 - \overline{\sigma}_e^2. \tag{25}$$

For EAP[θ_v|summed score], it is practical to compute

$$\overline{\sigma}_e^2 = \int E(\sigma_e^2)\phi(\theta)\,d\theta, \tag{26}$$

where

$$E(\sigma_e^2) = \sum_{\text{all } x} \sigma_e^2 L(x|\theta), \tag{27}$$

in which σ_e^2 is $SD^2[\theta|x]$, x is the summed score, and $L(x|\theta)$ is the theoretical joint likelihood for summed score x, computed from the trace lines as described in chapters 3 and 4.[7]

We then compute $\mathbf{S}^{\text{obs}}$, $\mathbf{S}^{\text{true}}$, and the regression-coefficient matrices $\mathbf{B}^*$ and $\mathbf{B}$ (using Eqs. 19–22) and compute the augmented estimates as

$$\widehat{\underline{\mathbf{EAP}}}[\theta] = \underline{\mathbf{EAP}}[\theta]. + \mathbf{B}(\underline{\mathbf{EAP}}[\theta]_i - \underline{\mathbf{EAP}}[\theta].)\,.$$

Regressed IRT Scale Scores Based on Summed Subscores for the Performance Assessment Part of the North Carolina Test of Computer Skills. The estimates of IRT ρ_v for the four subscales of the performance section of the North Carolina Test of Computer Skills are shown in Table 9.14; these differ little from the values of ρ_v computed for MAP[θ] for response patterns shown in Table 9.11. Similarly, the values of $\mathbf{S}^{\text{obs}}$ and $\mathbf{S}^{\text{true}}$, shown in Table 9.15, and the weights in the regression-coefficient matrices $\mathbf{B}^*$ and $\mathbf{B}$ (shown in Table 9.16), differ little from the corresponding values for the response-pattern IRT scale scores in Tables 9.12 and 9.13.

As a result, we are not surprised that the profiles based on EAP[θ| summed score] for each subscale for the three examinees plotted in Fig. 9.7 are very similar to the corresponding profiles based on MAP[θ] for response patterns in Fig. 9.5. Similarly, the profiles based on the empirical Bayes estimates of EAP[θ|summed score] for each subscale for those

---

[7]Marginal reliability is a better estimate to use for this purpose than the sample-based value computed using Eq. 18 for MAP[θ|response pattern]; however, in general, there are too many response patterns to permit practical computation of the summation in Eq. 27 over all response patterns, as opposed to all summed scores. For this (entirely practical) reason, we use different reliability estimates for the response-pattern and summed-score computations.

TABLE 9.14
Comparison of Subscale Reliabilities for the North Carolina Test
of Computer Skills Subscales Computed IRT Scale Scores (EAP[θ])
for Summed Scores, and the Regressed Estimates

	IRT ρ	*For IRT (Regressed)*
Keyboarding (KB)	.56	.74
Editing (ED)	.72	.78
Database (DB)	.65	.75
Spreadsheet (SS)	.73	.79

TABLE 9.15
S^{obs} and S^{true} for the IRT Summed Score Scale Scores EAP[θ]
for the North Carolina Test of Computer Skills,
Performance Assessment Tryout Form 1

	S^{obs}			
	KB	*ED*	*DB*	*SS*
KB	1.799			
ED	0.612	1.384		
DB	0.502	0.502	1.539	
SS	0.563	0.480	0.602	1.387

	S^{true}			
	KB	*ED*	*DB*	*SS*
KB	1.011			
ED	0.612	1.004		
DB	0.502	0.502	1.002	
SS	0.563	0.480	0.602	1.008

examinees are very similar to the corresponding profiles based on MAP[θ] for response patterns. Comparison of the reliability estimates for the empirical Bayes (regressed) IRT estimates in Tables 9.14 (for EAP[θ | summed score]) and 9.11 (for MAP[θ]) show that we obtain almost the same increase in reliability, whether we work with response-pattern or summed-score IRT scale scores.

Regressed IRT Scale Scores Based on Summed Subscores for a 1994 American Production and Inventory Control Society (APICS) Certification Examination. Figure 9.8 shows the subscale profiles for EAP[θ | summed score] for the 3PL model, along with the empirical Bayes subscale profiles, for the same three examinees previously plotted in Fig. 9.3 (for standardized subscores) and Fig. 9.6 (for response-pattern MAP[θ]s). For this

TABLE 9.16
B*, the Matrix of Weights That Are Used to Combine the Subscale
Scores MAP*[θ], and **B**, the Matrix of Weights That Are Used
to Combine the Subscale Scores EAP[θ], Into the Regressed Estimates,
for the IRT Summed-Score Scale Scores for the North Carolina Test
of Computer Skills, Performance Assessment Tryout Form 1

	B*			
	KB	*ED*	*DB*	*SS*
KB	**0.440**	0.174	0.073	0.136
ED	0.084	**0.644**	0.065	0.061
DB	0.050	0.091	**0.550**	0.143
SS	0.065	0.061	0.102	**0.634**

	B			
	KB	*ED*	*DB*	*SS*
KB	**0.783**	0.240	0.112	0.187
ED	0.149	**0.887**	0.100	0.084
DB	0.088	0.126	**0.843**	0.198
SS	0.116	0.084	0.157	**0.873**

Note. Each row gives the weights that multiply each of the four subscale scores to provide the regressed subscore estimate for that subscale. The largest weight in each row is emphasized in boldface.

highly unidimensional test with relatively unreliable subscale scores, it does not appear to matter much how the subscores are computed: Be they summed scores, response-pattern IRT scale scores, or IRT scale scores based on the summed scores, the subscore profiles vary widely when each subscale is considered separately, but they all collapse to a representation of the total score on the test when empirical Bayes methods are used.

Regressed IRT Scale Scores Based on Summed Subscores for the North Carolina End-of-Grade Test of Mathematics. This extended example summarizes the implementation of the augmented subscores system for the North Carolina End-of-Grade (NC EOG) mathematics tests for Grades 3–8. In a normal year of operation, the NC EOG tests are administered on a census basis to North Carolina students in those grades; approximately 90,000 students in each of the six grades respond to one of three randomly assigned forms. The total test scores are computed using the values of summed-score EAP[θ], as described in chapter 3, on a developmental scale that was constructed when the testing program began. Score reporting is done with linearly transformed (and rounded) EAP values reported as integers between (approximately) 100 and 200; within-grade averages range from about 140 for the third grade to about 170 for the eighth

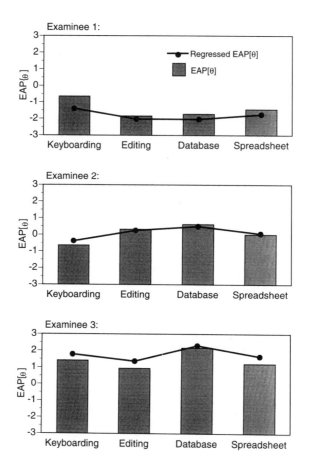

FIG. 9.7.   Values of EAP[θ] (shaded bars) and regressed (empirical Bayes) values of EAP[θ] (points) on the four subscales for three representative North Carolina Test of Computer Skills examinees.

grade. IRT calibration is used in lieu of equating to link the alternate forms, because the operational forms are preequated. Score reporting is done using a decentralized system that provides nearly immediate results; software in the scanning equipment for the multiple-choice bubble sheets computes the scale scores for each student's number-correct score using a table-lookup procedure.

After the testing program had been in operation for some years, a decision was made to add some variety of diagnostic, or subscore, reporting. Because the test specifications for the 80-item test forms were based on a structure that included seven "goals," the first plan was to produce a set of

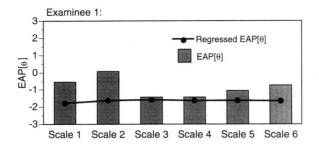

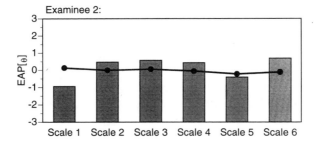

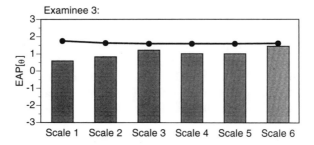

FIG. 9.8. Values of EAP[θ] (shaded bars) and regressed (empirical Bayes) values of EAP[θ] (points) on the six subscales for three representative APICS examinees.

seven subscores using the IRT versions of the methods described in this chapter. The seven goals were:

1. Numeration.
2. Geometry.
3. Patterns/pre-algebra.
4. Measurement.
5. Problem solving.
6. Statistics.

7. Computation (subdivided into symbolic computation and computation in context).

(A more complete description of the NC EOG tests is provided by Sanford, 1996).

More than adequate data were available to do the requisite preliminary calibrations: Many of the forms had already been administered operationally, and data sets with sample sizes in the 25,000–30,000 range were available. We used 10% random samples of those data sets to estimate the IRT item parameters (for the 3PL model), using only the items within each goal; then we used the entire samples to compute the regression weight matrices **B**. Using the operational data from 1996, we performed those analyses for three forms that had been administered in each of the six grades, for a total of 18 tests.

We expected some degree of consistency across forms, and even across grades, but that did not appear. The regression weights were not particularly consistent across forms, nor were they particularly interpretable— one would expect that often a particular goal score would have the highest weight involved in the computation with its regressed counterpart, but that did not happen often. Some rather detailed data analysis suggested that this was a consequence of the near-collinearity of the predictor set. The methods described in this chapter *are* multiple regression of each of the true subscale scores on the set of subscale scores. That means that these methods carry with them the potential difficulties that may be encountered in any application of multiple regression, and collinearity of the predictor variables is well known to lead to instability in the regression coefficients.

Given these results, the problem was reconsidered, and, based on indications from the first data analyses, a less linearly dependent set of subscores was defined: First, the "computation" goal was separated into two subscores, one for "symbolic computation" (conventional numerical arithmetic), hereafter called 7-C, and a second for "computation in context" (word problems emphasizing computation), now called 7-WP, because those two sections were among the least correlated of the parts of the tests. Geometry (Goal 2) was unchanged. Goals 1, 3, and 4 (numeration, patterns/pre-algebra, and measurement) were combined into a single subscore (called Goal 134); similarly, Goals 5 and 6 (problem solving and statistics) were combined into Goal 56.

Computation of the regression coefficients for this five-subscore system was much more reliable and consistent, even though there remains a substantial degree of collinearity. For example, Table 9.17 shows the eigenvalues of the matrix $\mathbf{S}^{true}$ for one of the test forms for Grade 4; 93% of the variance is accounted for with the first dimension. Nevertheless, we found

TABLE 9.17
Eigenvalues S^{true} for the Standardized Subscale Scores for the
North Carolina End-of-Grade Test of Mathematics, Grade 4, Form D

Number	Eigenvalue	Percent of Total
1	4.633	93
2	0.219	4
3	0.128	3
4	0.033	1
5	−0.010	—

that across the 18 grade/form combinations for the calibration year, the weight matrices (**B**) were reasonably consistent.

The augmentation substantially improved the reliability of the five subscores to be reported; for one example (again, a single form for Grade 4), Table 9.18 shows that the reliability for the original (unregressed) EAP values ranged from 0.65 to 0.87, whereas the reliability of the augmented scores ranged from 0.91 to 0.95. Because the purpose of this subscore computation was to report for each individual student, that higher level of reliability is good. Augmentation is most helpful for Goal 2, because (for example) there are only seven (explicitly) geometry items on a Grade 4 test, but the geometry score can be predicted well from the other subscales. The empirical Bayes technology produces more modest increases in reliability for Goal 7-C (symbolic computation), because that section is short and all of the other goals are represented by word problems—so there is strength to be borrowed, but not so much as for geometry. Augmentation also helps the reliability for Goal 134 relatively less, because that goal combination has a relatively large number of items.

For mathematics alone, the NC EOG testing program uses a total of 18 forms each year; if a different set of weight matrices was used for each form, the practical burden involved in the computation of the augmented subscores would be large. In addition, new forms of the tests are occasionally introduced, without previously being administered as intact forms.

TABLE 9.18
Number of Items, Subscale IRT Reliability, and Augmented Reliability,
for the Five Subscores for the North Carolina End-of-Grade
Mathematics Test, Grade 4, Form D

	Number of Items	IRT ρ	For IRT (Regressed)
Goal 7-C	12	.81	.91
Goal 7-WP	11	.78	.94
Goal 2	7	.65	.93
Goal 134	31	.87	.95
Goal 56	19	.83	.95

TABLE 9.19
Weight Matrix **B** for Grades 3, 4, 5, and 6 for the Five Subscores for
the North Carolina End-of-Grade Mathematics Test, Grade 4, Form D

Regressed Subscore	Subscore				
	Goal 7-C	Goal 7-WP	Goal 2	Goal 134	Goal 56
Goal 7-C	**0.63**	0.12	0.06	0.21	0.12
Goal 7-WP	0.13	**0.38**	0.04	0.23	**0.38**
Goal 2	0.11	0.07	0.33	**0.44**	0.22
Goal 134	0.13	0.13	0.16	**0.48**	0.28
Goal 56	0.09	0.27	0.10	**0.36**	0.35

Note. The largest weight in each row is emphasized in boldface.

For those reasons, some systematization of the weight matrices (**B**) was required to make the system work. After extensive data analysis, using retrospective data, we found that two weight matrices were sufficient: One of those (shown in Table 9.19) is an average of weight matrices for three forms in each of grades 3, 4, 5, and 6; a second weight matrix was used for the tests in grades 7 and 8. Within those blocks of grades, and with the set of subscales reduced to five, weight matrices for the individual forms tended to have coefficients that differed from the average values (like those shown in Table 9.19) by no more than 10% or so. Between the two blocks of grades (2–6 and 7–8), there were changes in the structure of the weights that tracked changes in relative emphases on the different parts of mathematics.[8]

In this system, there must be a large number of score-translation tables ("EAP tables"): one for each subscore within each form within each grade. For five subscales and three forms within six grades, that is 90 for each operational year. In the development of this system for the existing NC EOG testing program, that part could not be simplified. The (main) function of the EAP tables is to take the place of form equating at the level of subscales; the tests had not been constructed to be parallel down to the goal level, although they were nearly parallel at the level of the total score. As a result, the seven geometry items (for example) on one form could be somewhat more empirically difficult than the geometry items on another form for the same grade. We depended on the IRT methods described in chapter 3 to correct for that difference in difficulty, through the use of the scale-score transformation for each number-correct score.

---

[8]Data analysis used to make these decisions was not limited to the operational data from a single year. We calibrated the system using the operational data from 1996; then we used the weight matrices from that analysis to compute subscores from the 1997 data, which used different test forms. We also computed weight matrices from the 1997 data and compared those to the 1996 results.

Because this is a real operational test, and not an example for a book on test scoring, the question of the score-reporting scale arose. Although the basic computations were done on the standard score (z-score) scale, that is usually not regarded as an acceptable score-reporting scale—nobody likes to get a negative test score, and even +1.246 is not a particularly attractive value. We decided to use something very much like the traditional stanine scores (see, e.g., Anastasi & Urbina, 1997, p. 63), because they are widely considered interpretable by K–12 teachers and administrators. In addition, the integer (1–9) stanine scale does not give an excessive impression of precision for scores that, even with augmentation, are based on a relatively few item responses.

Bringing each test form's reported augmented subscores *exactly* onto the stanine scale, as defined by the traditional percentages of the distribution that are supposed to receive each integer score, would have produced another great multiplicity of cutpoint tables for this multigrade, multiform testing program. However, again we found substantial consistency across forms (within grades) in the cutpoints that needed to be used to yield a stanine-like transformation, so we were able to produce one table for each grade that could be used to transform the augmented (standardized) subscores onto the integer scale. An example of one of the tables of cutpoints is shown in Table 9.20.

Postscript. There are many components of this subscore-augmentation system for the NC-EOG mathematics tests that could, in some sense, be faulty. However, very few of those components can be investigated with the data that are normally collected in an operational testing program. Chief among those that cannot be conveniently investigated is validity— we assume that the more reliable augmented subscores are also more valid

TABLE 9.20

Pseudostanine Cutpoints for Grade 4 for the Five Subscores for the North Carolina End-of-Grade Mathematics Test, Grade 4, Form D

	Goal 7-C	Goal 7-WP	Goal 2	Goal 134	Goal 56
Integer Score is:	If regressed EAP is less than:				
1	−2.09	−1.99	−2.09	−2.12	−2.07
2	−1.09	−1.10	−1.03	−1.07	−1.09
3	−0.59	−0.65	−0.55	−0.59	−0.63
4	−0.08	−0.12	−0.08	−0.10	−0.11
5	0.47	0.44	0.41	0.43	0.44
6	0.91	0.91	0.85	0.88	0.91
7	1.20	1.27	1.20	1.26	1.28
8	1.40	1.57	1.51	1.58	1.59
9	If regressed EAP is higher.				

TABLE 9.21
Distribution of Integer Scores After Operational Administration
for Grade 4 for One of the Five Subscores for the
North Carolina End-of-Grade Mathematics Test

	Percent of Distribution		
Integer Score	Form H	Form O	Form P
1	0.0	0.0	0.0
2	4.5	5.7	5.4
3	9.5	10.6	10.6
4	14.8	15.6	16.1
5	20.0	20.4	21.2
6	19.5	17.8	18.8
7	14.4	12.5	12.2
8	9.8	8.8	7.5
9	7.5	8.6	8.1

than the original subscores would have been, but we cannot show that
without any clear validity criterion.

However, because three forms are randomly assigned within each
grade each year, we can investigate the degree to which the IRT alternate
form linking "works" to equate the scores across forms. Table 9.21 shows
the distribution of the integer (pseudostanine) scores for three forms of
the grade four test for one of the subscales. The 1998 administration of
the tests produced 30 such tables—one for each of the five subscores
within each of the six grades. All were fairly similar to the one shown in
Table 9.21, with roughly equal percentages of students receiving each integer score across the three forms.[9]

DISCUSSION

There has long been an interest in giving feedback to examinees that is
more diagnostic of strengths and weaknesses than is a single overall score.
In recent years, this interest has sometimes become a mandate. Yet restric-
tions on testing time preclude having subsections that are sufficiently long
to provide reliable scores. Many have judged that reporting unreliable

---

[9]The observant reader might wonder why there are (almost) no scores of 1 in Table 9.21.
There are two possible reasons: One is that the calibration of the IRT system was necessarily
done with retrospective data (from 1995, 1996, and 1997), and the data shown in Table 9.21
are from 1998; this is in the context of a testing program in which average scores have increased annually. To some extent, the lack of low scores is because the entire distribution of
scores moves upward each year. There were also some differences in the treatment of missing
responses between the retrospective data used to calibrate the system and the operational
data summarized in Table 9.21 that may account for some of the lack of very low scores.

scores is improper, for they would surely engender remedial actions on the part of examinees that might just be chasing errors of measurement. So the tack taken has been to eschew reporting unreliable subscores. It is well known that statistical stability (reliability) is a function of test length, and subscales are always short; thus was tied the Gordian knot. However, once one allows for the calculation of an estimate of a subscale score that is not strictly related to the number right on the items judged to be on that subscale, we are provided with the knife to cut that knot. In this chapter we have described how this can be accomplished in practice.

It seems worthwhile to comment briefly on the gains in subscore reliability possible on the APICS test. Whether or not this is good news depends strongly on why this test is so unidimensional. It is good news if mastery of the subject matter taps only a single aspect of proficiency. It is less welcome if the unidimensionality evolves from some odd anomaly of test construction practice. We cannot tell from these data what is the cause. However, traditional test construction practice, which insists that one measure of the worth of each candidate item is its biserial correlation with the rest of the test, does not foster the building of multidimensional tests. A sensible experiment would be to try to build a multidimensional test from the ground up, including items in each subsection that are highly correlated with others in that section but are as uncorrelated as possible with items from other sections. Of course, the relative value of test construction practices is measured best with validity data. We need to carefully measure the set of validity criteria about which the subscores are supposed to inform us, and see what kind of test does the job best.

The North Carolina Test of Computer Skills was explicitly built to be multidimensional; even so, there were substantial gains in the stability of each of the subscores using this technology. If, after observing the resulting score stability, it is decided that this is still not sufficient, the next recourse is to increase the length of some (or all) of the subtests. Interestingly, an increase in only one of the test sections may increase the reliability of all of the subscores sufficiently for the required purposes.

When Are These Scores Unsuitable? To answer this question we must return to the purpose of the test. In general there are three purposes for a test: measurement, contest, and prod. Most tests are used for more than one purpose. A final exam in a course is used both to assess a student's understanding of the course (measurement), and also to encourage the student to study and hence see the course as a whole rather than as a sequence of topics (prod). Placement tests are principally for measurement purposes, but also serve as prods. Most tests that have a strong diagnostic component share these goals. Admissions tests and tests used to award scholarships are principally contests, but they serve as prods for study as well, and require reasonable measurement characteristics.

We believe that all tests whose purpose is principally measurement are scored better using ancillary information. The reason behind this is that if the goal is measurement, we want the score to have the smallest possible error, which is best accomplished with this technology. High reliability may not appear to be as necessary for tests used as prods, except that a test will serve as a better motivator if the examinee believes that it actually measures what he or she knows—no one studies for a lottery. The closer that the test score comes to being a random number, the less it motivates careful preparation. Thus we conclude that if tests are used principally as prods it is better if their reliability is as high as possible, but it is not as crucial as when the test's purpose is principally measurement.

What about tests as contests? This is a more difficult question. A naive response is to suggest that for all purposes a more accurate measure is better than one that is less accurate. Indeed, we believe that is true when it is to everyone's benefit to have the most accurate answer (e.g., when a test is used for diagnosis and placement). But when the test is a contest, it is not to the advantage of a low-scoring examinee for the test to be accurate. In fact, for such persons a random number might be a fine measure, increasing their chances of winning to be the same as everyone else's. Issues of fairness also arise if the ancillary information is not under the control of the examinee. For example, we know that the mean scores of each of the United States on any standardized test are different from one another. Thus, we could reduce the error on an individual's test score if we also included an indicator variable for their state in the regression. But is it fair to prefer one person over another for a scholarship when their observed scores were identical but one lives in a higher scoring state? Even in this instance we could argue that if the test was readministered, the person from the higher scoring state is likely to do better than the person from the lower scoring state.

This brings us to the nub of the issue. Is the scholarship being awarded for performance on the test? Or is it for what that performance portends in terms of future accomplishments? If it is the latter, than we ought to use estimates of true score that utilize all information available.

However, most contests are not concerned with any long-term predictions (in the Olympics the gold medal goes to whoever was fastest that day, even if on the next 99 future dates that person is not likely to win), so prizes are awarded on the basis of observed score.[10] We agree with this, if it is a pure contest, but we believe that even in this extreme case reasonable

---

[10]Even to this rule, there are exceptions: In some subjectively judged competitions, such as figure skating, it is widely believed that past performances have an effect on judges' scores, effectively regressing the scores obtained on any given day toward an average of the performers' prior scores.

arguments can be made to use all information available. The only place where we believe that such adjustments ought not be made is in those situations in which we do not have acceptably accurate estimates of the parameters required to do the adjustment. One situation where this might be the case is when a test is being scored in a new subsample of the population. Suppose there is an ethnic classification for which the SAT-V and the SAT-M are uncorrelated (e.g., recent immigrant populations). It would not be proper to use the adjustment described in the first example within this subgroup. This is the only situation in which this procedure seems unambiguously inappropriate.

REFERENCES

Anastasi, A., & Urbina, S. (1997). *Psychological testing* (7th ed.). Upper Saddle River, NJ: Prentice-Hall.

Casella, G. (1985). An introduction to empirical Bayes data analysis. *American Statistician, 39*, 83–87.

Folske, J. C., Gessaroli, M. E., & Swanson, D. B. (1999, April). *Assessing the utility of an IRT-based method for using collateral information to estimate subscores.* Paper presented at the Annual Meeting of the National Council on Measurement in Education, Montreal.

Gessaroli, M. E. (1997, March). *Using multidimensional collateral item response information to aid in subscore reporting.* Paper presented at the Annual Meeting of the National Council on Measurement in Education, Chicago.

Green, B. F., Bock, R. D., Humphreys, L. G., Linn, R. L., & Reckase, M. D. (1984). Technical guidelines for assessing computerized adaptive tests. *Journal of Educational Measurement, 21*, 347–360.

Kelley, T. L. (1927). *The interpretation of educational measurements.* New York: World Book.

Kelley, T. L. (1947). *Fundamentals of statistics.* Cambridge, MA: Harvard University Press.

Longford, N. T. (1997). Shrinkage estimation of linear combinations of true scores. *Psychometrika, 62*, 237–244.

Mislevy, R. M., Johnson, E. G., & Muraki, E. (1992). Scaling procedures in NAEP. *Journal of Educational Statistics, 17*, 131–154.

Nishisato, S. (1984). Forced classification: A simple application of a quantification method. *Psychometrika, 49*, 25–36.

Sanford, E. E. (1996). *North Carolina End-of-Grade tests: Reading and Mathematics* (Tech. Rep. No. 1). Raleigh, NC: State Board of Education.

ten Berge, J. M. F., Snijders, T. A. B., & Zegers, F. E. (1981). Computational aspects of the greatest lower bound to the reliability and constrained minimum trace factor analysis. *Psychometrika, 46*, 201–213.

Vevea, J. L., Billeaud, K., & Nelson, L. (1998, June). *An empirical Bayes approach to subscore augmentation.* Paper presented at the annual meeting of the Psychometric Society, Champaign-Urbana, IL.

Yen, W. M. (1987, June). *A Bayesian/IRT index of objective performance.* Paper presented at the annual meeting of the Psychometric Society, Montreal.

References

Adams, R. J., & Khoo, S. T. (1992). *QUEST: The interactive test analysis system* [Computer program]. Melbourne, Victoria: Australian Council for Educational Research.

Allen, N. L., Mazzeo, J., Ip, S., Swinton, S., Isham, S. P., & Worthington, L. H. (1995). Data analysis and scaling for the 1994 Trial State Assessment in reading. In J. Mazzeo, N. L. Allen, & D. L. Kline (Eds.), *Technical report of the NAEP 1994 Trial State Assessment program in reading* (pp. 169–219). Washington, DC: Office of Educational Research and Improvement, U.S. Department of Education.

American Psychological Association (1985). *Standards for Educational and Psychological Testing*. Washington, DC: Author.

Anastasi, A., & Urbina, S. (1997). *Psychological testing* (7th ed.). Upper Saddle River, NJ: Prentice-Hall.

Andersen, E. B. (1973). Conditional inference for multiple choice questionnaires. *British Journal of Mathematical and Statistical Psychology, 26*, 42–54.

Andersen, E. B. (1977). Sufficient statistics and latent trait models. *Psychometrika, 42*, 69–81.

Andersen, E. B. (1980). *Discrete statistical models with social science applications*. Amsterdam: North Holland.

Andersen, E. B. (1997). The rating scale model. In W. van der Linden & R. K. Hambleton (Eds.), *Handbook of modern item response theory* (pp. 67–84). New York: Springer.

Andrich, D. (1978a). A rating formulation for ordered response categories. *Psychometrika, 43*, 561–573.

Andrich, D. (1978b). Application of a psychometric rating model to ordered categories which are scored with successive integers. *Applied Psychological Measurement, 2*, 581–594.

Andrich, D. (1988). *Rasch models for measurement*. Newbury Park: Sage.

Arbuckle, J. L. (1995). *AMOS for Windows: Analysis of moment structures (Version 3.5)*. Chicago, IL: SmallWaters.

Armor, D. J. (1974). Theta reliability and factor scaling. In H. L. Costner (Ed.), *Sociological Methodology 1973–1974*. San Francisco: Jossey-Bass.

Armstrong, R. D., Jones, D. H., Berliner, N., & Pashley, P. (1998, June). *Computerized adaptive tests with multiple forms structures*. Paper presented at the annual meeting of the Psychometric Society, Champaign–Urbana, IL.

Baker, F. B. (1992). *Item response theory: Parameter estimation techniques*. New York: Marcel Dekker, Inc.

Becker, R. A., & Chambers, J. M. (1984). *S: An interactive environment for data analysis and graphics*. Monterey, CA: Wadsworth.

Bennett, R. E., Rock, D. A., & Wang, M. (1991). Equivalence of free-response and multiple-choice items. *Journal of Educational Measurement, 28*, 77–92.

Bentler, P. M., & Wu, E. J. C. (1995). *EQS 5.4 for Windows*. Encino, CA: Multivariate Software.

Bergan, J. R., & Stone, C. A. (1985). Latent class models for knowledge domains. *Psychological Bulletin, 98*, 166–184.

Berkson, J. (1944). Application of the logistic function to bio-assay. *Journal of the American Statistical Association, 39*, 357–375.

Berkson, J. (1953). A statistically precise and relatively simple method of estimating the bioassay with quantal response, based on the logistic function. *Journal of the American Statistical Association, 48*, 565–599.

Binet, A., & Simon, T. (1905). Methodes nouvelles pour le diagnostic du niveau intellectuel des anormaux. *Annee Psychologique, 11*, 191–244.

Birnbaum, A. (1958a). *On the estimation of mental ability*. Series Report No. 15. Project No. 7755-23, USAF School of Aviation Medicine, Randolph Air Force Base, Texas.

Birnbaum, A. (1958b). *Further considerations of efficiency in tests of mental ability*. Series Report No. 17. Project No. 7755-23, USAF School of Aviation Medicine, Randolph Air Force Base, Texas.

Birnbaum, A. (1968). Some latent trait models and their use in inferring an examinee's ability. In F. M. Lord & M. R. Novick (Eds.), *Statistical theories of mental test scores* (pp. 395–479). Reading, MA: Addison-Wesley.

Bock, R. D. (1972). Estimating item parameters and latent ability when responses are scored in two or more latent categories. *Psychometrika, 37*, 29–51.

Bock, R. D. (1975). *Multivariate statistical methods in behavioral research*. New York: McGraw-Hill.

Bock, R. D. (1983). The mental growth curve reexamined. In D. J. Weiss (Ed.), *New horizons in testing* (pp. 205–219). New York: Academic Press.

Bock, R. D. (1997). A brief history of item response theory. *Educational Measurement: Issues and Practice, 16*, 21–33.

Bock, R. D. (1997). The nominal categories model. In W. van der Linden & R. K. Hambleton (Eds.), *Handbook of modern item response theory* (pp. 33–50). New York: Springer.

Bock, R. D., & Aitkin, M. (1981). Marginal maximum likelihood estimation of item parameters: Application of an EM algorithm. *Psychometrika, 46*, 443–458.

Bock, R. D., Gibbons, R., & Muraki, E. (1988). Full-information factor analysis. *Applied Psychological Measurement, 12*, 261–280.

Bock, R. D., Gibbons, R., Schilling, S. G., Muraki, E., Wilson, D., & Wood, R. (2000). *TESTFACT 3.0: Test scoring, item statistics, and full-information item factor analysis*. Chicago, IL: Scientific Software, Inc.

Bock, R. D., & Jones, L. V. (1968). *The measurement and prediction of judgment and choice*. San Francisco: Holden-Day.

Bock, R. D., & Mislevy, R. J. (1982). Adaptive EAP estimation of ability in a microcomputer environment. *Applied Psychological Measurement, 6*, 431–444.

Bock, R. D., Thissen, D., & Zimowski, M. F. (1997). IRT estimation of domain scores. *Journal of Educational Measurement, 34*, 197–211.

Bollen, K. A. (1989). *Structural equations with latent variables*. New York: Wiley.

Boomsma, A. (1983). On the robustness of LISREL against small sample sizes in factor analysis models. In K. G. Jöreskog & H. Wold (Eds.), *Systems under direct observation: Causality, structure, prediction (Part 1)*. Amsterdam: North-Holland Publishing Co.

Bradlow, E. T. (1996). Negative information and the three-parameter logistic model. *Journal of Educational and Behavioral Statistics, 21*, 179–185.

Bradlow, E. T., Wainer, H., & Wang, X. (1999). A Bayesian random effects model for testlets. *Psychometrika, 64*, 153–168.

Brennan, R. L., & Johnson, E. G. (1995). Generalizability of performance assessments. *Educational Measurement: Issues and Practice, 14*, 9–27.

Bridgeman, B., Morgan, R., & Wang, M. M. (1996). *Reliability of Advanced Placement Examinations* (RR 96-3). Princeton, NJ: Educational Testing Service.

Bridgeman, B., & Rock, D. A. (1993). Relationships among multiple-choice and open-ended analytical questions. *Journal of Educational Measurement, 30*, 313–329.

Brown, W. (1910). Some experimental results in the correlation of mental abilities. *British Journal of Psychology, 3*, 296–322.

Browne, M. W. (1972). Orthogonal rotation to a partially specified target. *British Journal of Mathematical and Statistical Psychology, 25*, 115–120.

Browne, M. W. (1982). Covariance structures. In D. M. Hawkins (Ed.), *Topics in applied multivariate analysis* (pp. 72–141). Cambridge: Cambridge University Press.

Browne, M. W. (1984). Asymptotically distribution-free methods for the analysis of covariance structures. *British Journal of Mathematical and Statistical Psychology, 37*, 62–83.

Browne, M. W., Cudeck, R., Tateneni, K., & Mels, G. (1998). *CEFA: Comprehensive exploratory factor analysis*. Columbus, OH: Department of Psychology, Ohio State University.

Burt, C. (1922). *Mental and scholastic tests*. London: P. S. King.

Calderone, J., King, L. M., & Horkay, N. (1997). *The NAEP guide*. Washington, DC: U.S. Department of Education, National Center for Education Statistics.

Camilli, G. (1994). Origin of the scaling constant $d = 1.7$ in item response theory. *Journal of Educational and Behavioral Statistics, 19*, 293–295.

Carroll, J. B. (1945). The effect of difficulty and chance success on correlations between items or between tests. *Psychometrika, 10*, 1–19.

Casella, G. (1985). An introduction to empirical Bayes data analysis. *The American Statistician, 39*, 83–87.

Cattell, R. B. (1956). Validation and intensification of the Sixteen Personality Factor Questionnaire. *Journal of Clinical Psychology, 12*, 205–214.

Cattell, R. B. (1974). Radial parcel factoring versus item factoring in defining personality structure in questionnaires: Theory and experimental checks. *Australian Journal of Psychology, 26*, 103–119.

Cattell, R. B., & Burdsal, C. A., Jr. (1975). The radial parcel double factoring design: A solution to the item-vs.-parcel controversy. *Multivariate Behavioral Research, 10*, 165–179.

Chen, W. H., & Thissen, D. (1997). Local dependence indices for item pairs using item response theory. *Journal of Educational and Behavioral Statistics, 22*, 265–289.

Christoffersson, A. (1975). Factor analysis of dichotomous variables. *Psychometrika, 40*, 5–32.

Cliff, N., & Caruso, J. C. (1998). Reliable component analysis through maximizing composite reliability. *Psychological Methods, 3*, 291–308.

College Entrance Examination Board. (1988). *Technical Manual for the Advanced Placement Program 1982–1986*. New York: Author.

Cook, L. L., Dorans, N. J., Eignor, D. R., & Peterson, N. S. (1985). *An assessment of the relationship between the assumption of unidimensionality and the quality of IRT true-score equating* (RR-85-30). Princeton, NJ: Educational Testing Service.

Cressie, N., & Holland, P. W. (1983). Characterizing the manifest probabilities of latent trait models. *Psychometrika, 48*, 129–141.

Cronbach, L. J. (1951). Coefficient alpha and the internal structure of tests. *Psychometrika, 16*, 297–334.

Cronbach, L. J. (1990). *Essentials of psychological testing* (5th ed.). New York: HarperCollins.

Davis, L. A., & Lewis, C. (1996). *Person-fit indices and their role in the CAT environment.* Paper presented at the annual meeting of the National Council on Measurement in Education, New York, April 9–11.

Dorans, N. J., & Lawrence, I. M. (1987). *The internal construct validity of the SAT* (RR-87-35). Princeton, NJ: Educational Testing Service.

Dorans, N., & Lawrence, I. M. (1991, November). *The role of the unit of analysis in dimensionality assessment.* Paper presented at the International Symposium on Modern Theories in Measurement: Problems and Issues, Montebello, Quebec, Canada.

Drasgow, F., Levine, M. V., & Williams, E. A. (1985). Appropriateness measurement with polytomous item response models and standardized indices. *British Journal of Mathematical and Statistical Psychology, 38*, 67–86.

DuBois, P. H. (1970). *A history of psychological testing.* Boston: Allyn & Bacon.

Education Commission of the States. (1970). *National Assessment of Educational Progress: 1969–1970 Science: National results and illustrations of groups comparisons.* Denver, CO: Author.

Ercikan, K., Schwarz, R., Weber, M., Ferrara, S., & Michaels, H. (1997, April). *The effect of integrated items on the validity and reliability of tests: Sciences and mathematics integration in a statewide performance assessment.* Paper presented at the Annual Meeting of the National Council on Measurement in Education, Chicago.

Feldt, L. S., & Brennan, R. L. (1989). Reliability. In R. L. Linn (Ed.), *Educational Measurement* (3rd Ed., pp. 105–146). New York: American Council on Education/Macmillan.

Finney, D. J. (1952). *Probit analysis: A statistical treatment of the sigmoid response curve.* London: Cambridge University Press.

Fisher, R. A. (1921). On the mathematical foundations of theoretical statistics. *Philosophical Transactions, A, 222*, 309–368.

Fisher, R. A. (1925). *Statistical methods for research workers.* Edinburgh: Oliver and Boyd.

Fisher, R. A. (1954). *Statistical methods for research workers.* (12th Ed.). New York: Hafner Publishing Co.

Fitzpatrick, A. R., Link, V. B., Yen, W. M., Burket, G. R., Ito, K., & Sykes, R. C. (1996). Scaling performance assessments: A comparison of one-parameter and two-parameter partial credit models. *Journal of Educational Measurement, 33*, 291–314.

Folske, J. C., Gessaroli, M. E., & Swanson, D. B. (1999, April). *Assessing the utility of an IRT-based method for using collateral information to estimate subscores.* Paper presented at the Annual Meeting of the National Council on Measurement in Education, Montreal.

Gessaroli, M. E. (1997, March). *Using multidimensional collateral item response information to aid in subscore reporting.* Paper presented at the Annual Meeting of the National Council on Measurement in Education, Chicago.

Gibbons, R. D., & Hedeker, D. R. (1992). Full-information item bi-factor analysis. *Psychometrika, 57*, 423–436.

Gorsuch, R. L. (1983). Factor analysis. Hillsdale, NJ: Lawrence Erlbaum Associates.

Green, B. F., Jr. (1950). A note on the calculation of weights for maximum battery reliability. *Psychometrika, 15*, 57–61.

Green, B. F. (1997, March). *Alternate methods of scoring computer-based adaptive tests.* Paper presented at the annual meeting of the American Educational Research Association, Chicago, IL.

Green, B. F., Bock, R. D., Humphreys, L. G., Linn, R. L., & Reckase, M. D. (1984). Technical guidelines for assessing computerized adaptive tests. *Journal of Educational Measurement, 21*, 347–360.

Gulliksen, H. O. (1950). *Theory of mental tests*, New York: Wiley. (Reprinted in 1987 by Lawrence Erlbaum Associates; Hillsdale, NJ).

Haley, D. C. (1952). *Estimation of the dosage mortality relationship when the dose is subject to error*. Stanford: Applied Mathematics and Statistics Laboratory, Stanford University, Technical Report 15.

Hambleton, R. K., & Rovinelli, R. J. (1986). Assessing the dimensionality of a set of test items. *Applied Psychological Measurement, 10*, 287–302.

Harlow, L. L. (1985). Behavior of some elliptical theory estimators with nonnormal data in a covariance structures framework: A Monte Carlo study. Unpublished doctoral thesis. University of California, Los Angeles.

Harmon, H. H. (1976). *Modern factor analysis* (Third Edition, Revised). Chicago, IL: University of Chicago Press.

Hattie, J., Krakowski, K., Rogers, H. J., & Swaminathan, H. (1996). An assessment of Stout's index of essential unidimensionality. *Applied Psychological Measurement, 20*, 1–14.

Hays, W. L. (1994). Statistics (Fifth Edition). Fort Worth, TX: Harcourt Brace.

Holland, P. W., & Rubin, D. B. (1982). *Test equating*. New York: Academic Press.

Hoskens, M., & De Boeck, P. (1997). A parametric model for local dependence among test items. *Psychological Methods, 2*, 261–277.

Hoyle, R. H. (1995). The structural equation modeling approach: Basic concepts and fundamental issues. In R. H. Hoyle (Ed.), *Structural equation modeling: Concepts, issues, and applications* (pp. 1–13). Thousand Oaks, CA: Sage Publications.

Hoyt, C. (1941). Test reliability estimated by analysis of variance. *Psychometrika, 6*, 153–160.

Hu, L., & Bentler, P. M. (1998). Fit indices in covariance structure modeling: Sensitivity to underparameterized model misspecification. *Psychological Methods, 3*, 424–453.

Hu, L., & Bentler, P. M. (1999). Cutoff criteria for fit indexes in covariance structure analysis: Conventional criteria versus new alternatives. *Structural Equation Modeling, 6*, 1–55.

Hucker, C. O. (1975). *China's imperial past : an introduction to Chinese history and culture*. Stanford, CA: Stanford University Press.

Jöreskog, K. G. (1967). Some contributions to maximum likelihood factor analysis. *Psychometrika, 32*, 443–482.

Jöreskog, K. G. (1973). A general method for estimating a linear structural equation system. In A. S. Goldberger & O. D. Duncan (Eds.), *Structural equation models in the social sciences* (pp. 85–112). New York: Academic.

Jöreskog, K. G., & Sörbom, D. (1995a). *LISREL 8 User's Reference Guide*. Chicago, IL: Scientific Software, Inc.

Jöreskog, K. G., & Sörbom, D. (1995b). *PRELIS: A program for multivariate data screening and data summarization*. Chicago, IL: Scientific Software, Inc.

Kaiser, H. F. (1958). The varimax criterion for analytic rotation in factor analysis. *Psychometrika, 23*, 187–200.

Kelderman, H. (1984). Loglinear Rasch model tests. *Psychometrika, 49*, 223–245.

Kelley, T. L. (1927). *The interpretation of educational measurements*. New York: World Book.

Kelley, T. L. (1947). *Fundamentals of statistics*. Cambridge: Harvard University Press.

Kendall, M. G., & Stuart, A. (1967). *The advanced theory of statistics, volume II: Inference and relationship (2nd Ed.)*. New York: Hafner Publishing Co.

Kim, H. R. (1994). *New techniques for the dimensionality assessment of standardized test data*. Unpublished doctoral dissertation, University of Illinois at Urbana–Champaign.

Klein, S. P., & Bell, R. M. (1995). How will the NCAA's new standards affect minority student-athletes? *Chance, 8(3)*, 18–21.

Klein, S. P., McCaffrey, D., Stecher, B., & Koretz, D. (1995). The reliability of mathematics portfolio scores: Lessons from the Vermont experience. *Applied Measurement in Education, 8*, 243–260.

Koretz, D., McCaffrey, D., Klein, S., Bell, R., & Stecher, B. (1992). *The reliability of scores from the 1992 Vermont Portfolio Assessment Program*. Interim Technical Report. Santa Monica, CA: Rand Institute on Education and Training.

Kuder, G. F., & Richardson, M. W. (1937). The theory of the estimation of test reliability. *Psychometrika, 2*, 151–160.

Lawley, D. N., & Maxwell, A. E. (1971). *Factor analysis as a statistical method*. New York: American Elsevier.

Lawrence, I. (1995). *Estimating reliability for tests composed of item sets*. (RR 95-18). Princeton, NJ: Educational Testing Service.

Lazarsfeld, P. F. (1950). The logical and mathematical foundation of latent structure analysis. In S. A. Stouffer, L. Guttman, E. A. Suchman, P. F. Lazarsfeld, S. A. Star, & J. A. Clausen, *Measurement and Prediction* (pp. 362–412). New York: Wiley.

Leslie, L. A., & Funk, C. E. (1935). *25,000 words spelled, divided, and accented*. New York: Funk & Wagnalls.

Li, H. (1997). A unifying expression for the maximal reliability of a linear composite. *Psychometrika, 62*, 245–249.

Li, H., & Wainer, H. (1997). Toward a coherent view of reliability in test theory. *Journal of Educational and Behavioral Statistics, 22*, 478–484.

Li, H.-H., & Stout, W. F. (1995, April). *Assessment of dimensionality for mixed polytomous and dichotomous item data: Refinements of POLY-DIMTEST*. Paper presented at the Annual Meeting of the National Council on Measurement in Education, San Francisco.

Linacre, J. M., & Wright, B. D. (1995). *A user's guide to BIGSTEPS*. Chicago: MESA Press.

Linn, R. L. (1993). Linking results of distinct assessments. *Applied Measurement in Education, 6*, 83–102.

Linn, R. L., & Burton, E. (1994). Performance-based assessment: Implications of task specificity. *Educational Measurement: Issues and Practice, 13*, 5–15.

Longford, N. T. (1997). Shrinkage estimation of linear combinations of true scores. *Psychometrika, 62*, 237–244.

Lord, F. M. (1952). A theory of test scores. *Psychometric Monographs*, Whole No. 7.

Lord, F. M. (1953). The relation of test score to the trait underlying the test. *Educational and Psychological Measurement, 13*, 517–548.

Lord, F. M. (1965). An empirical study of item-test regression. *Psychometrika, 30*, 373–376.

Lord, F. M. (1980). *Applications of item response theory to practical testing problems*. Hillsdale, NJ: Lawrence Erlbaum Associates.

Lord, F. M., & Novick, M. (1968). *Statistical theories of mental test scores*. Reading, Mass.: Addison Wesley.

Lord, F. M., & Wingersky, M. S. (1984). Comparison of IRT true-score and equipercentile observed-score "equatings." *Applied Psychological Measurement, 8*, 453–461.

Lukhele, R., Thissen, D., & Wainer, H. (1994). On the relative value of multiple-choice, constructed-response, and examinee-selected items on two achievement tests. *Journal of Educational Measurement, 31*, 234–250.

Lunneborg, C. E., & Abbott, R. D. (1983). *Elementary multivariate analysis for the behavioral sciences*. New York, NY: North-Holland.

MacCallum, R. C., Roznowski, M., & Necowitz, L. B. (1992). Model modifications in covariance structure analysis: The problem of capitalization on chance. *Psychological Bulletin, 111*, 490–504.

MacCallum, R. C., Browne, M. W., & Sugawara, H. M. (1996). Power analysis and determination of sample size for covariance structure modeling. *Psychological Methods, 1*, 130–149.

Masters, G. N. (1982). A Rasch model for partial credit scoring. *Psychometrika, 47*, 149–174.

Masters, G. N., & Wright, B. D. (1984). The essential process in a family of measurement models. *Psychometrika, 49*, 529–544.

Masters, G. N., & Wright, B. D. (1997). The partial credit model. In W. van der Linden & R. K. Hambleton (Eds.), *Handbook of modern item response theory* (pp. 101–122). New York: Springer.

Maxwell, A. E. (1977). *Multivariate analysis in behavioural research*. London: Chapman and Hall.

McDonald, R. P. (1967). Nonlinear factor analysis. *Psychometric Monographs* (No. 15).

McDonald, R. P. (1981). The dimensionality of tests and items. *British Journal of Mathematical and Statistical Psychology, 34*, 100–117.

McDonald, R. P. (1982). 1981, 1982 Linear versus nonlinear models in item response theory. *Applied Psychological Measurement, 6*, 379–396.

McDonald, R. P. (1985). *Factor analysis and related methods*. Hillsdale, NJ: Lawrence Erlbaum Associates.

McDonald, R. P. (1999). *Test Theory*. Hillsdale, NJ: Lawrence Erlbaum Associates.

McDonald, R. P., & Ahlawat, K. S. (1974). Difficulty factors in binary data. *British Journal of Mathematical and Statistical Psychology, 27*, 82–99.

McLeod, L. D. (1996). *Exploration of the use of the graded item response model in open-ended test assembly*. Unpublished master's thesis, University of North Carolina at Chapel Hill.

McLeod, L. D., & Lewis, C. (1999). Detecting item memorization in the CAT environment. *Applied Psychological Measurement, 23*, 147–160.

Mellenbergh, G. J. (1995). Conceptual notes on models for discrete polytomous item responses. *Applied Psychological Measurement, 19*, 91–100.

Mislevy, R. J. (1986). Recent developments in the factor analysis of categorical variables. *Journal of Educational Statistics, 11*, 3–31.

Mislevy, R. J. (1992). *Linking educational assessments: Concepts, issues, methods, and prospects*. Princeton, NJ: Educational Testing Service.

Mislevy, R. J., & Bock, R. D. (1982). Biweight estimates of latent ability. *Educational and Psychological Measurement, 42*, 725–737.

Mislevy, R. J., & Bock, R. D. (1990). *BILOG 3: Item analysis and test scoring with binary logistic models*. Chicago, IL: Scientific Software.

Mislevy, R. J., Johnson, E. G., & Muraki, E. (1992). Scaling procedures in NAEP. *Journal of Educational Statistics, 17*, 131–154.

Mislevy, R. J., & Wu, P. K. (1996). *Missing responses and IRT estimation: Omits, choice, time limits, and adaptive testing*. RR-96-30-ONR. Princeton, NJ: Educational Testing Service.

Moore, D. S., & McCabe, G. P. (1993). *Introduction to the practice of statistics*. New York: W. H. Freeman & Co.

Muraki, E. (1992). A generalized partial credit model: Application of an EM algorithm. *Applied Psychological Measurement, 16*, 159–176.

Muraki, E. (1993). *POLYFACT* [Computer program]. Princeton, NJ: Educational Testing Service.

Muraki, E. (1997). A generalized partial credit model. In W. van der Linden & R. K. Hambleton (Eds.), *Handbook of modern item response theory* (pp. 153–164). New York: Springer.

Muraki, E., & Bock, R. D. (1991). *PARSCALE: Parameter scaling of rating data* [Computer program]. Chicago, IL: Scientific Software, Inc.

Muraki, E., & Carlson, J. E. (1995). Full-information factor analysis for polytomous item responses. *Applied Psychological Measurement, 19*, 73–90.

Muthén, B. (1978). Contributions to factor analysis of dichotomous variables. *Psychometrika, 43*, 551–560.

Muthén, L. K., & Muthén, B. O. (1998). *MPLUS: The comprehensive modeling program for applied researchers, user's guide*. Los Angeles, CA: Muthén & Muthén.

Nandakumar, R. (1994). Assessing latent trait unidimensionality of a set of items—comparison of different approaches. *Journal of Educational Measurement, 31*, 1–18.

Nandakumar, R., & Stout, W. F. (1993). Refinements of Stout's procedure for assessing latent trait multidimensionaltiy. *Journal of Educational Statistics, 18*, 41–68.

Nandakumar, R., Yu, F., Li, H.-H., & Stout, W. F. (1998). Assessing unidimensionality of polytomous data. *Applied Psychological Measurement, 22*, 99–115.

National Academy of Education. (1993). *The Trial State Assessment: Prospects and realities.* Stanford, CA: Author.

Nishisato, S. (1984). Forced classification: A simple application of a quantification method. *Psychometrika, 49*, 25–36.

Norušis, M. J. (1993). *SPSS for Windows professional statistics release 6.0.* Chicago, IL: SPSS Inc.

Novick, M. R., & Jackson, P. H. (1975). *Statistical methods for educational and psychological research.* New York: McGraw-Hill.

Novick, M. R., & Lewis, C. (1967). Coefficient alpha and the reliability of composite measurements. *Psychometrika, 32*, 1–13.

Nunnally, J. C., & Bernstein, I. H. (1994). *Psychometric theory* (Third Edition). New York: McGraw-Hill.

Orlando, M. (1997). *Item fit in the context of item response theory.* Unpublished doctoral dissertation, The University of North Carolina at Chapel Hill.

Orlando, M., & Thissen, D. (2000). New item fit indices for dichotomous item response theory models. *Applied Psychological Measurement, 24*, 50–64.

Pedhazur, E. J. (1982). *Multiple regression in behavioral research* (Second Edition). New York: Holt, Rinehart & Winston.

Peel, E. A. (1948). Prediction of a complex criterion and battery reliability. *British Journal of Psychology, Statistical Section, 1*, 84–94.

Ramsay, J. O. (1989). A comparison of three simple test theory models. *Psychometrika, 54*, 487–499.

Ramsay, J. O. (1991). Kernel smoothing approaches to nonparametric item characteristic curve estimation. *Psychometrika, 56*, 611–630.

Ramsay, J. O. (1995). *TESTGRAF: A program for the graphical analysis of multiple-choice test and questionnaire data.* McGill University, Unpublished manuscript.

Ramsay, J. O., & Abrahmowicz, M. (1989). Binomial regression with monotone splines: A psychometric application. *Journal of the American Statistical Association, 84*, 906–915.

Ramsay, J. O., & Winsberg, S. (1991). Maximum marginal likelihood estimation for semiparametric item analysis. *Psychometrika, 56*, 365–379.

Rasch, G. (1960). *Probabilistic models for some intelligence and attainment tests.* Copenhagen: Denmarks Paedagogiske Institut. (Republished in 1980 by the University of Chicago Press of Chicago).

Rasch, G. (1961). On general laws and the meaning of measurement in psychology. *Proceedings of the Fourth Berkeley Symposium on Mathematical Statistics and Probability* (pp. 321–333). Berkeley, CA: University of California Press.

Rasch, G. (1966). An item analysis which takes individual differences into account. *British Journal of Mathematical and Statistical Psychology, 19*, 49–57.

Rasch, G. (1977). On specific objectivity: An attempt at formalizing the request for generality and validity of scientific statements. In M. Blegvad (Ed.), *The Danish yearbook of philosophy.* Copenhagen: Munksgaard.

Reckase, M. D. (1985). The difficulty of test items that measure more than one ability. *Applied Psychological Measurement, 9*, 401–412.

Reckase, M. D. (1997). A linear logistic multidimensional model for dichotomous item response data. In W. J. van der Linden & Ronald K. Hambleton (Eds.), *Handbook of item response theory* (pp. 271–286). New York: Springer-Verlag.

Reckase, M. D., & McKinley, R. L. (1991). The discriminating power of items that measure more than one dimension. *Applied Psychological Measurement, 15*, 401–412.

Reese, L. M. (1995). *The impact of local dependencies on some LSAT outcomes*. LSAC Research Report Series. Newtown, PA: Law School Admission Council.

Reise, S. P., & Flannery, W. P. (1996). Assessing person-fit on measures of typical performance. *Applied Psychological Measurement, 9*, 9–26.

Roussos, L. A., Stout, W. F., & Marden, J. I. (1998). Using new proximity measures with hierarchical cluster analysis to detect multidimensionality. *Journal of Educational Measurement, 35*, 1–30.

Samejima, F. (1969). Estimation of latent ability using a response pattern of graded scores. *Psychometric Monograph*, No. 17.

Samejima, F. (1972). A general model for free-response data. *Psychometric Monograph*, No. 18.

Samejima, F. (1977). The use of the information function in tailored testing. *Applied Psychological Measurement, 1*, 233–247.

Samejima, F. (1979). *A new family of models for the multiple choice item* (Research Report #79-4), Department of Psychology, University of Tennessee.

Samejima, F. (1995). Acceleration model in the heterogeneous case of the general graded response model. *Psychometrika, 60*, 549–572.

Samejima, F. (1997). Graded response model. In W. van der Linden & R. K. Hambleton (Eds.), *Handbook of modern item response theory* (pp. 85–100). New York: Springer.

Sanford, E. E. (1996). *North Carolina End-of-Grade Tests*. Raleigh, NC: North Carolina Department of Public Instruction.

Sanford, E. E. (1996). *North Carolina End-of-Grade tests: Reading and Mathematics* (Technical Report #1). Raleigh, NC: State Board of Education.

SAS Institute Inc. (1988). *SAS procedures guide, 6.03 edition*. Cary, NC: Author.

SAS Institute Inc. (1990). *SAS/STAT User's Guide, Version 6, Fourth Edition, Volumes 1 and 2*. Cary, NC: SAS Institute Inc.

Schmid, J., & Leiman, J. M. (1957). The development of hierarchical factor solutions. *Psychometrika, 22*, 53–61.

Shavelson, R. J. (1996). *Statistical reasoning for the behavioral sciences*. Boston, MA: Allyn and Bacon.

Shavelson, R. J., Gao, X., & Baxter, G. P. (1993). *Sampling variability of performance assessments*. CSE Technical Report 361. Los Angeles, CA: National Center for Research on Evaluation, Standards, and Student Testing (CRESST), Graduate School of Education, University of California at Los Angeles.

Sireci, S. G., Thissen, D., & Wainer, H. (1991). On the reliability of testlet-based tests. *Journal of Educational Measurement, 28*, 237–247.

Spearman, C. (1910). Correlation calculated with faulty data. *British Journal of Psychology, 3*, 271–295.

Stanley, J. C. (1957). KR-20 as the stepped-up mean item intercorrelation. In *14th Yearbook of the National Council on Measurement in Education* (pp. 78–92). Washington, DC: American Council on Education.

Stevens, S. S. (1951). Mathematics, measurement, and psychophysics. In S. S. Stevens (Ed.), *Handbook of experimental psychology*. New York: John Wiley & Sons.

Stout, W. (1987). A nonparametric approach for assessing latent trait unidimensionality. *Psychometrika, 52*, 589–617.

Stout, W., Habing, B., Douglas, J., Kim, H. R., Roussos, L., & Zhang, J. (1996). Conditional covariance-based nonparametric multidimensionality assessment. *Applied Psychological Measurement, 20*, 331–354.

Stroud, A. H. (1974). *Numerical quadrature and solution of ordinary differential equations*. New York, NY: Springer-Verlag.

Suen, H. K. (1990). *Principles of test theories*. Hillsdale, NJ: Lawrence Erlbaum.

Tabachnick, B. G., & Fidell, L. S. (1996). *Using multivariate statistics* (Third Edition). New York, NY: Harper Collins.

Tanaka, J. S., & Huba, G. J. (1984). Confirmatory hierarchical factor analyses of psychological distress measures. *Journal of Personality and Social Psychology, 46,* 621–635.

ten Berge, J. M. F., Snijders, T. A. B., & Zegers, F. E. (1981). Computational aspects of the greatest lower bound to the reliability and constrained minimum trace factor analysis. *Psychometrika, 46,* 201–213.

Thissen, D. (1982). Marginal maximum likelihood estimation for the one-parameter logistic model. *Psychometrika, 47,* 175–186.

Thissen, D. (1991). *MULTILOG user's guide: Multiple, categorical item analysis and test scoring using item response theory.* Chicago, IL: Scientific Software.

Thissen, D. (1993). Repealing rules that no longer apply to psychological measurement. In N. Frederiksen, R. J. Mislevy, & I. Bejar (Eds.), *Test theory for a new generation of tests* (pp. 79–97). Hillsdale, NJ: Lawrence Erlbaum Associates.

Thissen, D. (1998a, April). *Scaled scores for CATs based on linear combinations of testlet scores.* Paper presented at the annual meeting of the National Council on Measurement in Education, San Diego, CA,.

Thissen, D. (1998b, June). *Some item response theory to provide scale scores based on linear combinations of testlet scores, for computerized adaptive tests.* Paper presented at the annual meeting of the Psychometric Society, Champaign–Urbana, IL.

Thissen, D., Pommerich, M., Billeaud, K., & Williams, V. S. L. (1995). Item response theory for scores on tests including polytomous items with ordered responses. *Applied Psychological Measurement, 19,* 39–49.

Thissen, D., & Steinberg, L. (1984). A response model for multiple-choice items. *Psychometrika, 49,* 501–519.

Thissen, D., & Steinberg, L. (1986). A taxonomy of item response models. *Psychometrika, 51,* 567–577.

Thissen, D., & Steinberg, L. (1988). Data analysis using item response theory. *Psychological Bulletin, 104,* 385–395.

Thissen, D., & Steinberg, L. (1997). A response model for multiple choice items. In W. J. van der Linden & Ronald K. Hambleton (Eds.), *Handbook of item response theory* (pp. 51–65). New York: Springer-Verlag.

Thissen, D., Steinberg, L., & Fitzpatrick, A. R. (1989). Multiple choice models: The distractors are also part of the item. *Journal of Educational Measurement, 26,* 161–176.

Thissen, D., Steinberg, L., & Mooney, J. A. (1989). Trace lines for testlets: A use of multiple-categorical-response models. *Journal of Educational Measurement 26,* 247–260.

Thissen, D., Wainer, H., & Wang, X. (1994). Are tests comprising both multiple-choice and free-response items necessarily less unidimensional than multiple-choice tests? An analysis of two tests. *Journal of Educational Measurement, 31,* 113–123.

Thomson, G. H. (1940). Weighting for battery reliability and prediction. *British Journal of Psychology, 30,* 357–366.

Thurstone, L. L. (1925). A method of scaling psychological and educational tests. *Journal of Educational Psychology, 16,* 433–449.

Thurstone, L. L. (1927). A law of comparative judgment. *Psychological Review, 34,* 278–286.

Thurstone, L. L. (1937). Psychology as a quantitative rational science. *Science, 85,* 228–232.

Thurstone, L. L. (1947). *Multiple factor analysis.* Chicago, IL: University of Chicago Press.

Thurstone, L. L. (1959). *The measurement of values.* Chicago: University of Chicago Press.

Tierney, L. (1990). *LISP-STAT: An object-oriented environment for statistical computing and dynamic graphics.* New York: Wiley.

van der Linden, W., & Hambleton, R. K. (1997). *Handbook of modern item response theory.* New York: Springer.

van der Linden, W. J., & Hambleton, R. K. (1997). *Handbook of item response theory*. New York: Springer-Verlag.

Vevea, J. L., Billeaud, K., & Nelson, L. (1998, June). *An empirical Bayes approach to subscore augmentation*. Paper presented at the annual meeting of the Psychometric Society, Champaign–Urbana, IL.

Wainer, H. (1976). Estimating coefficients in linear models: It don't make no nevermind. *Psychological Bulletin, 83*, 213–217.

Wainer, H. (1983). Pyramid power: Searching for an error in test scoring with 830,000 helpers. *American Statistician, 37*, 87–91.

Wainer, H. (1999). Is the Akebono school failing its best students? A Hawaiian adventure in regression. *Educational Measurement: Issues and Practice, 18*, 26–35.

Wainer, H. (2000). Kelley's paradox. *Chance, 13*, 47–48.

Wainer, H., Dorans, N., Flaugher, R., Green, B., Mislevy, R. M., Steinberg, L., & Thissen, D. (1990). *Computerized adaptive testing: A primer*. Hillsdale, NJ: Lawrence Erlbaum Associates.

Wainer, H., & Kiely, G. L. (1987). Item clusters and computerized adaptive testing: A case for testlets. *Journal of Educational Measurement, 24*, 185–201.

Wainer, H., & Lewis, C. (1990). Toward a psychometrics for testlets. *Journal of Educational Measurement, 27*, 1–14.

Wainer, H., & Mislevy, R. J. (1990). Item response theory, item calibration, and proficiency estimation. In H. Wainer, N. Dorans, R. Flaugher, B. Green, R. Mislevy, L. Steinberg, & D. Thissen, *Computerized adaptive testing: A primer* (pp. 65–102). Hillsdale, NJ: Lawrence Erlbaum Associates.

Wainer, H., & Mislevy, R. J. (2000). Item response theory, item calibration, and proficiency estimation. In H. Wainer, N. Dorans, D. Eignor, R. Flaugher, B. Green, R. Mislevy, L. Steinberg, & D. Thissen, *Computerized adaptive testing: A primer (Second Edition)* (pp. 61–100). Hillsdale, NJ: Lawrence Erlbaum Associates.

Wainer, H., Sireci, S. G., & Thissen, D. (1991). DIFferential testlet functioning: Definitions and detection. *Journal of Educational Measurement, 28*, 197–219.

Wainer, H., & Thissen, D. (1987). Estimating ability with the wrong model. *Journal of Educational Statistics, 12*, 339–368.

Wainer, H., & Thissen, D. (1993). Combining multiple-choice and constructed response test scores: Toward a Marxist theory of test construction. *Applied Measurement in Education, 6*, 103–118.

Wainer, H., & Thissen, D. (1996). How is reliability related to the quality of test scores? What is the effect of local dependence on reliability? *Educational Measurement: Issues and Practice, 15*, 22–29.

Wainer, H., Wadkins, J. R. J., & Rogers, A. (1984). Was there one distractor too many? *Journal of Educational Statistics, 9*, 5–24.

Walsh, J. E. (1963). Corrections to two papers concerned with binomial events. *Sankhyā, Series A, 25*, 427.

Wiley, D. E. (1973). The identification problem for structural equation models with unmeasured variables. In A. S. Goldberger & O. D. Duncan (Eds.), *Structural equation models in the social sciences* (pp. 85–112). New York: Academic.

Williams, V. S. L., Rosa, K. R., McLeod, L. D., Thissen, D., & Sanford, E. (1998). Projecting to the NAEP scale: Results from the North Carolina End-of-Grade testing program. *Journal of Educational Measurement, 35*, 277–296.

Wilson, D., Wood, R., & Gibbons, R. D. (1991). *TESTFACT: Test scoring, item statistics, and item factor analysis*. Chicago, IL: Scientific Software, Inc.

Wilson, M., & Adams, R. J. (1995). Rasch models for item bundles. *Psychometrika, 60*, 181–198.

Wilson, M., & Wang, W.-C. (1995). Complex composites: Issues that arise in combining different modes of assessment. *Applied Psychological Measurement, 19,* 51–71.

Wingersky, M. S., Barton, M. A., & Lord, F. M. (1982). *LOGIST user's guide.* Princeton, NJ: Educational Testing Service.

Wright, B. D. (1994). IRT in the 1990s: Which models work best? *Rasch Measurement Transactions, 6,* 196–200.

Wright, B. D. (1996). Construct problems with descriptive IRT. *Rasch Measurement Transactions, 10,* 481.

Wright, B. D. (1997). A history of social science measurement. *Educational Measurement: Issues and Practice, 16,* 33–52.

Wright, B. D., & Linacre, J. M. (1992). *BIGSTEPS Rasch analysis* [Computer program]. Chicago, IL: MESA Press.

Yen, W. M. (1981). Using simulation results to choose a latent trait model. *Applied Psychological Measurement, 5,* 245–262.

Yen, W. M. (1984). Effect of local item dependence on the fit and equating performance of the three-parameter logistic model. *Applied Psychological Measurement, 8,* 125–145.

Yen, W. M. (1984). Obtaining maximum likelihood trait estimates from number-correct scores for the three-parameter logistic model. *Journal of Educational Measurement, 21,* 93–111.

Yen, W. M. (1986). The choice of scale for educational measurement: An IRT perspective. *Journal of Educational Measurement, 23,* 299–325.

Yen, W. M. (1987, June). *A Bayesian/IRT index of objective performance.* Paper presented at the annual meeting of the Psychometric Society, Montreal, Quebec, Canada.

Yen, W. M. (1993). Scaling performance assessments: Strategies for managing local item dependence. *Journal of Educational Measurement, 30,* 187–214.

Yen, W. M., Burket, G. R., & Sykes, R. C. (1991). Nonunique solutions to the likelihood equation for the three-parameter logistic model. *Psychometrika, 56,* 39–54.

Yen, W. M., & Ferrara, S. (1997). The Maryland school performance assessment program: Performance assessment with psychometric quality suitable for high stakes usage. *Educational and Psychological Measurement, 57,* 60–84.

Yung, Y. F., McLeod, L. D., & Thissen, D. (1999). On the relationship between the higher-order factor model and the hierarchical factor model. *Psychometrika, 64,* 113–128.

Zhang, J., & Stout, W. F. (1999a). Conditional covariance structure of generalized compensatory multidimensional items. *Psychometrika, 64,* 129–152.

Zhang, J., & Stout, W. F. (1999b). The theoretical DETECT index of dimensionality and its application to approximate simple structure. *Psychometrika, 64,* 213–249.

Author Index

A

Abbott, R. D., *5*
Abrahamowicz, M., *98*
Adams, R. J., *150, 174*
Ahlawat, K. S., *197*
Aitkin, M., *198*
Allen, N. L., *148*
Anastasi, A., *4, 383*
Andersen, E. B., 77, 148, 149
Andrich, D., 148, 149
Arbuckle, J. L., 224
Armor, D. J., 34
Armstrong, R. D., *281*, 321

B

Baker, F. B., 16, 81n, 101n
Barton, M. A., *114*
Baxter, G. P., *48*
Becker, R. A., *46*
Bell, R., *3*
Bell, R. M., *25n*
Bennett, R. E., *10*
Bentler, P. M., *223*, 224
Bergan, J. R., *174*
Berkson, J., 88
Berliner, N., *281, 321*
Bernstein, I. H., *4*
Billeaud, K., *154, 335, 352*
Binet, A., 79
Birnbaum, A., 74, 93, 258, 296
Birnbaum, Allen, 88
Bock, R. D., 5, *5, 6*, 9, 45, 78n, 83, 84, *89, 91*, 95n, *112, 113, 119, 136*, 146, 148n, 149, *150*, 174, *190, 197, 198, 200, 209, 228*, 321, *327, 375*
Bollen, K. A., 218
Boomsma, A., 221
Bradlow, E. T., 136, 175n, *211*
Brennan, R. L., *34, 35–38, 41, 48*
Bridgeman, B., *191, 254*
Brown, W., 30
Browne, M. W., *209*, 220, 221, *223, 238*, *246*
Burdsal, C. A., Jr., *218*
Burket, G. R., *136, 172*
Burt, C., 79, 80n, 82
Burton, E., 48

C

Calderone, J., *253*
Camilli, G., 89
Carlson, J. E., *12, 225, 228*
Carroll, J. B., 197
Caruso, J. C., *45n*
Casella, G., 247n, 346, 347
Cattell, R. B., 11, 218, *218*
Chambers, J. M., *46*
Chen, W. H., *175*
Christoffersson, A., 197
Cliff, N., *45n*
Cook, L. L., *218*
Cressie, N., 77
Cronbach, L. J., 4, 33, 35
Cudeck, R., *209, 238, 246*

D

Davis, L. A., *290*

401

Subject Index

405